Clinical Applications
of Cognitive Therapy

Clinical Applications of Cognitive Therapy

ARTHUR FREEMAN

University of Medicine and Dentistry of New Jersey
School of Osteopathic Medicine
Stratford, New Jersey

JAMES PRETZER AND
BARBARA FLEMING

Case Western Reserve University
School of Medicine
Cleveland, Ohio

AND

KAREN M. SIMON

Center for Cognitive Therapy
University of Pennsylvania
Philadelphia, Pennsylvania

Plenum Press • New York and London

Library of Congress Cataloging in Publication Data

Freeman, Arthur M.
    Clinical applications of cognitive therapy / Arthur Freeman . . . [et al.].
        p.   cm.
    Includes bibliographical references.
    ISBN 0-306-43311-7
    1. Cognitive therapy. 2. Personality disorders – Treatment. I. Title.
    [DNLM: 1. Cognitive Therapy. 2. Personality Disorders – therapy. WM 425 F855c]
    RC489.C63F73   1990
    616.89'142 – dc20
    DNLM/DLC   90-6706
    for Library of Congress   CIP

First Printing—March 1990
Second Printing—October 1990

For information about our audio products, write us at:
Newbridge Book Clubs, 3000 Cindel Drive, Delran, NJ   08370

The DSM-III-R diagnostic criteria are reprinted with
permission from the *Diagnostic and Statistical Manual of
Mental Disorders, Third Edition, Revised.* Copyright 1987
American Psychiatric Association.

© 1990 Plenum Press, New York
A Division of Plenum Publishing Corporation
233 Spring Street, New York, N.Y. 10013

Printed in the United States of America

Preface

Since Beck and his colleagues (Beck, Rush, Shaw, & Emery, 1979) published their classic work on the cognitive therapy of depression ten years ago, cognitive therapy has come of age. From the early clinical focus on a single diagnostic entity, the cognitive therapy model has been adapted to treat a wide variety of clinical problems and populations. Thus, a number of clinicians, including many trained at the Center for Cognitive Therapy at the University of Pennsylvania, have developed applications for the treatment of anxiety, personality, and eating disorders. They have adapted the model to work with couples, children, adolescents, and families as well as with schizophrenic inpatients. These clinicians have gone on to establish their own centers and take responsibility for training and supervising others. The present collaboration is just one result.

The title we have chosen for this volume is descriptive of the book's development as well as its utility. The authors, who are all practicing clinicians, have developed the theoretical and practical models found within on the firing line of the psychotherapeutic interaction. When specific techniques did not work, consultation was sought. If the techniques still did not produce the desired results, revisions were made again. The ultimate results of this process were then tested and evaluated in terms of treatment efficacy and practicality with other patients with similar diagnoses. This volume, then, is written with the practicing clinician in mind. And, whether the reader is a psychologist, psychiatrist, social counselor worker, psychiatric nurse, or pastoral counselor, he or she should find principles of case conceptualization and practical techniques which can be readily applied in daily practice.

While each of the authors has his or her own idiosyncratic style of therapy, all have maintained a fairly parochial view. We do not consider our work to be eclectic; we have not attempted to establish "rapprochement" with any other theoretical or practical model. Rather we view cognitive therapy as having boundaries that are elastic enough to allow the freedom of creativity within the cognitive therapy model.

This book has grown and matured as new ideas were tried, developed, and incorporated. We do not see it as the ultimate destination of cognitive therapeutic treatment, but as a milestone along the path. Many people must be acknowledged for their varied contributions to this volume. First and foremost, we wish to express our gratitude to Aaron T. Beck, M.D., director of the Center for Cognitive Therapy, and Professor of Psychiatry at the University of Pennsylvania. Tim has been teacher, mentor, colleague, and friend to all of us for many years. His contributions to psychotherapeutic theory in practice have earned him a place as one of the preeminant therapists of our time. Eliot Werner, medical and behavioral science editor at Plenum, has left his mark on this book in terms of his ideas, encouragement, and feedback. Our students and patients deserve special thanks, for it is through our interactions with them that we continue to learn, question, develop, and improve our therapeutic skills. Finally, Apple Computer deserves special thanks for its invention and development of the Macintosh, without which this and other writings might never have existed.

Our intention and hope is that our readers will be motivated to try these ideas and develop them further.

Contents

Clinical Applications of Cognitive Therapy

I

Introduction

In this section of the book, the underpinnings of the cognitive therapy model are presented and discussed. The purpose of this volume—to serve as a clinician's handbook for the application of the cognitive therapy model—is achieved in a stepwise fashion. The initial chapter addresses the issue of what cognitive therapy is, while debunking several of the most widely held myths and misconceptions. From the meaning of cognitive therapy, the book moves on to the important issue of clinician assessment. The use of both clinician interviews and a variety of self-monitoring techniques is discussed. The point is made that the effectiveness of cognitive therapy derives from a careful, self-correcting assessment and concep tualization process that must not be neglected.

The strategies and techniques described in the interventions chapter are prerequisite skills that the clinician reader can adapt to specific problems and populations. These techniques are arranged thematically in order to aid in this process. Furthermore, we offer clinical vignettes and verbatim interactions to illustrate the use of a variety of interventions both in this and in subsequent chapters.

The chapter on depression is designed to be an introduction for those readers not already familiar with the text *Cognitive Therapy of Depression* by Beck, Rush, Shaw, and Emery (1979). However, it also serves as an updated refresher course for those familiar with the earlier work.

The depression chapter leads naturally to a theoretical and clinical discussion of the treatment of suicide. The conceptualization, treatment strategies, and specific techniques are discussed in detail.

In the final chapter of Part II, the clinical problem of anxiety is addressed; a broad range of anxiety disorders is covered, including Generalized Anxiety, Obsessive Compulsive, Phobic, and Panic Disorders.

It is our hope that this stepwise approach of developing an understanding of the basic model, methods and ideas of conceptualization, and the translation of the conceptual model to practical treatment will prepare the therapist for the cognitive therapeutic treatment of the broad range of patients seen in clinician practice.

1

Cognitive Therapy in the Real World

It is Monday morning and a therapist looks at his schedule: "Let's see . . . at 9:00 I have a couple who haven't been able to extricate themselves from an on-again, off-again relationship; then I have a young executive recovering from depression complicated by alcohol abuse and Paranoid Personality Disorder. Next I go to the Family Practice Center to see a client with somatic symptoms of stress, a young father obsessed with the thought of harming his child, and a family with chronic conflict among adolescent children. Later I return to my office to see a dentist with chronic social anxiety, an agoraphobic housewife, and a CPA troubled by anxiety, depression, and outbursts of anger."

Although the monologue is imaginary, the caseload on that particular Monday was real and illustrates a major problem in the practice of Cognitive Therapy.* Practitioners of Cognitive Therapy have worked to develop and test specific treatment approaches for disorders such as unipolar depression, phobias and anxiety disorders, substance abuse, and so on, with excellent results (see Simon & Fleming, 1985). Unfortunately, the practicing therapist soon discovers that life is not that simple. Clients rarely present with a single problem for which there is a well-validated treatment protocol. More typically, clients enter treatment with multiple problems, with a variety of factors complicating therapy, or with problems for which empirically tested treatment approaches are not yet available. The clinician is then faced with the task of figuring out what to do. This book is written for the practicing clinician who must try to bridge the gap between controlled outcome studies and the complexities encountered in clinical practice. This initial chapter is designed both to orient the experienced cognitive behavioral clinician to the particular treatment approach advocated by the authors and to serve as an introduction to Cognitive Therapy for readers who are less familiar with recent developments in this field.

---

*A wide variety of "cognitive" and "cognitive-behavioral" therapies have been developed in recent years. In order to minimize confusion without creating the illusion that all cognitive therapies are equivalent, Aaron Beck's approach will be referred to as Cognitive Therapy. When cognitive therapies in general are referred to, lower-case letters will be used.

A COGNITIVE VIEW OF PSYCHOPATHOLOGY

The first task a practicing clinician faces is that of finding some way to understand the wide range of individual, couple, and family problems that he or she encounters. Cognitive Therapy is based on a straightforward, commonsense model of the relationships among cognition, emotion, and behavior in human functioning in general and in psychopathology in particular. Three aspects of cognition are emphasized: automatic thoughts, underlying assumptions, and cognitive distortions.

An individual's immediate, unpremeditated interpretations of events are referred to as "automatic thoughts" because they occur spontaneously and without apparent volition. One major premise of the cognitive view of human functioning is that automatic thoughts shape both individuals' emotions and their actions in response to events. For example, when Al, a secretary in his late 20s, was summoned to his superior's office, his immediate response was, "Oh God, I must have really blown it! I'm really in trouble now." According to the cognitive view, we would expect him to feel and act as though he was in serious trouble as long as he maintained this interpretation of the situation. If his interpretation of the situation is accurate, his responses are likely to be reasonably appropriate. However, if he is overestimating the extent to which he is in trouble or is completely mistaken, his emotions and actions are not likely to be appropriate to the situation. Cognitive Therapy is based on the observation that dysfunctional automatic thoughts that are exaggerated, distorted, mistaken, or unrealistic in other ways play a major role in psychopathology. If it is possible to identify the automatic thoughts that the client experiences in problem situations, this often provides a simple explanation for apparently incomprehensible reactions.

Often the dysfunctional thoughts that clients report are so extreme that it is hard for others to comprehend that intelligent, capable, well-educated individuals could believe such things without there being some "deep" reason behind it. For example, Al was convinced that he was going to be vigorously criticized and possibly fired despite his not being aware of having committed any major infractions and his not having received hostile criticism or unfair treatment from his supervisor previously. A second premise of Cognitive Therapy is that an individual's beliefs, assumptions, and "schemas"* shape the perception and interpretation of events. Al had grown up in a family in which he received many punitive reprimands, deserved and undeserved, while receiving little positive feedback. He

---

*In the literature on Cognitive Therapy, the terms *dysfunctional beliefs, underlying assumptions,* and *schemas* have been used interchangeably to refer to the individual's unspoken, and often unrecognized, assumptions. No consistent distinctions are drawn among these closely related terms, and in this work they will be treated as synonyms.

Table 1. Commonly Observed Cognitive Distortions

Dichotomous thinking—Things are seen in terms of two mutually exclusive categories with no "shades of gray" in between. For example, believing that one is *either* a success *or* a failure and that anything short of a perfect performance is a total failure.

Overgeneralization—A specific event is seen as being characteristic of life in general rather than as being one event among many. For example, concluding that an inconsiderate response from one's spouse shows that she doesn't care despite her having showed consideration on other occasions.

Selective abstraction—One aspect of a complex situation is the focus of attention, and other relevant aspects of the situation are ignored. For example, focusing on the one negative comment in a performance evaluation received at work and overlooking a number of positive comments.

Disqualifying the positive—Positive experiences that would conflict with the individual's negative views are discounted by declaring that they "don't count." For example, disbelieving positive feedback from friends and colleagues and thinking "They're only saying that to be nice."

Mind reading—The individual assumes that others are reacting negatively without evidence that this is the case. For example, thinking, "I just *know* he thought I was an idiot!", despite the other person's having behaved politely.

Fortune-telling—The individual reacts as though his or her negative expectations about future events are established facts. For example, thinking, "He's leaving me, I just know it!," and acting as though this is definitely true.

Catastrophizing—Negative events that might occur are treated as intolerable catastrophes rather than being seen in perspective. For example, thinking "Oh my God, what if I faint!" without considering that, whereas fainting may be unpleasant and embarrassing, it is not terribly dangerous.

Minimization—Positive characteristics or experiences are treated as real but insignificant. For example, thinking, "Sure, I'm good at my job, but so what, my parents don't respect me."

Emotional reasoning—Assuming that emotional reactions necessarily reflect the true situation. For example, deciding that because one feels hopeless, the situation must really be hopeless.

"Should" statements—The use of *should* and *have-to* statements to provide motivation or control behavior. For example, thinking, "I shouldn't feel aggravated. She's my mother, I *have* to listen to her."

Labeling—Attaching a global label to oneself rather than referring to specific events or actions. For example, thinking, "I'm a failure!", rather than "Boy, I blew that one!"

Personalization—Assuming that one is the cause of a particular external event when, in fact, other factors are responsible. For example, assuming that a supervisor's lack of friendliness is a reflection of her feelings about the client rather than realizing that she is upset over a death in the family.

came to assume that attention from authority figures was almost certain to be hostile and punitive and his response to being summoned to his supervisor's office was shaped by this preconception. A third premise of Cognitive Therapy is based on Beck's (1976) observation that errors in logic or "cognitive distortions" are quite prevalent in clients suffering from a number of different disorders (see Table 1). These cognitive distortions can lead individuals to erroneous conclusions even if their perception of the situation is accurate. If the situation is perceived erroneously, these distortions can amplify the impact of the misperceptions. For example, Al tended to view others as either completely benevolent or completely hostile (dichotomus thinking, see Table 1). Because his supervisor was not *always* kind and considerate, Al concluded that because she was not completely benevolent, she must be hostile. This, in combination with his assumptions about authority figures, contributed to his anticipation of punishment.

The cognitive model is not simply that "thoughts cause feelings and actions." It is recognized that emotions can influence cognitive processes and that behaviors can influence the evaluation of a situation by modifying the situation itself or by eliciting responses from others. Another factor in the cognitive model is the impact of mood on cognition. A number of studies of the impact of mood on cognition have produced evidence that an individual's mood can significantly bias recall and perception (for a recent review see Isen, 1984). For example, Bower (1981) found that sadness facilitated recall of sad events in subjects' lives, whereas happiness facilitated recall of happy events. Moods other than sadness and happiness have not been the subject of extensive empirical research, but clinical observation suggests that other moods such as anxiety and anger may also bias perception and recall in mood-congruent ways. Because both biased recall and biased perception of events would tend to elicit more of the same mood, it appears that the tendency of mood to bias cognition in a mood-congruent way could easily tend to perpetuate a mood regardless of its initial cause.

Automatic thoughts, underlying assumptions, cognitive distortions, and the impact of mood on cognition combine to set the stage for a self-perpetuating cycle (presented graphically in Figure 1) that is observed in many disorders. An individual may hold dysfunctional assumptions that predispose him or her to psychopathology without their having any noticeable effect until a situation relevant to the assumptions arises. However, when a relevant situation arises, the dysfunctional assumptions, in combination with any cognitive distortions, contribute to problematic automatic thoughts. These dysfunctional automatic thoughts elicit a corresponding mood, the nature of which depends on the content of the automatic thoughts. This mood then biases recall and perception in such a way that the individual is likely to experience additional dysfunctional automatic thoughts, intensifying his or her mood. As the mood intensifies, it further biases recall and perception and easily becomes self-perpetuating. In Al's case, his negative preconceptions about authority figures and his tendency toward dichotomous thinking caused no problems except when he interacted with authority figures. When he received the summons already discussed, he quickly became both depressed and anxious in response to his anticipation of punishment. Once he became somewhat depressed and anxious, he began to focus selectively on past transgressions that might be grounds for disciplinary action, and he overlooked his overall good work

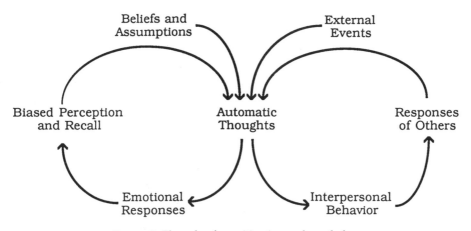

FIGURE 1. The role of cognition in psychopathology.

record. By the time he met with his supervisor, Al was convinced that he would be fired and was quite upset. He was amazed to discover that his supervisor only wanted to reassign some of his responsibilities.

Dysfunctional automatic thoughts influence the individual's behavior as well as his or her mood. The impact of automatic thoughts on interpersonal behavior and the subsequent responses of others can either serve to perpetuate or terminate the problem. For example, it no doubt is obvious that Al's anticipation of hostility and punishment from his supervisor affected his interaction with her and with his co-workers. Had his supervisor noticed nonverbal indications of his anxiety and depression, she might have become suspicious and more likely to criticize his performance. On the other hand, she might have expressed sympathy and concern, which would have been incompatible with his preconceptions about her. As it happened, his subjective distress elicited no response from her, and on this occasion the interpersonal aspects of the problem were negligible.

It is important to note that the cycle presented in Figure 1 need not start with the combined effects of dysfunctional beliefs and an event relevant to those beliefs. If dysfunctional automatic thoughts were elicited by objectively negative events or if a particular mood were elicited by biochemical changes, the same cycle could result. Similarly, regardless of the point at which the cycle started, cognition plays an important role in the cycle and often is a productive point for intervention.

PRINCIPLES OF COGNITIVE THERAPY

The cognitive view of psychopathology, including the model of the interactions among cognition, mood, and behavior presented in Figure 1, suggests a variety of possible intervention points. Usually the initial goal of therapy would be to break the cycle or cycles that perpetuate and amplify the client's problems. This could be done by modifying the client's automatic thoughts, improving the client's mood, working to eliminate the biasing impact of mood on recall and perception, or changing the client's behavior. A combination of these interventions could break the cycle(s) that perpetuate the problems and alleviate the client's immediate distress. However, if the therapist only worked to break this cycle, the client would be at risk for a relapse whenever he or she experienced events similar to the ones that precipitated this episode. In order to achieve lasting results, it is also important to modify the beliefs and assumptions that predispose the client to his or her problems and to help him or her plan effective ways to handle situations which might precipitate a relapse.

Although Cognitive Therapy is closely identified with interventions designed to modify automatic thoughts, this is only one of many possible approaches to intervention. As will be seen in subsequent chapters, Cognitive Therapy with any particular client is likely to involve interventions designed to modify mood and interventions intended to achieve behavior change as well as interventions focused primarily on cognition.

Given the range of possible intervention points and the complexity of many clients' problems, it is not surprising that Cognitive Therapy is most effective when the therapist thinks strategically about intervention. This process involves forming a clear conceptualization of the client and his or her problems and using this as a basis for selecting the most productive targets for intervention and the most appropriate intervention techniques. When the therapist intervenes without pausing to develop a conceptualization of the client's problems and without using that conceptualization to select the most appropriate interventions, much time and effort can be expended on interventions which prove ineffective or minimally relevant. For example:

A trainee was attempting to treat a medical student whose presenting problem was discomfort with public speaking. However, she found that the client objected to the relaxation exercises she proposed and did not practice the relaxation exercises at home as she had instructed him to. When she reviewed the case with her supervisor, it became clear that the client's discomfort with public speaking was due to a fear of fainting and that, from the client's point of view, the use of relaxation exercises missed the point completely. The client cooperated much more eagerly with interventions which more directly addressed his fear of fainting. Later, when the case conceptualization had been shared with the client and he could see how relaxation training fit into the overall treatment plan, he was more willing to comply with relaxation exercises.

The strategic approach to Cognitive Therapy is quite unlike therapies in which the therapist uses a standard therapeutic approach with all clients in the hope that by being "therapeutic in general" he or she will eventually address the most important issues. It is also quite different from technique-oriented approaches where Intervention A is automatically used with Problem A and Intervention B is automatically used with Problem B. The cognitive therapist strives to develop an individualized treatment approach for each client, based on an understanding of that particular client. Although Cognitive Therapy uses a wide range of intervention techniques, many of which were developed by practitioners of other theoretical orientations, Cognitive Therapy is not simply an "eclectic" approach. As will be seen in the chapters describing intervention with a wide range of disorders (Chapters 4–13), these interventions are used for specific purposes based on a cognitive conceptualization of the client and following a systematic treatment plan.

There are a wide variety of approaches that could be used to implement this strategic form of therapy. The approach used in Cognitive Therapy has been described as "collaborative empiricism" (Beck, Rush, Shaw, & Emery, 1979). The therapist endeavors to work with the client to help him or her to recognize the cognitions and other factors that cause problems for the client, to test the validity of the thoughts, beliefs, and assumptions that prove important, and to make the needed changes in both cognition and behavior. Although it is clear that approaches ranging from philosophical debate to operant conditioning can be effective with at least some clients, collaborative empiricism has substantial advantages. By actively collaborating with the client, the therapist minimizes the resistance and oppositionality that is often elicited by taking an authoritarian role, yet the therapist is still in a position to structure each session as well as the overall course of therapy so as to be as efficient and effective as possible.

Collaboration can be greatly facilitated by relying on a process of "guided discovery" rather than direct confrontation. By asking a series of simple questions, it is possible to guide the client so that he or she develops an understanding of his or her problems, explores possible solutions, and develops a plan for dealing with the problems. For example, such questions as the following: "So you were standing there at the party wanting to join in but feeling really awkward. Do you remember what was going through your head?" "One thought you mentioned was, 'If I open my mouth, I'll make a fool of myself.' Do you have any evidence as to how often you'd say foolish things if you spoke up more often at parties?" "Suppose you did say something foolish, how would you expect the others to react?" "If you said something foolish and the others laughed, you'd feel embarrassed, but what would be the lasting consequences?" could guide a social phobic through the process of pinpointing and challenging automatic thoughts without using direct confrontation.

Guided discovery maximizes client involvement in therapy sessions and minimizes the possibility of the client's feeling that the therapist is attempting to impose his or her own ideas on the client. In addition, this approach makes it possible for the client to learn a method for understanding and solving his or her own problems. Thus, guided discovery can prepare the client to deal with future problems on his or her own whereas approaches in which the therapist simply provides the solutions and persuades the client to adopt them are less likely to equip the client with the skills needed to deal effectively with new problems as they arise.

THE PROCESS OF COGNITIVE THERAPY

In order to take a strategic approach to addressing the client's problems, the therapist must develop an understanding of the client and his or her problems. Therefore, the first step in Cognitive Therapy is an initial assessment that provides a foundation for subsequent interventions. By beginning with a systematic evaluation, the therapist can develop an initial conceptualization quickly rather than waiting for an understanding of the client to develop gradually over the first few months of therapy and thus can be in a position to intervene effectively early in therapy. This conceptualization is the foundation for an individualized treatment plan that allows the therapist to be selective and efficient in employing the wide range of interventions and techniques that are available.

It is also important for the therapist to use the initial therapy sessions to establish a solid foundation for therapy before plunging into interventions. The effectiveness of any psychotherapy depends on a relationship of confidence, openness, caring, and trust established between client and therapist, and this is no less true for Cognitive Therapy. The cognitive therapist takes an active, directive role in treatment and thus can work actively to develop the therapeutic relationship rather than waiting for it to develop gradually over time. With many clients, this is more easily said than done. Discussions of the complexities and difficulties encountered in the therapeutic relationship are found in many of the treatment chapters, particularly in those discussing the treatment of clients with personality disorders.

In order to collaborate effectively, therapist and client must agree on goals for therapy. Therefore, following the initial evaluation, the therapist works with the client to specify goals for therapy and to prioritize them. These goals include the problems that the client wishes to overcome and the positive changes he or she wants to work toward and should be operationalized clearly and specifically enough so that both therapist and client can tell if progress is being made. For example:

Frank, a depressed salesman, initially stated his goal for therapy as, "to become the best I can be." When stated in that way, the goal was quite vague and abstract. It also was clearly unmanageable considering that Frank was so depressed that he could not manage to revise his resume or do household chores. After considerable discussion, Frank and his therapist agreed on more specific goals including feel less depressed and anxious, decrease amount of time spent worrying, and actively hunt for a job (revise resume, actively search for job openings, complete applications for appropriate openings, etc.).

With clearer, more concrete goals, it is much easier for the therapist to select appropriate interventions and for both therapist and client to see if they are making progress towards achieving the goals.

Once the goals for therapy are clear, it is necessary for therapist and client to decide which goal or goals to focus on first. It generally requires little additional effort to prioritize the client's goals at the same time as the goals of therapy are clarified. This involves considering the client's preferences regarding which issues to work on first, the therapist's conceptualization, which problems seem most likely to respond to early interventions, and any practical considerations that are relevant. There is considerable advantage in working initially toward a goal that appears manageable even if it is not the goal that is most important to the client. If it proves possible to make demonstrable progress toward a valued goal, the client will be encouraged, and this will increase his or her motivation for therapy. The process of jointly agreeing on goals and priorities maximizes the likelihood that therapy will accomplish what the client is seeking. At the same time, it establishes the precedent of the therapist's soliciting and respecting the client's input while being open regarding his or her own views. Thus it lays the foundation for therapist and client to work together collaboratively, and it makes it clear to the client that his or her concerns are understood and respected. The time and effort spent on establishing mutually agreed upon goals and priorities is more than compensated for by the resulting increase in client involvement, decrease in resistance, and decrease in time and effort wasted on peripheral topics.

One issue that is important in a collaborative approach to therapy is to introduce the client to the therapist's conceptualization of the problems and to his or her approach to therapy. Although this could be done as a "minilecture" about psychopathology and psychotherapy, it is generally easier and more effective to use a guided discovery approach and to base the explanation on the thoughts and feelings the client reports experiencing on a particular occasion when his or her problems were occurring. If the client does not have a clear memory of his or her thoughts and feelings in a problem situation, it often is possible to use the thoughts and feelings experienced at some other point, such as while waiting for the session to begin or at a particularly emotional point during the session. It is wise to reserve more didactic explanations for occasions where the client is not able to report his or her thoughts and feelings clearly enough for this to form the basis of the explanation.

When a more didactic explanation is necessary, explanations based on concrete examples can be quite useful. For example:

Imagine that you're walking through the woods on a pleasant spring morning, and you go around a bend in the trail and see a bear standing there. Obviously you're going to have an emotional reaction and you're going to do something. What isn't obvious to many people is that your emotions and your actions are based on your interpretation of the situation.

Suppose that before you left camp you heard that Joe drove into town to rent a bear costume. Your reaction when you see the bear is going to be very different if you didn't know that. But just because Joe has a bear costume doesn't mean that's him on the trail ahead of you. Until you're close enough to see if this bear has a zipper down the front, your reactions are going to depend on whether you decide it's Joe or a real bear on the trail ahead of you. If you're wrong you may be in for a big problem.

As people go through their day-to-day lives, they're constantly interpreting the situations they run into. When people have problems, sometimes it's because they're misinterpreting events and reacting in ways that don't fit the situation, and sometimes it's because they see the situation clearly but don't have a good way to handle it. In Cognitive Therapy we find that it can be really useful to look at the thoughts that run through people's heads at the times when their problems flare up and to figure out whether their interpretations of what's going on are useful or not. It the person is misinterpreting events, it can be useful to help him or her learn to recognize when the interpretations are off target and learn to see events more clearly. If it turns out that he or she is seeing things clearly but doesn't have good ways of handling the problems that come up, then it's useful to help find better ways of dealing with the problems. How does that sound to you?

One of the primary interventions used in Cognitive Therapy is teaching the client to identify the specific automatic thoughts that occur in problem situations, to recognize the effects these thoughts have on his or her emotions and behavior, and to respond effectively to those thoughts that cause difficulty. Negative, self-deprecating, or other problematic thoughts typically are a habitual part of the client's life and come "fast and furious" without the client necessarily being aware of their presence or their relationship to his or her distress. By using the interview and self-monitoring techniques discussed in Chapter 2, the client can learn to recognize dysfunctional thinking and its impact on moods and actions as a preliminary to learning ways to develop control over it. A colleague reported the following interaction:

During the first session, I had asked my client how often he thought that he had negative thoughts. His response was that he had them at times but only infrequently. Given his BDI of 38, my thinking was that he would have many, many more. He estimated no more than 2 to 3 a day. As a homework assignment I asked him to record as many of his thoughts as possible. I estimated that he probably had several negative thoughts a day, and that by the end of the week he would probably have 50 thoughts recorded. He quickly responded, "I'll never be able to do it. It would be too hard for me. I'll just fail." My response was to indicate that he already had 3 and only needed 47 more.

The client's limited awareness of his constant stream of negative thoughts was obvious when he expected to have 2 to 3 per day but produced 3 in a few seconds. After helping the client to recognize his ongoing stream of thoughts, the therapist was then able to help him learn how to record the thoughts so that they could be reviewed in therapy sessions and go on to introduce the idea of responding to dysfunctional thoughts.

Clients often find their negative automatic thoughts to be quite believable, even after their detrimental impact is clear. Thus the therapist's next task is to help the client to look critically at his or her automatic thoughts. This is most effective when done through guided discovery, as in the following example:

Therapist: One of the thoughts you said runs through your head when you're sitting at home was, "I'm a failure." A total failure?

Client: Yeah. I can't seem to do nothing right.

Therapist: I can see how sitting at home and thinking that would be pretty depressing. Not only do you feel bad about what you've done with your life so far but it doesn't seem like that would give you much hope for the future.

Client: It don't seem like there's nothing I can do.

Therapist: What is it that convinces you that you're a total failure?

Client: Just look at me. . . . I didn't finish school. I got two kids on welfare and I can't hardly keep them fed.

Therapist: Yeah, things are really rough for you and being stuck with no job and no money sure isn't success, but I'm wondering if that means you're a total failure. . . . One thing you mentioned when you were telling me what your day was like was that you make a point of giving your kids three square meals a day. Does that count as a failure?

Client: No, I guess that's something good.

Therapist: It sounds pretty worthwhile to me. I know there are plenty of mothers in your neighborhood who don't manage to do that. Is there a chance that there are other worthwhile things about you that you're not giving yourself credit for?

Client: I guess so. The neighbor kids sure like to come over to see me.

Therapist: When you're sitting at home and thinking, "I'm a failure," you feel pretty depressed. How do you think you would feel if you were thinking something like, "I've failed at some things, but I do some good things too"?

Client: (smiling slightly) I wouldn't feel nearly so bad.

Therapist: And which is closer to the truth?

Client: What you said.

As can be seen from the example, the process of looking critically at automatic thoughts leads naturally to the idea of "talking back" to dysfunctional thoughts. This involves generating adaptive alternatives to the dysfunctional automatic thoughts and using these alternative views to counteract the negative impact of the dysfunctional thoughts as they occur in problem situations. In the initial stages of therapy, clients generally record their automatic thoughts as they occur in problem situations, work with the therapist to develop effective responses, and then try to use these responses in new situations. As the client develops increasing skill in responding to dysfunctional thoughts, he or she begins to develop responses between sessions soon after the problem situations occur and eventually is able to recognize and respond to dysfunctional thoughts as they occur.

Homework assignments are used extensively throughout Cognitive Therapy. It is obvious that a client who does some of the work of therapy on his or her own between sessions will accomplish more than one who waits for his or her weekly hour with the therapist. In addition, a client, in the course of his or her daily life, is in a position to collect data and test the effects of cognitive and behavioral changes in a way that would be difficult to do within the therapy session. As will be seen in Chapter 3, noncompliance often occurs when homework assignments are used. However, rather than being a problem, noncompliance is often quite useful in identifying problems in the therapist–client relationship and in identifying the factors that block the client from making the desired changes. For example:

Doug, a young accountant, experienced chronic problems with procrastination which were so severe that he had lost three jobs because he was unable to complete his work on schedule. Early in therapy it became clear that part of the problem stemmed from his reluctance to perform any task less than perfectly, and Doug and his therapist agreed that it would be very helpful if he could become comfortable performing tasks less than perfectly when appropriate.

Because Doug was unemployed at the time, it was not possible to use his job as an arena for working on this issue, so it was agreed that Doug's hobby of model-plane building would be a good starting place. After some discussion, it was agreed that he would begin by starting to assemble a new model, intentionally doing it less perfectly than he normally would, and monitoring his thoughts and feelings while doing so. When he returned for the next therapy session Doug reported that he had been too busy to begin working on the model. When he and the therapist explored this, he explained that in order to work on the model he would need to completely unpack the boxes in his workroom (having moved recently), set up his workbench, carefully arrange the lighting, and arrange all of his tools in their proper places. He was trying to arrange everything perfectly so that he could assemble a model imperfectly!

This made it very easy for the therapist to point out how pervasive Doug's perfectionism was and the way in which it transformed simple tasks into major projects. Doug responded with increased motivation for working to change his perfectionism and was able to make steady progress thereafter.

It was emphasized earlier that it is important to address the client's underlying assumptions as well as intervening to counteract dysfunctional thoughts, improve mood, and change behavior problems. Otherwise it is possible to resolve the client's current problems but still leave the client prone to relapse. Clients usually find it difficult to identify the assumptions that are behind their dysfunctional thoughts and maladaptive behavior patterns but the importance of identifying and addressing the client's dysfunctional assumptions can easily be seen in the following example:

Edith, a successful academic, sought therapy because of a long-standing tendency to worry excessively about her health, the health of family members, and any threats to the safety of family members. She had been in therapy twice previously and had found therapy useful with other problems, but it had had little effect on her worries. She expressed considerable dissatisfaction with a previous therapist who had confronted her worries directly. Both she and the rest of her family were in good health, and her worries consistently proved unnecessary yet they were very persistent.

In exploring the pros and cons of eliminating her worries the therapist said, "It's clear that you'd stand to gain a lot by worrying less. What disadvantages would there be to getting rid of the worries?" Without pausing to think the client blurted out, "Then I would get sick!" Subsequent discussion made it clear that she held a strong belief that worrying served to forestall disaster. She had been unable to give up her worries because she believed this would jeopardize the safety of her family and herself.

Even though Edith knew intellectually that this idea was not logical, she could not convince herself that it was untrue, in part because she could cite a number of occasions on which she worried noticeably less than usual and misfortune followed. As she and her therapist examined this view logically and tested it in practice, she became increasingly convinced that it was untrue and was able to work successfully to control her worries.

In theory, effectively modifying the client's basic assumptions and any dysfunctional interaction patterns should leave him or her no more prone to future problems than anyone else. However, even if these interventions were completely effective, they would not render the client immune to future difficulties. Therefore, Cognitive Therapy closes with explicitly working to prepare the client to deal with future set backs. This work, based on Marlatt and Gordon's (1985) research on relapse prevention, consists of helping the client to become aware of high-risk situations, to identify early warning signs of impending relapse, and to develop explicit plans for handling high-risk situations and heading off potential relapse.

It is particularly valuable to explore the client's expectations regarding future problems and to address any unrealistic expectations. Often clients who have overcome significant problems through therapy are quite enthusiastic and hope or expect never to have similar problems again. If the client leaves therapy with this expectation, he or she may misinterpret subsequent difficulties and react with, "Oh my God, I'm depressed again! Cognitive Therapy didn't work, it really is hopeless." It is obvious that unrealistically optimistic expectations regarding the long-term effects of therapy could easily predispose the client to overreact when he or she encounters future problems. If it is possible to help the client to adopt the more realistic view that all people encounter problems from time to time, but that Cognitive Therapy has equipped him or her with the skills needed to cope effectively with problems, the risk of his or her overreacting to future setbacks should be decreased and potential relapses may be avoided.

Preferably, when the client has attained his or her goals for therapy, work on relapse prevention has been completed, and when the client's progress has been maintained long enough for him or her to have a reasonable amount of confidence that he or she will be able to cope with problems as they arise, the decision to terminate is made. In the typical case, the therapist and client agree to "taper off" by shifting from weekly sessions to biweekly and, possibly, monthly sessions when the time for termination is near. This not only makes the ending of therapy less abrupt but also provides therapist and client an opportunity to discover how well the client handles problems without the therapist's help and to discover whether any additional issues need to be addressed. In the hopes that early intervention with future problems may forestall major difficulties, the client is offered the opportunity to return for "booster sessions" if problems arise.

The Structure of a Cognitive Therapy Session

Each element of the structure of Cognitive Therapy sessions is designed to maximize the collaboration between therapist and client while working efficiently toward the client's goals. The practice of investing a few minutes at the beginning of each session to agree on an agenda that is followed unless it is explicitly modified is quite valuable in making the best use of the available time while remaining responsive to the client's wants and preferences. Having agreed upon an agenda for the session does not prevent the client from digressing onto other topics. However, having an agreed-upon agenda makes it possible for the therapist to gently but firmly limit the digressions and return the discussion to more productive topics without seeming authoritarian or controlling. If the client resists the therapist's efforts to use session time productively, the therapist can easily make it clear that by working to focus the session productively he or she is working with the client toward their shared goals rather than arbitrarily trying to take charge of the session. The use of a mutually agreed-upon agenda also minimizes the occurrence of the "hand-on-the-doorknob" phenomenon such as when, in the closing seconds of the session, the client says, "Oh, by the way, I think I'm gay," or in some other fashion raises an important topic when there is much too little time to address it. With many clients, an explicit discussion of "what we want to be sure to get to today" will identify the important issues so that therapist and client

Agenda Setting
Review client's current status, events of the past week
Solicit feedback regarding previous session

Review homework from previous session

Focus on main agenda item(s)

Develop new homework
Solicit feedback regarding current session

FIGURE 2. The structure of a typical session.

can decide how to best allocate the time. If a client introduces an important topic at the close of the session anyway, the therapist can respond to nonemergency topics with a statement like, "Gee, that sounds really important to you. It's a shame we don't have time to do it justice. Let's be sure to get it on the agenda next time." The client will quickly get in the habit of thinking ahead about how he or she wants to use the session.

Figure 2 shows the structure of a typical Cognitive Therapy session. It is simplest for therapist and client to quickly agree on the agenda for the session before delving into the events of the week or the client's current concerns. A quick review of major events since the last session is obviously valuable in enabling the therapist to monitor progress and identify any pressing problems that may have been overlooked in agenda setting. A review of homework from the previous session is important because most clients will understandably do homework only if it is used in the session and because even a brief amount of time spent reviewing the homework can help the client get more out of it. Each of these "housekeeping" functions is typically completed in a few minutes, and the bulk of the session then may be devoted to one particular issue or may be divided among several issues. The final work of the session consists of collaboratively developing a new homework assignment and then getting feedback from the client about the therapy session.

It may seem unusual that the client's feedback is solicited at two points during the therapy session. By soliciting feedback about the previous session toward the beginning of a session and soliciting feedback about the current session at the end of the session, the therapist increases the chances of identifying interpersonal problems or client dissatisfactions in time to address them before they disrupt therapy. It takes little time to solicit feedback unless there is a problem to discuss and, if there is a problem, the time needed to resolve it is well spent.

THE COMPLEXITIES ENCOUNTERED IN PRACTICE

When reading through an outline of the principles of Cognitive Therapy, the practice of this type of therapy can seem fairly straightforward. Actually, this is often not the case. Clients frequently present with very complex problems, with several coexisting problems, or with problems for which no "standard" approach has been developed and tested. In these cases the therapist is faced with the task of tailoring the cognitive approach to meet the needs of a particular client. For example:

Helga was a 25-year-old Czechoslovakian immigrant who was referred for therapy by her lawyer following her third conviction for shoplifting. She had a long history of episodes during which she would impulsively steal small items from department stores, often discarding them later. She was a generally law-abiding individual with strong religious values and professed an inability to control her impulse to steal. While she expressed a desire to stop stealing, she was reluctant to enter therapy because "I don't believe in it" and because she doubted that it would be helpful. She accepted referral for therapy primarily because her lawyer thought that doing so might help her avoid a jail sentence.

In addition to the problems presented by Helga's being an unwilling client and having a poor command of English, the therapist had no previous experience treating kleptomania and was not aware of any reports of Cognitive Therapy having been used as a treatment for kleptomania. However, after a series of telephone calls revealed that there were no local therapists who were fluent in Czech and that the one local therapist known to be experienced in treating kleptomania was unavailable, it was concluded that a trial of Cognitive Therapy was at least as promising as the other options open to Helga.

The initial phase of therapy consisted of spending considerable time attempting to develop a collaborative relationship by using the approach to developing collaboration with clients who are not receptive to therapy that is outlined in Chapter 10. The initial evaluation had not proven very helpful in understanding the stealing both because Helga described each episode as occurring spontaneously without any precipitant and because she was unable to describe any thoughts or feelings that preceded the stealing or coincided with it. Thus the second stage of therapy consisted of a detailed assessment of the client's episodes of stealing.

Helga was asked to record thoughts and feelings associated with mild impulses to steal as they occurred as well as any actual episodes of stealing. Over the course of several weeks of self-monitoring, it gradually became clear that the impulse to steal arose at times when Helga was quite angry over situations unrelated to the stealing. The impulses were accompanied by thoughts about "getting even" and thoughts expressing the belief that others' mistreatment of her justified the stealing. A close look at the situations that angered her and at the ways in which she handled anger revealed that she frequently felt abused and mistreated in fairly ordinary situations, directed her anger at "the system" rather than at the individual whom she saw as mistreating her, believed that she was helpless to do anything about the mistreatment, and failed to make use of appropriate options for handling situations she was angry about. As she saw it (at times when she was angry) she was being mistreated by "the system" and was therefore justified in retaliating by stealing from department stores since they were another part of "the system."

Given this understanding of her impulsive stealing, it was possible to develop a treatment plan that focused on the key elements of her problem. This included working to improve her impulse control (using the techniques discussed in Chapter 8), working to get her to focus on the specific situation that elicited her anger rather than "the system" in general, helping her to recognize and challenge the cognitive distortions that amplified her anger over situations that others would find aggravating rather than infuriating, and helping her learn more adaptive ways to handle situations that angered her. Interventions included identifying and challenging the cognitions that blocked adaptive responses as well as improving her skills in assertion, clear communication, and effective problem solving.

Over the course of 20 sessions her impulse control improved, she became more effective in handling problem situations, and she reported that the impulse to steal had become less and less frequent and then vanished. Although it was not possible to document conclusively that she was not stealing, both her lawyer and her probation officer were convinced that she had made sufficient progress to permit termination of therapy, and since termination she has gone for over 2 years without an arrest.

It is with complex or atypical clients such as Helga that the need for a strategic approach to intervention is most obvious. In working with clients who have multiple problems or with clients who have personality disorders, no empirically validated treatment protocols are available, and the therapist can easily feel overwhelmed and confused if he or she does not approach the client systematically. If such clients were rare, it might make sense to reserve the strategic approach for clients who are clearly complex or with whom a "standard" approach proves ineffective. However, difficult clients are anything but rare and, in addition, a strategic approach to Cognitive Therapy is helpful with "easy" clients as well. With all clients, an individualized treatment approach provides the therapist with an opportunity to improve the effectiveness and efficiency of therapy.

MISCONCEPTIONS ABOUT COGNITIVE THERAPY

A number of myths and misconceptions about Cognitive Therapy are encountered frequently. Among the most common of these are the following:

1. *Cognitive Therapy is "the power of positive thinking."* If anything, Cognitive Therapy is "the power of realistic thinking." While convincing oneself or one's client that everything is wonderful can cheer one up for the time being, this approach has several disadvantages. First, it is often difficult to convince people of things that are not true. Second, the results tend to be temporary because reality is likely to confront the individual sooner or later. Finally, actions based on views that are unrealistically optimistic can be just as maladaptive as actions that are based on unrealistically negative views. Although viewing problem situations realistically may be less cheery than a "Pollyanna" approach, it is almost always less negative than the client's view and lays a good foundation for effective coping.

2. *The cognitive theory of psychopathology claims that negative thoughts cause psychopathology.* From Figure 1 it should be obvious that although negative thoughts are seen as one part of a cycle, we do not assume that cognition is all that is important. Life events, social interactions, and any biochemical disorders play important parts in clients' problems as well. The cycles that perpetuate clients' disorders can be initiated at any point in the cycle. However, once a cycle has begun, cognition plays an important role and provides a promising point for intervention.

3. *Cognitive Therapy is simple.* Although the theory behind Cognitive Therapy is one which many people find quite reasonable and easy to understand, the practice of Cognitive Therapy is anything but simple. People are complex and, as the chapters on personality disorders show, intervening effectively can be quite complicated despite the simplicity of the theory.

4. *Cognitive Therapy is talking people out of their problems.* Many therapists are aware of Albert Ellis's disputational approach to challenging clients' irrational beliefs (e.g., Ellis & Greiger, 1977) and assume that Cognitive Therapy uses a similar approach. However, despite the theoretical similarities between the two approaches, Cognitive Therapy relies on "guided discovery" rather than debate (Dryden, 1984; Ellis, Young, & Lockwood, 1987). Our opinion is that when the therapist works with the client to help him or her to look critically at his or her views, the client is likely to be less resistant and is more likely to develop the skills needed to analyze future problems on his or her own.

5. *Cognitive Therapy ignores emotion and behavior.* Although the therapy's name is Cognitive Therapy, it might be more accurately called "Cognitive-Behavioral-Emotive Therapy." Although cognitions are the direct targets in Cognitive Therapy, therapeutic success is measured by corresponding change in emotion and behavior.

6. *Cognitive Therapy ignores the past.* It would be more accurate to say that Cognitive Therapy pays only as much attention to the past as is necessary. We find that while the client's previous experiences may be the foundation of his or her current problems, it is often possible to resolve the problems by focusing primarily on the present. If "here-and-now" inter-

ventions are effective, there is no need to use the client's time and money to explore the past. However, when working to challenge strongly held dysfunctional beliefs that resist here-and-now interventions, exploration of the origins of the beliefs can be both enlightening and effective.

7. *Cognitive Therapy is superficial.* It is true that Cognitive Therapy focuses on achieving the client's specific goals for therapy rather than automatically working for major personality changes. However, this does not necessarily mean that the resulting changes are limited or trivial. For example, a depressed, perfectionistic engineer recently sought treatment for chronic procrastination. Therapy focused on his depression, perfectionism, and procrastination over the course of 19 sessions. At the close of treatment he had not only experienced substantial improvement with the problems upon which therapy had focused but also was more emotionally expressive, more able to empathize with others, and more comfortable with intimacy in relationships. Cognitive Therapy can be superficial or deep, depending on the client's goals and the nature of the problems being addressed.

8. *The therapeutic relationship is unimportant in Cognitive Therapy.* Not only is a good therapeutic relationship essential for collaborating effectively with a client, but the interpersonal relationship between therapist and client can be very powerful for challenging the client's dysfunctional beliefs and assumptions regarding interpersonal relationships.

9. *Cognitive Therapy is finished in 15 sessions or less.* A number of outcome studies of Cognitive Therapy have limited the duration of therapy to 12 to 20 sessions for methodological reasons, so some readers have mistakenly concluded that Cognitive Therapy always lasts 12 to 20 sessions. Cognitive Therapy tends to accomplish results relatively quickly, but the duration of therapy depends on the nature of the client's problems, his or her level of motivation, and the degree to which the client's life situation complicates therapy. It can range from a few sessions to several years.

10. *Cognitive Therapy means no medication.* Although Cognitive Therapy alone has been found to be as effective as pharmacotherapy in the treatment of unipolar depression (see Simon & Fleming, 1985), it has also been found to work well in combination with psychotropic medication (Murphy, Simons, and Wetzel, 1984). Medication is definitely recommended in combination with Cognitive Therapy for clients with Bipolar Disorder, psychosis, and clients who are so depressed that they are unresponsive to verbal interventions. With other clients, the decision needs to be made on a case-by-case basis.

11. *Cognitive Therapy is just a collection of techniques.* Cognitive Therapy has developed a wide variety of specific techniques (for example, see Burns, 1980) and also has borrowed freely from other therapies. However, the therapist who focuses solely on applying techniques will encounter many situations where "cookbook" application of techniques proves inef-

fective. It is important to base interventions on an understanding of the client and his or her problems and to use interventions strategically rather than becoming preoccupied with techniques.

12. *The goal of Cognitive Therapy is to eliminate emotion.* Actually, the goal of Cognitive Therapy is to have emotion be proportional to the situation and to have the client be able to handle the emotion adaptively. In many situations, one goal of therapy is to "tone down" emotional overreactions; however, working to help the client recognize and understand his or her emotional reactions is often an important part of doing this. On the other hand, overcontrolled, unexpressive clients often become more "in touch" with their feelings as a side effect of Cognitive Therapy even when it is not one of their major goals.

13. *Cognitive Therapy is only appropriate for bright, intellectually oriented clients.* It is sometimes assumed that only bright, middle-class clients can benefit from interventions based on looking critically on dysfunctional thoughts. This is not at all the case. Cognitive Therapy has been used effectively with disadvantaged clients including clients who have had little formal education or who are illiterate. It is true that it is easiest to work with bright, well-educated, psychologically minded, highly motivated clients, but this is true for all therapies. With clients who have difficulty with abstract thinking, it is simply necessary to rely less on purely verbal interventions and more on using behavioral interventions to achieve cognitive change.

14. *Cognitive Therapy is not useful for seriously disturbed clients who need inpatient treatment.* Since Cognitive Therapy was developed primarily in outpatient settings and has been studied most extensively in outpatient settings, some have assumed that it is not appropriate for seriously disturbed clients. Although inpatient treatment typically consists of medication, supportive counseling, and occupational and expressive therapies, Cognitive Therapy can be used quite effectively in inpatient settings even in acute care with seriously disturbed clients. Various clinicians around the world have begun a literature regarding the application of Cognitive Therapy in inpatient settings and report promising results. The interested reader is referred to: Bowers (1988); Coché (1987); Freeman & Greenwood (1987); Greenwood (1983); Perris et al. (1987); and Perris (1988).

THE CLINICAL APPLICATION OF COGNITIVE THERAPY

This book is intended to help the practicing clinician apply Cognitive Therapy effectively with the complex problems encountered in clinical practice. This is not a simple task. However, if a therapist understands the basic principles of Cognitive Therapy, develops a comprehensive conceptualization of each client, incorporates cognitive principles into the structure of therapy sessions, and is not misled by myths and misconceptions, Cognitive Therapy can provide an effective and comprehensible approach to working with the full range of clients encountered in clinical practice.

II

The Clinical Practice of Cognitive Therapy

When the principles of Cognitive Therapy discussed in the preceding chapter are presented in workshops and training programs, they strike many therapists as straightforward and reasonable. This leads some therapists to conclude that applying these principles in clinical practice is simply a matter of learning some new techniques and using them. However, the effective application of Cognitive Therapy requires several important factors: a clinical assessment, which provides a basis for developing an understanding of the client and his or her problems; a strategic intervention plan based on this conceptualization; and a wide range of cognitive and behavioral interventions, which can be used flexibly in executing the intervention plan. Many therapists find that the practice of Cognitive Therapy involves their making some changes in their basic approach to clients as well as making more superficial changes, such as explicitly setting agendas and using some new interventions.

Fortunately, those who make the effort required to master this approach report finding it well worth the effort. The cognitive perspective provides a conceptual framework that makes therapy with complex clients less confusing and frustrating. In addition, cognitive techniques prove to be powerful tools for both alleviating current distress and accomplishing the lasting changes needed to head off future problems. Cognitive Therapy is most widely known as a short-term treatment for depression, and the effectiveness of time-limited Cognitive Therapy with severe depression has been well documented (e.g., Simon & Fleming, 1985). However, this treatment approach has proven to be quite versatile and is used effectively with problems ranging from phobias to personality disorders.

This initial section provides a detailed discussion of the assessment skills and therapeutic techniques that form a foundation for a strategic approach to intervention, followed by chapters detailing the application of Cognitive Therapy to depression, suicidality, and anxiety disorders. The second section covers Cognitive Therapy with each of the personality disorders, discussing assessment, conceptualization, and intervention strategies and providing case examples. The final chapter provides guidelines for developing, assessing, and maintaining skill in the practice of Cognitive Therapy for those who do not have access to training programs or who are interested in going beyond the training they have received.

2

Clinical Assessment in Cognitive Therapy

A short, plump, middle-aged woman enters the office, eyes red from crying. She explains that she "just can't handle" her boss at work whom she describes as a "schizophrenic" and as being hostile and critical for no reason. By her description, she has been feeling somewhat depressed, has been breaking into tears unexpectedly, has been experiencing panic attacks related to work, and "just can't go to work." She mentions that she was hospitalized for the treatment of depression several years ago but says that her current problems seem different from the problems she had then.

A therapist meeting a new client for the first time is faced with a complex task. Somehow, the therapist must form an initial understanding of the client, figure out how to be helpful, develop a good working relationship, and, at the same time, handle the practical details of working together. The task of understanding an individual and his or her problems is a difficult one. After all, the client is not likely to be able to provide a clear and concise analysis of his or her problems and may well be unable or unwilling to provide the detailed information that the therapist needs. The task facing the therapist in Cognitive Therapy is further complicated by the need to go beyond behavioral assessment or the collection of historical information to the assessment of the client's thoughts, feelings, beliefs, and underlying assumptions.

Although the task of assessment may be difficult, it plays a crucial role throughout the course of Cognitive Therapy. The initial assessment of the client's symptomatology, history, current functioning, and goals for therapy forms the foundation for the understanding of the processes that produce and maintain the client's difficulties and thus is the basis for the initial treatment strategy. Throughout treatment, the therapist constantly tests and refines his or her understanding of the client, revises this conceptualization as the client changes (and as flaws in the conceptualization are discovered), tests the effectiveness of interventions, and monitors the progress of therapy. The ongoing need for assessment does not end even when therapy ends. The client will need to develop the ability to monitor his or her own progress in order to maintain and build upon the gains made in therapy.

THE PROCESS OF CLINICAL ASSESSMENT

If by "clinical assessment" we mean the process of collecting and organizing information, then some form of assessment is a part of all psychotherapeutic interactions. The therapist observes, listens, and asks questions, interprets the resulting information in terms of his or her theoretical beliefs and previous experience, and bases subsequent interventions on the conclusions reached. When the client smiles and says, "I'm sorry I'm late, Doctor. I hope you're not upset," the psychoanalyst must decide, "Shall I interpret the resistance, the transference, or neither?"; the nondirective therapist must decide, "Shall I respond with unconditional positive regard, congruence, or reflection?"; and the cognitive therapist must decide, "Shall I explore the beliefs and assumptions behind this statement or just respond to it directly and go on with the session?" Clinical assessment can be quick and implicit or more careful and deliberate but whichever form it takes, assessment provides the basis for therapeutic intervention.

Many therapists rely primarily on an informal assessment process of simply observing whatever emerges in the course of therapy and interpreting it in terms of their own experience. The informal observations of experienced clinicians can be quite rich and remarkably accurate; however, informal assessment has several major drawbacks. First, because the information is not collected systematically, important information may be overlooked, or a biased picture may be created. Second, informally collected information can easily be influenced by a variety of factors, such as the therapist's verbal and nonverbal cues or the client's concerns and inhibitions, without the biases being noticed. Third, it is difficult to compare informally collected information from one client with similar information from another client or with information collected from the same client on another occasion. (For example, is a client who is "bummed out" more or less depressed than one who is feeling "pretty down"? Is a shift from feeling "bummed out" to feeling "not too good" an improvement or not?) Finally, it takes an extended period of time to develop a reasonably complete conceptualization of a client on the basis of informal assessment. This may not be a problem with undirected long-term therapies but a directed, strategic therapy such as Cognitive Therapy requires a clear conceptualization of the patient early in treatment to form a basis for early intervention. A more systematic approach to assessment can overcome these problems without interfering with the process of therapy.

Much of what has been written on the topic of cognitive assessment or on assessment in cognitive-behavioral therapy has been written from a research-oriented perspective (e.g., Arnkoff & Glass, 1982; Glass & Arnkoff, 1982; Kendall & Korgeski, 1979; Merluzzi, Glass, & Genest, 1981). These authors have much to contribute. However, there are important differences between assessment for use in research and assessment for use in clinical practice. In particular, the psychometric characteristics of measures are of great importance in research due to the requirements of statistical analyses, the need to be able to reach firm conclusions on the basis of a limited amount of data, and the desire to generalize findings beyond the individuals being assessed. Reliability and validity are of obvious value in clinical assessment as well; however, the most crucial question is whether the assessment procedure proves useful and practical with individual clients. Assessment techniques that provide rich data that is difficult to quantify may be quite valuable in clinical assessment but may not be acceptable for research use. Conversely, techniques that provide reliable, valid numerical scores may be ideal for research use but be of limited value in clinical practice.

In fact, assessment data that is of limited reliability or unknown validity can often be useful clinically because, ideally, clinical assessment is a self-correcting process. If therapist and client work together to collect needed information and interpret it and then implement therapeutic interventions based on their resulting conceptualizations, the results of their interventions serve as a source of corrective feedback. Successful interventions both accomplish desired changes and provide evidence of the clinical utility of the conceptualizations on which the interventions were based. Unsuccessful or partially successful interventions highlight areas in which the current conceptualizations are not adequate. Observation of the actual effects of the unsuccessful interventions and of the factors that influenced this outcome can serve as a basis for a revised conceptualization that can again be tested in practice. When clinical assessment is integrated with intervention in this way, this self-correcting process can make the most of rich data, even if the reliability and validity of a particular observation or self-report are uncertain. In order for this process to function effectively, the therapist and client must simply remember that their conceptualizations are hypotheses based on uncertain data and be alert for data that is inconsistent with their hypotheses.

TARGETS OF ASSESSMENT

In considering the focus of assessment, it is important to distinguish between an initial assessment and an ongoing clinical assessment in therapy. In the initial assessment, the therapist's goal is to obtain specific information about the client's problems, background, and goals for therapy in order to form an initial conceptualization, determine whether or not Cognitive Therapy is an appropriate treatment approach, and formulate an initial treatment plan. This calls for obtaining considerable information in a limited amount of time and is most easily done through a semistructured interview, supplemented by questionnaire data. In contrast, the focus of assessment in ongoing therapy is determined by the specific problem being addressed in therapy at the moment with the goal of obtaining detailed, specific information rather than a broad overview.

Assessment in the Initial Evaluation

The challenge for the therapist during an initial evaluation is to obtain enough information to permit the development of an early treatment plan without taking an unreasonable amount of time or sacrificing attention to the development of a good working relationship. Table 2 lists the topics ideally covered in an initial evaluation. This list of topics may appear both exhaustive and exhausting, but it is important to remember that the clinician's task is to obtain an *overview* of each area and to go into detail only if it is clear that detailed information is needed. With practice, it is possible to cover these topics in about an hour and a half while remaining emotionally responsive and beginning to develop a therapeutic relationship.

A balance between structure and flexibility is needed in order to be both efficient and sensitive in the initial interview. Without the therapist actively structuring the interview, an extremely verbal client could easily spend many weeks telling his or her story, whereas a less verbal client might finish quickly but fail to mention important information. On the other hand, a therapist who rigidly adheres to a preconceived structure risks appearing insensitive and alienating the client. The therapist's task can be simplified if he or she constructs an initial evaluation form that outlines the major points to be covered and provides sufficient space for recording the client's responses. By using such a form the therapist is freed from the task of remembering both the topics to be covered and the client's responses and thus can be more sensitive and responsive. With the outline to aid in maintaining structure, the therapist is free to cover topics whenever they fit naturally with the client's story without fear of forgetting to cover other important topics.

An important issue that is often overlooked in initial evaluations is the assessment of substance abuse. Alcohol abuse and the abuse of both prescription drugs and "street" drugs are widespread and can have an important impact on treatment for other problems as well as being substantial problems in their own right. It is important that such problems be detected early in treatment because therapy for other problems is likely to prove ineffective while active substance abuse persists.

TABLE 2. Topics to be Covered in an Initial Evaluation

Presenting problem
  Nature of problem(s), precipitants, course, client's understanding of problem, previous
  attempts at dealing with problem.
Current life situation
  Living situation, work, interests and activities, use of leisure time, family relationships,
  level of satisfaction with current life.
Developmental history
  Family history: descriptions of parents, relationships with parents, relationships with sib-
  lings, major events during childhood.
  School/occupational history: level of achievement, satisfaction, enjoyment, interests, career
  choices, problems.
  Social history: peer relationships in childhood, adolescence, adulthood; sexual relation-
  ships, sexual identity and preferences, dating, serious relationships, and marriage in-
  cluding description of partners and any relationship problems.
Traumatic experiences
  Disruptions of family relationships; medical, psychological, or substance abuse problems
  within the family; physical or sexual abuse.
Medical history
  Current health, time since last checkup, current medications, known allergies to medica-
  tions, previous medical problems, substance abuse, family history of medical problems,
  psychological problems, and/or substance abuse.
Psychiatric history
  Previous therapy or counseling (when? with whom? why? what was helpful/unhelpful?
  were there any problems with therapy?); previous occurrences of current problems; their
  course and outcome.
Mental status
  Appearance, attitude, behavior, mood and affect, speech and thought, perception, intellec-
  tual and cognitive functioning.
Client's goals for therapy
  State clearly and specifically, prioritize.
Client's questions and concerns

In assessing substance abuse, the goal is to determine if substance abuse is a problem for the client and to determine if it is a problem of sufficient severity that it needs to be addressed before focusing on other problems. Individuals with a substance abuse problem typically are slow to recognize the extent of the problem and frequently will deny the existence of the problem despite clear evidence to the contrary. Thus it is important for the therapist to look for evidence of a problem (such as interpersonal, work, financial, or legal problems stemming from substance abuse, in-ability to control drug use, development of tolerance, withdrawal symp-toms, etc.) rather than simply asking if there is a problem. It is also impor-tant to frame the questions so as to encourage acknowledgment of problems ("How often do you get drunk?" instead of "You don't get drunk, do you?"). Table 3 presents examples of the types of questions that

TABLE 3. Examples of Questions Useful in Assessing Substance Abuse

---

Personal concerns
  "Do you ever feel guilty about your drinking?"
  "Have you ever tried to cut back on your drinking or quit drinking?" (If so: Why? What happened? Did you resume? If so, why?)
Interpersonal problems
  "Does your (wife/husband) ever worry or complain about your drinking?"
  "Have you ever lost friends because of drinking?"
Work/financial/legal problems
  "Have you ever gotten into trouble at work because of drinking?"
  "Have you ever been arrested for things you did while drinking?"
Loss of control
  "Do you ever end up drinking more than you intend to?"
  "Can you stop drinking without a struggle after one or two drinks?"
Indications of tolerance or withdrawal
  "How much does it take for you to get drunk?"
  "How much do you need to drink before you start to feel it?"
  "What's the most you ever have to drink?"
  "What's the longest you go without drinking?" "What happens when you don't have anything to drink?"

---

often prove useful in assessing the presence and impact of substance abuse. Although the questions in this table are worded to assess alcohol abuse, similar questions would be appropriate for assessing abuse of other substances.

If it is clear that substance abuse is a problem of sufficient magnitude that it must be addressed before working on other problems, considerable therapeutic work may be needed before the client will accept this recommendation. It may be important to challenge such misconceptions as "I can't be an alcoholic, I only drink beer" and "I'm not an alcoholic, I quit drinking for 6 weeks." It may also be important to share with the client the evidence that the therapist has observed. If it is not clear whether substance abuse is the top-priority problem or not, a trial period during which therapist and client test to see whether the client can abstain and can successfully make use of therapy without first working on the drug or alcohol problem may be quite useful.

ASSESSMENT DURING THE COURSE OF THERAPY

Cognition, emotion, and behavior are the three aspects of human functioning that are of prime importance in Cognitive Therapy and that are the targets of assessment in ongoing therapy. The therapist's goal is to assess the client's cognitive, emotional, and behavioral responses in problem situations in sufficient detail to permit clear conceptualization of the problem and strategic planning of interventions. This is not a simple task.

Many different aspects of cognition are potentially of interest including: self-statements, attributions, expectations, self-efficacy expectations, irrational beliefs, basic assumptions, schemata, mental images, and current concerns. To further complicate the picture, these categories are not mutually exclusive. For example, the thought, "He's going to be mad at me because I'm so dumb," is a self-statement that includes an expectation ("He's going to be mad at me"), an attribution ("because I'm so dumb"), is suggestive of an efficacy expectation ("I'm dumb, therefore I won't do well at tasks requiring intelligence"), and a current concern ("I don't want him to be mad at me."). Fortunately, it is not necessary for the therapist to draw fine distinctions between different categories of cognitions in clinical practice. The focus is on the client's immediate, spontaneous cognitive response in a particular situation, not on a specific type of cognition. The questions being addressed are "what is the client's immediate cognitive response in the problem situation?" and "what cognitions coincide with intensification in the client's symptoms?"

The focus in assessing emotion is determined largely by the client's goals for therapy. Those emotions that play an important role in the client's problem or that occur in problem situations are the emotions that need assessment. The therapist's goal is to develop a clear understanding of the emotions that the client experiences and of their intensity. It is generally most productive to focus on changes in the intensity of emotion or changes in the type of feeling rather to attempt to assess the client's overall mood. Clients may initially report a global mood that they describe as unchanging or as fluctuating only randomly but a careful assessment often provides a very different picture. For example:

A middle-aged history professor complained of a chronic depressed mood which he described as stable and unchanging. He reported that he felt no pleasure or sense of accomplishment in any activities and said that this had been the case for years. The therapist asked him to collect additional data concerning the relationship between his activities and his mood by recording the activity he was engaged in, his level of enjoyment, and the level of his feeling of accomplishment each waking hour. To the surprise of both therapist and client this self-monitoring revealed a number of activities which were quite enjoyable and satisfying at the moment but which the client tended to overlook or devalue in retrospect.

As with cognition and emotion, the focus in assessing behavior in Cognitive Therapy is on the client's actions in problem situations. The therapist's goal is to understand clearly what the client did, when, and in what context. The importance of clear, specific information cannot be overemphasized. A client's description of behavior may be misleading if the therapist is not careful to obtain specific information. For example:

A timid bookkeeper who was working toward being more assertive opened the session by expressing strong concerns over the possible repercussions of having "told off" a colleague at work. When he was asked to describe his actual behavior in detail, it turned out that he had actually said, "Isn't that rushing things a bit?" in a very appropriate way, but that in his anxiety about assertion he mislabeled his behavior as aggressive.

Assessment Techniques

In assessing cognition, emotion, and, to a lesser extent, behavior we are forced to rely primarily on client descriptions despite knowing that these reports can easily be inaccurate, biased, censored, or fabricated. These obvious problems with reliance on self-report measures have raised important concerns that have received considerable discussion in recent years (Ericsson & Simon, 1980), and it seems clear that the method used in eliciting descriptions of internal processes exercises a strong influence on the validity of the descriptions. In clinical practice, the ultimate test of the value of self-reports is their utility in predicting or controlling behavior (Kendall & Hollon, 1981). If interventions based on the reports are effective, this demonstrates that the client's reports are useful whether or not their accuracy can be confirmed.

Over the years, many techniques have been developed for assessing cognition (Merluzzi et al., 1981), emotion (Levi, 1975), and behavior (Cone & Hawkins, 1977). Unfortunately, a great number of these techniques are impractical for regular clinical use due to the time, effort, and expense involved. The following is a survey of selected assessment techniques that prove both useful and practical in clinical practice.

Clinical Interview

The technique for assessing cognition, emotion, and behavior that is most frequently used in clinical practice is the interview. The therapist systematically or unsystematically asks the client to describe the thoughts, feelings, and actions that occurred in the situation under discussion and hopes to receive an accurate report. This task may seem simple and straightforward, but the importance of obtaining valid information complicates it considerably.

There is currently a controversy over whether it is at all possible for individuals' reports of their cognitions to be useful (Ericsson & Simon, 1980; Nisbett & Wilson, 1977; White, 1980). Although there is evidence that clients who are appropriately motivated and trained can provide useful data about behavior (Linehan, 1977), it has been argued that many important cognitions are not accessible to self-monitoring and that individuals' reports concerning their own cognitions are often no more accurate than are inferences made by naive observers (Nisbett & Wilson, 1977). Ericsson and Simon (1980) have reviewed the empirical literature bearing on these points and their analysis supports the conclusion that the way in which therapists obtain clients' reports of cognitions has a strong influence on the validity and usefulness of the reports but that properly obtained reports can be quite useful.

The following guidelines are designed to facilitate obtaining complete, accurate, and useful descriptions of client cognitions:

1. *Motivate the client to be open and forthright.* Make sure that it is clear that providing full, honest, detailed reports is in the client's interest by (a) providing a clear rationale for seeking the information, (b) demonstrating the relevance of the information being requested to the client's goals, and (c) demonstrating the value of clear, specific information by explicitly making use of the information.

2. *Minimize the delay between event and report.* This will result in more detailed information and will reduce the amount of distortion due to imperfect recall. For events occurring outside of the therapist's office, use an *in-vivo* interview or self-monitoring techniques when possible.

3. *Provide retrieval cues.* Review the setting and the events leading up to the event of interest either verbally or by using imagery to improve recall.

4. *Avoid possible biases.* Begin with open-ended questions that ask the client to describe his or her experience without suggesting possible answers or requiring inference. Focus on "What happened?" not on "Why?" or "What did it mean?" Do not ask clients to infer experiences they cannot remember. Wait until after the entire experience has been described to test your hypotheses or ask for specific details.

5. *Encourage and reinforce attention to thoughts and feelings.* Clients who initially have difficulty monitoring their own cognitive processes are more likely to gradually develop increased skill if they are reinforced for accomplishments than if they are criticized for failures. Some clients may need explicit training in differentiating between thoughts and emotions, in attending to cognitions, or in reporting observations rather than inferences.

6. *Encourage and reinforce acknowledgment of limitations in recall.* If the therapist accepts only long, detailed reports, this increases the risk of the client's inventing data in order to satisfy the therapist. It is important for the therapist to appreciate the information the client can provide and to encourage the client to acknowledge his or her limits in recalling details because incomplete but accurate information is much more useful than detailed reports fabricated in order to please the therapist.

7. *Watch for indications of invalidity.* Be alert for inconsistency within the client's report, inconsistency between the verbal report and nonverbal cues, and inconsistency between the report and data obtained previously. If apparent inconsistencies are observed, explore them collaboratively with the client without being accusatory or judgmental.

8. *Watch for factors that may interfere.* Be alert for indications of beliefs, assumptions, expectancies, and misunderstandings that may interfere with the client's providing accurate self-reports. Common problems include (a) the fear that the therapist will be unable to accept the truth and will become angry, shocked, disgusted, or rejecting if the client reports his or her experiences accurately; (b) the belief that the client must do a perfect job of observing and reporting the experiences and that he or she is a failure if the reports are not perfect from the beginning; (c) the fear that the information revealed in therapy may be used against the client or may give the therapist power over him or her and (d) the belief that it is dangerous to closely examine experiences involving strong or "crazy" feelings for fear that the feelings will be intolerable or will "get out of control."

Kendall (1981) argues that open-ended questions may not provide cues of sufficient strength to attain recall of all available information and suggests that assessment techniques that provide clients with possible cognitions (or emotions, or behaviors) to endorse or reject may facilitate a more complete recall of information. Although it is true that providing more detailed retrieval cues should facilitate recall, questions that suggest possible cognitions, emotions, or behaviors are more likely to bias clients' responses than are open-ended questions. If increased recall is gained at the cost of decreased accuracy, this strategy for improving recall may be counterproductive. In general, techniques for improving recall that do not suggest possible responses are preferable. Of the techniques included in these guidelines, minimizing the delay before obtaining the report, providing recall cues by reviewing the stimuli eliciting the event of interest, using self-monitoring techniques, and planning *in vivo* experiences for the specific purpose of collecting data all provide ways of enhancing recall while minimizing possible biases.

The task of assessing emotional responses through clinical interview can be particularly complex. For example:

A young woman requesting treatment for depression presented a description of her difficulties that did not coincide with the therapist's understanding of depression. After some confusion, the therapist asked her to describe what it felt like to be "depressed". She described episodes of abruptly feeling "really miserable" with sweating palms, pounding heart, trembling, and nausea. In short, she described a panic attack, not depression. It quickly became clear that she used the term *depression* to refer to all unpleasant sensations and did not differentiate between depression, anxiety, and anger.

Clients often may have difficulty labeling emotions, may label emotions idiosyncratically, or may have difficulty noticing mild emotions. Inconsistencies between reported emotions and nonverbal cues, actions, or reported cognitions make it possible to detect these difficulties and take remedial action. It is not unusual for the therapist to need to devote some time to helping clients develop greater skill at detecting and expressing emotions or helping clients differentiate between thoughts and emotions. With the therapist providing feedback concerning nonverbal indications of emotion in facial expression, voice tone, or action, most clients learn to identify and describe emotions fairly quickly.

In-Vivo Interview and Observation

A major problem with the clinical interview as an assessment technique is that clients must rely on recall in order to provide information about events occurring outside the therapy session and therefore important information can easily be forgotten or distorted. Unfortunately, most events of interest to the therapist occur outside of the therapist's office. One possible solution is for the therapist to accompany his or her client into the problem situation and both to conduct an interview and to observe carefully as the events of interest occur. This approach effectively eliminates the limitations imposed by extensive reliance on memory and can quickly provide much valuable information. However, the therapist's presence in the problem situation may have an important impact on the situation or the client's response. In addition, in-vivo expeditions may entail a substantial investment of the therapist's time (and thus the client's money). When it is feasible, in-vivo interview and observation can be quite productive.

Self-Monitoring

A second method for reducing the need to rely on recall for information regarding cognitions, emotions, and behavior occurring outside the therapist's office is self-monitoring. A variety of methods have been developed for recording events as they occur. These include maintaining a diary or journal (Mahoney, 1977), making audiotape recordings (Craighead, Kimball, & Rehak, 1979), and completing structured questionnaires (Schwartz & Gottman, 1976) among others.

The Dysfunctional Thoughts Record (DTR), often referred to as a "thought sheet," is the most frequently used approach to self-monitoring in Cognitive Therapy (Beck et al., 1979; Burns, 1980). The "three-column" DTR is a chart that provides a simple, open-ended framework to aid clients in recording information regarding the stimulus situation, emotional responses, and cognitions. Its simplicity renders it quite versatile, and the instructions can easily be tailored to suit virtually any clinical situation.

For example:

Dianne was a young woman who entered treatment complaining of problems with both depression and anxiety. Initially, she was not able to specify the situations that elicited her depression or anxiety, and she was unable to describe her thoughts and feelings in enough detail to be useful. Because the need for more detailed information was already clear to the client, the DTR was introduced to her with a dialogue similar to the following:

Therapist: Well, it seems clear that our first step will need to be getting a better picture of just when your problems flare up and what's going on then, so that we can figure out how to deal with them. How does that sound to you?

Dianne: That makes sense.

Therapist: The problem with trying to figure things out here in the office is that it's hard for you to remember all the detailed information we need. (Client nods) Now it would have been easier to remember the details if you had known ahead of time that we were going to talk about these things, but you'd still be stuck relying on memory, and it would be easy to lose track of the details.

Dianne: Yeah.

Therapist: The obvious solution would be to write down the stuff you want to remember, then you don't have to worry about forgetting. What do you think about that?

Dianne: I'll try it.

Therapist: There's one particular format I generally recommend to people because it makes keeping track of the information we need easier. How about if I show it to you and see what you think?

Dianne: Sure.

Therapist: (Showing Dianne a blank DTR form) This is really just three columns on a sheet of paper. In the first column you'd briefly describe what the situation is, just the facts without any commentary on it, like "in bed after alarm clock goes off Monday morning." Does that make sense?

Dianne: Yeah, that's pretty straightforward.

Therapist: In the next column you'd write down what you're feeling . . . sad, happy, anxious, whatever. You might just feel depressed, for example, or you might feel depressed, and anxious, and discouraged all at once, so you'd write all three down. Also, it turns out that it's useful to have an idea how strong these feelings are. That's not an easy thing to put down on paper. The best way we've been able to come up with is to rate each feeling on a scale from 1 to 10 where a 10 is the strongest you've ever felt that particular feeling and a 1 is a feeling that's just barely noticeable.
              For example, if you woke up Monday morning feeling discouraged, you'd write down "discouraged"; then you'd think of the most discouraged you've ever felt (which would be a 10) and compare how you're feeling Monday morning with that. A 5 would be about half that discouraged, an 8 or 9 would be feeling pretty intensely discouraged, and a 2 or 3 would be feeling mildly discouraged. It's not precise but it gives us a clear enough idea to be useful. Does that sound like something you could try?

Dianne: I guess I can do that.

Therapist: Most people find it's a bit awkward at first but that they get used to it pretty quickly.

Dianne: Okay.

Therapist: In the third column you'd write down what we call your "automatic thoughts." That's your immediate reaction that just pops into your head without any particular line of reasoning leading up to it, without you particularly intending to think it. It turns out that the immediate thoughts are most useful for understanding people's problems and figuring out how to deal with them. Just pay attention to the thoughts that come to you right away and write them down whether or not there's an obvious connection between the thoughts and your problem.

It's most helpful if you can write the thoughts down just the way they ran through your head, quoting them as much as possible. If the thought you notice Monday morning is, "God, I don't want to get up! The day's gonna be a drag," it will be more useful to write it down just like that than to paraphrase it as, "I didn't want to get up because it seemed like a bad day." Does that make sense?

Dianne: Yeah, I think so.

Therapist: Most people find it takes a little practice to get smooth at noticing the thoughts running through their heads and writing them down. That's not the sort of thing people usually do very often.

The final thing that would be useful to know would be how much you believe each of the thoughts you write down. You've probably noticed that a lot of the thoughts that run through your head are real believable but that there are some thoughts that you've got doubts about or don't believe at all right as you think them. So the last thing is to rate how much you believe each thought right as you think it from 0 to 100%, where 100 means you're absolutely certain it's true and 0 means you don't believe it at all.

Dianne: Do I try to write down everything that happens?

Therapist: That's a good question. Because we're trying to understand your periods of anxiety and depression, what would probably be most useful would be to watch for times when you start feeling noticeably more anxious or depressed and record this information then. Because there's a limit to how much we can discuss in a session, writing down two or three events a day would end up being plenty. However, two or three times a week would still be helpful. How does that sound?

Dianne: I'll try it.

Dianne returned with the DTR seen in Figure 3. She and her therapist were then able to review the incident in more detail using the interview techniques discussed and obtain additional information. At the same time, the therapist was

Situation Briefly describe the situation	Emotion(s) Rate 0-100%	Automatic Thought(s) Try to quote thoughts then rate your belief in each thought 0-100%
I had just taken my trash out Monday nite - I realized I had forgotten something so I took another bag out later and set the bag in the back. I ran into my landlord there & we were talking about the animals going out there at nite. When I went upstairs he put the trash in the cans. I saw this from my kitchen window.	Depression 50%	Why was I so stupid not to think to put the trash in the cans & close them tight so the animals couldn't get at it. He probably thinks I'm so stupid. I'm always doing stupid things around him. He might not want me for a tenant anymore since I think he has an idea I've been sick with my nerves.

FIGURE 3. Sample Dysfunctional Thought Record.

able to provide constructive feedback that improved Dianne's subsequent use of the DTR. The data from this, and other situations that Dianne monitored, made it possible for her therapist to develop a clear understanding of her problems relatively quickly.

In the example, a hypothetical example was used to explain the use of the DTR to Dianne. It can be particularly effective for the therapist to use an actual incident that the client has described in presenting the DTR. When the therapist anticipates asking the client to complete the DTR as a homework assignment, he or she can make a point of recording a situation that is discussed in the course of the session in DTR format. Then, when the DTR is explained, the therapist can easily show how the DTR was used as a simple way to record the information the client provided.

Clients typically find the DTR easy to use once they have an opportunity to practice using it, and they typically use it effectively once it is clear to them that the DTRs prove useful. Some individuals need training in differentiating between thoughts and feelings or in rating the intensity of feelings and the degree to which they believe the automatic thoughts. In such cases jointly completing a DTR or two during a therapy session and providing nonpunitive feedback on subsequent attempts to use the DTR is generally sufficient. Sometimes clients have difficulty completing their initial DTR because of a fear that "I won't do it right." This problem can be minimized by addressing this fear when self-monitoring is first assigned and making it clear that the client need not complete the form perfectly or "right" in order for it to prove useful.

Thought Sampling

The techniques for *in-vivo* thought sampling that have been developed in recent years by Klinger (1978) and by Hurlburt, Leach, and Saltman (1984) provide a method for obtaining a picture of an individual's typical pattern of cognitions rather than focusing on responses in problem situations. The basic procedure used by these investigators is to provide the client with an electronic device that sounds a tone at random intervals and to instruct the client to immediately record whatever cognitions are occurring when the tone sounds. The resulting sampling of cognitions is independent of environmental or subjective stimuli and thus should be unbiased. A large enough sample of cognitions should provide reliable data regarding overall cognitive patterns.

A variety of methods have been used for recording cognitions, including having clients dictate their cognitions into a tape recorder, instructing them to write down their cognitions in a notebook, and asking them to complete structured questionnaires. A simple method for use in clinical practice would be to use the alarm function on an inexpensive digital watch to provide the cue for thought sampling and to use the DTR for recording the situation, thoughts, and feelings at that moment. In order to maintain an unbiased sampling procedure, it would be important to set the watch's alarm to sound according to a random schedule.

This procedure can also be valuable when the situational or cognitive cues associated with the problem being treated are not clear. For example:

A middle-aged factory foreman had made good progress in therapy by using DTRs to identify dysfunctional cognitions related to episodes of anger and depression and then "talking back" to the cognitions. However, he began to experience a vague depressed mood that seemed not to be related to any clear stimuli. He was unable to identify situations or cognitions related to the depressed mood and therefore was asked to use a thought sampling procedure to collect additional data. When he returned for his next therapy session, a review of the cognitions he had recorded revealed constant ruminative thoughts centering on a theme of "I'm too tired to . . . ." It gradually became clear that these ruminative thoughts were responsible for his decreased motivation to deal with problems actively and his increased depression.

There are some disadvantages to using the thought sampling procedure. It can be intrusive, it generally will produce much irrelevant data along with the useful data, and, unless well planned, can be reactive. However, if a cross-section of the client's thoughts is needed or if it is not clear what cues elicit the client's response, this procedure may be worth considering. In order to increase the likelihood of the client's complying with the thought sampling procedure, it may be important to identify the aspects of the procedure that the client expects to find difficult, uncomfortable, or embarrassing and then to plan how the client can deal with these eventualities.

Techniques for Assessing Beliefs and Assumptions

The task of identifying the dysfunctional beliefs and underlying assumptions that contribute to the client's problems is complicated by the fact that these cognitions typically are not accessible to direct self-report. Although these cognitions underlie the automatic thoughts and cognitive distortions assessed by the preceding techniques, the individual's beliefs and assumptions are often reflected only indirectly in the content of his or her thoughts. Thus the clinician usually must rely on inference rather than observation in identifying key beliefs and assumptions.

One approach to identifying dysfunctional beliefs and assumptions is to wait until a large sample of automatic thoughts has been collected through interview and self-monitoring and then to look for recurrent themes or patterns among these thoughts. For example, if a client says on one occasion, "I'm a worthless failure," at another time reports thinking,

"If I can't succeed at this, what good am I to anybody?", and during a more optimistic period reports thinking, "I'll make my quota and show them I'm not as worthless as they think I am," the therapist might hypothesize that the client holds a belief equating worth with success. There would be obvious problems with the therapist's simply assuming that his or her inference is true. However, the inference can be tested by considering whether it is consistent with the client's behavior, by obtaining the client's feedback, and by observing the effects of interventions based on this inference. Returning to our example, if the client has a history of striving to succeed and becoming depressed in response to failure, if the client endorses the therapist's statement that "it sounds like you operate on the assumption 'If I'm not successful, I'm worthless'," and if interventions based on the assumption that the client holds this belief prove effective, the therapist has grounds for concluding that his or her inference is accurate.

Another approach to identifying dysfunctional beliefs and assumptions is the "vertical arrow" or "downward arrow" technique described by Burns (1980). In this technique, therapist and client choose an apparently important automatic thought as a starting place and then, rather than considering whether the thought is valid or not, they consider the implications if the thought were true. For example:

A middle-aged man was almost completely immobilized by doubt over his ability to successfully perform even ordinary tasks. When faced by an assignment at work or a chore at home he would wonder "Can I do it or not?" and be extremely reluctant to attempt the task. After selecting a specific situation where this thought occurred, the downward arrow technique was used to understand the dysfunctional belief behind the client's strong reluctance to attempt any task where he was not certain of complete success:

Therapist: So, when it's time to start on the report, the thought "Can I do it or not?" comes up and you can't get yourself to start working on it. Suppose you were to try working on it and found out that you couldn't do it. What would that mean?

Client: If I can't do something worthwhile I'm a failure.

Therapist: A complete failure?

Client: Yes.

Therapist: And if you *were* a complete failure, what would that mean?

Client: I'm no good to anybody.

Therapist: So, it sounds like your view is, "If I try to do something and can't, that means I'm a total failure and no good to anybody." No wonder you can't get yourself to try things if you aren't sure you'll succeed.

As with the first approach to identifying dysfunctional beliefs and assumptions, it is important to treat the results of the downward arrow technique as hypotheses to be tested, particularly because the decision of how far to pursue the chain of *what ifs* is quite subjective. However, this technique has the advantage of being comprehensible to the client and providing a method that he or she may be able to use independently.

Self-Report Questionnaires

The assessment techniques discussed thus far can be quite useful but definitely are not "quick and easy." A number of investigators have attempted to develop assessment techniques that are more economical to use, by constructing a variety of self-report questionnaires. These measures typically can be self-administered by clients and have numerical scoring systems intended to permit easy interpretation of responses. They are designed to have significant advantages over other assessment techniques but unfortunately have limitations as well.

Endorsement-Type Questionnaires. A large variety of questionnaires have been developed in which respondents are presented with specific responses and are asked to either indicate the extent to which they agree or disagree with each alternative, indicate which of several alternatives is most typical of them, or indicate the frequency with which each response occurs. This approach has been used widely in the assessment of irrational beliefs (Glass & Merluzzi, 1981), self-statements (Kendall & Hollon, 1981), and other cognitive variables.

Unfortunately, there are a number of problems with this type of questionnaire. One problem is that a questionnaire may seem to cover its target area thoroughly but overlook important content areas because they have not been encompassed by theory or noted by the persons who developed the questionnaire. Even when the item pool is generated empirically in order to minimize this risk, no forced-choice measure can encompass all possible options, and there remains a risk of biasing or limiting the client's responses by providing a limited number of alternatives to endorse. The numerical scoring systems that make these questionnaires so convenient for research use can limit their clinical utility by combining the client's responses into a numerical score that obscures much of the useful information. Finally, it is difficult to know whether a client's responses on this type of questionnaire accurately reflect the client's day-to-day cognitions, reflect the client's self-perception, or reflect the impression the client wishes to create.

Endorsement-type questionnaires may be useful at times as a method for quickly surveying areas of possible interest. However, it is not clear that this generally would save time and energy because a more detailed assessment would be needed if clinically significant responses are noted.

Free-Response Questionnaires. Another type of self-report questionnaire is that in which the client is simply instructed to record his or her responses to a situation or to open-ended questions and is provided with unstructured space in the questionnaire to do so. One example of this approach is the "thought listing" procedure reviewed by Kendall and Hollon (1981) in which respondents are simply instructed to write "everything that went through your mind" regarding a given situation.

The free-response format has an advantage in that it minimizes the possibility of the investigator's preconceptions' biasing or limiting clients' responses. Unfortunately, free-response questionnaires have many of the same disadvantages as the clinical interview, and the rating systems used to quantify responses for research are too time consuming to be practical for clinical use. These questionnaires are best viewed as self-administered clinical interviews and the same guidelines that apply to interviewing should apply to the construction and administration of these measures.

Self-Report Measures of Symptomatology. A variety of questionnaires that assess target symptoms have been developed that can be quite useful for monitoring progress in therapy. Regular monitoring of target symptoms can provide regular feedback on the effectiveness of therapy and can also provide a useful cue for occasions on which sudden changes (which may be worth exploring) have occurred.

The Beck Depression Inventory (BDI, Beck 1978) is a self-report measure that frequently proves useful clinically:

John, a young lawyer, started his eighth session of Cognitive Therapy by expressing deep hopelessness. He reported that after feeling better for a few weeks, he was depressed once again. He expressed the conviction that therapy had accomplished nothing and that there was no hope of overcoming his depression. John had been asked to complete the BDI in the waiting room before each therapy session, and his therapist noted that his current BDI score (18) was considerably lower than his initial score (32). As John compared his responses on the two occasions, he was quickly able to see that although he was indeed depressed again, much of his improvement persisted, and his progress in therapy had not been "wiped out." He and the therapist were then able to focus on the recent exacerbation of his depression rather than needing to spend much of the session addressing his hopelessness.

Short, self-administered questionnaires such as the BDI or the state form of the State-Trait Anxiety Inventory (Speilberger, Gorsuch, & Sucherne, 1970) can easily be used on a regular basis to monitor progress in therapy and can be particularly valuable for quickly spotting times when therapist and client are "stuck" and are making little progress. However, it is necessary to use such measures critically and to compare the numerical score against the client's report and the clinician's observations. Both discrepancies between the numerical score and other data and unexpected fluctuations in scores should be explored carefully.

Diagnostic Inventories. With the publication of DSM-III and DSM-III-R, a large number of paper-and-pencil measures, as well as structured and semistructured interviews have been developed with the intent of assisting in diagnosis (see Reich, 1987b). Many of these measures show promise for use in both research and in clinical practice. However, virtually all of them will require additional development and validation before they are ready for widespread clinical use.

Traditional Psychological Testing

Objective and projective psychological tests have traditionally been rejected by clinicians with behavioral and cognitive-behavioral orientations because it was believed that such approaches could have little validity and usefulness (Sobel, 1981). However, intelligence tests, projective techniques, and personality inventories all have considerable potential for assessing cognitive variables that are of interest to the therapist, and many of these measures have more evidence of reliability and validity than the self-report measures typically used by behavioral and cognitive-behavioral clinicians (Sundberg, 1981).

Simply looking through clients' responses on projective tests, such as the Thematic Apperception Test (Murray, 1943), suggests potential for using these approaches to obtain information useful to the cognitive therapist. For example, Al, a 17-year-old boy in an alcohol treatment program, responded to one TAT card (3BM) saying, "It looks like he has a real drug problem or something and is about at the bottom of the elevator. Looks like he's beyond help; so he'll probably die." This response seems to provide an indication that the client is experiencing significant hopelessness about overcoming his drinking problem that could interfere with motivation for treatment or contribute to a risk of suicide if not addressed. This type of interpretation is of doubtful reliability or validity but can prove clinically useful if it is used to generate hypotheses about the client that are subsequently tested.

Some systems for interpreting the MMPI produce interpretative statements that are easily translated into a cognitive framework. For example, among other things, the interpretation of Al's MMPI profile suggested that he was likely to place a high value on status and recognition, to feel a strong need to be around other people, and to act without considering the consequences of his actions. Interestingly, it also indicated that despite his apparent hopelessness about overcoming his drinking problem, he was not particularly depressed. This information, if valid, could facilitate development of an appropriate treatment plan.

Contemporary objective and projective psychological tests offer many advantages, including the use of actuarial data to aid in interpretation of results, the ability to guard against attempts to mislead the therapist, and the option of using computerized interpretation services. Unfortunately, the interpretation of traditional objective and projective personality tests has not yet been approached systematically from a cognitive point of view and, as a result, use of these measures can require a considerable amount of translation on the clinician's part. Some approaches to interpretation are so heavily psychodynamic in orientation that attempts at translation are difficult if not impossible (for example: Bellak, 1975; Gilberstadt, & Duker, 1965), whereas other approaches are much more easily used in a cognitive framework (Caldwell & O'Hare, 1975; Hill, 1972). Still, even if the task is not difficult, the validity of the interpretation may suffer in translation.

At present, a cognitive therapist who is trained in the interpretation of measures such as the TAT, the MMPI, and the Holtzman Inkblot Technique, and who is able to integrate them into a cognitive framework, may find them quite useful as part of the initial evaluation, particularly with complex clients. If cognitively oriented investigators work on methods for interpreting objective and projective tests within a cognitive-behavioral framework this could provide a valuable resource. However, for the present, clinicians must either rely on their own skills at fitting current interpretive systems into a cognitive framework or do without these measures.

CONCLUSION

Overall, the clinical interview and self-monitoring techniques appear to be the most generally useful assessment strategies for the cognitive therapist. These techniques are eminently practical and, when done skillfully, can provide a wealth of useful data. It is true that these data may or may not be reliable and valid, but if the conceptualizations which are developed on the basis of this information are tested in practice, this limitation can be overcome. In clinical practice, if interventions based on assessment data work consistently over time, the data are valid enough. Conversely, if the intervention fails, either the assessment, the interpretation of the data, or the execution of the intervention is insufficient and further work is needed.

At this point, self-report measures of symptomatology can be useful in the initial evaluation or for monitoring progress in therapy, thought sampling may be useful on occasion, and traditional psychological tests may be useful to those who are trained in interpreting them. However, the myriad of measures of cognitive variables that have been developed in recent years are generally more valuable for research use than in clinical practice, and even the most promising need further development. As Sundberg (1981, p. 8) writes:

All new instruments produced, like the traditional tests, must be subjected to questions about reliability, validity, norms, social desirability, and test-taking attitudes. They should also be scrutinized for their incremental utility. That is, questions such as the following should be asked: Do new cognitive measures add any validity to predictions and other operations beyond that provided by old procedures? If they do, are they more efficient, less time consuming, or easier to administer?

However, by and large, researchers developing new and promising approaches to assessing cognition have overlooked the need for validity studies and guidelines for clinical interpretation in their rush to investigate areas of particular interest (Glass & Merluzzi, 1981). Fortunately, clinical interview and self-monitoring work quite well in practice, so the clinician need not suffer while waiting for researchers to refine additional assessment techniques.

3

Cognitive and Behavioral Interventions

Once the therapist and client have jointly agreed upon treatment goals, the therapist will need a range of skills and techniques in order to implement the overall treatment strategy. The goal of this chapter is to describe the wide range of techniques that are used in Cognitive Therapy. The techniques will be broadly categorized as "cognitive" and "behavioral." However, it is important to remember that a behavioral technique, such as assertion training, can be used to accomplish cognitive changes (i.e., changes in expectancies regarding the consequences of assertion), as well as changes in interpersonal behavior. Similarly, cognitive techniques are often intended to produce changes in behavior as well as cognition. Therefore, in our descriptions of these techniques, we will distinguish between those that *primarily* produce changes in cognition and those that *primarily* produce changes in behavior.

COGNITIVE TECHNIQUES

Not surprisingly, cognitive interventions play a central role in Cognitive Therapy. Early in therapy, the therapist and client work to identify and modify dysfunctional automatic thoughts and cognitive distortions. Later in therapy, the client's maladaptive beliefs and assumptions become the focus of attention. A wide range of specific techniques have been developed for use in modifying these cognitions. Although many of these techniques can be used effectively to change automatic thoughts, cognitive distortions, and underlying assumptions, the techniques are categorized according to the type of cognition they are most commonly used to modify.

Techniques for Challenging Automatic Thoughts

As was discussed in Chapter 1, the process of identifying and challenging automatic thoughts is central to cognitive therapy. The use of the

Daily Record of Automatic Thoughts

Date	Situation Briefly describe the situation	Emotion(s) Rate 0–100%	Automatic Thought(s) Try to quote thoughts then rate your belief in each thought 0–100%	Rational Response Rate degree of belief 0–100%	Outcome Re-rate emotions

FIGURE 4. Five-column Dysfunctional Thought Record.

Dysfunctional Thought Record (DTR), or "thought sheets," in monitoring and recording automatic thoughts was discussed in Chapter 2. With the addition of columns in which the client can record his or her "rational responses" and rerate his or her emotions after developing these responses to the automatic thoughts (see Figure 4), thought sheets can be used as a format for challenging the automatic thoughts as well as being used for self-monitoring.

Typically, after the client has learned to use thoughts sheets to record the automatic thoughts that occur in problem situations, the therapist and client work together to look at them critically, and to develop more adaptive alternatives to those thoughts that are found to be unrealistic or dysfunctional. These are then listed on the thought sheet as rational responses. Although the goal is for the client to develop the ability to identify dysfunctional automatic thoughts as they occur and to generate effective responses quickly, most clients find this task to be difficult enough that it is necessary to approach this goal in a series of steps. At first, many clients are able to look critically at their automatic thoughts only with the therapist's assistance. With practice, clients become able to review their automatic thoughts and develop written rational responses soon after problem situations have passed, needing limited help from the therapist. Next, clients find that they are able to look critically at their automatic thoughts even when they are quite upset, as long as they do it in writing. Finally, clients reach the point where they can develop effective responses to automatic thoughts "in their heads" and only need to write out the thoughts and responses when particularly difficult problems arise.

Once the client becomes able to generate rational responses soon after the problem has arisen, an immediate index of the effectiveness of the responses is provided by the client's rerating of the intensity of his or her emotions. If the intensity of the problematic emotions has dropped substantially, the responses have been effective; if the intensity has changed little, the responses have been ineffective. It is important for the client to be able to generate rational responses that are convincing and that address each of the major points raised in the automatic thoughts.

A wide variety of techniques for challenging automatic thoughts have been developed and because no single technique is universally effective, the therapist needs to master a wide range of these techniques. A number of the most widely used of these techniques are discussed next.

Understanding Idiosyncratic Meaning. It is not safe for the therapist to assume that he or she completely understands the terms used by the client without asking for clarification. For example, if a group of 100 professionals were asked to indicate what they meant by "depression," we would not get identical responses. Similarly, one cannot be sure exactly what a client means when he or she uses words like *depressed, suicidal, anxious,* or *upset.* In order to be able to intervene effectively, it is important for the therapist to make sure that he or she is not merely in the right ballpark in understanding the client's terminology but that the therapist is right on target. The process of clarifying the client's words might be called the "Columbo Technique." The TV character played by Peter Falk in the television series of the same name solved crimes not by drawing inferences (à la Sherlock Holmes or Hercule Poirot) but rather by assuming that there was a great deal that he did not know and was willing to ask what appeared to be obvious or even "dumb" questions. For example:

Client: I'm stupid, really dumb!

Therapist: You call yourself stupid and dumb. Just what does mean·to be dumb? What does being stupid mean to you?

Client: You know D-U-M-B. You know what dumb is, don't you? I'm stupid, really stupid.

Therapist: I know what I mean when I use the term *dumb*, but it would be important to know what *you* mean by the term.

Client: Someone stupid screws everything up, they don't do anything right, nothing works out for them.

Therapist: And how does that fit you?

Client: Well, maybe I don't screw everything up, but nothing much has been working out for me lately.

Therapist: So is that being dumb or having a run of bad luck?

Guided Association/Guided Discovery. Through a simple sequence of questions, such as "Then what?", "What would that mean?", "What would happen then?", the therapist can help the client explore the significance he or she sees in events. This collaborative, therapist-guided technique stands in opposition to the technique of free association basic to psychoanalysis, which involves unguided speech that, it is assumed, will eventually get to areas of conflict and concern. The guided discovery technique involves the therapist working with the client to understand the connections between the client's ideas, thoughts, and images. For example:

Therapist: What would happen if you gave her a call?

Client: I can't do that!

Therapist: Do you have any image of what would happen if you did call?

Client: She'd laugh.

Therapist: And then what would happen?

Client: I'd feel like a fool.

Therapist: And then what?

Client: I'd be embarrassed, terribly embarrassed.

Therapist: If you were to call, and she laughed and you felt embarrassed, what would that indicate to you?

Client: I'm a complete idiot. What girl in her right mind would want to go out with me?

Examining the Evidence. One effective way to challenge a dysfunctional thought is to examine both the extent to which the thought is supported or disconfirmed by the available evidence and whether other interpretations would better fit the evidence. This process not only involves examining the evidence but also involves considering the source of the data and the validity of the client's conclusions, as well as considering whether the client is overlooking available data. Many clients begin with a conclusion such as "I'm no good" and then selectively focus on evidence that supports their conclusion. By examining the evidence, the client's conclusion can be more easily challenged and altered. For example:

Client: It's hopeless. I'll never get better. I'm going to live the rest of my life in this awful state of depression.

Therapist: You say that you'll never get any better. That you'll always be this way. Have you ever felt better, less depressed?

Client: Yeah, but that was long ago. I spoke to someone who really knows this stuff, and he said that I can expect to be this way forever.

Therapist: Who was that person? Was this person one of your previous therapists?

Client: Not exactly, but he really knows.

Therapist: Who was this?

Client: One of the guys on the psych unit. He told me that he knew lots of guys like me and they never got better.

Therapist: Was this someone on the staff or a patient?

Client: One of the patients.

Therapist: It sounds like you're taking his opinion pretty seriously. Have you heard any other opinions about your depression?

Client: The doctor who referred me to you said Cognitive Therapy could help me.

Therapist: Who do you think knows more about you odds of getting out of this depression?

Client: I guess it's obvious now that you point it out.

Challenging Absolutes. By taking an idea literally, or to its full extreme, the therapist can often help the client to move to a more moderate statement of his or her views. A corresponding moderation in the intensity of emotional responses typically follows. Absolutes such as never, always, no one, everyone, and so on are often easy targets. Clients often complain initially that the therapist is only drawing semantic distinctions; however, "I've got some real problems at work, but I'm good at some of what I do" has a very different impact from "I'm totally incompetent." For example:

Client: No one would help me, no one cares.

Therapist: No one? No one in the whole world?

Client: Well, maybe my parents would care, but no one else.

Therapist: Let's start with that. It's not true that no one would care, someone would, your parents would, anyone else?

Client: Well, Sue and Jan call me and ask if they can help. They seem to care, but no one else does.

Therapist: So it sounds like it would be pretty realistic to say, "My parents and Sue and Jan care and will help me if I need it, but I can't count on most other people." How do you feel when you look at things that way?

Client: That's not nearly as bad.

Considering the Odds. Clients often focus on the outcome they fear most and react as though this worst possible outcome is certain. It can be quite useful to examine the likelihood of the events they fear. For example:

Therapist: So, the thought that is most frightening to you is "He'll never come back." Do you have any idea how likely it is that he'll never come back?

Client: After the fight last night he probably won't.

Therapist: Have the two of you had fights like last night before?

Client: Yeah, I guess we fight a lot.

Therapist: And has there been a time so far when he's gone away angry and never come back?

Client: No, either he comes back to me or I go to him.

Therapist: Do you see any reasons why last night's fight should be different from the others?

Client: No, I guess not.

Therapist: So what does that tell you about the chances of his never coming back?

Client: I guess it's not too likely, is it?

Reattribution. A common statement made by clients is "It's all my fault" (or "It's all his/her fault"). Although one cannot dismiss this out of hand, it is unlikely that a single person is totally responsible for everything that happens in a particular situation. Some clients take responsibility for events and situations that are only minimally attributable to them, whereas others tend to always blame someone else and take no responsibility. The therapist can help the client distribute responsibility more equitably among the relevant parties, often with substantial reductions in guilt or anger as the result. For example:

Client: It's all my fault. I really screwed things up this time. If I could only have handled things differently, the relationship could have worked. If only I hadn't been so demanding. It could have been good, I blew it. What's left?

Therapist: There's much that you did both good and bad in the relationship. Is it *all* your fault that things didn't work out?

Client: Yeah. Who else?

Therapist: What part did Alicia play in the breakup? Did she do anything to contribute to the difficulty? I know that you feel that it was all your fault. I think it would be helpful to examine just what you contributed and what Alicia contributed to the ending of this relationship.

Client: No, it's my fault.

Therapist: Did Alicia do anything at all to contribute to the problem?

Client: You mean besides being a bitch?

Therapist: Let's start with that . . .

Turning Adversity to Advantage. Clients often are quicker to identify the disadvantages resulting from life changes than to recognize their advantages. Explicitly checking to see whether an event has good as well as bad aspects can have a major impact. There are times that even a seeming disaster can be used to advantage. Losing one's job may seem like a disaster but may, in some cases, be the entry point to a new job or even a new career. Having a deadline imposed may be seen as oppressive and unfair but may be used as a motivator. This technique involves asking the client to look to see if there is a silver lining to the cloud. Given that the depressed individual often does the opposite and finds a dark lining to every silver cloud, looking for the kernel of positive in a situation can be very difficult for many clients. They may simply not see the positive, and if the therapist points out positive aspects, they may react with greater negativity. It is important for the therapist to make a point of identifying only realistically positive sides to negative events and to avoid the tendency to become overly optimistic in response to the client's negativity. For example:

Client: Now that I've lost him, what do I do?

Therapist: With him gone, what keeps you in Philadelphia? You've thought of other cities, in fact we've spoken of wanting to move. In fact, you've disliked living here but stayed here because of Larry.

Client: That's true, now I don't have to sweat leaving. There's no guy to leave. It is freeing. I hate living in the city. But I don't know whether I'm ready to do something new at this point.

Therapist: Let's explore that.

Direct Disputation. Although Cognitive Therapy generally advocates guided discovery rather than directly challenging the client's views, there are times when direct confrontation is necessary. This is most likely to arise when a client is seriously suicidal and the therapist must directly and quickly work to challenge his or her hopelessness. Direct confrontation also can be useful in other situations in which the therapist must intervene quickly and the client is not willing or able to participate actively in the process. Disputation and debate are potentially dangerous tools because it can be difficult to present a convincing argument without seeming to demean, nag, or browbeat the client, and without the discussion simply becoming an intellectual debate. It is generally a good idea to encourage as much collaboration as possible, to emphasize data rather than abstract logic or philosophical principles, and to switch back to guided discovery as soon as is feasible. For example:

Client: I'm going crazy. My mind is going. What am I going to do? I've got to do something before my mind is totally gone. I feel that I need to just run away. Maybe that will help.

Therapist: I understand that you are terrified of going crazy, but obviously I'm not as concerned as you are. Would you like to know why?

Client: I guess so.

Therapist: The reason that I'm not afraid of your going crazy is that this isn't the way craziness starts. You're anxious and very scared, but those are not signs of craziness. Being afraid of craziness is very different from being crazy.

Client: You mean I'm not crazy?

Therapist: No, you're not crazy!

Externalization of Voices. The client can get very effective practice in responding adaptively to dysfunctional thoughts by having the therapist role-play the part of the client's dysfunctional thoughts and having the client practice more adaptive responding. A necessary foundation for this exercise is a thorough discussion of ways of responding effectively to the particular dysfunctional thoughts in question, and it may help to have the therapist first model responding to dysfunctional thoughts that the client presents. After this, the therapist can express a series of the client's dysfunctional thoughts for the client to respond to. It is usually most effective to start with dysfunctional thoughts that the client finds relatively easy to handle and then build up to more problematic ones presented powerfully and dramatically. For example:

Therapist: I'd like to be your negative voice. I'd like you to be a more positive and functional voice.

Client: I'll try.

Therapist: Okay. Let's begin. "You really don't know what you're talking about!"

Client: That's not true. There are times that I may be over my head, but overall, I really do know my stuff.

Therapist: "If you're so smart, what are you doing in this dead end job?"

Techniques for Eliminating Cognitive Distortions

Techniques that can be used to change cognitive distortions can obviously be used to challenge automatic thoughts, as well. However, these techniques are especially good at reducing the client's belief in the value or truthfulness of specific distortions. They, therefore, have a specialized value that we would like to emphasize.

Labeling of Distortions. Many clients find it useful to label the particular cognitive distortions that they notice among their automatic thoughts and find that simply doing this weakens the emotional impact of the thoughts. A list of distortions such as the one in Chapter 1 can be provided to the client. *Feeling Good* (Burns, 1980) is also an excellent self-help book that can be useful in educating clients about cognitive distortions. Once the client understands what each distortion is, he or she can watch for examples of "personalizing," "mind reading," and so on, among his or her automatic thoughts. For example:

Client: He really doesn't care. I can tell. If he cared he would call. He probably thinks that I'm not worth it.

Therapist: What are you doing?

Client: What do you mean?

Therapist: What are you doing right now as you think about him?

Client: You mean like in the book?

Therapist: Yes. Like in the book.

Client: Mind reading?

Therapist: Mind reading!

Client: I guess I am.

Therapist: Can you really read his mind and know exactly what he's thinking?

Client: (Laughing) Hey, I'm depressed, not crazy!

Decatastrophizing. An outcome that is fairly unlikely can be quite upsetting if it is so negative that it would be intolerable were it to happen. For example, if you were to hear your physician say, "There's only a 10% chance that you have a brain tumor," you probably would not be very reassured. If the client is reacting as though the outcome he or she fears would be completely devastating, the therapist can work to help the client see whether he or she is overestimating the catastrophic nature of the situation. Questions that might be asked of the client include: "What is the worst that can happen?" or "If it does happen, how will your life be different three months from now?" It is important that this technique be used with gentleness and care so that the client does not feel ridiculed or made fun of by the therapist. For example:

Client: She'll think I'm an idiot. A moron. A loser.

Therapist: And if she does, how bad would that be?

Client: It *would* be awful.

Therapist: I understand that it would be embarrassing and feel bad, but what would be awful about it?

Client: It just would be.

Therapist: Let's think that through. . . . What consequences would it have if she were to think you were an idiot other than embarrassment?

Client: I guess it would be mostly embarrassing.

Therapist: And being embarrassed is really unpleasant for you. Does it have any lasting effects?

Client: I guess not.

Challenging Dichotomous Thinking. With clients who see things as "all or nothing," a technique for breaking down the dichotomy can be quite useful. Abstract discussions of whether things are ever really black and white often have little emotional impact. However, two techniques can be quite useful in reducing dichotomous thinking.

When dichotomous thinking is relatively mild, the simple process of *scaling* can be used. In this process, the client rates the intensity of emotions or the validity of automatic thoughts relative to the extreme ends of the continuum. This can help the client both to recognize the "in-between" levels and to reduce habitual dichotomous thinking. Because the client has been manifesting extreme thoughts and extreme behaviors, any movement toward moderation is usually quite helpful. For example:

Therapist: If you put your sadness on a scale of 1–100, how sad are you?

Client: 90 to 95.

Therapist: That's a lot. Can you think of the saddest you've ever been in your life? When was that?

Client: That's easy. When my mother died.

Therapist: How sad were you then?

Client: 100!

Therapist: Can you remember a time that you were not sad at all?

Client: Not really.

Therapist: No time at all?

Client: Well, on my fifth birthday, I got a train set.

Therapist: Good. Let's label that 0 for sadness. Use those two events, your fifth birthday party as 0 sadness and your mom's death as 100 sadness. Compared to those events, how sad are you now?

Client: Well, compared to that this is a 50, maybe 45.

When dichotomous thinking is more firmly entrenched, a more powerful intervention is needed. This involves first confirming that the client sees the issue in question dichotomously and then developing an operational definition, in the client's own words, of each pole of the dichotomy. Once this has been done, it is possible to examine the available data to determine if the topic in question is truly dichotomous or not. For example:

Therapist: It sounds as though you see people as being either completely trustworthy or not trustworthy at all with nothing in between.

Client: Sure, you can either trust somebody or you can't.

Therapist: As you see it, what are the characteristics of a completely trustworthy person? For example, if a Martian came down knowing nothing of humans, what should he look for to decide who could be trusted.

Client: Well. . . . Trustworthy people follow through on what they say.

Therapist: Some of the time? All of the time?

Client: All of the time. They never lie. They don't let anything interfere with doing what they say they will. They don't let you down or hurt you.

Therapist: Does that cover it, or is there more than that to trustworthiness?

Client: That's about it.

Therapist: What would be a good label for the other extreme, the people who aren't trustworthy?

Client: Treacherous.

Therapist: And what would the characteristics of treacherous people be?

Client: They don't follow through on what they say.

Therapist: From what you said about the characteristics of untrustworthy people, it sounds like they'd lie and deceive a lot. Am I right?

Client: Yeah, all the time. They try to take advantage of you when there's a chance. They try to hurt you then come up with excuses. They get your hopes up then let you down.

Therapist: Does that pretty much cover it?

Client: Yeah.

Therapist: Let's see how this works in practice. Let's take your sister-in-law. Which category would she fall in?

Client: Oh, I can trust her.

Therapist: Does she meet the full criteria for trustworthiness? Don't I remember you being really upset last week that she hadn't called when she said she would?

Client: I guess she doesn't follow through on everything she says.

Therapist: So does that mean she's "treacherous," lying and deceiving all the time and so on.

Client: No, she's pretty nice.

Therapist: Hmm. She doesn't seem to fall 100% in either category. Suppose we imagine a 0 to 10 scale where 0 means completely treacherous and 10 means absolutely, completely trustworthy. Where would you rate her?

Client: She'd be about an 8.

Therapist: How about your mother?

Client: She's not as reliable. She'd be about a 6.

Techniques for Changing Underlying Assumptions

The first step in effectively modifying dysfunctional beliefs and assumptions is to identify these cognitions using the methods discussed in Chapter 2 and to help the client to recognize his or her negative effects. Once this has been done, the cognitive techniques discussed as ways of challenging automatic thoughts can also be used effectively for challenging dysfunctional underlying assumptions. In addition, it can be very useful to help the client write a new assumption as an alternative to the dysfunctional assumption.

Writing an Alternative Assumption. Even after a client recognizes the assumptions that have been shaping his or her behavior and understands the ways in which they are dysfunctional, he or she may be unable to find an adaptive alternative view. The client may simply "draw a blank" when trying to think of a more adaptive belief or may assume that the only alternative is to go to the opposite extreme. It can be quite helpful for the therapist to help the client to formulate a written alternative and test it against the available evidence. For example:

Therapist: So it's pretty clear that you've been operating on the assumption that "I've got to be truly outstanding, and nothing short of that is worthwhile." And that that has been causing a lot of your problems with motivation. If that view is unrealistic and causes problems, what would be a better view to live by?

Client: "I'm just mediocre and that's it. I may as well quit trying for more than that."

Therapist: What effect do you think it would have on your motivation if you were to assume that?

Client: Hmm, I guess there wouldn't be much point to trying anything.

Therapist: So that view doesn't sound like much of an improvement. Do any other alternatives come to mind?

Client: What else is there?

Therapist: Let's try to think that through. Is it true that nothing short of outstanding is worth doing? For example, when I play softball I'm not outstanding but I have a good time. Is that worth doing?

Client: I guess it is if you want to have a good time.

Therapist: What does that suggest to you?

Client: That some things are worth doing even if you aren't great at them?

Therapist: Let's see if we can work this out clearly enough to put down on paper. What sorts of things might be worth doing even if you aren't outstanding?

Mental Imagery Techniques

Not all automatic thoughts are verbal in nature. It can be important to assess the content of any mental images that occur in problem situations and to deal with any dysfunctional images that occur. Whether or not mental images play an important role in the client's problems, mental imagery can be used in responding to dysfunctional thoughts, as a way of practicing new behaviors, or as a way of reducing problematic emotional responses.

Replacement Imagery. If the client experiences dysfunctional images in problem situations, one option is to help him or her to generate more adaptive alternative images to replace the dysfunctional ones. For example:

Therapist: When you anticipate going into the grocery store, do you get any images or pictures in your mind?

Client: I see myself having a panic attack, screaming at the top of my lungs, and running out of the store, leaving all the groceries in the cart and pushing people aside as I rush out. Everyone is staring at me, saying that I must be a lunatic.

Therapist: Has that ever actually happened?

Client: No. I get real anxious, but even if I have a panic attack I'm able to leave quietly without attracting much attention.

Therapist: Do you have any idea what effect it would have if you were able to replace the image of running out screaming with the image of leaving quietly?

Client: I guess I'd be a heck of a lot more comfortable with that, and it would be more realistic too.

Cognitive Rehearsal. By visualizing an event in the mind's eye, the client can imaginally practice particular behaviors without encountering the practical problems or risks that sometimes make it difficult to practice new behaviors in real-life situations. By realistically imagining himself or herself in a scene, the client can explore a range of possible responses, select the most promising one, and practice it to some extent. For example:

Therapist: I'd like you to close your eyes and picture speaking with your girlfriend. Can you picture that?

Client: Yeah. I don't like it.

Therapist: Like what?

Client: What I'm seeing.

Therapist: What do you see? Describe it.

Client: I see her listening to me and then turning away. I start crying and begging her to stay, and then I start feeling embarrassed and want to die.

Therapist: How does she react when you start crying and begging?

Client: It just turns her off more.

Therapist: Let's try to construct a picture of a way that you'd like to be able to react. What would you would like to see happen?

Client: I'd like her to listen and understand.

Therapist: Yeah, if she listens and understands, there's no problem. How would you like to handle it if she turns away?

Client: I don't want to beg, I need to stand up for myself.

Therapist: Do you think that would go better?

Client: Yeah. She'd respect that more, and I'd feel a lot better about it.

Therapist: So what would you actually say to her?

Client: (After further developing the imaginary scene) That sounds pretty good to me, but I'm not sure I could pull it off in real life.

Therapist: What if you were to practice it in imagination several times? Would that help you remember the things you want to say?

Client: I bet it would.

Desensitization and Flooding Imagery. Ever since Wolpe's pioneering work (1958), mental imagery has been used in a variety of ways to reduce or eliminate problematic emotional responses, especially anxiety. In systematic desensitization (Goldfried, 1971), the client proceeds through a hierarchy of imagined scenes starting with a situation that elicits only mild levels of anxiety. The client imagines the scene repeatedly, while practicing relaxation techniques, until he or she is comfortable while imagining the situation. The client then proceeds in a stepwise fashion until he or she is comfortable imagining the situations that initially would have been most frightening. Flooding in imagery (Stampfl & Levis, 1967, 1969) is a similar approach in which the hierarchy of scenes is dispensed with and the client imagines being in the situations that would be most intensely frightening to him or her for an extended period until the anxiety gradually subsides. Both of these techniques have been widely used clinically and have been demonstrated to be effective with a range of problems.

Coping Imagery. It is possible to combine the desensitization or flooding approaches already discussed with cognitive rehearsal by having the client imagine a problem situation, imagine that the problems which he or she fears occur, and then imagine tolerating the anxiety and coping effectively with the situation. This combined approach makes it possible to "decondition" the emotional responses and improve coping skills at the same time. For example:

Therapist: Now close your eyes and relax, and I'll start to guide you through the scene.

Client: Okay.

Therapist: The prof has just started passing out the math exam, and you're sitting there in your usual seat waiting to get your copy of the exam. Do you have a clear image of that?

Client: Yeah, I can see the room real clear. Everybody's sort of quiet and tense.

Therapist: How do you feel?

Client: I'm pretty tense.

Therapist: Remind yourself to use the relaxation exercise you've been practicing and go ahead and do it, then continue imagining and signal when the exam gets to you by raising your finger the way we discussed. . . . Now you look at the exam, and you realize you don't have the foggiest idea how to solve the first problem. It's something you should know how to do, but you can't remember anything about it.

Client: Oh God!

Therapist: How do you feel?

Client: I'm really tense. I'm starting to break into a sweat, and my stomach doesn't feel too good.

Therapist: Okay, stay with those feelings. Do you remember how you want to handle this situation?

Client: Yeah, remind myself there's no need to panic, I can come back to that one later, then try to stay calm and go on to the next one.

Therapist: Try that as you imagine the exam. . . . How are you feeling?

Client: It's working. I'm not nearly as tense, and I can think a lot clearer. Maybe one of the other questions will remind me how to do that first one.

Therapist: Great! Let's go on with that second question. Imagine that you pretty much remember how to do it but can't remember all the details. How do you want to handle that?

When using a "coping imagery" approach, it is important to remember that effective coping does not guarantee success. Therapist and client should prepare for failure as well as success. In the case illustrated here, the client found it quite useful to imagine both discovering that he had done well on the exam and discovering that he had failed the course despite his efforts. He found that both situations elicited problematic emotions (imagining success initially evoked anticipation of future, even harder exams while imagining failure initially elicited harsh self-criticism) that he could then prepare to cope with.

Techniques for Controlling Recurrent Thoughts

Clients are often troubled by recurrent dysfunctional thoughts such as chronic worries and ruminations. When this is the case, it is often useful to help them find ways of controlling the recurrent thoughts (Note: These techniques alone are often not effective in controlling obsessions. See the discussion of Obsessive-Compulsive Disorder in Chapter 6 for approaches to treating obsessions.)

Thought Stopping. Dysfunctional thoughts often have a snowball effect. One dysfunctional thought may elicit another and, if the process continues unimpeded, the client may be unable to respond to the thoughts effectively, simply because dysfunctional thoughts occur faster than he or she can develop responses. When this is the case, the client can be taught how to interrupt the flow of thoughts in order to deal more effectively with both the thoughts and the situation. The process is actually quite simple: The client simply interrupts the stream of thoughts with a sudden stimulus, imagined or real, then switches to other thoughts before the stream of dysfunctional thoughts resumes. However, because most clients have been advised repeatedly "Don't worry about it!" and have been unable to do so, a simple explanation of the technique is generally not credible and thus is ineffective. The technique is much more effective when demonstrated to the client:

Therapist: It sounds like these thoughts are really upsetting to you, and if there was some way to stop them you'd feel a lot better.

Client: I know, Doc, but I've tried to get them out of my head and I just can't.

Therapist: I'd like to try something. Can you get those thoughts started now.

Client: I guess so. I just keep thinking about the plane crashing. God, I'm sweating just thinking about it. I'm really getting upset.

Therapist: (Slapping the desk loudly) *Stop!*

Client: —I —I — Okay.

Therapist: Take a second to catch your breath. . . . How are you feeling?

Client: Boy, that got intense fast.

Therapist: Are the thoughts still running now?

Client: No, they're gone.

Therapist: What just happened? What allowed you to stop?

Client: The noise, I guess. You startled me.

Therapist: So it's hard to just stop the thoughts, but a dramatic enough stimulus can break the flow. . . . How do you think it would work if you were to be the one shouting "stop"?

Client: I don't know. I guess it might work.

Therapist: Let's try it.

After the client has seen that the technique works, the explanation of the technique becomes credible, and the client can learn to use more versatile stimuli such as imagining a shouted "stop!" or snapping a sturdy rubber band worn around his or her wrist. Thought stopping is easiest to use when the stream of thoughts is just beginning, and clients often find that they may need to do it periodically and to combine it with the following technique.

Refocusing. Although clients often find that it is very hard to stop thinking about their pressing concerns, there is a limit to how many things a person can think about at once. By completely occupying his or her mind with neutral or pleasant thoughts, it is possible for the client to block dysfunctional thoughts for a period of time. Any cognitive activity with which the client can occupy his or her mind will have this effect whether it involves counting, focusing on calming and pleasant images, focusing on external stimuli, or engaging in some activity that requires concentration. Although this technique excludes the dysfunctional thoughts only for a limited period of time, it can be very useful in allowing the client to establish some control over his or her thinking and in allowing him or her to "take a break" from the dysfunctional thoughts. Also, if used conscientiously, it seems to have the effect of reducing the frequency of rumination in general. Increased compliance may be gained by emphasizing this to ruminative clients.

This technique can be particularly useful in several different contexts. When thought stopping is effective in disrupting the stream of dysfunctional thoughts but the client finds that the thoughts resume quickly, refocusing can be used to keep the dysfunctional thoughts from resuming immediately. When worries or dysfunctional thoughts make it difficult for the client to get to sleep, imagining a pleasant, relaxing scene can block the thoughts or worries long enough for the client to get to sleep. Finally, when the client's symptom is maintained by the stream of dysfunctional thoughts, a refocusing technique such as the "outward focus" technique used in controlling panic attacks (see Chapter 6) can disrupt the stream of thoughts long enough for the symptom to subside.

Scheduling Worries. When a client's concentration or mood is negatively affected by recurrent thoughts or worries that are frequent but do not form an unbroken stream, it is often possible to gain control over the worries by scheduling specific time periods for the thoughts or worries and using the focusing technique discussed to postpone these thoughts until the allotted time. For example:

Therapist: It may sound strange, but one approach that often works well when people are bothered by their worries interfering with accomplishing their work and enjoying their free time is to schedule times to worry when it won't interfere too much and then postponing their worries until them.

Client: What do you mean?

Therapist: Well, rather than getting immersed in your worries whenever your mind happens to drift onto an upsetting subject, you decide that you are only going to get immersed at a particular time during the day. You make an agreement with yourself that you will set aside a specific time for your worries and that you will stop them and refocus your thinking any time you start to worry other than in the time period you have decided upon. For some people, it's not as big a struggle to stop thinking about something when they know that they will be getting a chance to think about them soon. How does that sound to you?

Client: That makes sense.

Therapist: What we'd need to do is figure out a reasonable schedule to start with, then try it out to see how it works for you. Do you have any ideas what sort of schedule would be good to try?

Client: I don't know. I don't seem to go very long without worrying.

Therapist: It can take a certain amount of trial and error to find a good schedule. Often scheduling 10 or 15 minutes every few hours is a good starting place.

Client: That sounds good. I could use my breaks and lunch.

Therapist: Let's try that and see how it works; then you can adjust it if you need to. The important thing is to have a clear agreement with yourself about when you'll plan to worry next and then to follow through on it. It's normal, particularly at first, to have worries pop up and have to intentionally set them aside until the right time. If you find it really hard to postpone the worries, you may be trying to go too long between worry sessions, and you might need to schedule more frequent times to worry.

If it has been established that the thoughts or worries are completely unnecessary, it should be possible to gradually lengthen the interval between worry periods and simultaneously shorten their duration, eventually eliminating them. If the thoughts or worries involve topics about which the client does need to think in order to make decisions, plan a course of action, or resolve conflicting thoughts and feelings, it may be possible to replace time spent worrying with time spent on effective problem solving.

Cognitive Techniques for Changing and Controlling Behavior

When maladaptive behavior is an important component of the client's problem, it might seem that interventions would need to be primarily behavioral. However, a number of cognitive interventions are used primarily for their impact on behavior.

Anticipating the Consequences of One's Actions. Many clients handle problem situations much less effectively than possible because they fail to accurately anticipate the consequences of their actions. Despite the obvious disadvantages of acting without forethought, many otherwise capable and effective clients act out of habit, act on impulse, or otherwise fail to think clearly in problem situations. If a client shows a generalized inability to plan effectively, a comprehensive intervention such as problem-solving training may be required. However, when he or she is able to deal effectively in many other areas of life, quick improvement in means–end thinking and subsequent changes in behavior often results simply from clarifying the client's goals in particular problem situations and directing his or her attention to the likely consequences of alternative courses of action. For example:

Joan, a graduate student in art history, complained of chronic problems with being overwhelmed by her workload. After all, when a paper was due she "had" to read all relevant books and journals so that she could write a "truly comprehensive" paper.

When asked if being comprehensive was a more important goal than getting a good grade, preparing for a career in academia, or reducing her workload to manageable proportions, she responded, "Gee, I never thought of it that way." She concluded that her top priorities were mastering her field and preparing for an academic career. Her therapist then asked about her observations regarding the consequences of attempts to write "truly comprehensive" papers. She quickly concluded that such attempts were invariably counterproductive and willingly agreed to try approaching her assignments differently.

Inducing Dissonance. When what one thinks and what one feels are in conflict, anxiety is the result (Festinger, 1957). Although there are several explanations of this cognitive dissonance phenomenon, it is sufficient to recognize that it exists and can be used. Actions, feelings, or beliefs cause dissonance when they conflict with personal, family, cultural, or religious values. A therapist can induce dissonance by highlighting these conflicts and then can help the client to resolve the dissonance in an adaptive way. For example, a client who believes that his or her death will be meaningless or go unnoticed is likely to experience little dissonance as he or she contemplates suicide. If the therapist draws the client's attention to the likely effects of his or her death on children or family, the therapist can induce dissonance. This will usually deter the client from making a suicide attempt and motivate the client to look for another solution. For example:

Therapist: What effect will this have on your kids?

Client: They'll survive.

Therapist: I'm sure that they will survive, but with what effect? How will what you do influence how they think, feel, or behave in the future?

Client: I don't want to think of it.

Therapist: I know, but it is something that's there, that you've got to at least look at.

Client: Why? Why do I have to look at it? Once I'm gone. . . .

Therapist: Once you're gone, the effects will linger.

Considering the Pros and Cons. When an informal look at the consequences of the client's actions is ineffective, working with the client to explicitly list the advantages and disadvantages of maintaining a particular belief, behavior pattern, or course of action as well as separately listing the advantages and disadvantages of at least one promising alternative can be quite useful. This can help clients make more adaptive choices, improve motivation for change, identify impediments to change, and help the client to achieve a broader perspective. For example:

Client: I can't stay in this marriage. If I stay, I'll die.

Therapist: There are many parts to the relationship from what you've described in the past, both good and bad. So far you've been pretty uncertain about what you want to do.

Client: You're right. I just can't make up my mind.

Therapist: Let's explore the possibilities. We can work at making two lists, the first can be the advantages and the disadvantages of staying with Steve. The second can look at the advantages and disadvantages of leaving.

Client: Aren't they the same?

Therapist: We'll see. There will be some overlap, but I think the lists will show some very different ideas too. It sounds like right now you see lots of disadvantages to staying with Steve. What disadvantages come to mind?

The client may argue initially that there is no point in considering the pros and cons of changing feelings, actions, or thoughts that he or she cannot control. However, there is considerable value in weighing the pros and cons of proposed change before investing time and energy in attempting to achieve it. If the client concludes that the change would be a good idea, then the therapist and client can work together to develop whatever control over feelings, actions, or thoughts is needed.

Self-Instructional Training. Meichenbaum (1977) has developed an extensive model for understanding the role of self-instructions in controlling impulses and behavior. According to Meichenbaum's view, children normally develop the ability to use self-instructions to control impulses and behavior by moving from overt repetition of instructions to overt verbalization of self-instructions to subvocalization of self-instructions and finally to the use of self-instructions without verbalization. However, some individuals either have failed to master the use of self-instructions or fail to use self-instructions effectively. When a client has problems with impulse control, explicit training in self-instruction may help him or her to develop more skill in self-control. Once therapist and client have developed a set of instructions that, if followed, would result in more adaptive behavior, the client can start at first by repeating the self-instructions out loud. With practice, the client can learn to use the instructions without needing to say them out loud, and eventually the instructions can become automatic. For example:

Therapist: How can you deal more effectively with Jon (the son) when he starts to act up?

Client: What do you expect me to do? I just act this way.

Therapist: Would you like to be able to act differently?

Client: Sure, but I just respond. I need some space. I want to throw him out of the window.

Therapist: What would happen if you could tell yourself the following: "I need to just walk away and not respond. I need to walk away and not respond."

Client: Well, if I listened to myself, I would probably be in far better shape.

Therapist: That's interesting! If you could tell yourself, very directly, very forcefully to leave the situation, both you and Jon would do better. Is that so?

Client: I suppose. But how can I talk rationally to myself when I'm so angry?

Therapist: Let's practice some and see if you can get to where you can do that.

Self-Motivation. Clients often present a lack of motivation as one of their primary problems or attribute their failure to take necessary actions to a lack of motivation. Often this problem is actually due to fears about the consequences of the actions or is due to indirectly expressed anger and resentment (see Chapter 13). However, many clients, particularly depressed ones, experience problems that are largely due to a lack of motivation. When this is the case, it is possible to help the client learn to develop greater motivation.

Both a feeling of enthusiasm or motivation and goal-directed behavior result when the individual can see actions that will lead to attainment of a valued goal and is reasonably confident that attempts at attaining the goal can be successful. Individuals who lack motivation typically do not have clear goals in mind, have not identified a course of action that will result in their attaining the goals, or doubt their ability to succeed at the endeavor. If the therapist can help clarify the client's goals, help him or her to develop a plausible plan for attaining the goals, and increase his or her expectancy of success, the client's motivation will be enhanced. For example:

Client: I know I should be working on the project, but I just can't get myself to.

Therapist: You said a few minutes ago that one thought that runs through your head when you're procrastinating is "why bother?" Do you have an answer for that? Is there any point to "bothering" with the project?

Client: I'm supposed to do it; they've assigned me to it.

Therapist: And you've tried to get started on it by telling yourself that you have to, you're supposed to. How well has that worked so far?

Client: Obviously, it hasn't worked at all.

Therapist: Suppose there were some legitimate reasons why this project was worth bothering with. . . . Do you think that might make a difference?

Client: Like what?

Therapist: Are there any good reasons for bothering with it that you see right off the bat?

Client: I'll get in trouble if I don't.

Therapist: That sounds like a possible reason to bother with it. Do you see any other reasons?

Client: Not really.

Therapist: How do you feel while you're in the office procrastinating?

Client: I'm usually pretty bored and afraid of getting caught.

Therapist: Do you have any idea how you'd feel if you were working away on the project and making headway on it?

Client: I certainly wouldn't be afraid of getting caught. I usually get wrapped up in my work pretty quickly and enjoy it some.

Therapist: Suppose that tomorrow when you want to get to work, you remind yourself: "Even though I'd rather not have this project, I'll probably feel better working on it than killing time," "The sooner I get started, the sooner I'll be done with it," "If I do a good job, maybe they'll give me something more interesting to do next," and so on. What effect do you think that would have?

Client: It should make it a heck of a lot easier to get started.

Of course, any fears or unexpressed resentments that play a role in the client's failure to act may need to be addressed as well.

BEHAVIORAL TECHNIQUES

Behavioral techniques can be used in several ways within Cognitive Therapy. They can be used straightforwardly to achieve behavior change they may be needed to teach the skills necessary for the client to reach his or her goals, or they may be used primarily to achieve cognitive change. It is beyond the scope of the present volume to describe the full range of behavioral techniques available to the clinician (see Bellack & Hersen, 1985; Bellack, Hersen, & Kazdin, 1982). We will instead discuss a number of techniques that most frequently prove useful in Cognitive Therapy.

The balance of cognitive to behavioral techniques depends on the particular symptom being addressed and on the overall goals of therapy. A useful heuristic for estimating the cognitive versus behavioral focus of the therapy is for the therapist to make a subjective estimate of the degree of the client's pathology or lack of effective coping skills. In general, the more severe the problem, the greater the emphasis on behavioral work, and the less severe the problem, the more cognitive the approach (see Figure 5). Note that even with the least severe problems, some of the work will be behavioral, and that with the most severe problems, some of the work will be cognitive. Other factors that influence the balance between cognitive and behavioral techniques include the client's responsiveness to verbal interventions and the extent to which anxiety plays an important role in the client's problems. Clients who do not respond well to verbal interventions because of intellectual limitations or communication difficulties may require greater reliance on behavioral interventions. When anxiety is a significant component of the client's problems, *in vivo* exposure to the situations that elicit the anxiety is often essential for effective treatment.

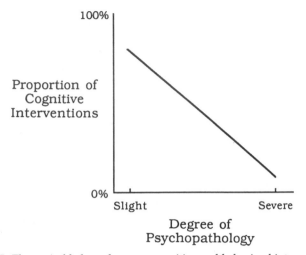

FIGURE 5. The typical balance between cognitive and behavioral interventions.

Techniques Used Primarily for Behavior Change

Graded Task Assignments. Many clients feel overwhelmed by the tasks that face them and see themselves as unable to change their behavior and/or powerless to change the situations in which they find themselves. The tasks the client faces can be made less overwhelming and more manageable by helping the client to approach them systematically and to break large tasks into manageable subtasks. By utilizing a "shaping" strategy, with each small step moving the client closer to the eventual goal, we can often help the client who has been immobilized by anxiety or depression to begin to expand his or her activities in a gradual manner. For example:

Roger, a married man in his late 60s, had been quite inactive for some time. He reported that whenever he considered trying any activity his immediate thought was "I can't do that, that's too much for me," and that he invariably decided not to attempt the activity. When his therapist asked for a specific example when this had occurred, Roger reported that for some time he had wanted to clean out the basement and that several times in the past week he had considered starting on it but had given up. In describing the amount of effort that it would require to complete the task, Roger said "It's an incredible mess. It must be about 30 by 60, and it's literally packed to the ceiling. We've just been storing odds and ends down there for years. There's no way I could clean that place out." However, when asked how hard it would be to take one box from the basement, sort out the things that were worth saving, and discard the rest, Roger's response was, "That wouldn't be too hard as long as I took my time." His therapist then asked, "Suppose you took care of just one box a day. . . . What would happen?" And Roger responded, "Sooner or later I'd get it cleaned up. But I could do more than one box a day, and I could get my son to help."

At the close of the session, he agreed to try working on the basement one box at a time and to be careful not to overload himself. Over the next several weeks he found that he was able to make steady progress on cleaning the basement and that he was able to successfully use the same approach with other tasks as well.

With many clients, progress on the small steps is quite reinforcing and results in substantial improvement in mood and motivation. However, for some clients, especially those who are demanding and perfectionistic, their response to small sequential steps is often "so what?", "big deal," or "it's not enough." Often this can be addressed by reminding the client that the small steps he or she has completed are steps toward a larger, worthwhile goal.

Activity Scheduling. Another situation in which clients often feel over-whelmed and helpless is when they have not had the forethought to plan ahead in order to use their time effectively, to choose among conflicting priorities, and to allocate time for relaxation and enjoyment as well as work. When the problem is mild, an unstructured discussion of these issues may be sufficient; but it often is valuable to address these issues more systematically by using the Activity Schedule (Figure 6). This form

	Mon	Tues	Wed	Thurs	Fri	Sat	Sun
6 a.m.							
7 a.m.							
8 a.m.							
9 a.m.							
10 a.m.							
11 a.m.							
12 p.m.							
1 p.m.							
2 p.m.							
3 p.m.							
4 p.m.							
5 p.m.							
6 p.m.							
7 p.m.							
8 p.m.							
9 p.m.							
10 p.m.							
11 p.m.							
12 p.m.							

Figure 6. The Activity Schedule.

provides a simple way for clients to record the ways in which they use their time as well as relevant information regarding mood. A detailed assessment of the client's use of his or her time can be used to identify inefficiencies and to reevaluate the client's choices among conflicting priorities. Once the client has developed some ideas of how to better utilize his or her time, the Activity Schedule form can be used prospectively to write out a plan for using time effectively and to monitor the effectiveness of this intervention.

Clients often find that by reviewing their use of time, it is possible to both be more productive and have more free time. For example:

Tom was a retired classical pianist who complained that there was simply not enough time in his day for some of the activities that would help in alleviating his depression, such as exercising and playing his piano. When he completed an Activity Schedule at his therapist's request, the therapist noticed that over 3 hours a day were occupied by activities that Tom labeled *morning ritual* and *after dinner ritual*. This very orderly, meticulous man had developed a ritualized sequence of household chores, personal hygiene activities, and meditation exercises that he performed methodically twice a day. As therapist and client reviewed these activities, their value to the client, and the negative impact of devoting so much time to the activities, the client chose to drop some of his rituals and streamline the rest. As a result he was able to find time to exercise and practice the piano each day and had additional free time to spend with his wife and on his hobbies.

Social Skills Training. When a client describes having social difficulty, the therapist cannot assume that the client is being unrealistically pessimistic in anticipating negative reactions from others. He or she may lack important social skills that must be learned in order for interpersonal interactions to go well. The therapist can work to help clients gain social skills that they have not mastered in the course of their development. These skills might include dressing appropriately, learning how to shake hands and make eye contact, learning how to start a conversation and be a good listener, and so on. In addition to directly teaching the needed skills, the therapist can facilitate their development through audiotaped or videotaped feedback, through within-session practice (e.g., role playing), and then through graded task assignment. When it is feasible, a group setting can be particularly useful for social skills training. For a more detailed discussion of social skills training methods see Curran and Monti (1982) and Kelly (1982).

Assertiveness Training. Many unassertive individuals are inhibited from becoming more assertive by their expectancies regarding the reactions of others rather than by actual skill deficits. However, assertion training can be quite useful for two reasons. First, many unassertive individuals are relatively unskilled at assertion and can benefit from polishing their skills.

Second, assertion training can be an effective way to challenge the client's expectancies regarding the consequences of assertion. One can discuss the advantages of assertive behavior at length, but if it is possible to induce the client to try acting assertively and observe the consequences, this will produce cognitive change much more quickly than will verbal intervention alone. For a detailed description of assertion training techniques, see Bower and Bower (1976), Jakubowski and Lange (1978), and Lange and Jakubowski (1976).

Behavioral Rehearsal. It can often be useful to help clients develop or polish a variety of skills in addition to social skills and assertion. Session time can be used to practice behaviors such as discussing a problem with a significant other, disciplining a child, or saying farewell to a friend. This practice allows the therapist to give feedback and coach the client on more effective responses. This strategy may be used for skill building, to practice existing skills, or to increase the client's comfort in dealing with the situations. In individual therapy, this is usually done by role playing the interaction, having the therapist take either the client's role to model the desired behavior or take the role of the person with whom the client is interacting. It is not easy to both play a role realistically and provide useful feedback; therefore, when an appropriate individual is available to assist with the role-play or group therapy is feasible, it may be advisable for the therapist to coach the client without enacting a role himself or herself. For many clients, learning to rehearse behaviors as a way of preparing for situations with which they expect to have difficulty is extremely helpful (Bower & Bower, 1976).

Techniques Used Primarily to Change Mood or Emotion

Activity Scheduling. Activity scheduling was discussed as a way of helping clients manage their time more effectively. The same technique can also be used effectively for another purpose. Initial interventions with seriously depressed clients can be quite difficult if they respond slowly (or not at all) to the therapist's questions and are quite inactive outside of therapy. If it is possible to improve the client's mood somewhat, he or she will usually become more responsive to verbal interventions and will be easier to engage in therapy. It is obvious that the use of antidepressant medication is one possible way to improve the client's mood.

Another strategy is to increase the client's activity level because an increase in activity level often produces an immediate improvement in mood. The main problem with this option is that seriously depressed clients are usually quite apathetic and inactive and can be quite difficult to motivate. When working with inpatients, the staff can actively intervene to increase the client's activity level. Therapists working with outpatients must find some way to induce clients to voluntarily increase their activity level unless family members can be recruited to help.

The "self-motivation" strategy discussed earlier in this chapter can be quite useful for this purpose. As long as the rationale for increasing the client's activity level is presented convincingly, the client can increase his or her chances of successfully increasing his or her activity level by reminding himself or herself of the purpose of increased activity and the evidence that this will prove helpful.

Therapist: Have you noticed any times when you've felt particularly depressed during the past week?

Client: — Yesterday I felt really lousy.

Therapist: At the time when you were feeling particularly lousy, what were you doing.

Client: Nothing, just sitting and thinking about my daughter.

Therapist: I understand that you've been feeling depressed constantly for months now. Do you remember any times in the past week when you've been a bit less depressed?

Client: Not really.

Therapist: Were there any times when you ended up doing something active despite your depression?

Client: Monday, my sister talked me into going shopping.

Therapist: How did you feel while you were out shopping?

Client: I was still depressed.

Therapist: How did your level of depression then compare with the way you were feeling yesterday when you were particularly depressed?

Client: It wasn't nearly that bad.

Therapist: So one of the times when you've felt the worst this week was when you were just sitting and thinking. At another time when you were more active, you felt depressed but a bit less depressed. A lot of people find that when they're depressed, if they can be more active, it helps them feel less depressed. Does that seem to be true for you?

Client: I guess so, but I can't get myself to do anything.

Therapist: That's often part of the problem. When people are depressed, they usually don't feel like doing anything and find it hard to get themselves to be active even if they're sure it will help. Would you like to learn a simple way to make it easier to motivate yourself to take action?

Client: What is it?

Therapist: To motivate a person to take action is for them to see something they want and the steps that will get it. When people are depressed, they often find it hard to be clear on the specific things they want in a particular situation. They also find it hard to believe that their actions will accomplish anything, so they don't see any point to taking action. But there's something we can do about that. Suppose you're sitting at home and thinking. One thing we know is that you'd like to feel less depressed. Right?

Client: Yeah.

Therapist: And you know from your own experience as well as what I've told you that being more active is likely to result in your feeling less depressed. . . . What effect do you think it would have if while you were sitting at home you were to say to yourself, "Boy, I sure don't feel like doing anything but I'd like to feel less depressed, and I know that if I get up and get involved in doing something I'll end up feeling better"?

Client: I guess it would make it a lot easier to get in gear.

Therapist: What do you think of trying this out to see how it works for you? (client nods) Do you have any ideas what activities would be good to try?

The therapist would then proceed to identify a range of activities in which the client could engage. Obviously it is important for the activities to be ones that would be practical for the client to engage in, that would not be overly ambitious, and that the client would be willing to try. The activities that tend to have the most beneficial impact on mood seem to be those that occupy the client's mind, involve some exertion or exercise, are potentially enjoyable, or are seen as "worthwhile." Once a range of appropriate activities has been identified, the Activity Schedule can be used to develop a plan for the client to follow and to monitor the client's activities and their impact on his or her mood.

It is important for the client to realize that increased activity is not intended to be "fun" or to eliminate his or her depression completely. The goal of this intervention is to improve the client's mood so that he or she will be more able to participate actively in therapy and to become more responsive to verbal interventions. If the client expects more than this, he or she will be disappointed and may erroneously conclude that the intervention was a failure.

In-Vivo Exposure. For many problems, the most effective manner of intervention may involve therapist and client working together in the actual situations in which the client's problems arise. The advantages of *in-vivo* observation for collecting data were discussed in Chapter 2, and it seems obvious that intervention *in vivo* makes it impossible for the therapist to tailor treatment to the demands of the situation and to obtain immediate feedback regarding the effects of the intervention. As will be seen in Chapter 6, *in-vivo* interventions are particularly useful for reducing excessive anxiety. Agoraphobia, social phobia, and social anxiety difficulties respond well to the therapist working with the client in the very situations where the client is most anxious.

Relaxation and Breathing Exercises. The use of progressive relaxation, focused breathing, or meditation can be helpful as a way for clients to gain a sense of control over their anxiety and to lower their anxiety level. However, clients with clinically significant levels of anxiety typically require additional interventions that address the cognitive and behavioral aspects of their excessive anxiety (see Chapter 6). Bernstein and Borkovec (1976) provide a good primer for those who are not familiar with these widely used techniques. Relaxation techniques can include the use of imagery (Edwards, 1989; Freeman, 1981), progressive muscle relaxation (Benson, 1975; Wolpe, 1958), autohypnosis (Davis, Eshelman, & McKay, 1982), and patterned breathing, as well as a variety of other strategies.

Shame-Attack Exercises. Many clients worry a great deal about what other people will think of them and go to great lengths to avoid situations that might prove embarrassing. Shame-attack exercises, which are favored by Ellis (1969) and his colleagues (Grieger & Boyd, 1980; Wessler & Wessler, 1980), are a method for reducing excessive sensitivity to the reactions of others. This technique involves having clients intentionally perform activities that are likely to attract unfavorable attention in order to test the client's catastrophic thinking about the importance of what others will think. For example, if a client tries loudly calling out each stop while riding on the subway or leading a banana down the street on a leash, he or she generally discovers that most people do not respond in extreme ways and that if someone does notice and think poorly of him or her, the consequences are minimal. The shame-attack experiences that offer the greatest value are exaggerations of experiences that are similar to ones that the client may actually wish to perform because this is likely to enhance generalization. After all, there is limited value in becoming comfortable doing ape imitations in public if one is still uncomfortable eating at nice restaurants for fear of using the wrong fork. Grieger and Boyd (1980, p. 153) outline four conditions for the optimal use of the shame attack. (1) The exercises should be used regularly after the identification of the irrational ideas. (2) The client should generate the exercise rather than the therapist concocting the most absurd or bizarre experiences. (3) The therapist must closely monitor the client's experience so that the client does not engage in dangerous or life-threatening behaviors. (4) The therapist needs to follow up on the results of the exercise and review the results or insights gained by the homework.

Behavioral Techniques Used Primarily to Achieve Cognitive Change

Behavioral Experiments. One of the most powerful ways to achieve cognitive change is to obtain evidence from personal experience that is incompatible with the target cognition. In Cognitive Therapy, this is most often done through designing a behavioral experiment in which the client intentionally tests the validity of his or her views. In order to do this, it is necessary to clearly specify the belief or expectancy being tested and then to operationalize it so that it can be tested unequivocally in a way that is both likely to be successful and is practical. For example:

Therapist: It sounds like your basic idea is, "I've got to do whatever is socially expected, or people will get upset with me." What do you think, is that true?

Client: I don't know. I've always done what I was supposed to.

Therapist: How could you find out if this idea is true or not?

Client: I guess I could try doing something that's not expected and see what happens.

Therapist: That sounds like a reasonable idea. What would be a good thing to try?

Client: I guess I could do somersaults down the hallway at work.

Therapist: Could you actually get yourself to do that in real life?

Client: God, no! I'd be too scared.

Therapist: How about starting with something more trivial that you could actually get yourself to try?

(After some discussion)

Therapist: So we're agreed, you're going to try wearing a tie that clashes with your suit and see if people at work get upset. . . . How will you know whether they're upset or not?

A well-designed behavioral experiment can be very effective, particularly when the client accepts the therapist's point of view intellectually but is not yet convinced "on a gut level." However, it is important for the therapist to explore the conclusions the client draws on the basis of the behavioral experiment as well as the results of the experiment because clients frequently fail to draw conclusions that seem obvious to the therapist or draw conclusions that do not follow logically from the results of the experiment.

Fixed Role Therapy. Often clients want to wait until their emotional responses or their beliefs change before changing their behavior. For example, an unemployed client might prefer to apply for jobs only after he or she feels confident about succeeding. Unfortunately, this could mean a long wait. Often it is easier to feel differently or believe differently as a result of acting differently than it is to change feelings and beliefs without first changing behavior. One application of this principle is fixed role therapy, a technique usually associated with Kelly's (1955) personal construct theory. As practiced in Cognitive Therapy, this technique consists of the therapist and client identifying the ways in which the client would behave differently if the desired feeling or belief were present. The client then agrees to try acting "as if" the desired feeling or belief were present. For example:

Carrie, a college freshman, complained of low self-esteem that inhibited her academically and in her personal life. After cognitive interventions were only partially effective, she and her therapist identified a number of ways in which she thought she would act differently if she had higher self-esteem. These included asking more questions in class, being more assertive with roommates, and dressing more dramatically. With some hesitation she agreed to try acting in those ways despite her low self-esteem. When she returned to therapy the following week, she reported proudly that not only had these behaviors proven successful but that she also was feeling much less insecure and more able to fully believe that she was a likeable and capable person.

Role Reversal. When the client's extreme reactions are based on a lack of understanding or a misunderstanding of the other person's point of view, it can be quite useful to reverse the roles so that the client is required to try to take on the other person's role within the session. This can be done verbally (e.g., "How do you think you'd feel if your boyfriend just said 'Okay' in that situation?") or in imagination. However, with clients who are willing to try role playing, it can have a particularly strong impact if the client attempts to act out the other person's side of the interaction while the therapist, having been coached by the client, acts out the client's role. One of two outcomes are common. Often the client obtains a new and much more accurate understanding of the other person's point of view, which he or she is then able to use both in responding to dysfunctional thoughts and in dealing with the other person more effectively. On other occasions, the client's misunderstandings and misperceptions persist. If this is the case, it is possible for the therapist to point out the differences between the client's enactment of the other person's role and the other person's actual behavior as evidence that that person reacts very differently from the client's expectations. Then the therapist and client can go on to try to develop a more accurate understanding of the other person.

Bibliotherapy. Reading appropriate books in conjunction with therapy can be very helpful for some clients. Books like *Feeling Good* (Burns, 1980), *A New Guide to Rational Living* (Ellis & Harper, 1975), *Cognitive Therapy and the Emotional Disorders* (Beck, 1976), *Coping with Depression* (Beck & Greenburg, 1974), *Talk Sense to Yourself* (McMullin & Casey, 1975), *Getting Undepressed* (Emery, 1988), or *Woulda, Coulda, Shoulda* (Freeman & DeWolf, 1989) can consolidate points made in therapy sessions and help the client do much of the therapy work on his or her own. It should be stressed that the bibliotherapy should be used as only one part of the overall psychotherapy and not as an alternative to effective intervention on the part of the therapist. It is important for the therapist to monitor the client's understanding of the material he or she has read, to correct misconceptions, and to help the client implement the changes discussed in the readings. No matter how eloquent an author may be, his or her words have no effect until they are put into practice.

Conclusions

A review of the full range of therapeutic techniques that can prove useful in Cognitive Therapy is far beyond the scope of this chapter. However, some of the more frequently used techniques are described here. In addition to the references cited in connection with specific techniques, several volumes may be useful to clinicians. *Feeling Good* (Burns, 1980) is written as a self-help book; however, it describes a wealth of specific interventions and can be a useful resource for therapists as well as being useful as a reading for clients. Another source for ideas regarding cognitive interventions is the *Handbook of Cognitive Therapy Techniques* (McMullin, 1986), a "how-to" guide that discusses 80 specific intervention techniques. Among the many works describing behavioral interventions, Rimm and Masters (1979) and Nay (1976) provide discussions of a great variety of intervention techniques.

The wide range of therapeutic techniques that can be used within Cognitive Therapy provides the therapist with a valuable resource. However, it is important for the therapist not to become preoccupied with techniques and attempt to apply them without a clear conceptualization of the client's problems and a strategic plan for intervention. A therapist who is able to develop an accurate understanding of his or her client and then think strategically will be able to develop effective interventions even if he or she knows few established techniques. On the other hand, a therapist who has mastered many techniques but applies them without a conceptualization of the client to guide his or her intervention will often find that ostensibly powerful techniques prove ineffective.

4

The Treatment of Depression

A discussion of the treatment of depression has a special place in any book on Cognitive Therapy. Depression was, after all, the first problem area to which Beck (1967, 1976) applied Cognitive Therapy. It is also the clinical problem that has been most extensively studied in terms of the efficacy of Cognitive Therapy (Simon & Fleming, 1985). Finally, depression, by itself and in combination with other disorders, is arguably the most common problem seen in clinical practice (Seligman, 1975).

The term *depression* refers to a broad range of affective disorders. Rather than being a unitary phenomenon, it is a highly complex, multidimensional clinical syndrome. In its clinical presentation, depression may be mild or severe, obvious or masked, episodic or chronic. Depression has emotional and behavioral manifestations, as well as distinctive cognitive patterns and neurochemical changes. There can be chronic, low-level depression with very subtle symptoms, or severe depression with definite and extremely problematic symptoms. The clinical symptomatology of depression is observed in every age, racial, and ethnic group, both sexes, and across the socioeconomic spectrum. Depression manifests itself both interpersonally and intrapersonally and can have major impact on the individual, the couple, and the family (Freeman, Epstein, & Simon, 1986).

The goal of this chapter is twofold. For readers who are familiar with Cognitive Therapy of depression, it will refresh their knowledge, while also discussing aspects of Cognitive Therapy of depression that have not been emphasized in previous discussions of this subject. For readers who are not familiar with Beck's approach to depression (Beck, Rush, Shaw, & Emery, 1979), it will provide an overview of Cognitive Therapy of depression and will introduce many of the concepts, strategies, and interventions that will be adapted in subsequent chapters for use with other disorders.

ASSESSMENT

Because depression is not a unitary phenomenon, the clinician is faced with the task of discriminating between a number of related disorders

ranging from Adjustment Disorder with Depressed Mood through Dysthymic Disorder and Cyclothymic Disorder to Bipolar Disorder, Depressed, and Major Depression. The assessment process is further complicated by the fact that complaints of depression can be secondary to other
disorders and that depressed individuals may present symptoms of other
disorders rather than complaining of depression. The distinctions between
these various disorders are not academic; they can have important implications for intervention. Fortunately, the detailed information provided by
the type of initial evaluation described in Chapter 2 provides the information needed to draw these distinctions.

Consider the following case example:

"Frank" was a 45-year-old, married man with three children who had been
employed as a machine tool salesman. At the time when he sought treatment,
Frank had been unemployed for several months and was feeling quite depressed
and hopeless over his career difficulties and the prospect of not being able to
provide well for his family. He had become increasingly withdrawn and inactive,
was unable to job hunt effectively, and spent most of his time sitting around the
house brooding about his problems and feeling miserable.

The mildest of the various forms of depression is Adjustment Disorder
with Depressed Mood (see Table 4). In this form of depression, an individual whose premorbid functioning has been unremarkable experiences
an identifiable stressor and becomes depressed, but his or her depression
does not satisfy the diagnostic criteria for other disorders. It is sometimes
assumed that no intervention is needed with adjustment disorders because
they tend to be time limited without intervention. However, if effective
intervention can decrease the client's distress, speed recovery, improve the
outcome, and decrease the risk of the client's problems progressing to the
point where they qualify for a more serious diagnosis, then it could be

TABLE 4. DSM-III-R Diagnostic Criteria for Adjustment Disorder
with Depressed Mood

A. A reaction to an identifiable psychosocial stressor (or multiple stressors) that occurs within
   3 months of onset of the stressor(s).
B. The maladaptive nature of the reaction is indicated by either of the following:
   1. Impairment in occupational (including school) functioning or in usual social activities
      or relationships with others
   2. Symptoms that are in excess of a normal and expectable reaction to the stressor(s).
C. The disturbance is not merely one instance of a pattern of overreaction to stress or an
   exacerbation of one of the mental disorders previously described.
D. The maladaptive reaction has persisted for no longer than 6 months.
E. The disturbance does not meet the criteria for any specific mental disorder and does not
   represent Uncomplicated Bereavement.

Table 5. DSM-III-R Diagnostic Criteria for Dysthymic Disorder

A. Depressed mood for most of the day, more days than not, as indicated either by subjective account or observation by others, for at least 2 years.
B. Presence, while depressed, of at least two of the following:
   1. Poor appetite or overeating
   2. Insomnia or hypersomnia
   3. Low energy or fatigue
   4. Low self-esteem
   5. Poor concentration or difficulty making decisions
   6. Feelings of hopelessness
C. During a 2-year period of the disturbance, never without the symptoms in A for more then 2 months at a time.
D. No evidence of an unequivocal Major Depressive Episode during the first 2 years of the disturbance.
E. Has never had a Manic Episode or an unequivocal Hypomanic Episode.
F. Not superimposed on a chronic psychotic disorder, such as Schizophrenia or Delusional Disorder.
G. It cannot be established that an organic factor initiated and maintained the disturbance.

quite valuable. In Frank's case, his initial reaction to being fired would have satisfied the diagnostic criteria for this disorder, but his depression soon progressed further.

Dysthymic Disorder (Table 5) and Cyclothymic Disorder (Table 6) are characterized by more chronic and persistent problems than result from an adjustment disorder but milder symptomatology than either Major Depression or Bipolar Disorder. It would be natural to assume that Dysthymic Disorder and Cyclothymic Disorder would respond to treatment more quickly than Major Depression and Bipolar Disorder because the symptoms are milder and result in less impairment. However, the high instance of substance abuse among clients with Cyclothymic Disorder and the high incidence of personality disorders among clients with Dysthymic Disorder greatly complicate and slow treatment.

Table 6. DSM-III-R Diagnostic Criteria for Cyclothymic Disorder

A. For at least 2 years, presence of numberous Hypomanic Episodes and numerous periods with depressed mood or loss of interest or pleasure that did not meet Criterion A of Major Depressive Episode.
B. During a 2-year period of the disturbance, never without hypomanic or depressive symptoms for more than 2 months at a time.
C. No clear evidence of a Major Depressive Episode or Manic Episode during the first 2 years of the disturbance.
D. Not superimposed on a chronic psychotic disorder, such as Schizophrenia or Delusional Disorder.
E. It cannot be established that an organic factor initiated and maintained the disturbance.

In fact, the individual with Dysthymic Disorder is probably the most difficult depressed patient to treat. This client gains little pleasure from life without being severely debilitated and often without having obvious precipitants for his or her depressed moods. Severely depressed clients are powerfully motivated to change by the intensity of their distress, though the severity of their depression may initially mask this motivation to change. However, the dysthymic experiences a much more tolerable level of distress and thus is less motivated to change. Furthermore, initial interventions with seriously depressed clients often produce noticeable changes early in therapy, and when client's level of depression changes from a BDI score of 32 to a score of 21, there is great clinical change. The client feels better, does more, and thinks differently and is encouraged to persist in therapy because it obviously is helping. With dysthymic clients, initial changes usually are slower and less obvious. When the dysthymic goes from a BDI score of 13 to an 11, the change is barely noticeable, and the client sees little indication that therapy is accomplishing anything. Given the small changes, whatever motivation for treatment the client had initially tends to disappear altogether.

The DSM-III R (APA, 1987) criteria for Major Depressive Disorder are given in Table 7. As can be seen, this is the diagnosis given for severe, episodic depressions that are extremely incapacitating for the individual. It is sometimes assumed that clients who are this severely depressed need antidepressant medication or hospitalization or some more "powerful"

TABLE 7. DSM-III-R Diagnostic Criteria for Major Depressive Disorder

At least five of the following symptoms have been present during the same 2 week period and represent a change from previous functioning; at least one of the symptoms is either (1) depressed mood, or (2) loss of interest or pleasure. (Do not include symptoms that are clearly due to a physical condition, mood-incongruent delusions or hallucinations, incoherence, or marked loosening of associations.)

1. Depressed mood most of the day, nearly every day, as indicated either by subjective account or observation of others
2. Markedly diminished interest or pleasure in all, or almost all, activities most of the day, nearly every day
3. Significant weight loss or weight gain when not dieting (e.g., more than 5% of body weight in a month), or decrease or increase in appetite nearly every day
4. Insomnia or hypersomnia nearly every day
5. Psychomotor agitation or retardation nearly every day (observable by others, not merely subjective feelings of restlessness or being slowed down)
6. Fatigue or loss of energy nearly every day
7. Feelings of worthlessness or excessive or inappropriate guilt (which may be delusional) nearly every day (not merely self-reproach or guilt about being sick)
8. Diminished ability to think or concentrate or indecisiveness, nearly every day
9. Recurrent thoughts of death (not just fear of dying), recurrent suicidal ideation without a specific plan, or a suicide attempt or a specific plan for committing suicide

TABLE 8. DSM-III-R Diagnostic Criteria for Bipolar Disorder

A. Current (or most recent) episode involves the full symptomatic picture of both Manic and Major Depressive Episodes (except for the duration requirements of 2 weeks for depressive symptoms), intermixed or rapidly alternating every few days.
B. Prominent depressive symptoms lasting at least a full day.

---

intervention rather than "talking therapy." In fact, Cognitive Therapy works well even with clients who are quite severely depressed, and it has been found to be at least as "powerful" as the other treatment options (see Simon & Fleming, 1985, for a recent review of research on the effectiveness of Cognitive Therapy). At the time of his initial evaluation, Frank clearly met the diagnostic criteria for Major Depression. He reported a constant depressed mood and appeared quite depressed; he reported that he no longer felt any interest in or enjoyment from his usual activities; he had a constant problem with waking in the early morning hours and being unable to get back to sleep; he reported chronic fatigue; and he felt totally worthless.

Bipolar Disorder is perhaps more widely known by the older term, Manic-Depressive Disorder. Many persons assume that this disorder is characterized by a regular alternation between manic and depressive episodes but in actuality the essential feature of Bipolar Disorder is a history of one or more manic episodes accompanied by one or more depressive episodes. From the diagnostic criteria shown in Table 8, it is clear that the pattern of manic and depressive episodes can vary considerably from client to client. The presence of manic episodes complicates treatment of depressed clients who have a Bipolar Disorder. First, clients usually fail to come in for therapy during manic episodes despite the degree of impairment that can result from a manic episode. Second, no cognitive interventions have been demonstrated to be effective in treating manic episodes. Therefore, there is a consensus that Cognitive Therapy is an appropriate treatment for depressive episodes in clients with Bipolar Disorder as long as appropriate medication is used to control the manic episodes.

It is important to note that both Cyclothymic Disorder and Dysthymic Disorder can co-occur with Bipolar Disorder or Major Depression. When a sufficiently detailed history of the client's symptoms is available, it is possible to diagnose both disorders by examining the pattern of symptomatology over time. However, often a detailed history is not available, and the Cyclothymic or Dysthymic Disorder is not apparent until the client's Major Depressive Episode has been at least partly treated.

Although the term *masked depression* is not a diagnostic label, it still is a concept that the clinician needs to consider. When a client complains of being "blue," "down," or "sad," his or her depression is easy to recognize.

However, individuals differ widely in the extent to which they are able to recognize and express their emotions and in the extent to which they are willing to acknowledge having psychological problems. Depressed individuals may seek help either without recognizing their depressed mood or without being willing to admit that they are depressed. When this is the case, they are likely to present "nonpsychological" symptoms such as sleeping difficulty, eating problems, loss of appetite, loss of libido, or a lack of motivation without mentioning feelings of sadness or depression. Often if these individuals are asked directly about depressed mood, periods of tearfulness, and so forth, it is possible to determine if they are indeed depressed. In addition, the Beck Depression Inventory (see Chapter 2) can be useful in determining the extent to which a client's complaints correspond to symptoms of depression. Obviously, when a client's "medical" complaints are symptoms of depression, effective treatment of the depression should alleviate the symptoms.

Conversely, a client's depressed mood may reflect a "secondary depression," where the depressed mood is a response to some other medical or psychiatric problem (Shaw, Vallis, & McCabe, 1985). Problems ranging from cardiac surgery to agoraphobia can elicit a depressed mood or a full depressive disorder as a reaction to either the actual impact the problem has on the client's life or the client's expectations about the effects it will have. Whether the depression is primary or secondary, cognitive therapy techniques can be used for treatment of the depression. However, when depression is a response to another psychiatric disorder, it may be more appropriate for therapist and client to focus most of their efforts on treating the primary disorder because the depression is likely to lift if the primary disorder can be resolved.

Cognitive Therapy can also be applied to helping clients deal with objectively tragic or saddening life problems. Many life situations cause realistic sadness, frustration, or grief. For example, Holmes and Rahe (1976) found the death of a loved one to typically be the most powerful stressor that persons experience. DSM-III-R (p. 361) states that individuals experiencing "uncomplicated bereavement" frequently suffer a full depressive episode and may enter therapy for associated symptoms. Assessment of the client who is responding to a life crisis does not differ from that of any other client. The therapist must assess the degree to which the client's response is realistic as well as any distortions in the client's thinking that aggravate the situation. When dysfunctional beliefs and cognitive distortions do not disrupt the normal grieving process, support and reassurance from the therapist may be sufficient. However, when cognitions about the loss intensify the grief or block the normal grieving process, Cognitive Therapy can be quite useful.

Even when a client presents with classic symptoms of depression, it is important for the therapist to be certain that depression is, in fact, the problem. A wide range of medical problems can contribute to depression or produce symptoms that mimic depression. Therefore, if the client has not had a complete physical exam in the past year, he or she should be directed to get one early in treatment to rule out the possibility that a medical disorder is involved. Obviously, treating a low thyroid level or congestive heart failure with Cognitive Therapy or with any other psychotherapy will be ineffective and may even constitute malpractice.

As outlined in the Beck Depression Inventory, a wide variety of symptoms are associated with depression, including feelings of sadness and depression, pessimism, and hopelessness, feelings of failure, dissatisfaction with activities, guilt, dissatisfaction with self, self-criticism, suicidality, tearfulness, irritation, loss of interest in others, difficulty making decisions, dissatisfaction with appearance, lack of motivation, early-morning waking, fatigue, loss of appetite, weight loss, overconcern with health, and decreased sexual desire. In addition to the distinction between the various diagnostic categories, the therapist must also assess the pattern of depressive symptomatology for a particular client.

Two individuals coming for treatment may have identical levels of depression, but the particular constellation of symptoms on the BDI may be very different. If both individuals have a score of 25 (out of 63), it would indicate a moderate to severe clinical depression. However, for one individual, the major manifestation of his or her depression might be interpersonal, whereas for the other the manifestations might be intrapersonal. The individual whose symptom picture is primarily interpersonal might have difficulty because of a loss of libido, loss of interest in other people, and a general dissatisfaction and boredom with everything. The patient whose symptom picture is primarily intrapersonal might have problems with self-blame, guilt, self-criticism, disappointment, and self-hate. Both of these patients might have other symptoms in common such as feelings of hopelessness, with a corresponding risk of suicidality for both. Any number of combinations of symptoms may occur and account for much variability between one depressed client and the next. When the therapist understands the client's symptom pattern, interventions can be selected that focus on the specific problem areas that are posing difficulties for the client.

In addition to correct diagnosis and assessment of the pattern of depressive symptomatology, the therapist must also determine whether the client can be effectively treated with outpatient psychotherapy or whether he or she should be hospitalized. This, of course, would depend upon the client's level of functioning, support system, and suicidality, among other factors. Hospitalization is most commonly needed when the client is suicidal and interventions within the session have not been sufficiently effective to alleviate the risk of a suicide attempt. This is discussed more fully in Chapter 5.

CONCEPTUALIZATION

The cognitive view is that depression is characterized by a "cognitive triad" of a negative view of the self, a negative view of the world,* and a negative view of the future (Beck, 1976; Beck et al., 1979). This cognitive triad is manifested in the content of the individual's "automatic thoughts," his or her immediate, involuntary, nonreflective cognitive response to a situation. In Frank's case, he made many negative statements that reflected these automatic thoughts, such as "I'm not good enough," "I've never really been successful," "I'll never get anywhere," and "I'll fail," and he believed these statements implicitly. These views contributed to Frank's depressed mood, his low motivation for job hunting ("I'm not good enough. I'll fail. Why bother?"), and to his pervasive sense of hopelessness and dissatisfaction.

If Frank's negative views had been accurate, his mood and his actions would have been easy to understand. However, when the situation was examined in detail, it turned out that Frank lost his job as part of a major work force reduction resulting from a recession. Not only had the layoff been based on seniority rather than on any lack on Frank's part, but he actually had received very positive evaluations on the job and had been promoted regularly before the firm's economic difficulties. Frank's former supervisor had a high opinion of his abilities and expressed confidence that Frank would be able to get a good job and do well in it. By all accounts (except Frank's), his view of himself as a failure, his pessimistic outlook, and his subsequent lack of motivation were completely unrealistic. How could an intelligent, well-educated man develop such an unrealistically negative view of himself?

The cognitive view argues that an individual's schemas, beliefs, and assumptions constantly and automatically shape his or her perceptions and interpretations of events. In the course of growing up, Frank had been taught, both explicitly and implicitly, that success was essential for one to be worthwhile, to be liked, and to enjoy life. In addition, he had been taught that the way to succeed was to set very high standards and to push very hard in trying to meet those standards. Consequently, he viewed most situations in terms of success and failure, had a lifelong pattern of setting unrealistically high standards for himself, and tried to do things perfectly. These beliefs and assumptions predisposed him to be unreasonably self-critical and to react strongly to perceived failures.

Frank's cognitive distortions intensified the impact of his dysfunctional beliefs. He was particularly prone to the distortions of "dichotomous

---

*It is important to note that Beck uses the phrase *negative view of the world* to refer to the depressed individual's negative view of his or her personal experience, not a negative view of the world in general.

thinking" and "labeling". For example he viewed success and failure in absolute terms. As he saw it, anything that was not a complete success was clearly a total failure, and if he failed at a task, then he was a failure. Because being laid off, whatever the reason, was not success, then by definition he was a failure. This view of himself had a broad impact. After all, what prospective employer would choose to hire a failure? Frank's view was that even if he was able to fool someone into hiring him, it would lead inevitably to disaster because he was a failure. Thus it was not surprising that Frank was unable to motivate himself to actively apply for another job. From his point of view, job hunting seemed futile at best and potentially disastrous.

The combination of his unrealistically high standards for himself and his dichotomous thinking about success and failure was particularly devastating for Frank. Because his standards for judging his performance as success were excessively severe, he was doomed to frequently fall short of his standards. When the "failure" was relatively minor, Frank simply became quite upset with himself and redoubled his efforts, but each time a significant "failure" occurred Frank would begin to consider himself a complete failure. He would then expect to fail at anything he tried and would lapse into a depression. This pattern of cognitions had been responsible for his history of recurrent episodes of depression in response to perceived failures.

The third factor that completed the picture of Frank's depression was the impact his mood had on his cognition. As discussed in Chapter 1, perception and evaluation of personally relevant events is negatively biased during depression. Thus Frank showed a tendency to selectively recall previous failures and shortcomings and to be biased toward interpreting ambiguous situations negatively. Because both recall of sad events and biased perception of events would tend to elicit a depressed mood, the tendency of moods to bias cognition in a mood-congruent way perpetuated and amplified Frank's depressed mood.

These three factors set the stage for the "downward spiral of depression" (Figure 7). In Frank's case, his schemas and basic assumptions about failure and self-worth predisposed him to depressive reactions when confronted by "failure." When he was laid off, these beliefs about the significance of failure were activated, and a stream of negative automatic thoughts about himself, his situation, and his future prospects resulted. Given his proclivity for dichotomous thinking, these negative thoughts were quite extreme and seemed completely plausible to him. These negative thoughts then elicited a depressed mood that further biased Frank's perception and recall in a depression-congruent way. This resulted in his selectively remembering past failures while overlooking experiences that were inconsistent with his negative views. Thus his thoughts became increasingly negative, his mood increasingly depressed, and so on. As a

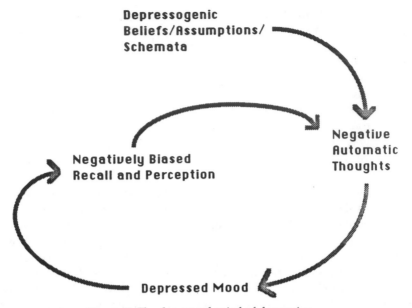

FIGURE 7. The downward spiral of depression.

result, it was possible for Frank's reaction to being laid off to spiral from shock and disappointment to significant depression over a short period of time.

A number of additional factors commonly tend to perpetuate depressions once they occur. The depressed individual's lack of motivation often results in a decrease in activity that has several effects: The unoccupied time provides additional opportunity for depressing ruminations, the depressed individual may become concerned or self-critical over his or her decreased productivity, and the individual has fewer experiences that he or she might possibly enjoy or find worthwhile. Also, the changes in the depressed individual's behavior as well as his or her expressions of depressed mood may affect interpersonal interactions in a way that is likely to perpetuate the depression.

STRATEGIES FOR INTERVENTION

The cognitive conceptualization of depression in terms of the "downward spiral of depression" suggests that it is important to break the depression-perpetuating cycle of *negative automatic thoughts* → *depressed mood* → *biased recall and perception* in order to alleviate the depression. This cycle can be broken at any point. Thus Frank's therapist hypothesized that if Frank could be induced to take a more balanced view of himself, his experiences, and his future prospects, or if his mood could be improved, or if the biasing impact of his depressed mood on perception and recall could be counteracted, the cycle that perpetuated his depression could be broken, and his depression should subside. However it can be seen from Figure 7 that if Frank and his therapist accomplished only this without modifying his dysfunctional beliefs, Frank would still be at risk for a relapse whenever he experienced a setback or failure that could restart the downward spiral. In order to achieve lasting results, it would be necessary to modify the beliefs and assumptions that predisposed Frank to depression and to help him plan effective ways to handle situations that might precipitate a relapse.

The general strategy of first attempting to disrupt the cycles that perpetuate the client's depression and then attempting to modify the beliefs and assumptions that predispose the individual to depression can be implemented in many ways within the framework of "collaborative empiricism" outlined in Chapter 1. A wide variety of techniques for modifying automatic thoughts, dysfunctional beliefs and assumptions, dysphoric moods, and maladaptive behavior are available to the therapist. If it is possible to develop a clear understanding of each client and use this as a foundation for an individualized treatment plan, the therapist can intervene more effectively than if he or she uses a "standard" approach to all depressed clients.

COGNITIVE AND BEHAVIORAL TECHNIQUES

After working to establish a collaborative therapeutic relationship, Cognitive Therapy for depression often begins either with behavioral interventions designed to improve the client's mood or with cognitive interventions focused on identifying and challenging dysfunctional automatic thoughts. In Frank's case, his depression was so intense that he was largely inactive at home and was fairly unresponsive during the session. Frank's answers to the therapist's questions were slow and terse and he was not able to participate actively in a collaborative approach to dealing with his problems. This led the therapist to conclude that it would be quite useful to focus initially on improving Frank's mood in the hope that this would increase his responsiveness to verbal interventions and his motivation to take an active part in therapy. Despite Frank's lethargy, it was possible to use a guided discovery approach to analyzing the differences between times when Frank's depression was particularly intense and times when it was less intense and to demonstrate that his level of activity had an important impact on his mood. This made it possible to introduce Frank to activity scheduling (Chapter 3) in a way that resulted in his being willing to try it as a "homework assignment."

When Frank tried to intentionally be more active despite his depression, he quickly discovered that by simply increasing the number of things that he did each day, he was able to improve his mood substantially. Although this intervention did not eliminate Frank's depression or his procrastination, it resulted in Frank's being much more responsive and motivated during sessions and provided him with clear evidence that he was not helpless in the face of his depression. At this point, it was possible to engage Frank more actively in collaboration and clarify his goals for therapy.

The productive targets for initial cognitive interventions can be selected by paying special attention to the cognitive triad, the client's negative views of self, world, and future. Just as symptoms differ, the relative importance of issues relating to self, world, and future differ for each client. By assessing the importance of each of the three factors, the therapist can determine which of the three to emphasize in initial interventions. In addition, another aspect of the early phase of therapy is to orient the client to the cognitive view of depression and to establish a collaborative relationship. This assessment of the roles of each aspect of the cognitive triad in the client's depression can be visualized in a way that can be used to help the client have a better understanding of the focus of the therapy.

The cognitive triad can be pictured as an equilateral triangle. One can draw a perpendicular line from each of the three sides (Figure 8), with the degree of importance of a particular factor represented by the length of the line such that the shorter the line, the greater the degree of importance of that factor for the individual and the longer the line, the less important that particular factor is. Thus, the intersection of the three lines will be closest to the factor or factors that are most strongly represented in the client's cognitions. For example, a client who voices many statements reflecting low self-esteem and a negative view of his or her experiences but who does not emphasize a negative view of the future would be seen as having problems primarily with negative views of self and world and would be represented graphically by Pattern "A" in Figure 8. The client's concerns would be voiced by statements reflecting low self-esteem and negative views of world and experience. When questioned about current hopelessness and suicidality, this client might say, "Kill myself? Oh, No! I'll just continue to live my poor, miserable life because I deserve to." It must be remembered, of course, that the representation of negative thoughts of the self, world, and future can change at any time. Thus, the therapist should not be lulled into complacency regarding the future suicidal potential of a client who is not currently hopeless.

If the client's concerns focus primarily on self and future, the verbalizations might include those reflecting low self-esteem and suicidal thoughts, for example, "What good am I? I deserve to die. The world seems to get along pretty well; it's me that is at variance with the rest of the

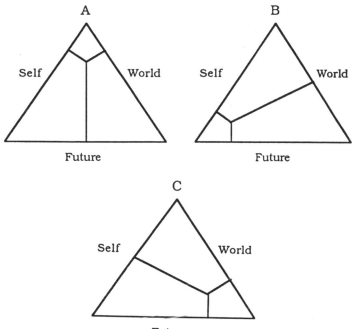

FIGURE 8. Graphic representation of the relative importance of components of the cognitive triad.

world." In Frank's case, by far the most important aspect of the cognitive triad was his negative view of himself. He was preoccupied with the belief that he was a complete failure, and to a lesser extent with the belief that he was doomed to remain a failure. His view of the world was the least distorted of the three aspects of the cognitive triad but was also the aspect on which he focused the least. This is shown in Pattern "B" in Figure 8.

Finally, if the client's concerns involve a negative view of the world and the future (Pattern "C"), a view that is common among clients who have Axis II diagnoses as well, the client's verbalizations might include a diatribe against the ills and evils of the world and a multitude of reasons as to why the client is powerless to improve things. When asked about self-esteem or personal contributions to their difficulty, this type of individual will often go on in great detail about how he or she has tried and not succeeded because of the world's problems and present him or herself as an innocent victim.

Interventions directed toward challenging negative automatic thoughts typically play a major part in Cognitive Therapy with depressed clients. In working with Frank, the therapist's next goal was to demon-strate the connection between automatic thoughts and mood to Frank and to work to help him learn to challenge his negative automatic thoughts. This was done by asking Frank to identify a point in the past when he had experienced a noticeable increase in his depressed mood and then pinpointing the automatic thoughts that occurred in that situation as follows:

Therapist: Can you think of a particular point in the past week when you became noticeably more depressed? A time when your mood took a turn for the worse?

Client: Um . . . I guess I got pretty depressed Thursday morning.

Therapist: What was the situation at the time when your mood shifted?

Client: Let me think. . . . The mail had just come, and I was sitting on the couch flipping through it.

Therapist: Do you remember what thoughts were running through your mind as you sat there flipping through the mail?

Client: No, I don't think anything was on my mind.

Therapist: Let's try something that should make it easier to remember whatever you might have been thinking. What I'm going to ask you to do is imagine that situation over again as realistically as you can. People often find that that makes it easier to remember the details. How does that sound?

Client: Ok.

Therapist: So settle back in a comfortable position, close your eyes to shut out distractions, and let yourself relax. . . . Now I'd like you to imagine being back in that situation as realistically as you can. It's Thursday morning, the mail has just come, and you're flipping through it. Imagine the room just the way it was on Thursday, the mail in your hands, the whole situation. . . . How do you feel as you imagine that?

Client: I'm starting to feel depressed like I did then.

Therapist: What thoughts are running through your head?

Client: I'm thinking about the bills.

Therapist: What I'd like you to do is try to quote the thoughts as much as possible in the same words as when they ran through your head because sometimes the wording can make a big difference.

Client: "Look at all these bills! I'll never be able to pay them off. How's Jack ever going to go to college?"

Therapist: Ok. Stop imagining and open your eyes. Do you think those thoughts might have something to do with your getting more depressed right then?

The therapist was then able to explain the cognitive view of the impact of automatic thoughts on mood using Frank's reactions to illustrate his points. He was then able to introduce the idea of challenging negative automatic thoughts as follows:

Therapist: When you went ahead and opened the mail, how did it turn out?

Client: Well, they weren't all bills, and it wasn't as bad as I expected.

Therapist: Are you going to be able to pay them off?

Client: Yeah. I'm getting unemployment, and my wife works part time so we haven't had to dip into our savings yet.

Therapist: How do you think you would have felt if instead of thinking "I'll never be able to pay them off," you'd been thinking "These damn bills are a pain It's a good thing I've got unemployment and some money in the bank"?

Client: I'd probably have felt better.
Therapist: Which would have been closer to the truth?
Client: That they're a pain.

After discussing the merits of looking critically at automatic thoughts and "talking back" to the ones that are exaggerated or distorted, the therapist was able to demonstrate the use of the Dysfunctional Thought Record (Chapter 2) by showing Frank how the therapist had recorded Frank's thoughts on a DTR sheet. Frank's next homework assignment was to use the DTR to record his automatic thoughts at times when his mood worsened and to begin reading Feeling Good (Burns, 1980) in addition to maintaining his increased activity level.

One of the most frequently used strategies in Cognitive Therapy is that of developing adaptive responses to dysfunctional thoughts (see Chapter 3). In Frank's case, negative thoughts relating to his self-worth, judgments of his performance, and the futility of trying to find another job frequently occurred at the times when he became more depressed. Most of Frank's negative thoughts were not actually true (as is the case with most depressives), and therefore could be challenged with specific disconfirming evidence from his life. By correcting exaggerations and distortions in his automatic thoughts, Frank was able to improve his mood considerably. However, as Frank examined his automatic thoughts, he discovered some of them to be "true, but not useful." For example, Frank experienced periods during which he ruminated over the possibility that his savings might eventually be exhausted. Although such an eventuality was possible and would have posed a serious problem were it to occur, Frank's periods of ruminating about this were very depressing to him and did nothing to forestall the problem. Dysfunctional thoughts of this type can be handled adaptively by the client's learning to control the occurrence of these thoughts through techniques such as "thought stopping" and "scheduling worries," through replacing them with more adaptive thoughts, or through developing effective plans for preventing or handling the anticipated problem. In Frank's case, he found that when he took active steps to find a new job, these worries subsided.

Often the automatic thoughts or themes among automatic thoughts that come up most frequently are the most important to address. Frank's conviction that he was "a complete failure" was a recurrent theme among the thoughts that he recorded on the DTR and thus was selected as the next target for intervention. This view of himself probably could have been addressed in the abstract through a philosophical analysis; however, it was simpler and more powerful for the therapist to guide Frank to examine the evidence bearing on the question of whether Frank was indeed a complete failure. The therapist discovered that Frank had been laid off, purely on the basis of seniority, in a work force reduction after years of being one of the better salesmen at his firm and of providing well for his family. Once this evidence had been made explicit, Frank no longer accepted the view that he was "a complete failure" and instead endorsed the view that he had failed at some things and succeeded at others.

The discussion of success and failure highlighted Frank's long-standing tendency to set unrealistically high standards for himself and the negative consequences this had for him. The therapist chose to intervene here by examining the pros and cons of holding very high standards for oneself. Frank initially expressed a strong conviction that it was necessary to do his work perfectly in order to be successful, but as he and his therapist considered the available evidence, he quickly realized that this approach resulted in considerable stress and pressure, resulted in his often becoming preoccupied with trivial imperfections in his work, and resulted in his interpreting performance with which his superiors were quite pleased as being inadequate. In addition to continuing to use DTRs, he agreed to try a behavioral experiment (Chapter 3) of doing a "good but not perfect" job on several household tasks in order to test whether setting more moderate standards for himself was actually a good idea.

Noncompliance with homework assignments can be very useful in identifying important issues that have not yet been addressed. It was at this point in therapy that Frank suddenly found himself unable to get around to doing the homework despite having been quite reliable about doing it previously. At the same time, he began experiencing upsetting visual images and disturbing dreams of himself ending up as a vagrant. When he and his therapist examined the thoughts that occurred when he tried to do his homework and when the images occurred, they uncovered an intense fear that if Frank relaxed his perfectionism at all, the consequences would be disastrous. Once the fear was identified, Frank and his therapist were able to challenge it successfully, and Frank's work on reducing his perfectionism then proceeded without a hitch.

At this point in therapy, Frank's depression had subsided to nonclinical levels and he had begun active job hunting. When the client's goals for therapy have been attained and he or she is free of depression, it may seem that the time for termination has arrived. However, if therapy is stopped before identifying and challenging the client's dysfunctional assumptions and preparing him or her to handle future setbacks, he or she will continue to have a predisposition toward depression. The middle stage of Frank's therapy began with identifying the basic assumptions that predisposed him to depression by looking for patterns among the automatic thoughts collected thus far in therapy and use of the "downward arrow" technique (Chapter 2). Once the assumptions were identified, it was possible to help Frank to look at them critically, to work to develop more adaptive alternative beliefs, and to test them through behavioral experiments (Chapter 3). For example, one of Frank's basic assumptions that had been uncovered in examining his difficulty through the antiperfectionism homework assignments was the idea that in order to succeed he must constantly set very high standards for himself and work as hard as possible or, in his own words, "If I quit pushing I might end up there [as a vagrant on a streetcorner]." When asked whether he had any evidence that would support this view Frank pointed to his poor performance when depressed. However, the therapist was able to remind Frank that they knew from previous sessions that he did not lower his standards for himself or quit trying to force himself to work hard when he was depressed; the problem was that when he was depressed this approach to motivating himself was ineffective. In fact, the approach to self-motivation that had proven effective in overcoming his inactivity and procrastination included setting moderate, clearly manageable goals rather than high standards for himself and focusing on what he hoped to accomplish through the activity rather than pushing himself or dwelling on the bad consequences that would occur if he did not act. After reviewing his experiences in several other situations, it was clear to Frank that the available evidence was incompatible with his initial assumption.

Although this review of the evidence did not completely eliminate his belief in the assumption that a more positive, less pressured approach to work would lead to disaster, it prepared Frank to test the assumption through a "behavioral experiment" in which he tried his new approach to self-motivation with job hunting tasks and compared the results with the results he had achieved by setting high standards and putting a lot of pressure on himself. He was surprised to discover that the new approach not only was much more pleasant but also resulted in his completing more applications and being able to present himself more confidently in interviews. After this experience, he no longer accepted his former assumption that it was necessary to set high standards for himself and constantly push himself.

Work on relapse prevention generally focuses on clearly identifying situations that would be likely to present a risk of relapse and pinpointing early warning signs of relapse. The next step is to develop plans for coping with those situations should they arise. With Frank, it was already clear that work-related "failures" were the primary situation in which there would be a risk of another depression. From a review of Frank's response to earlier work-related setbacks, he and his therapist learned that a consistent early sign that he was starting down the path to depression was when he began to feel increasingly pressured and to focus solely on work. Knowing this, he and his therapist were able to formulate a plan for handling setbacks that included intentionally resisting his tendency to withdraw and become inactive, using adaptive self-statements (such as "Failing at one task doesn't make me a failure in general" and "The thing to do is to plan ahead rather than dwelling on this setback"), taking active steps to deal with the situation, rereading the portions of *Feeling Good* (Burns, 1980) that he had found particularly useful, and returning to therapy for a "booster session" if necessary.

Particular attention was paid to Frank's expectations regarding future problems. Initially he expected never to feel depressed again and was at risk for reacting to a future period of sadness or depression with thoughts like, "Oh my God, I'm depressed again! Cognitive Therapy didn't work, it really is hopeless." Obviously, these unrealistically optimistic expectations regarding the long-term effects of therapy might be encouraging initially but could predispose him to relapse when he encountered future problems. His adoption of the more realistic view that Cognitive Therapy had equipped him with the skills he needed to cope effectively with depression and to prevent depressed moods from becoming major problems decreased the risk of his overreacting to future setbacks and should decrease the risk of relapse.

The final stage of therapy is termination. It is usually a collaborative process during which therapy sessions are gradually scheduled less frequently so that therapist and client have an opportunity to see whether the gains achieved in therapy persist without frequent intervention by the therapist. In Frank's case, termination was more abrupt than usual because soon after he and his therapist began discussing termination he began a new job some distance away and was unable to come in for therapy at the times when the therapist could be available. Therefore it was necessary to handle the final steps of work on relapse prevention and termination by telephone. At the close of therapy, Frank had been completely free of depression for 3 weeks, had been able to actively pursue job hunting without procrastination, had resumed his normal family and social activities, had begun a new job about which he was enthusiastic, and was experiencing substantially less stress and pressure than he had previously experienced when starting other jobs. Because termination had been more abrupt than usual, there had not been an opportunity to observe how Frank coped with a significant setback or failure, but he had a clear plan for handling failures adaptively, was confident that he would be able to do so, and was comfortable with the idea of returning for a booster session if necessary.

CONCLUSION

Because Beck originally developed Cognitive Therapy specifically for the treatment of depression, it is not surprising that the majority of outcome studies of Cognitive Therapy have involved the treatment of depression. In controlled outcome studies, Cognitive Therapy has been found to be an effective treatment for depression, to be at least as effective as treatment with antidepressant medication and often to be superior, and possibly to have a lower dropout rate than treatment with antidepressant medication (Simon & Fleming, 1985). In almost all comparisons between Cognitive Therapy and alternative treatment approaches, Cognitive Therapy has been found to be at least as effective as the alternatives and often more effective.

The cognitive approach to the treatment of depression is not only a well-developed, well-validated approach to effectively treating an important problem, it is also the "standard" Cognitive Therapy approach that serves as a foundation for the cognitive approach to other, more complex disorders. Thus a solid understanding of Cognitive Therapy of depression is strongly recommended.

5

The Treatment of Suicidal Behavior

Cognitive Therapy with a suicidal client is quite different from therapy with a depressed client who is not suicidal. Even the most experienced therapist reacts with a surge of emotion when it becomes clear that a client is seriously considering taking his or her own life. The suicidal client presents the therapist with a life and death crisis that demands an immediate response and in which the possible consequences of ineffective interventions are obvious. At the same time, Cognitive Therapy's collaborative approach can be difficult to implement when the client is seriously considering suicide and the therapist has the conflicting goal of keeping the client alive. Finally, it can be difficult to use a guided discovery approach when the client's motivation for therapy is questionable and the therapist feels realistic pressure to intervene quickly.

Given the pressure the therapist is under and the potential seriousness of the situation, it is essential for the therapist to have a clear understanding of suicidal thinking and behavior to guide effective intervention. A large body of clinical lore regarding suicide has been developed over the years (Freeman & White, 1989). Some of these beliefs are valid and useful, whereas others are myths that can contribute to the therapist's underestimating the risk of suicide, having difficulty in developing a conceptualization of the problem, and most serious of all, having difficulty in developing and implementing effective treatment strategies. Some beliefs about suicide that are common among clinicians include the following:

1. *Suicide is a "cry for help."* It is certainly true that some clients threaten suicide or make ostensible suicide attempts in an attempt to demonstrate the magnitude of their distress and obtain the help they feel they need. However, if this was generally the case, few clients would make potentially lethal suicide attempts because one can hardly receive help after one is dead. It is far more useful to view a suicide attempt as a statement that the individual sees few or no other options left to effect a change in his or her life. The strong relationship between hopelessness and suicide that has been found in a number of studies suggests that suicidality is often an

indication that the client has concluded that he or she is beyond help rather than being a "cry for help."

2. *Suicide is hostility turned inward.* The traditional psychodynamic conceptualization of suicide is that the suicidal individual is so enraged and furious at some significant other that he or she wishes to kill them. However, rather than turning the rage and murderous intent on the object of the anger, the suicidal individual is forced, by virtue of socialization, to kill himself or herself. Similarly, the traditional view of depression is that it also results from hostility turned inwards. Little evidence has been found to support either of these views. In fact, Beck initially developed his cognitive view of depression after first unsuccessfully attempting to provide empirical support for the psychodynamic view of depression by analyzing the content of the dreams of depressed individuals (see Beck, 1976). He found that the dreams of depressives were characterized more by themes of defeat and deprivation than by the expected indications of hostility turned inwards.

3. *Suicide risk can be determined from history and demographic characteristics.* Most clinicians are aware that suicide rates vary with sex, age, social support, and other factors; and attempts have been made to use factors such as these to develop criteria for estimating suicide risk (e.g., Patterson, Dohn, Bird, & Patterson, 1983). Although criteria based on these factors can improve judgments about suicide risk made by relatively unsophisticated assessors (Patterson *et al.*, 1983), this approach is of limited utility when used on a case-by-case basis. These factors are relatively stable over time, although suicide risk can fluctuate widely. Therefore, overreliance on these factors will lead to overestimation of suicide risk with some clients and underestimation of suicide risk with others. For example, all depressed males over 45 who are unmarried and socially isolated would obtain a score on Patterson's scale that would suggest that hospitalization should be considered due to suicide risk. Conversely, many of the authors' clients who have been at high risk for suicide or who have made suicide attempts would not have been classified as high risk on the basis of background characteristics alone.

4. *Clients are more likely to make suicide attempts as they get less depressed.* It is true that the client who is so severely depressed that he or she cannot get out of bed is not likely to have the energy to plan and carry through a suicide attempt. As this client becomes less depressed, he or she will have more energy and may make a suicide attempt if his or her suicidality persists while the depression lifts. The more typical depressed individual, however, does not become more suicidal as his or her depression lifts; instead he or she becomes increasingly hopeful and commensurately less suicidal as problems are overcome.

5. *The risk of suicide is higher at holiday times.* The popular media have, over the years, focused on holiday time as a time of increased depression

and suicide. There is, in fact, no evidence that there is higher rate of suicide, psychiatric hospitalization, or depression at the holiday seasons. As a matter of fact, the suicide rate and rate of suicide attempts are higher in the spring (Lester, 1983).

6. *If you talk openly about the topic of suicide with clients, you might "put the idea in their heads."* Novice therapists often fear that talking explicitly about suicide may give the client an idea that he or she had not considered previously. As a result, they are inclined to avoid talking about suicide in order to avoid responsibility for any negative consequences. This fear might make sense if clients were generally unaware of suicide. However, the possibility of suicide is not a closely held secret. Any client who is even remotely at risk for attempting suicide will have considered this option long before the therapist raises the topic. Abundant clinical experience shows that explicit discussions of suicide in therapy make it possible to address the issues directly and therefore are much more likely to reduce the risk of suicide than to increase it.

7. *Talking about suicide decreases the risk.* This belief is based on a "hydraulic" model of psychological functioning that assumes that talking about an impulse dissipates the energy. Thus talking about suicide would automatically eliminate the need to act on the self-destructive impulse. However, simply talking about an impulse does not necessarily make it disappear. A discussion of suicide may decrease the risk of a suicide attempt, increase the risk, or have no effect depending on the content of the discussion and the client's reaction to it. Thus simply discussing suicide is not necessarily an effective intervention; it is also important to address the client's motivation for suicide and develop viable alternatives to suicide.

8. *If the client was serious about suicide, he or she would not bring it up in therapy.* It certainly is natural to assume that a client who is serious about suicide will not bring it up in therapy because the therapist is likely to interfere. Thus it is possible to conclude that willingness to talk about suicide shows that the client isn't "really" serious. However, a high proportion of persons who go on to commit suicide do, in fact, directly or indirectly communicate their intent to significant others (Robins, Gassner, Kayes, et al., 1959). However, evasiveness in talking about suicide does not necessarily mean that the risk of suicide is low.

9. *If someone is serious about suicide you cannot stop them.* Although it is true that even hospitalization cannot permanently prevent a person who is determined to commit suicide from finding an opportunity to do so, this does not mean that the therapist is helpless when confronted by a seriously suicidal client. For one thing, episodes of serious suicidality tend to be time limited; thus simply delaying a suicide attempt may allow time for the immediate crisis to pass. The key to intervening effectively with a seriously suicidal client is to challenge the client's conclusion that suicide is the most promising option he or she has rather than trying to make suicide impossi-

ble. If the client who seriously intends to take his or her own life begins to believe that he or she has better options than suicide, the situation will be much easier to deal with.

10. *Suicide "gestures" need not be taken seriously.* Often, suicide attempts are labeled as "gestures" when it appears to the clinician that the client's intent was not to die but rather to elicit some sort of reaction from significant others. The individual who makes a suicide attempt and then immediately calls a hospital, who carefully times his or her attempt so as to be discovered in time, or who "attempts suicide," using a method that is clearly nonlethal may well intend to achieve some desired effect rather than intending to die. However, even if the client's intent has been carefully assessed, there are two good reasons not to simply dismiss the act as a "gesture." First, a client can miscalculate and die even if this was not his or her intent. Second, if the "gesture" does not achieve the desired response from others and the therapist does not intervene effectively, the client may progress to more and more extreme actions. The fact that a client's last suicide attempt was nonlethal does not guarantee that the next one will be nonlethal as well.

11. *Suicidal clients must immediately be started on medication.* Many non-medical therapists react to suicidality by immediately referring the client to a psychiatrist for antidepressant medication to limit the suicidality. However, most antidepressant medications require from 1 to 3 weeks before they have a substantial antidepressant effect. If a client is imminently suicidal, the medication may well be too late, even though it might be useful as a part of longer term treatment. Also, tricyclic antidepressants can be quite lethal in overdose and may provide a convenient means for suicide. Antidepressant medication can be useful, but it is neither necessary nor sufficient in the treatment of suicidality.

12. *Suicidal clients must be hospitalized.* Related to the medication myth is the notion that the suicidal client must be immediately hospitalized. It is obvious that hospitalization will be required if the therapist is not able to intervene effectively enough to eliminate the immediate danger to the client. However, if hospitalization is the therapist's primary response to suicidality and other interventions are not tried first, clients will often be hospitalized when less drastic interventions could have been effective.

ASSESSMENT

An immediate and complete clinical assessment of suicide risk is important both as a part of the initial evaluation and whenever indications of possible suicidality appear. Detecting early signs of increasing suicidality can require considerable sensitivity to subtle distinctions in meaning on the therapist's part. For one client, the statement, "I would like to die," may mean that he or she finds the idea of death attractive as an escape from his or her problems but would not do anything to hasten his or her demise. For another client, the same statement may indicate that he or she intends to take active steps toward suicide or even has started implementing his or her plan. The client who updates his or her will, begins wrapping up the unfinished details of life, or begins giving away possessions may well be in the process of implementing a suicide plan and merits an evaluation. Likewise, expressions of increasing hopelessness or vague comments such as "If I'm still around next month, I'll. . . ." can be important warning signs. If the clinician can recognize early indications of increasing suicidality, he or she may be able to intervene before a crisis arises. However, even the most sensitive clinician cannot assume that he or she understands the significance of possible indications of suicidality without directly asking the client about them and discussing his or her intentions. When in doubt, assess.

In assessing suicidality, it is important for the clinician to obtain information regarding the client's thoughts about suicide, his or her intentions regarding suicide, any plan that the client has formed, and relevant background information. The Scale of Suicidal Ideation (SSI; Beck, Kovacs, & Weissman, 1979) provides a useful framework for assessing these content areas. This measure is intended for use as a structured interview with the clinician asking the necessary questions to obtain the information sought by each item. Although it is possible to obtain a numerical score on the SSI, the numerical scoring is used primarily for research purposes. In clinical practice, the content of the client's responses is more useful than the numerical ratings. It seems obvious that the risk of suicide increases when the client's wish to die is stronger than his or her wish to live, when he or she strongly wants to attempt suicide, when he or she sees no significant deterrents to suicide, has developed a potentially effective plan for suicide, and has made the necessary preparations. Also a history of previous "serious" suicide attempts increases the risk of another serious attempt. Note that the SSI simultaneously assesses the client's suicidality at the time of the interview, as well as the client's perception of how he or she might have responded to the same questions at a time of greater crisis. It is important to assess both of these points in time because the client who is feeling somewhat better at the time of the assessment may become substantially more suicidal if his or her mood deteriorates again.

It is important to distinguish clearly between thoughts of suicide, suicidal intent, and lethality of method in assessing suicidality because the three can be quite independent of each other. For example:

A young woman presented for therapy tearfully saying "Help me, I'm suicidal." A careful assessment revealed that she experienced nearly constant thoughts of suicide but found these thoughts distressing and repugnant rather than appealing. She did not wish to die and in fact was terrified that she would attempt suicide despite not wanting to do so.

Despite her conviction that she was suicidal, this young woman actually suffered from obsessions regarding suicide and was not at all suicidal (for further discussion of obsessions see Chapter 6).

Use of a nonlethal method in a suicide attempt can create the impression that the attempt was "manipulative" and not serious, but it is important to assess the client's intent rather than jumping to conclusions:

A young woman despondent over a lost love made all the plans to die of asphyxiation. She closed the kitchen window tightly and stuffed kitchen towels around the door to make it airtight. She then turned on the oven and put her head in the oven so that she could breathe deeply of the gas. Her oven, however, was electric and all she did was singe her hair. Her intent was most serious, although her problem solving and impulse control were flawed.

Because her intent was very serious even though her method was not lethal, without effective intervention, this client might well have learned from her experience and have chosen a more lethal method for her next attempt.

Similarly, an action that is intended as a suicide gesture rather than being taken with the intention of dying can still be fatal if the client miscalculates. For example:

Gina, a 17-year-old who had a history of chronic conflict with her mother, took an overdose in the hopes of making the extent of her distress clear to family and caregivers with no intent of dying. She chose Tylenol for her overdose, believing it to be harmless but nearly died from severe liver damage.

It is important to take "manipulative" suicide attempts seriously, not only because they can prove fatal despite the client's intentions but also because there is no guarantee that "serious" attempts will not follow. Some months after her near death, Gina took another Tylenol overdose knowing full well that it was potentially lethal and intending to die.

An evaluation of the client's overall level of depression can provide information useful in assessing suicidality. If the Beck Depression Inventory is used, the clinician can measure overall level of depression, while also getting a sense of the specific symptoms of depression by looking at specific items endorsed by the client. The client's responses to Items 2 (hopelessness) and 9 (suicidality) are of particular value.

It is also important to assess the client's level of hopelessness. This often can be done simply by asking the client directly how much hope he or she has that his or her problems will be overcome. Also, the Hopelessness Scale (HS) has proven to be a useful measure of hopelessness and to be strongly related to suicidality (Beck, Kovacs, & Weissman, 1975).

A number of historical points are worth considering in assessing the potentially suicidal client: (1) Is there a history of suicide attempts? (2) When was the last attempt? (3) What have been the circumstances of previous attempts? (4) Is there a family history of suicide or suicide attempts? The maxim, "The best predictor of future behavior is past behavior," is important to remember in working with clients with a history of previous suicide attempts. The risk of a suicide attempt increases as the client's current life situation becomes more similar to situations in which he or she has made previous attempts.

CONCEPTUALIZATION

It is often assumed that suicide is directly linked to depression because the vast majority of persons who attempt suicide or commit suicide show signs of depression. However, recent research has made it increasingly clear that the major precipitant of suicide is hopelessness (Beck, Steer, Kovacs, & Garrison, 1985). In fact, when the relationship between hopelessness and suicide is taken into account, no relationship between depression and suicide remains. The apparent relationship between depression and suicide is due primarily to the high incidence of hopelessness among depressed individuals.

The finding of a strong association between suicide and hopelessness makes suicide quite understandable. If a person is suffering but has the strong hope that tomorrow things will improve, the suffering becomes more tolerable. However, when an individual believes that he or she has no more options left and that he or she faces a choice between interminable misery and a quick death, death may appear to be a welcome relief. For example:

Kathy, a divorced mother of one, arrived in her therapist's office in tears without an appointment. She told the receptionist that she would wait as long as necessary but that she had to see her therapist; she couldn't go home. When her therapist met with her, Kathy revealed that she was sure that if she had gone home she would have started her car in a closed garage and have committed suicide through carbon monoxide inhalation.

As Kathy saw it, problems at work had gotten so bad that "I can't go back!", but without a job she would be unable to provide for herself and her son. She had not thought carefully about what would happen if she quit her job but was convinced that it would be so intolerable that death would be preferable. She was certain that there was no way to resolve her dilemma and that suicide was the only viable option open to her.

By far the majority of suicidal individuals hold the belief that there is no hope of things improving and therefore no longer any reason for continuing life. They see suicide as the only way of obtaining relief from intolerable misery. Although suicide is an option for any person, the majority of individuals never exercise this option because they see more promising ways of dealing with their problems. Suicide is at the bottom of most people's list of options and only becomes an issue as the individual exhausts other options and gets closer to the bottom of his or her list. When any individual feels that he or she has no further options, suicide is likely unless the individual is inhibited by powerful deterrents such as religious beliefs, concern about the effects that suicide would have on family members, or fear of death.

Hopelessness is not the only factor that can lead to suicidality. Some individuals who are intensely angry but who are unskilled at handling anger think of suicide as a way of punishing the source of their anger. For example:

Mary, a 32-year-old mother of two, came into therapy one day talking of suicide but appearing more angry than depressed. When asked if any event had precipitated her thoughts of suicide, she described a series of slights by her husband and her in-laws. When asked what suicide would accomplish, she talked of how her family would finally realize how badly they had mistreated her and would be overcome with guilt and regret.

This type of suicidality does bear some resemblance to the traditional view that suicide is hostility turned inwards. However, this type of motivation for suicide is much less common than hopelessness, and, in actuality, hopelessness plays a role here as well. The session with Mary made it clear that she saw no other way to vent her anger with her family or to induce them to treat her better in the future. If she had seen viable alternatives to suicide, she would not have seriously considered suicide.

Another type of motivation for suicide might be termed the histrionic suicide. This is a suicide attempt that is motivated primarily by a desire for stimulation, excitement, or attention. Some individuals crave activity and excitement and when feeling anxious, nervous, "itchy," or bored, they seek out "exciting" activities such as consuming drugs or alcohol in quantity, speeding in cars or motorcycles, engaging in high-risk sports such as sky diving, or deliberately entering dangerous situations. These acts are often interpreted by therapists as quasi-suicidal because they risk physical injury or loss of life. Sometimes the suicidal elements of these actions are more blatant as in the following example:

Jack was a 27-year-old male who reported that when feeling itchy or nervous he had only two ways of coping with these feelings. One option was to drive his car at great speeds, often exceeding 100 m.p.h. His second strategy was to drive along back roads to small highway bridges over streams or creeks and then to jump from the bridges. Either alternative was usually exciting enough to take the edge off of his nervousness, and he was never injured. However, an auto accident or an unexpected rock in the stream could easily have been lethal.

Histrionic attempts may appear flamboyant or manipulative, and the client may have little or no intention of dying. However, even when manipulation and attention seeking are the major elements, the possibility of a histrionic attempt being lethal exists, and the self-destructive potential of these actions still needs to be taken seriously.

A final group of individuals attempts suicide as a direct result of command hallucinations, that is, voices from within that command the individual to commit suicide. The voices are usually experienced as quite compelling, and rather than expressing a desire to die, the client feels that he or she must obey the voices. No cognitive theory of psychosis or psychotic symptomatology has been developed to date, so there is no clear conceptualization to guide interventions with these clients. Despite this, some cognitive techniques can prove useful in combination with appropriate medication.

STRATEGIES FOR INTERVENTION

With all suicidal clients, it is imperative to take whatever steps are needed to prevent a suicide attempt. However, it is often possible to intervene effectively enough within a single session to make hospitalization unnecessary. If initial interventions are effective, it may be possible to continue working with the client on an outpatient basis and to take precautions that are sufficient but less disruptive of therapy.

The approach to assessing suicidality discussed provides a good foundation for intervention with suicidal clients. An important first step is to identify the client's motivation for suicide. It is then necessary to help him or her consider whether suicide is a promising method for attaining his or her goals. This is done by directing the client to consider whether there are disadvantages to suicide that outweigh its perceived advantages, and whether there are better alternatives for attaining his or her goals. When the client becomes a willing participant in a serious discussion regarding whether suicide is in his or her interest, it is possible for the therapist to challenge the distortions and misconceptions that have led the client to conclude that suicide is his or her best (or only) option. This straightforward approach results in the therapist and client discovering that suicide is not the most promising approach to the client's problems, and it is usually possible to persuade the client to make a firm commitment to refrain from suicide at least long enough to explore the other alternatives.

If it is possible to reach the point where the client makes a believable commitment to refrain from suicide attempts while the therapist and client try other approaches to overcoming the client's problems, the therapist and client can then take steps to minimize the risks of a suicide attempt should a crisis arise and begin working on the client's problems using the usual

Cognitive Therapy approach. If the client will not make a believable commitment to refrain from suicide, is not willing to take steps to dismantle his or her suicide plan, or if the client makes it clear that he or she is still planning to attempt suicide, the therapist must take decisive action. The options at that point include voluntary or involuntary hospitalization and contacting the client's significant others to involve them in intervention. It is the therapist's responsibility to do all that is within his or her power to minimize the risk of suicide.

When hospitalization proves necessary, the therapist may face several problems as a result. First, hospitalization can be difficult to arrange if the client is not willing to agree to a voluntary admission. In most states, if it cannot be clearly demonstrated that the client is an *imminent* danger to him- or herself or to others, the client cannot be hospitalized involuntarily. Nonmedical therapists who are not able to hospitalize clients themselves are sometimes frustrated by having clients whom they see as being in need of involuntary hospitalization being refused admission because the admitting physician does not agree with their assessment. Also, clients who wish to leave the hospital can often manage to be discharged within a few days simply by acting as if they are no longer suicidal. Furthermore, being hospitalized has a number of effects on the suicidal client, some positive, some negative. Among the potentially positive effects are the following: (1) it will place the seriously suicidal client in a generally safe environment where he or she can be closely observed (although clients can, and do, make suicide attempts in hospitals). (2) Placing a client in the hospital allows the outpatient therapist to share responsibility for the client's survival with other professionals. (3) The client in the hospital can be stabilized on medication more easily. (4) The client in the hospital may be taken out of an overwhelmingly stressful home, job, or general life situation. Some of the potentially negative effects are (1) The client in the hospital is often removed from family and other available support systems. (2) The client may be stigmatized by a psychiatric hospitalization. (3) The client may be upset with the therapist over involuntary hospitalization (although, of course, it is better to have an upset client than a dead one). (4) The therapist may have difficulty continuing his or her work with the client unless the admitting physician is cooperative. The therapist needs to carefully consider the setting that the client will be placed in, the long-term effect of the hospitalization, and his or her responsibility to the client and the client's family. Adverse reactions can be minimized by obtaining the client's consent when possible and by pointing out the ways that the therapist's actions are in the client's best interest. However, these strong actions risk offending some clients to the point that they will terminate therapy. This should not deter the therapist from taking necessary action. After all, a live client will have the opportunity to see another therapist; a client's suicide eliminates the possibility of further therapy in a most tragic manner.

The question of whether to involve a suicidal client's significant others in intervention raises difficult questions that must be decided on a case-by-case basis. Although the legal aspects of this situation may vary somewhat from state to state, confidentiality does not preclude sharing of information if the client presents a danger to himself or others and the therapist is not able to intervene in such a way that the danger is eliminated. In fact, the therapist is likely to discover that he or she is legally obligated to notify significant others rather than simply notifying authorities if a substantial danger to self or others persists.

No matter how effective the initial interventions with a potentially suicidal client may appear, the therapist cannot rely on a single session of intervention. It is essential for the therapist to reassess the client's suicidality following the interventions, to develop a plan of action that the client is willing to commit herself or herself to, to take steps to minimize the possibility of an impulsive suicide attempt, to arrange timely follow-up, and to periodically reassess suicidality until it is clear that the crisis has passed.

COGNITIVE AND BEHAVIORAL TECHNIQUES

It is important for the therapist not to overlook the therapist–client relationship in his or her hurry to respond quickly to a client's suicidality. Assessment and intervention will proceed most smoothly if the therapist is perceived as an individual who can be trusted, who is supportive, re-sourceful, and available, and who is allied with the client. The therapist's openness and lack of self-consciousness in asking directly about the client's thoughts of suicide and in utilizing the data from relevant measures, from the client's history, and from clinical observation can serve to build confidence in the therapist and put the client at ease. One client reported, after the initial crisis intervention interview, "I really felt uncomfortable when you asked all those questions. But you touched on all the thoughts I was having but that I was afraid to say, thinking that you would think that I was crazy for having those thoughts. When you asked me those questions so directly, I knew that you must of asked them before and that maybe I wasn't so crazy, just really upset."

Initially, the suicidal client and his or her therapist are likely to have conflicting goals in mind because the client is at least considering suicide and the therapist's primary goal is to keep the client alive. This obviously makes it difficult to use a collaborative approach unless therapist and client can identify a goal toward which both are willing to work. Often the goal of trying to determine whether suicide is a good idea or not is a good starting place. For example:

It sounds like you're pretty certain that suicide's the best option you have in this situation. This is something which I think is important to take seriously. With most decisions, people have the option of changing their minds if it turns out that they've made a poor choice but with suicide you don't get to try something else if it turns out that you weren't thinking clearly. Would you be willing to take a look at whether suicide is really the best option you have?

With this rationale, it is usually possible to take a collaborative approach with even seriously suicidal clients.

The therapist is then in a position to clarify the client's motivation for suicide and his or her expectations regarding the likely consequences of suicide. The full range of interventions that are used in looking critically at automatic thoughts can be used in looking critically at the client's views regarding suicide. Whatever the motivation for suicide, it can be quite valuable to help the client to look carefully at the evidence supporting his or her conclusion that suicide is necessary and will accomplish the desired ends, as well as looking at the alternatives to suicide.

Intervening with the Hopeless Suicidal Client

When hopelessness is a significant part of the client's motivation for suicide, it is important to help the client verbalize his or her hopelessness and then to look critically at his or her conviction that the situation is hopeless. What evidence convinces the client that the situation is hopeless? Will the hopeless situation last forever? Is it unchangeable? Might there be options for dealing with his or her problems that the client has overlooked? When clients are helped to examine their situation, they are often able to see the distortions in their logic and discover that the situation is not nearly as hopeless as it appeared. For example:

When Kathy, the divorced mother of one, mentioned before, first described her dilemma to her therapist, she was convinced that because she felt she couldn't return to her job but couldn't support herself and her son without a job, the situation was truly hopeless. However, when she and her therapist carefully examined the situation in detail, it became clear that Kathy and her son would not perish immediately if she quit her job. Actually she had a number of alternatives: She could live off her savings for a few months and look for a new job; her parents would help her out financially if she really needed it; and if all else failed, she could go on welfare.

Once it was clear that the situation was difficult rather than hopeless, her suicidality subsided, and her mood improved considerably. Such other assumptions as, "They'll be better off without me," "Nobody will miss me," or "I'd be better off dead" can often be handled in a similar way.

In addition to questioning what would be accomplished by suicide, it is important for the therapist to work to identify significant reasons not to commit suicide. It is obvious that one of the major drawbacks to suicide is that the individual forfeits the rest of his or her life. However, this is seen as a good reason to refrain from suicide only if the individual has a significant amount of hope that life can be worth living. With hopeless individuals in particular, it is important to identify reasons to refrain from suicide that do not rely on hope for the future. These deterrents to suicide may include the likely effects of the client's suicide on family and friends, religious prohibitions regarding suicide, fear of surviving an attempt but being seriously injured, concern about what others will think, and so on. It is usually necessary for the therapist to take an active role in generating possible deterrents, but this can be done most effectively if the therapist works to engage the client in the process rather than simply listing the reasons he or she sees for the client not to commit suicide.

Explicitly listing the advantages and disadvantages of suicide and separately listing the advantages and disadvantages of continuing to live can be an effective way of integrating the results of these interventions. This will have the additional benefit of providing the client with a concise summary of the conclusions reached during the session, to which he or she can refer if suicide should again start to seem like a promising option. For example, the thought, "I would be better off dead," can have an enormous impact as long as it is accepted without critical examination; and clients may have difficulty challenging such thoughts on their own if they have not been in treatment long. A concise summary of the major conclusions reached in therapy can be quite useful to clients when suicidal thinking reemerges between sessions.

In initial interventions with hopeless clients, it is not necessary for the therapist to attempt to convince the client that all problems will be overcome, that the alternatives to suicide will definitely be successful, or even that suicide is always unacceptable as an option. All that is necessary is (1) to raise sufficient doubt regarding the merits of suicide and (2) to identify sufficiently promising alternatives to suicide so that (3) the client is willing to make a commitment to refrain from suicide attempts while (4) the therapist and client explore other options. It is important for the therapist to accept the client's skepticism and not to encourage unrealistically optimistic expectations that are likely to lead to sudden disappointment. Reluctant clients are often more willing to agree to refrain from suicide for a reasonable period of time if the therapist points out that by agreeing to this approach the client is not giving up suicide as an option. For better or worse, the client will always have the option of choosing to commit suicide later should it ever turn out that suicide is the best option available to him or her.

Cognitive Therapy generally emphasizes a guided discovery approach rather than a more confrontational, disputational approach. However, when the therapist is faced with a hopeless client who is not willing to participate actively in the process described, it is important to actively dispute the client's distortions and misconceptions and to present possible alternatives to suicide even if this must be done with minimal participation by the client. There are important advantages to involving the client in this process as much as possible, but if guided discovery is not feasible, direct disputation may prove effective. If it is effective, then the therapist should be able to shift to a more collaborative approach as the client becomes more willing to look at alternatives to suicide.

Once it is clear that suicide is not a promising option and that there are important reasons not to commit suicide, the client may still see no viable alternatives to suicide. It is also important for the therapist to help the client to identify the possible alternatives. If the therapist only takes the approach of trying to elicit options from the client, a rather limited list is likely to be generated. If the therapist takes a brainstorming approach and raises possibilities of his or her own and encourages the client to consider options that at first glance seem absurd or unworkable, it is possible to generate a much larger pool of possible alternatives to suicide to choose from. Options that strike the client as unworkable may well prove to have more potential than was immediately apparent or may suggest other, more feasible options.

Having explored the perceived advantages and disadvantages of suicide as well as having identified alternatives to suicide, the stage is set for the therapist and client to agree on a course of action and pursue it. An important part of this agreement is the client's making a believable commitment to refrain from suicide for a reasonable period of time during which therapist and client will work to overcome his or her problems. The agreement should also include the client's agreeing to call and talk with the therapist (not just leaving a message) before actually doing anything to harm him- or herself. Some therapists make a practice of having the client sign a written contract containing these and other provisions, and doing so would have an advantage with clients who take written agreements more seriously than verbal agreements. However, the key element is the agreement and the clinician's judgment as to whether the client's commitment is genuine, rather than the contract *per se*. This point is emphasized by one client's response to the therapist's suggestion that he sign a written contract, "So what are you going to do if I kill myself, sue me?" The contract, whether spoken or written, is not intended to be enforceable but is one stage in a collaborative approach to dealing with suicidality.

The therapist and client should try to anticipate any situations that would be likely to produce a sudden increase in suicidality and plan how the client can best cope with them should they arise. An important early intervention is to work with the client to dispose of any available means for suicide that the client may have selected. This might include steps such as asking an individual who collects guns and who had planned to shoot himself to turn the guns over to the police, to place the guns in the custody of a reliable significant other, or even to bring them in to the therapist. The purpose of such precautions is not to make suicide impossible to but decrease the risk of an impulsive suicide attempt by making the means of suicide less accessible. It is best to design precautions so that it is possible to confirm that the client has complied with them, because otherwise the therapist may face some difficult decisions. For example:

> One client reported that he had three handguns loaded and available to use in a planned suicide attempt. After a rather lengthy discussion, he agreed to turn the guns over to his brother who would keep them indefinitely. The client was asked to call the therapist that evening to confirm that the guns had indeed been turned over to his brother. Instead what the client reported was that he had changed his mind and rather than turning the guns over to his brother, he had gone down to the river, tossed the guns, in a paper bag, over the side and watched them sink beneath the waves.

The therapist had no way of confirming whether the guns had actually been disposed of or not and therefore had to decide whether the client's assertions were true on the basis of little or no data.

If the preceding interventions have been effective and hospitalization is not needed, the recently suicidal client is likely to need closer follow-up than most clients. It is not unusual for cognitive therapists to meet with a client two or three times per week during times of crisis or to arrange scheduled telephone contacts between sessions. It is important for the therapist or a colleague to be accessible to handle crises as they arise even if that means the client calls late at night or on weekends. If sufficient therapist–client contact is scheduled throughout the week, emergency phone calls should be held to a minimum.

With this foundation, Cognitive Therapy can then proceed much as it would if the client had not been suicidal. It is usually best for therapist and client to work first on issues that are related to the motivation for suicide, which are important to the client, and on which there is a good chance of making noticeable progress quickly. In addition, it is important for the therapist to be alert to any indications of increasing suicidality and to repeat these interventions if a setback or crisis should produce a renewed risk of suicide.

Intervening with the Angry Suicidal Client

When suicidal impulses are a product of intense anger at oneself or others and are motivated by a desire to punish oneself or others, it is clear that the optimal solution is to help the client develop more adaptive ways of handling intense anger. However, because it is likely to take considerably more than a single session to accomplish this, it is important to deal effectively with the immediate crisis first.

Once it is clear to therapist and client that suicide would be an attempt to punish oneself or others, therapist and client are in a good position to consider whether suicide is likely to be the best option for doing so. This is likely to include an examination of the client's expectations about the consequences of a suicide attempt, the degree to which he or she is certain that suicide will have the desired impact, the deterrents to suicide, and alternative ways to accomplish the desired results. It is also important to question whether the desired results are important enough to be worth the client's risking his or her life. The client may not have considered the fact that suicide attempts that are not intended to be fatal can still be lethal.

If it is possible to identify alternatives to suicide that the client would find emotionally satisfying and would be willing to try, these can be substituted for suicide as a way of "buying time" so that it is possible to work to help the client develop more adaptive ways of handling anger. Even alternatives that the therapist would not normally suggest are worth considering such as throwing a temper tantrum, writing a nasty letter to the person who is the object of his or her anger, or marking his or her wrists with a marking pen rather than slitting them. Although these are not very appropriate ways of handling anger, they are much better than suicide. Once the client has agreed to refrain from suicide a certain period of time, it is important to proceed with agreeing on a treatment plan, dismantling any preparations for suicide, and periodically monitoring suicidality, as discussed.

Many clients who consider suicide out of anger rather than hopelessness manifest characteristics of Borderline Personality Disorder, and the treatment ideas discussed in Chapter 8 may prove useful in working with them even if the client does not completely meet the criteria for Borderline Personality Disorder. In particular, the client is likely to have problems with impulse control and the methods for increasing impulse control discussed in Chapter 8 are likely to be helpful.

Intervening with the Histrionic Suicidal Client

As with the angry suicidal client, in working with the histrionic suicidal client it is important to identify the functions that would be served by a suicide attempt and to consider whether suicide is really a promising means for accomplishing those ends. Whether the goal of a suicide attempt is to reduce anxiety, to achieve a desired response from significant others, or simply to obtain stimulation and excitement, the process of exploring the pros and cons of a suicide attempt, the deterrents to suicide, and alternatives to suicide that has been discussed can be quite useful.

In working with these clients, it is important for the therapist to be aware of his or her reactions to them. On one hand, when the client's talk of suicide seems manipulative, particularly if there is a history of apparently manipulative suicide attempts, it is easy to conclude that he or she is not "really" suicidal but is just being manipulative. One must remember that if the client feels that his or her threats of suicide are not being taken seriously, he or she may feel that it is necessary to take more extreme steps in order to be taken seriously. On the other hand, histrionic clients can sometimes be quite skilled at inducing others to come to their aid, and the therapist can easily slip into trying to "rescue" the client rather than working to get the client to take an active part in therapy. To be effective, the therapist needs to avoid both extremes. Additional suggestions for working with histrionic clients can be found in Chapter 9.

Intervening with Clients Experiencing Command Hallucinations

Intervention with clients who are suicidal due to command hallucinations is quite different from intervening with other suicidal clients in that the primary intervention is pharmacological, that is, the use of antipsychotic medication. Often, medication alone is effective in reducing or eliminating command hallucinations, and cognitive interventions are directed toward increasing the client's compliance with the medication regimen. In addition, it is possible to work cognitively to increase the client's ability to cope effectively with the voices once the medication has substantially reduced their floridly psychotic symptoms.

The therapist working with clients having command hallucinations needs to know the precise nature of the commands. Thus the client must be questioned directly about the content and nature of the commands as well as his or her ability to resist them. Once the nature of the commands is understood, it is important to help the client examine whether obeying the commands is a good idea. Individuals suffering from command hallucinations usually have never stopped to consider what would be accomplished by obeying the voices and and what would happen if they refused. By raising this question the therapist can start to lay a foundation for the client's choosing not to obey the voices rather than feeling compelled to obey. Sometimes, an approach as simple as "What evidence do you have as to whether it is a good idea to obey the voices or not? Have they given you good advice in the past?" can be quite effective in clearly establishing that resisting the commands is a good policy.

Next, the therapist and client need to develop a plan for coping with the command hallucinations. If the client has already discovered some partially effective strategies such as staying active or keeping his or her mind occupied, these can be incorporated into the plan. Clients often find it useful to minimize the amount of unstructured time in their day, to explicitly remind themselves that they do not have to do what the voices say, and to remind themselves that the voices give poor advice. It also can be useful to help the client "talk back" to the commands either through refusing directly, for example, "I don't have to. I won't, I won't, I won't," or through more sophisticated responses such as "I'm not going to. Suicide is sinful, and it would hurt my family. And besides, if I can hold on till my new job starts, money won't be so tight, and I'll be able to get my own apartment again." It can be particularly useful to have the client write a summary of the most convincing arguments for resisting the voices and of the most promising coping strategies to aid him or her in remembering the plan for coping with the voices. It is also important to take steps to reduce the risk of an impulsive suicide attempt as discussed.

If the client is chronically psychotic, then Cognitive Therapy is likely to be of greatest value in increasing the client's compliance with his or her medication regimen and in helping the client deal more effectively with problem situations that arise. If the psychotic symptoms are acute and subside once the immediate crisis is over, then the usual cognitive approach to the client's remaining problems should prove effective.

Conclusions

A seriously suicidal client presents even the most seasoned therapist with a crisis situation in which he or she must respond quickly and effectively while under considerable pressure. If it is possible to understand the client's motivation for suicide and then to help the client consider whether suicide is really the best way to achieve his or her ends, this usually averts the immediate crisis and provides an opportunity for therapist and client to work on the more general life. It is important to remember, however, that obtaining knowledge, mastering effective techniques, and gaining clinical experience do not render one omnipotent or infallible.

Therapists often have considerable difficulty coping with the suicide of one of their clients, in part due to the intensity of their own reactions and in part because of the reactions of colleagues. Certainly, some degree of self-examination as well as a wide range of emotional reactions on the therapist's part is both inevitable and healthy following any negative outcome in therapy. However, therapists are not immune to dysfunctional beliefs and cognitive distortions and many go from thinking. "There must have been something I could have done! What did I miss?," to thinking, "How can I call myself a therapist? I can't help anybody," without giving the same attention to their successes as to their failures and without acknowledging factors outside their control that complicated intervention. At times like these, a therapist can benefit from a dose of his or her own medicine, whether self-administered or provided by a consultant, supervisor, colleague, or his or her own therapist.

6

Anxiety Disorders

Interest in the anxiety disorders has increased greatly in the past few years with the recognition that anxiety disorders are among the most prevalent psychiatric conditions. The results of a recent epidemiological survey indicate that phobias are the most frequently occurring DSM-III disorders among women and the second most frequent among men (Myers, Weissman, Tischler, Holzer, Leaf, Orvaschel, Anthony, Boyd, Burke, Kramer, & Stoltzman, 1984). In addition, the problem of anxiety goes far beyond just the DSM-III anxiety disorder diagnoses. Complaints of anxiety are among the most common problems among clients seeking help from general medical practitioners, far outnumbering other emotional or behavioral problems. One study showed anxiety as the fifth most common reason for visits to a primary care physician, ahead of all other emotional concerns (Marsland, Wood, & Mayo, 1976). These statistics only include those people whom primary care physicians recognize as having anxiety and those people who are actively seeking help. Beyond this, individuals with severe anxiety and panic often present to health practitioners with any one of a number of related physical problems (e.g., headaches, irritable bowel syndrome, difficulty breathing) and the majority of people with anxiety problems simply never seek help.

Although anxiety is one of the most common of emotional responses, it need not be problematic at all. When experienced in moderate intensity, anxiety can serve to motivate, energize, and mobilize the individual to heights of performance and spectacular deeds. Many people claim to "work best under pressure," that is, when their anxiety level is high enough to motivate them to exert additional effort. It is only when the anxiety level is so high that it debilitates the individual or causes emotional or physical discomfort that anxiety becomes a problem.

ASSESSMENT

At first glance, it seems that differential diagnosis of anxiety disorders would be a simple, straightforward task. If people report a fear of flying, they must be simple phobics; if they cannot leave home, they must be agoraphobics. In actuality, however, the distinctions are much more complex, and a simple checklist of symptoms is not sufficient to adequately diagnose anxiety disorders or to determine the most useful type of treatment. Upon careful assessment, for example, symptoms of fear of flying *may* turn out to be part of a broader agoraphobic syndrome; staying at home *could* turn out to be due to depression rather than agoraphobia; and fear of people *could* be part of a Borderline Personality Disorder rather than a Social Phobia.

The diagnoses of anxiety disorders have been changed significantly in DSM-III-R. One major change is that Agoraphobia and Panic Disorder are no longer two separate diagnostic categories (as in DSM-III, APA, 1980). The essential feature of Panic Disorder is still the presence of recurrent, unexpected panic attacks, but in DSM-III-R (see Table 9), Panic Disorder can exist with or without Agoraphobia (defined as the fear of being where escape might be difficult or help not available in the event of a panic attack). There is also a separate category of Agoraphobia without History of Panic Disorder. The presence of panic attacks alone is not sufficient evidence to conclude that a client has an anxiety disorder, much less Panic Disorder. A past study found that 34% of normal young adults had experienced at least one panic attack in the previous year (Norton, Harrison, Hauch, & Rhodes, 1985), and panic attacks have been found to be present in varying degrees in a wide range of disorders (Boyd, 1986). When the panic attacks are due to another disorder such as Schizophrenia or Somatization Disorder, the diagnosis of Panic Disorder is not made. Also, the presence or absence of panic attacks is insufficient to distinguish *among* the anxiety disorders. In Simple Phobia or Social Phobia, the person may have panic attacks, but these occur only in the presence of specific phobic stimuli. The diagnosis of Panic Disorder is made only when attacks are unexpected and do not occur immediately before or during exposure to a specific situation that almost always causes anxiety.

The distinction between Panic Disorder with and without Agoraphobia can be a difficult one if the agoraphobic avoidance is mild. When asked if they avoid many situations, clients with panic attacks may answer "No," leading one to conclude that they have Panic Disorder without Agoraphobia. However, patterns of avoidance may be subtle or may have continued for so long that the client does not recognize the avoidance. It may be necessary to specifically ask about the frequency of their involvement in a number of activities (e.g., driving on freeways, flying, traveling far away from home, attending concerts, plays, and sporting events), both alone and accompanied, and about any special conditions needed to enable them to face feared situations (e.g., having a glass of water available when speaking in public), in order to accurately ascertain the extent of the Agoraphobia.

TABLE 9. DSM-III-R Diagnostic Criteria for Panic Disorder

A. At some time during the disturbance, one or more panic attacks (discrete periods of intense fear or discomfort) have occurred that were (1) unexpected, i.e., did not occur immediately before or on exposure to a situation that almost always caused anxiety and (2) not triggered by situations in which the person was the focus of others' attention.

B. Either four attacks, as defined in Criterion A, have occurred within a 4-week period, or one or more attacks have been followed by a period of at least a month of persistent fear of having another attack.

C. At least four of the following symptoms developed during at least one of the attacks:
   1. Shortness of breath (dyspnea) or smothering sensations
   2. Dizziness, unsteady feelings, or faintness
   3. Palpitations or accelerated heart rate (tachycardia)
   4. Trembling or shaking
   5. Sweating
   6. Choking
   7. Nausea or abdominal distress
   8. Depersonalization or derealization
   9. Numbness or tingling sensations (parathesias)
   10. Flushes (hot flashes) or chills
   11. Chest pain or discomfort
   12. Fear of dying
   13. Fear of going crazy or of doing something uncontrolled

   Note: Attacks involving four or more symptoms are panic attacks; attacks involving fewer than four symptoms are limited symptom attacks (see Agoraphobia without History of Panic Disorder).

D. During at least some of the attacks, at least four of the C symptoms developed suddenly and increased in intensity within 10 minutes of the beginning of the first C symptom noticed in the attack.

E. It cannot be established that an organic factor initiated and maintained the disturbance, e.g., amphetamine or caffeine intoxication, hyperthyroidism.

   Note: Mitral valve prolapse may be an associated condition, but does not preclude a diagnosis of Panic Disorder.

   Agoraphobia: Fear of being in places or situations from which escape might be difficult (or embarrassing) or in which help might not be available in the event of a panic attack. (Include cases in which persistent avoidance behavior originated during an active phase of Panic Disorder, even if the person does not attribute the avoidance behavior to fear of having a panic attack.) As a result of this fear, the person either restricts travel or needs a companion when away from home or else endures agoraphobic situations despite intense anxiety. Common agoraphobic situations include being outside the home alone, being in a crowd or standing in line, being on a bridge, and traveling in a bus, train, or car.

Social Phobia is a fear of exposure to the scrutiny of others, particularly the fear of embarrassment or humiliation due to one's actions while others are watching (see Table 10). Although seemingly straightforward, the diagnosis of Social Phobia can be a complex one to make. The presence of social anxiety in and of itself is not sufficient to warrant the diagnosis of Social Phobia. For example, social anxiety resulting from intense fear of intimacy

TABLE 10. DSM-III-R Diagnostic Criteria for Social Phobia

A. A persistent fear of one or more situations (the social phobic situations) in which the person is exposed to possible scrutiny by other and fears that he or she may do something or act in a way that will be humiliating or embarrassing. Examples include being unable to continue talking while speaking in public, choking on food when eating in front of others, being unable to urinate in a public lavatory, hand trembling when writing in the presence of others, and saying foolish things or not being able to answer questions in social situations.

B. If an Axis III or another Axis I disorder is present, the fear in A is unrelated to it, e.g., the fear is not of having a panic attack (Panic Disorder), stuttering (Stuttering), trembling (Parkinson's disease), or exhibiting abnormal eating behavior (Anorexia Nervosa or Bulimia Nervosa).

C. During some phase of the disturbance, exposure to the specific phobia stimulus (or stimuli) almost invariably provokes an immediate anxiety response.

D. The phobic situation(s) is avoided or is endured with intense anxiety.

E. The avoidant behavior interferes with occupational functioning or with usual social activities or relationships with others, or there is marked distress about having the fear.

F. The person recognizes that his or her fear is excessive or unreasonable.

G. If the person is under 18, the disturbance does not meet the criteria for Avoidant Disorder of Childhood or Adolescence.

Specify generalized type if the phobic situation includes most social situations and also consider the additional diagnosis of Avoidant Personality Disorder.

in a person with Borderline Personality Disorder or from hypersensitivity to potential rejection in a person with Avoidant Personality Disorder would not necessarily lead to a separate diagnosis of Social Phobia. There must be a persistent fear of one or more situations in which the person is exposed to possible scrutiny by others and fears that he or she may act in a way that will be humiliating or embarrassing. Social Phobias often include fear that one's anxiety will be noticed by others. Thus a social phobic may be unwilling to write in the view of others for fear that his or her hand will tremble or may avoid social situations for fear of being so nervous that he or she will perspire excessively.

One difficult but important differential diagnosis is that between Social Phobia and Paranoia. Social phobics are often concerned that people are watching them and talking about them and thus might be diagnosed as paranoid. However, it would be more appropriate to consider these individuals as acutely self-conscious rather than paranoid. These clients are often so worried about people noticing their anxiety that they feel as if they are the center of attention. However, unlike individuals with true Paranoia, they do not ascribe malicious intentions to other people and do not feel that they are in danger of anything worse than humiliation.

Both agoraphobics and social phobics often become anxious in public but in different ways and for different reasons. Social phobics are not concerned about having panic attacks, as are agoraphobics, and generally do not feel a need to be accompanied by a friend or family member. Although agoraphobics often do worry about embarrassing themselves in public by having a panic attack, they can be distinguished from social phobics by the fact that they worry not only about embarrassment but also about being unable to escape from the situation or unable to get help if they do panic.

A Simple Phobia is a persistent fear of a specific object or situation and is usually quite circumscribed (see Table 11). Fears of specific stimuli such as heights, insects, snakes, and so on are quite common but would be considered to be Simple Phobias only if the fear and/or avoidance resulted in significant impairment or distress. Simple phobias encountered in clinical practice range from the commonplace, such as fear of flying, to the idiosyncratic, such as fear of the wind. It is important to remember that if the consequence that the individual fears is embarrassment or humiliation, a diagnosis of Social Phobia is likely to be more appropriate than a diagnosis of Simple Phobia. For example, most clients who enter therapy complaining of a fear of breaking into a sweat in social situations would not be classified as Simple Phobia (fear of sweat) but, rather, as Social Phobia because they are actually less concerned about sweat *per se* than they are that others will notice their excessive perspiration and that they will then be humiliated and embarrassed.

When a client seeks therapy for what appears to be a fear or phobia, it is important to ascertain whether the symptoms involve compulsive rituals or not. For example, many clients who report a fear of germs or dirt have developed elaborate hand washing or cleaning rituals as a result of their fears. It is often necessary to explore this area carefully because clients may be so used to their extensive strategies for preventing harm that they no longer view them as rituals and may not think to mention them. Even if

TABLE 11. DSM-III-R Diagnostic Criteria for Simple Phobia

A. A persistent fear of a circumscribed stimulus (object or situation) other than fear of having a panic attack (as in Panic Disorder) or of humiliation or embarrassment in certain social situations (as in Social Phobia).

Note: Do not include fears that are part of Panic Disorder with Agoraphobia or Agoraphobia without History of Panic Disorder.

B. During some phase of the disturbance, exposure to the specifc phobic stimulus (or stimuli) almost invariably provokes an immediate anxiety response.

C. The object or situation is avoided or endured with intense anxiety.

D. The fear or the avoidant behavior significantly interferes with the person's normal routine or with usual social activities or relationships with others, or there is marked distress about having the fear.

E. The person recognizes that his or her fear is excessive or unreasonable.

F. The phobic stimulus is unrelated to the content of the obsessions of Obsessive Compulsive Disorder or the trauma of Post-Traumatic Stress Disorder.

TABLE 12. DSM-III-R Diagnostic Criteria for Obsessive-Compulsive Disorder

A. Either obsessions or compulsions:

   Obsessions—1, 2, 3, and 4:

   1. Recurrent and persistent ideas, thoughts, impulses, or images that are experienced, at least initially, as intrusive and senseless, e.g., a parent's having repeated impulses to kill a loved child, a religious person's having recurrent blasphemous thoughts
   2. The person attempts to ignore or suppress such thoughts or impulses or to neutralize them with some other thought or action
   3. The person recognizes that the obsessions are the product of his or her own mind, not imposed from without (as in thought insertion)
   4. If another Axis I disorder is present, the content of the obsession is unrelated to it, e.g., the ideas, thoughts, impulses, or images are not about food in the presence of an Eating Disorder, about drugs in the presence of a Psychoactive Substance Use Disorder, or guilty thoughts in the presence of a Major Depression

   Compulsions: 1, 2, and 3:

   1. Repetitive, purposeful, and intentional behaviors that are performed in response to an obsession, or according to certain rules or in a stereotyped fashion
   2. The behavior is designed to neutralize or to prevent discomfort or some dreaded event or situation; however, either the activity is not connected in a realistic way with what it is designed to neutralize or prevent, or it is clearly excessive
   3. The person recognizes that his or her behavior is excessive or unreasonable (this may not be true for young children; it may no longer be true for people whose obsessions have evolved into overvalued ideas)

B. The obsessions or compulsions cause marked distress, are time consuming (take more than an hour a day), or significantly interfere with a person's normal routine, occupational functioning, or usual social activities or relationships with others.

---

fears and phobias do exist, if a person also has significant obsessions or compulsions, she or he would be diagnosed as having an Obsessive-Compulsive Disorder (see Table 12) rather than a phobia. Treatment for the rituals would generally need to precede any treatment addressed at the fears or phobias.

The criteria for Generalized Anxiety Disorder are much more specific in DSM-III-R than they were in previous diagnostic systems (see Table 13); however, the use of the term *generalized* still leads many to mistakenly assume that the anxiety is continuous, pervasive, and "free floating." Careful cognitive and behavioral assessment of individuals with Generalized Anxiety Disorder makes it clear that there are definite variations in the presence and intensity of anxiety, depending on the situation and cognitions of the client at the time. Even though it is common for clients to initially experience their anxiety as occurring spontaneously for no apparent reason, the concept of free-floating anxiety (i.e., anxiety that occurs "out of the blue" for no reason) does not seem to be borne out when careful assessment takes place. With systematic monitoring of both behaviors and

TABLE 13. DSM-III-R Diagnostic Criteria for Generalized Anxiety Disorder

A. Unrealistic or excessive anxiety and worry (apprehensive expectation) about two or more life circumstances, e.g., worry about possible misfortune to one's child (who is in no danger) and worry about finances (for no good reason), for a period of six months or longer, during which the person has been bothered more days than not by these concerns. In children and adolescents, this may take the form of anxiety and worry about academic, athletic, and social performance.

B. If another Axis I disorder is present, the focus of the anxiety and worry in A is unrelated to it, e.g., the anxiety or worry is not about having a panic attack (as in Panic Disorder), being embarrassed in public (as in Social Phobia), being contaminated (as in Obsessive Compulsive Disorder) or gaining weight (as in Anorexia Nervosa).

C. The disturbance does not occur only during the course of a Mood Disorder or a psychotic disorder.

D. At least 6 of the following 18 symptoms are often present when anxious (do not include symptoms present only during panic attacks):

Motor tension
1. Trembling, twitching, or feeling shaky
2. Muscle tension, aches, or soreness
3. Restlessness
4. Easy fatigability

Autonomic hyperactivity
5. Shortness of breath or smothering sensations
6. Palpitations or accelerated heart rate (tachycardia)
7. Sweating or cold clammy hands
8. Dry mouth
9. Dizziness or lightheadedness
10. Nausea, diarrhea, or other abdominal distress
11. Flushes (hot flashes) or chills
12. Frequent urination
13. Trouble swallowing or "lump in throat"

Vigilance and scanning
14. Feeling keyed up or on edge
15. Exaggerated startle response
16. Difficulty concentrating or "mind going blank" because of anxiety
17. Trouble falling or staying asleep
18. Irritability

E. It cannot be established that an organic factor initiated and maintained the disturbance, e.g., hyperthyroidism, Caffeine Intoxication.

cognitions, it becomes apparent that the anxiety was indeed triggered by particular stimuli, although often by thoughts or interoceptive cues that may not be obvious to the external observer.

Post-Traumatic Stress Disorder (PTSD) has received much attention in recent years due to the high incidence of PTSD among combat veterans. However, it should be noted that PTSD can occur following any extraordinary traumatic event such as a natural disaster, a major accident, or a

Table 14. DSM-III-R Diagnostic Criteria for Post-Traumatic Stress Disorder

A. The person has experienced an event that is outside the range of usual human experience and that would be markedly distressing to almost anyone, e.g., serious threat to one's life or physical integrity; serious threat or harm to one's children, spouse, or other close relatives and friends; sudden destruction of one's home or community; or seeing another person who has recently been, or is being, seriously injured or killed as the result of an accident or physical violence.
B. The traumatic event is persistently reexperienced in at least one of the following ways:
   1. Recurrent and intrusive distressing recollections of the event (in young children, repetitive play in which themes or aspects of the trauma are expressed)
   2. Recurrent distressing dreams of the event
   3. Sudden acting or feeling as if the traumatic event were recurring (includes a sense of reliving the experience, illusions, hallucinations, and dissociative [flashback] episodes, even those that occur upon awakening or when intoxicated)
   4. Intense psychological distress at exposure to events that symbolize or resemble an aspect of the traumatic event, including anniversaries of the trauma
C. Persistent avoidance of stimuli associated with the trauma or numbing of general responsiveness (not present before the trauma), as indicated by at least three of the following:
   1. Efforts to avoid thoughts or feelings associated with the trauma
   2. Efforts to avoid activities or situations that arouse recollections of the trauma
   3. Inability to recall an important aspect of the trauma (psychogenic amnesia)
   4. Markedly diminished interest in significant activities (in young children, loss of recently acquired developmental skills such as toilet training or language skills)
   5. Feeling of detachment or estrangement from others
   6. Restricted range of affect, e.g., unable to have loving feelings
   7. Sense of a foreshortened future, e.g., does not expect to have a career, marriage, or children, or a long life
D. Persistent symptoms of increased arousal (not present before the trauma), as indicated by a least two of the following:
   1. Difficulty falling or staying asleep
   2. Irritability or outbursts of anger
   3. Difficulty concentrating
   4. Hypervigilance
   5. Exaggerated startle response
   6. Physiologic reactivity upon exposure to events that symbolize or resemble an aspect of the traumatic event (e.g., a woman who was raped in an elevator breaks out in a sweat when entering any elevator)
E. Duration of the disturbance (symptoms in B, C, and D) of at least 1 month.

Specify delayed onset if the onset of symptoms was at least 6 months after the trauma.

victimization (see Table 14). Clinically, it is valuable to distinguish between PTSD resulting from a single traumatic event and PTSD resulting from recurrent trauma. Persons with PTSD stemming from recurrent trauma appear to be much more difficult to treat effectively.

In making a DSM-III-R diagnosis, as well as in the treatment of anxiety disorders, cognitive assessment is especially important because the same outward behavior patterns and reported fears may reflect very different disorders depending on the personal meaning of the situations to the client. Any given phobic stimulus may be part of a Simple Phobia, Social Phobia, or Panic Disorder, depending on the cognitions behind the fear. Two clients seeking treatment for driving phobia, for example, may have different disorders depending on their cognitions. One client may report only such thoughts as "I could have an accident and die," "People drive like maniacs," and "This is too dangerous," indicating a Simple Phobia. The second client may report all these cognitions plus thoughts like "What if I have a panic attack and can't get home?" "I'll be stuck on the highway all alone" and "No one will be there to help me," indicating the possibility that the client may be agoraphobic and be likely to have other areas of avoidance as well.

Cognitive assessment with anxiety clients can be challenging because they are frequently unaware of their thoughts related to their anxiety and avoidance. When asked exactly what they are afraid of or nervous about, the most typical response is, "I don't know, I just feel afraid" or, "I don't have any particular thoughts, I just feel bad." One client who complained of a fear of bridges insisted that she had no thoughts whatsoever about bridges, knew there was nothing to be afraid of, and just got an intense physical feeling of fear any time she approached a bridge. Given the frequent lack of awareness of cognitions, it may be necessary to be creative in eliciting automatic thoughts from anxiety clients. In this case, the therapist started off using the fairly traditional approach of simply asking what thoughts ran through the client's mind as she approached a bridge. When that was ineffective, the therapist decided to try using imagery by asking the client to close her eyes and imagine herself driving toward a particular bridge while the therapist described the scene in detail. When the client was able to vividly imagine herself approaching the bridge, she was able to report all the physical feelings of fear that she was experiencing and in the midst of her descriptions of her feelings she reported the thought, "What if I fall off the edge?"

If imagery is not vivid enough to elicit automatic thoughts, it may be useful to use *in-vivo* exposure (actually going into the feared situation with the client) for the purpose of collecting automatic thoughts. With the therapist along to help focus the client's attention on thoughts and with the level of anxiety rising as the object or situation becomes closer, most clients are able to report some of their cognitions. In some cases, role playing can be useful in eliciting automatic thoughts, especially those occurring in interpersonal situations.

Because many clients have been told by family and friends that their fears are silly, they may be inhibited from disclosing their automatic thoughts. They know the thoughts are irrational and are often concerned about being rejected by the therapist. The therapist can reassure the client that although thoughts may sound silly on the surface, those fears can be very intense and just as strong as if a gun were put to their head.

Cognitive assessment is generally discussed in terms of assessing verbal thought. In a study of anxiety, however, 90% of clients reported visual images of being in danger prior to and concomitant with their anxiety (Beck, Laude, & Bohnert, 1974). Many clients who have difficulty pinpointing specific verbal automatic thoughts will be able to graphically describe images of disaster when asked whether they get any pictures, images, or scenes that flash through their mind when they are anxious. Therefore, assessment of imagery should always be a part of cognitive assessment of anxiety. Just as imagining a scene in systematic desensitization evokes similar emotional reactions to those that would be experienced if exposed to the actual stimulus, so too does imagining a catastrophe evoke emotional responses similar to those that would occur in reaction to an actual catastrophe. Therefore, in Cognitive Therapy it is just as important to be able to pinpoint and modify mental imagery as it is to pinpoint and modify verbal automatic thoughts.

Given the wide variety of physical symptoms experienced by clients with anxiety disorders, it is crucial to have the client receive a complete physical examination to rule out physiological disorders that require medical treatment. DSM-III-R has introduced the diagnosis of Organic Anxiety Syndrome that is marked by prominent, recurrent panic attacks or generalized anxiety caused by a specific organic factor. Certain endocrine disorders can cause symptoms similar to anxiety disorders, as can withdrawal from substances such as sedatives or alcohol and intoxication from caffeine or amphetamines. These conditions would be given the diagnosis of Organic Anxiety Syndrome and not be considered anxiety disorders. The practice of requiring a physical examination before giving a diagnosis of anxiety disorder is important in ruling out Organic Anxiety Syndrome, but it has other important advantages in the treatment of anxiety disorders as well. Many anxiety clients have catastrophic thoughts about their symptoms, thinking they are dying or having a stroke or heart attack. It is crucial for both the client and the therapist to know whether there is a rational basis for the fears or not. Thus having a thorough physical examination can be the first step in challenging the catastrophic thoughts.

It is also important to pay careful attention to symptoms of depression when dealing with clients with anxiety disorders. Depressive symptoms are quite common in anxiety clients, especially in clients with Panic Disorder or Obsessive-Compulsive Disorder, and frequently the symptoms are severe enough to fit the DSM-III-R criteria for Major Depression. In fact, when attempting to conduct a study that required subjects with agoraphobia but without symptoms of depression, one of the authors found it almost impossible to find such subjects even among a sample of hundreds of agoraphobics.

The crucial distinction to make when a person shows symptoms of both an anxiety disorder and depression is whether the depression is primary or secondary. If the client has no history of Major Depression prior to the onset of the anxiety disorder, if the depression clearly began after the agoraphobia, or if he or she reports that the depression is due to the limitations resulting from agoraphobia, then the person would be given both the diagnoses of Panic Disorder with Agoraphobia and Major Depression and the depression would be considered secondary to the agoraphobia. In such cases, treatment primarily focusing on agoraphobia would be appropriate, although it may be necessary to address some aspects of the depression early in the treatment. If, however, the depression predated the agoraphobia or is clearly independent of it, the depression would not be considered secondary to the agoraphobia and successful treatment of the agoraphobia would not be expected to alleviate the depression. Obviously, if the client is avoiding situations because he or she is too depressed and cannot deal with the outside world, then the individual would not be given a diagnosis of Panic Disorder, and treatment for depression would be more appropriate.

Many clients use alcohol or other substances to reduce their anxiety, often to the point of abuse or dependence. Because these clients often underreport their use of these substances, it is crucial to get a careful and detailed history of the client's use of alcohol and other substances and to ask specific questions about his or her current practices. Research has consistently provided evidence of state-dependent learning (e.g., Eich, 1977), and this indicates that any type of desensitization procedures administered under the influence of alcohol may not generalize to a dry state. Thus, any alcohol or substance abuse would need to be treated before an anxiety treatment program is likely to be beneficial. Even clients who do not actually abuse alcohol may count on its availability as a coping strategy and, if so, they will need to stop using alcohol in this way and learn alternative coping strategies in order for treatment to be effective.

CONCEPTUALIZATION

Anxiety is a part of everyday life and in many situations can be functional. Anxiety is generally considered a normal reaction if it is aroused by a present danger and if it dissipates when the danger is no longer present. If the degree of anxiety is greatly disproportionate to the danger or if no objective danger is present, then the reaction is considered to be abnormal. The precise boundaries between what is considered to be normal and abnormal anxiety are defined to a large degree by social norms.

According to Beck's cognitive theory of psychopathology (Beck, 1976), the thinking of the anxious client is dominated by themes of danger. The client anticipates threats to self and family, and those threats can be either physical, psychological, or social in nature. In phobias, the anticipation of physical or psychological harm is confined to specific situations. The fears are based on the client's exaggerated conception of specific harmful attributes of these situations. The phobic is not afraid of the situation or object in and of itself but rather is afraid of the consequences of being in the situation or in contact with the object. In Generalized Anxiety Disorder and Panic Disorder, the client anticipates danger in situations that are less specific and therefore more difficult to avoid. Thus, the thinking of the anxious client is characterized by repetitive thoughts about danger that take the form of continuous verbal or pictorial cognitions about the occurrence of harmful events.

A number of cognitive distortions are particularly common in anxious clients and tend to amplify their anxiety:

1. *Catastrophizing.* Anxious clients tend to dwell on the most extreme negative consequences conceivable, assuming that a situation in which there is any possibility of harm constitutes a highly probable danger. Simple phobics tend to expect disaster in the form of physical harm when faced with a specific situation or object, social phobics expect more personal disaster in the form of humiliation and embarrassment, and agoraphobics expect disaster as the consequence of their own internal experience of anxiety or panic attacks.

2. *Personalization.* Anxious individuals often react as though external events are personally relevant and are indications of a potential danger to him or her. Thus, if an anxious client hears about a car accident, she or he may decide that he or she is likely to have a car accident as well.

3. *Magnification and minimization.* When anxious, individuals tend to focus on signs of danger or potential threat to the exclusion of other aspects of the situation. Thus the anxious client tends to emphasize any aspects of a situation that might be seen as dangerous and minimize or ignore the nonthreatening or rescue factors in a situation.

4. *Selective abstraction.* The anxious person often focuses on the threatening elements of a situation and ignores the context.

5. *Arbitrary inference.* The anxious client frequently jumps to dire conclusions on the basis of little or no data. For example, a client may assume that any unusual feeling in the body must be a heart attack or that any turbulence means the airplane will crash.

6. *Overgeneralization.* The client may view a time-limited situation as lasting forever (i.e., "this panic attack will never end"), may assume that because a particular problem has occurred previously it is bound to reoccur frequently or may assume that if he or she had any difficulty in a particular situation that shows that the situation is dangerous.

Research has demonstrated that certain beliefs are characteristic of anxious individuals (Deffenbacher, Zwemer, Whisman, Hill, & Sloan, 1986; Zwemer & Deffenbacher, 1984). In a nonclinical population, these authors found that anxious individuals tended to believe that if something is or may be dangerous or fearsome, one should be terribly upset about it and continually think and worry about it (anxious overconcern), that one has to be thoroughly competent, adequate, and achieving in order to be worthwhile (personal perfection), that it is horrible when things are not the way they would like them to be (catastrophizing), and that it is easier to avoid than to face life's difficulties (problem avoidance). In a clinical study of the beliefs of phobics, Mizes, Landolf-Fritsche, and Grossman-McKee (1987) found that in addition to anxious overconcern and problem avoidance already discussed, phobics also endorsed the belief that it is essential to be loved and approved by all significant others (demand for approval). Significant, but weaker, correlations were found between level of phobic avoidance and both the idea that the past determines present feelings and behaviors that cannot be changed (helplessness) and the idea that one must do well at everything to be worthwhile (high self-expectations). Although research is not yet available on clinical populations of different types of phobics, it seems clear from clinical observation that social phobics are ruled by the belief that it is a dire necessity to be loved by everyone for everything they do. They also seem to hold the underlying assumption that it is essential to appear strong and in control at all times, and that any demonstration of weakness or anxiety is disastrous. Agoraphobics seem to be especially concerned with the issue of control and to hold the underlying assumption that one must have certain and perfect control over things. They also tend to hold a generalized belief that the world is threatening if confronted independently and that security from danger must be ensured either through the availability of a loved one or by being extremely cautious.

A cognitive model of anxiety (Figure 9) demonstrates how a number of cognitive factors work together in the development and maintenance of anxiety. An individual's perception of each situation he or she encounters is shaped by his or her beliefs and assumptions and can be biased by any cognitive distortions that occur. If a situation is perceived as presenting some degree of risk of threat, the individual automatically evaluates the degree of threat present as well as his or her capacity for handling the situation satisfactorily. Although the perception of threat elicits anxiety, belief in one's own self-efficacy (or ability to cope in that particular situation) moderates the perception of threat and hence the anxiety. Thus if one perceives a stimulus as dangerous but is convinced that he or she will be able to safely deal with the danger, the stimulus is seen as less of a threat and causes less anxiety. However, if one has low self-efficacy and feels incapable of dealing with the potential danger, anxiety is increased. Take

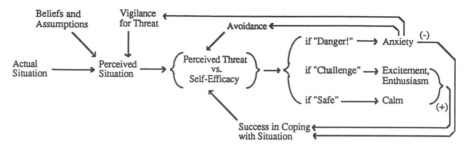

FIGURE 9. A cognitive model of anxiety.

the example of two people looking down from a steep cliff. One person is an experienced mountain climber. She can see that there is the risk of falling and that it would be dangerous to fall. However, she knows from her experience that she has the skills she needs to cope with the situation, so she experiences a sense of challenge, excitement, and enthusiasm. The other person has never done any mountain climbing before. He sees the threat of falling but, in addition, perceives that he does not have the ability to cope with the situation. Instead of a sense of challenge, he is overwhelmed with the sense of danger and experiences intense anxiety. A person's sense of self-efficacy is shaped by one's experience. If one perceives a situation as dangerous and is able to cope successfully with the situation, one's sense of self-efficacy is increased. The next time a similar situation is approached, that person is likely to feel less anxious and more able to cope. If, however, one experiences intense anxiety and is not able to cope effectively, one's sense of self-efficacy is decreased, and similar situations are likely to be viewed as even more dangerous in the future.

Intense anxiety tends to produce involuntary vigilance for signs of danger and, if any indications of danger are perceived, an involuntary fixation of attention on these danger signs. When one is objectively in danger, it seems only natural to focus one's attention on the danger until a solution has been found. However, the client with an anxiety disorder is unrealistically anxious and thus often is vigilant for signs of danger or is preoccupied with perceived dangers when this is not at all adaptive. As a result, the amount of attention remaining for focusing on specific tasks, recall, or self-reflection can be greatly restricted, and the client may well complain of inability to concentrate or of forgetfulness.

When faced with the experience of intense anxiety, an individual may choose to avoid or escape from the stimulus seen as dangerous. This can be a very effective short-term strategy and can successfully reduce anxiety for the moment. However, it has its cost. Because avoidance does nothing to change the perception of the stimulus as dangerous, the appraisal of threat is unmodified, and the stimuli continues to be seen as dangerous. In addition, avoidance does not help to increase self-efficacy. The client learns that the anxiety-provoking stimulus can be avoided but has no evidence that he or she is capable of handling it in any other, more direct way. Thus when again faced with the stimulus, the person may believe that he or she has no alternative but to again avoid or escape the situation. Thus avoidance reinforces future avoidance of the same and similar situations. Over time, consistent avoidance of problem situations can lower self-efficacy and increase the individual's anxiety. These patterns of avoidance can lead to any of the phobic disorders, the type of phobia differing primarily in the situations that elicit the anxiety and in the consequences that are feared.

If, instead of avoiding, the individual attempts to cope with the perceived danger through vigilance and worry and no catastrophe follows, he or she may conclude that the vigilance and worry proved effective. This pattern of response to perceived or anticipated threats can easily become habitual and result in frequent periods of stress and anxiety due to rumination about such threats. If such a pattern becomes sufficiently ingrained and the resulting anxiety becomes sufficiently intense, Generalized Anxiety Disorder could develop.

Obsessions go far beyond the distressing worries and rumination characteristic of individuals with Generalized Anxiety Disorder and are produced by a somewhat different pattern of cognitions. Most individuals occasionally experience thoughts, images, or impulses that they find repugnant. If the individual can accept that this experience is just a part of being human, no problem arises. However, if an individual believes that certain thoughts, feelings, or impulses are totally unacceptable, perhaps because they are a sign of insanity or moral depravity, then when such a thought, feeling, or impulse occurs, it is likely to be followed by catastrophic cognitions such as "God! How could I think such a thing? Only a freak would think that!" These cognitions elicit strong emotional reactions, including anxiety, and because anxiety produces an involuntary fixation of attention on signs of danger and vigilance for signs of danger (i.e., unacceptable thoughts), the individual can quickly become preoccupied with his or her unacceptable thoughts. This preoccupation tends to generate additional thoughts, images, or impulses on the same theme, and the flow of unacceptable cognitions can quickly become quite intense.

Compulsions arise when the individual tries a behavior or cognitive response that reduces his or her anxiety in the short run without dealing with the situation effectively. In this case, the anxiety soon returns, and the individual can easily become involved in a pattern of repeating the behavior or thought in order to obtain short-term anxiety relief without ever dealing effectively with the situation. One situation in which this is particularly likely to develop is when the individual is incorrectly attributing his or her anxiety to the situation at hand. For example, if an individual's belief that he or she is "dirty" is due to guilt over some transgression rather than being due to soiled hands, hand washing obviously will not eliminate the feeling of dirtiness, but it may provide enough temporary relief to become addicting. It has often been noted that clients with compulsions are often quite unwilling to acknowledge particular actions or feelings that they believe to be totally unacceptable. Obviously, an individual who is unwilling to acknowledge the problematic actions or feelings will be unable to deal with these directly and effectively and can easily become dependent on any strategy that provides temporary relief. Unfortunately, for many of these individuals, the relief is only momentary, and the "solution" becomes much worse than facing their "unacceptable" behavior or feelings would have been. Cognitive compulsions such as compulsive counting or compulsively repeating a particular prayer can develop as a way of blocking unacceptable thoughts, images, or impulses from awareness and then become "addictive" in the same way as compulsive acts.

PTSD can be conceptualized in terms of the individual's partially effective, partially dysfunctional attempts to avoid recalling his or her traumatic experiences. Individuals with PTSD attempt to avoid stimuli that might arouse recollections of the traumatic event(s) and attempt to avoid thoughts and feelings associated with the trauma, yet they are plagued by very distressing intrusive memories of the event(s). It is quite understandable that an individual who has undergone traumatic experiences would fear memories of the event and attempt to avoid them because these recollections are intensely distressing. However, he or she encounters the same problem as the person who is plagued by obsessions. The fear of memories, images, thoughts, and feelings associated with the traumatic event(s) results in a focus of attention on these cognitions and vigilance for stimuli that might elicit them. At the same time, the individual's determined avoidance of the cognitions blocks him or her from realizing that they are not dangerous, simply quite distressing.

Cognitive-behavioral theorists have devoted considerable effort to the task of developing and validating a theoretical model of Panic Disorder with Agoraphobia. Figure 10 presents a cognitive view of agoraphobia created by combining elements from the theories of agoraphobia presented by Goldstein and Chambless (1978) and by Mathews, Gelder, and Johnston (1981). This model is intended as a flow chart of the development of an anxiety disorder and is not meant to imply causality. The middle level of the chart illustrates the process of the development of the anxiety disorder, with the top and bottom levels showing predisposing and contributing factors.

People, particularly those with high levels of trait anxiety, may at some point in their lives experience a traumatic experience or an increase in stress that raises their anxiety to the point where new or more severe physical symptoms occur. This is particularly likely if the person already has a medical condition that is aggravated by stress and that has vague,

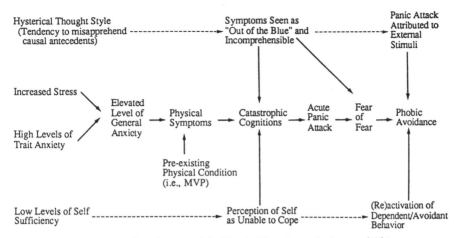

FIGURE 10. Cognitive model of Panic Disorder with Agoraphobia.

confusing symptoms.* Regardless of whether the symptoms experienced by the client are due to the interaction between increased anxiety and a vague physical condition or simply result from intensified anxiety, when the person notices these new and strange physical symptoms, he or she may begin to suspect that something is seriously wrong. These suspicions increase the client's anxiety and because the symptoms of concern are aggravated by anxiety, the symptoms increase in intensity. As the symptoms get worse, the suspicions seem to be confirmed, and they are replaced by catastrophic thoughts about the symptoms such as "I'm having a heart attack! I must be dying!" or "Oh no, I'm going to go crazy!" These thoughts serve to further increase the anxiety, intensifying the severity of the symptoms and stimulating further catastrophic thoughts. At the same time, the individual's increased attention to his or her physical sensations also aggravates the symptoms and makes them appear more severe and frightening. The anxiety symptoms and the fearful thoughts about the symptoms form a cycle that can spiral to peak levels of anxiety very quickly and produce an acute panic attack during which the individual is *certain* that he or she is dying, going crazy, or going "out of control."

---

*One physical condition that has been the source of much controversy recently in relation to anxiety disorders has been mitral valve prolapse. This is a generally benign heart condition that is often asymptomatic but that produces vague symptoms in some individuals. Empirical research into the relationship between mitral valve prolapse and agoraphobia have been conflicting with some studies showing a relationship and other studies failing to find such a relationship (summarized in Gorman, Shear, Devereux, King, and Klein, 1986). Whether a statistical connection between agoraphobia and mitral valve prolapse is substantiated or not, this syndrome is illustrative of how any physical syndrome with vague symptoms not clearly understood by the client can be part of the development of agoraphobia.

Once a panic attack has occurred, the person may become so fright-ened of having subsequent attacks that he or she begins to anticipate the possibility of future panic attacks, excessively monitors his or her internal state, and hence increases the likelihood of continued panic attacks. If the process stops here, the client might be seen as having a Panic Disorder without Agoraphobia. However, the person may associate the panic with the particular situation in which panic attacks have occurred and begin to avoid that and similar situations. Also, he or she may anticipate needing help when a panic attack occurs and therefore avoid being alone. This avoidance may make the individual more comfortable initially but, as noted previously, avoidance can easily decrease self-efficacy and is likely to gradually make the problem worse. This cycle can develop into the full syndrome of Panic Disorder with Agoraphobia and might eventually pro-gress to the point where the individual is completely housebound. For example:

Jenny was a 28-year-old married female who was a housewife with a 3½-year-old son. Her husband was the pastor of a church in a small southern town. Jenny sought treatment because she had been having severe panic attacks for the past 2 years, and her life had become increasingly restricted. She was afraid of any situa-tion out in public where she felt she might be trapped and unable to get home. She avoided stores, church, restaurants, waiting in line, theaters, and traveling alone. This had severely limited her life, and she felt depressed about it and had gained 20 lb in the past 2 years.

Jenny described herself as always having been "high-strung," but this had never been a problem for her in the past. As she saw it, her problems had begun about 2 years before during a church service when she got very light-headed, dizzy, her heart pounded, her hands got cold and clammy, she felt terrified and felt she had to leave. She left in the middle of her husband's sermon and was very embar-rassed. This was the first in a series of panic attacks that always occurred when Jenny was out in public.

The first panic attack occurred at a time when Jenny had just moved from a large city to a small town, her son had just become a toddler, and her husband had a new parish and was spending much less time with her. However, Jenny did not attribute her physical symptoms to the stress she was under. Instead, she saw them as coming totally out of the blue and thought that it must be a physical problem. She sought medical attention, was diagnosed as having mitral valve prolapse, and her physician prescribed 150 mg of Imiprimine per day. She felt somewhat better on the medication but still had panic attacks and avoided a range of situations.

Two additional variables (shown in Figure 10) have been hypothesized by Goldstein and Chambless (1978) as predisposing an individual to con-tinue through this entire process and develop Panic Disorder with Agora-phobia. The tendency to misapprehend causal antecedents (labeled *hys-terical thought style* by Goldstein and Chambless) may increase the possibility that the anxiety symptoms will seem to come "out of the blue" and be totally incomprehensible. If Jenny had been able to think about her symptoms systematically and to draw accurate connections between cause and effect, she might have noticed her initial physical symptoms and thought, "Boy, I must really be under a lot of stress. Maybe I should take it easy for a while." This reaction would not have raised her anxiety level and thus would not have contributed to a panic attack. However, Jenny had a very impressionistic thought style and did not even realize that she had been under stress when the symptoms began until possible stressors were explored in detail in therapy 2 years later. Because she had drawn no connection between her increased stress and the physical symptoms, the symptoms seemed mysterious and frightening to her and thus were more likely to lead to catastrophic cognitions. A person who has difficulty thinking analytically is likely to look haphazardly for reasons for the symptoms, tending to attribute responsibility to the situation rather than to stress and anxiety. This makes it more likely that avoidance will ensue.

Low levels of self-sufficiency and self-efficacy can also predispose an individual to developing the full agoraphobic syndrome. A person who tends to be self-sufficient certainly could experience a panic attack if the situation were right, but he or she would then be likely to try dealing actively with the problem rather than avoiding situations associated with the panic attack and/or relying on others for security. The person who generally feels incapable of handling problems on his or her own is more likely to assume that there is nothing that he or she can possibly do to deal with the situation

STRATEGIES FOR INTERVENTION

The primary goal in treating clients with anxiety disorders is to eliminate both the client's disproportionate fears and any maladaptive patterns of avoiding or preventing anxiety that the individual may have developed. However, this is not easily done because the fears and the dysfunctional behaviors tend to perpetuate each other. The task is further complicated by the fact that rational responses do not have the same impact on anxiety as on other problematic emotions. It is quite common for a client to understand intellectually that he or she is in no danger but to continue to feel quite anxious and to avoid the feared situation.

The conceptualization of anxiety disorders presented in Figures 9 and 10 suggests a variety of points where useful intervention can occur. The client's overall level of anxiety can be reduced by training him or her in anxiety-reduction skills. The client's catastrophic cognitions regarding the feared situation, the anxiety symptoms, memories, thoughts, images, and the like and any hysterical thought style can all be challenged through cognitive restructuring. Avoidance, whether behavioral or cognitive, can be modified through intentionally exposing the client to the stimuli he or she fears (in collaboration with the client, of course). Finally, the client's sense of self-efficacy and self-sufficiency can be increased through cognitively challenging any unrealistically harsh appraisals of his or her capacities and through training in coping skills such as assertion. Each of these points of possible intervention can have an impact on the entire process of the anxiety disorder, but a more powerful impact is achieved when several aspects of the anxiety process are modified at the same time.

In general, individuals with anxiety disorders have allowed anxiety to take over their lives, investing a great deal of time and energy trying to fight, control, and/or avoid the anxiety. One widely used treatment tactic is to ask clients to give up their "control" of anxiety and instead to accept the experience of anxiety and expose themselves to situations in which their anxiety would be heightened. As they do so and discover that the consequences are not as catastrophic as they initially expected, the anxiety gradually fades away. However, in order to enable clients to face the situations they fear, it is necessary to first challenge their appraisal of threat cognitively. As long as clients truly believe that exposing themselves to the feared situation will cause them to risk dying, "going crazy," being humiliated, and so forth, they will not expose themselves to the situation, no matter how hard the therapist tries to encourage them. Only when the belief that disaster is inevitable has been effectively challenged, at least to some extent, will clients be willing to initiate approach behavior.

Exposure to the phobic stimulus, whether it is exposure to a single situation, a wide range of situations, or a range of internal cues, is a central part of the treatment of anxiety disorders. This exposure can be done in imagery or in the actual situations the client fears; it can be done in gradual steps or all at once, and it can be done as part of homework assignments or with the therapist's assistance. The coping skills used to reduce the client's general level of stress can be used to help reduce his or her anxiety during exposure to feared situations, but it is the experience of encountering the feared situations in such a way that disaster does not follow that is crucial.

Training in coping skills and exposure to phobic situations are not only useful in reversing avoidance and weakening the connection between the situation and the experience of anxiety. These interventions also serve to increase the client's sense of self-efficacy, leaving clients with a new sense that they can indeed cope with situations. These interventions are especially powerful because they provide the client with concrete accomplishments that provide particularly convincing evidence of self-efficacy (Bandura, 1977). An increase in self-efficacy should not only lower the client's anxiety level and contribute to improved coping but also should help reduce the client's likelihood of developing further anxiety reactions.

The process of monitoring and challenging dysfunctional thoughts is useful as a coping strategy in the situation where the client becomes anxious and also has the added effect of altering the client's "hysterical thought style." Cognitive restructuring can help him or her learn to take the time to look critically at the thoughts and feelings generated in various situations, thus reducing the tendency to automatically jump to conclusions and misunderstand the relationships between cause and effect. This facilitates more effective problem solving and reduces the likelihood of similar problems occurring in the future. (See Chapter 9 for additional suggestions for modifying a global, impressionistic thought style.)

Another type of intervention that has received much attention in recent years is the use of medication, especially for reducing or eliminating panic attacks. These medications are not necessarily incompatible with Cognitive Therapy; in fact, there is some research that indicates that medications may facilitate the process of exposure by helping the client be more willing to approach anxiety-provoking situations (summarized in Barlow & Waddell, 1985). However, because the relapse rates for medication treatment alone are alarmingly high and because many antianxiety medications are potentially addicting, the use of medication alone is not a sufficient treatment for any of the anxiety disorders. When medications are used in conjunction with Cognitive Therapy, it is important that the client be faded off the medication while Cognitive Therapy is still in progress to prevent relapse. At that time, any fears about discontinuing the medication can be addressed, and behavioral experiments can be performed to demonstrate convincingly to the client that progress can be maintained even without the medication.

COGNITIVE AND BEHAVIORAL TECHNIQUES

Many clients with anxiety disorders are frightened in part because their problems seem incomprehensible. Therefore, it can be quite valuable to begin treatment by educating the client about anxiety. After the initial evaluation, the therapist can explain the symptoms of anxiety to the client in detail, basing the explanation on the client's personal experience as much as possible. This brief didactic presentation helps the client to feel understood and to have confidence in the therapist as well as establishing a rationale for the interventions that will follow. Most clients with anxiety symptoms have been to many different medical and mental health professionals without receiving clear explanations and without feeling that aynone understands their problems. They often feel that their problems are unique and are quite reassured to discover that other people have had similar problems and have been successfully treated. A clear explanation can also be the first step in decatastrophizing the presence of the symptoms and helping clients become less excessively concerned with them.

One way to give anxious clients some relief while also beginning to challenge the belief that they are helpless and cannot handle situations is to increase their self-efficacy by teaching them specific skills to help them reduce their own anxiety. Rather than just challenging their feelings of helplessness verbally, learning coping skills provides convincing evidence that the client can, in fact, cope with anxiety. Once the client feels armed with tools that make him or her more adequate to deal with anxiety, he or she may be more likely to be willing to attempt some exposure to anxiety-provoking situations. Thus training in coping skills can serve two distinct purposes: (1) to actually help the person reduce anxiety and thus make exposure more comfortable and (2) to build the person's self-efficacy and make him or her more willing to try confronting his or her fears. Coping skills that are especially useful in reducing anxiety include relaxation methods and outward focus techniques.

A wide variety of relaxation training methods are useful clinically, ranging from simple deep breathing methods to elaborate, highly technical biofeedback procedures. (See Bernstein and Borkovec, 1976, for a good introduction to relaxation techniques.) The most important variable seems not to be which technique is used but, rather, that whatever technique is chosen is practiced consistently and that the client has faith in it. Any relaxation method that is practiced regularly with confidence will help the client achieve deeper levels of relaxation. The choice of relaxation method is important, however, because of the importance of teaching a method that will engage the client and is likely to maintain interest and cooperation. Taking a careful history of previous attempts at learning relaxation and eliciting current cognitions about relaxation are crucial steps needed before deciding which relaxation method is most likely to be effective with a particular client. Factors to consider include whether the individual finds a simple deep breathing method too boring or has difficulty keeping his or her mind from wandering (indicating a need for a somewhat more complex method, possibly with a tape recording to use to focus attention), whether he or she experiences physical pain that would make methods involving muscle tensing too uncomfortable, or whether his or her tension tends to build in one area of the body that is particularly difficult to relax (indicating possible benefits of tensing and then relaxing that area or using biofeedback regarding tension in that particular muscle group).

Relaxation can be helpful for clients with the full range of anxiety disorders and serves to reduce generalized anxiety, increase self-efficacy, and provide a coping tool for use when facing particularly stressful or anxiety-provoking situations. It also tends to increase clients' awareness of early stages of anxiety, so that they may be able to begin to deal with their anxiety while it is still reasonably low and prevent their symptoms from intensifying. It is important for the client to have realistic expectations about the likely effects of relaxation training. Clients with Generalized Anxiety Disorder may find that relaxation methods alone may help bring about a significant change in their symptoms; but for phobic clients, relaxation is only a first step in the treatment and cannot be expected to have a major impact on the symptoms in and of itself. In particular, although relaxation can be useful in preventing panic attacks by lowering the client's overall level of anxiety, once a panic attack has started, most clients do not find relaxation helpful in coping with the panic itself.

One of the major coping techniques used for the reduction of anxiety has often been referred to as "diversion" or "distraction." This terminology has led some therapists to criticize the technique as providing a way for the person to "escape" from the realities of the current situation and to see it as another mode of avoidance. Using the term *outward focus* makes the true purpose and usefulness of this technique more obvious. An excessive focus on the client's internal state serves to make the anxiety symptoms more severe and to decrease the more appropriate focus on the world outside of the client's body. Changing one's focus to specific items and events in the external world, however, is a very appropriate return to reality, rather than an avoidance of it. Although it can be very difficult for clients to simply ignore their symptoms, they can be taught the skill of focusing their attention on something specific outside of their body as an alternative to excessively focusing on their internal state. This technique is useful for most anxiety clients whenever they find their anxiety increasing and want to disrupt the cycle that amplifies it. Although it is very difficult for an individual to simply "stop worrying," it is not difficult to block catastrophic thoughts about one's internal symptoms by focusing on something else and occupying one's mind with that for a few minutes. This technique is particularly useful for clients who experience panic attacks because it is one coping skill that can be used effectively in the midst of even the strongest panic attack, often diffusing the panic in a matter of seconds.

When teaching outward focus as a coping technique, the therapist has the client rate his or her anxiety at a time when he or she is quite anxious, then instructs him or her to focus on some item in the office such as a lamp or pencil sharpener. The client is asked to describe the item in detail as if describing it to a Martian who has never seen a lamp before. What is its size, shape, color, texture? How would it look from different angles? What writing does it have on it? After this has continued for a few minutes, the client is again asked to rate his or her level of anxiety, which hopefully is lower than before the exercise, and the rationale for focusing on non-threatening stimuli in order to block the cognitions that amplify his or her anxiety is explained. Other forms of outward focus that are useful in public situations can also be explained such as "eavesdropping" on the conversations of strangers, counting the number of people wearing red, singing along with songs on the car radio, watching for out-of-state license plates, and so forth. The client is then encouraged to practice this technique between sessions, whenever he or she has a panic attack, in order to both demonstrate its effectiveness and to become more skilled at using the technique. With social phobics, it is especially useful to help them learn to use focusing on the details of the face of the person they are taking to as a form of outward focus. With practice, this technique can be used to reduce anxiety during a conversation without anyone else noticing.

Intervention with Jenny occurred at many different points. Initially, she was taught relaxation and outward focus to lower her general level of anxiety. For Jenny, any focus on breathing in the relaxation was not helpful, because if she focused her attention on her breathing, she started to worry about whether she was breathing "right" or not. Instead, she learned an autogenic method where she focused on relaxing various muscle groups. She found that learning to change her focus of attention through the use of outward focus was particularly helpful to her because it changed her natural pattern of focusing on her symptoms. Together, graded exposure and training in coping skills led to early success and feelings of self-efficacy, so that each session started out with her proudly announcing all the accomplishments of the week.

Even while the therapist is educating the client about anxiety and teaching coping skills, he or she should be collecting data about the client's automatic thoughts and images. Learning to identify automatic thoughts is a crucial early step in Cognitive Therapy with anxiety. Once the client has learned to identify these automatic thoughts and images, possibly using the dysfunctional thought records discussed in Chapter 3, the full range of techniques can be used to challenge these thoughts. The therapist can also help the client challenge his or her thoughts by providing factual information that the client does not have (for example, facts about the physical consequences of physical symptoms or statistics about the odds of being killed in an airplane crash) and by helping the client explore possible rescue factors in the situation.

Jenny's treatment quickly moved to cognitive work to address her fear of the fear and catastrophic cognitions. Her main fears were of having a panic attack and either passing out or embarrassing herself in public. She began to write Dysfunctional Thought Records during the week whenever she attempted to do hierarchy items and at any other times that she felt particularly anxious. An example of an early DTR is shown in Figure 11. What she reported as being the most helpful in challenging her automatic thoughts was learning to distinguish specific symptoms of anxiety and other, normal feelings of discomfort from a full panic attack. In the past, if she noticed that she was feeling dizzy, for example, she would automatically conclude that she was going to have a full panic attack, pass out, and humiliate herself. As she got skilled at identifying and challenging her automatic thoughts, however, she was able to notice one symptom, check to see if there was any way she could understand why she might be having that symptom (stress from rushing around too fast, son cranky, fight with husband, expecting her period, etc.) and practice some coping skills to reduce the symptom.

Daily Record of Automatic Thoughts

Date	Situation Briefly describe the situation	Emotion(s) Rate 0–100%	Automatic Thought(s) Try to quote thoughts then rate your belief in each thought 0–100%	Rational Response Rate degree of belief 0–100%	Outcome Re-rate emotions
	Before shopping at Jacobson's	Anxious 65	I haven't been here since I had a panic attack here. What if I panic again?	There's no reason to believe I'll panic again. Besides, if I get anxious, I can do relaxation and concentrate on my shopping and I'll survive.	Anxious 20
	While shopping at Jacobson's	Anxious 25	I feel a bit disoriented and wobbly. Am I starting to panic?	The floor is made of plank and uneven. This may be just a natural response.	Anxious 0
	At church, sitting in the middle in a crowded service	Anxious 50	My heart is pounding	I'll be all right even if my heart pounds a great deal. (It didn't.)	Anxious 0
			Without Joey here with me, I have no excuse to leave.	If I want to leave, I can even if Joey isn't here.	

FIGURE 11. A thought sheet from Jenny, an agoraphobic client.

One useful experience that occurred coincidentally after her sixth therapy session was that she was driving alone with her son, and her car broke down far away from home. Despite all her fears of what would happen if she were trapped away from home, she handled the situation appropriately. Later, as she looked back on that experience, she could see that she had been realistically anxious but had not panicked; and she was able to refer back to that experience throughout treatment whenever she began to confuse feelings of anxiety with panic.

Because catastrohizing is one of the major cognitive distortions in anxiety disorders, decatastrophizing is one of the major cognitive interventions. Through Socratic questioning, the therapist helps the client explore what could actually happen in the situation. In the treatment of anxiety disorders, the most commonly asked question is, "What is the worst that could happen?" The therapist has the client spell out in detail what he or she sees as the ultimate consequences so that the therapist and client can consider whether it would be possible to cope with the situation if the worst were to happen.

Amy came into treatment for her fears of eating and drinking in public that were severely limiting her life. As she was planning to go out for coffee with some friends (including Sarah, a woman she did not know well), she had been able to identify the thought, "What if I get upset and really start shaking?" She and the therapist explored the likelihood of that happening and concluded that it was possible (because that had happened before) but not very likely (because she had been quite anxious in a number of situations but had not had a severe shaking episode in a long time). The therapist then moved on to explore the worst possible scenario by asking, "Well, let's just say that you did get so upset that you shook harder than you ever have before. What's the worst what could happen?" Amy replied, "Sarah might notice and ask what's the matter with me." The therapist then asked, "And if she did notice and ask you, what's the worst that could happen?" Amy said, "I could be so nervous that I couldn't even answer her!" Again, the therapist asked, "And if that did happen, what is the worst that would happen next?" This time Amy thought for a second and answered, "Well, I'd be terribly embarrassed, and Sarah would probably think I was weird." Once more, the therapist asked, "And what's the worst that could happen then?" After thinking some more, Amy replied, "Well, Sarah might not want to have any more to do with me, but the other people there are my friends and probably would understand." Finally, the therapist asked, "And if that did happen?" Amy concluded, "I'd feel embarrassed, but I do have plenty of good friends, so I'd live without Sarah as a friend. Besides, if she's that narrow minded, who needs her anyway?"

In addition to challenging and modifying the verbal automatic thoughts, clients may need to learn how to modify images because images often have a strong effect on their anxiety.

As Amy's thoughts in this situation were discussed further, she was able to describe in detail an image she had of herself looking like one of the schizophrenic clients she had seen in a psychiatric hospital. The therapist was then able to use several techniques to begin to challenge that image. Amy was asked to practice acting very anxious in front of a mirror, and she was able to see the difference between looking anxious and looking "crazy." She was also asked to reimagine that picture of herself, but this time give the image a different ending. This time, she imagined herself using her coping skills and ending up looking and feeling much more relaxed. She and her therapist also worked on decatastrophizing her image, exploring what would happen in the unlikely event that she did end up looking that "crazy," and she came to a similar conclusion as when her verbal thoughts were challenged: Sarah might not want anything to do with her, she might even make some disparaging remarks, but that would have little lasting effect on Amy's life. Challenging that image also helped to identify another one of Amy's fears: that if she became extremely anxious, she would, in fact, go crazy. This fear was then challenged as well.

Other techniques that can be helpful in modifying imagery include using thought stopping to turn off the image, time projection (imagining the situation 6 months, a year, or several years from the present), developing a positive image to be substituted for the dysfunctional one and used for coping, and using imagery to practice coping skills.

Exposure techniques are an essential component of Cognitive Therapy with anxiety disorders. Purely verbal interventions have only a limited effect on problems involving significant anxiety. In order for treatment to be effective, the client must repeatedly confront the situation he or she fears, tolerate the anxiety, and cope effectively with both the situation and the anxiety. This exposure can be gradual, as in systematic desensitization, or massed, as in flooding, but it is quite important. After all, the most effective way to challenge thoughts is through behavioral experiments and the testing of specific hypotheses. Most exposure assignments serve as ways of testing the client's cognitive assumptions and expectations.

Although graded exposure hierarchies may be used both via imagery in the office or *in vivo*, the rationale for the use of these assignments is quite different from that presented by the strict behaviorists using similar techniques. These homework assignments are not used to "decondition" the connection between the stimulus and anxiety, but, rather, as a powerful way of challenging the client's thoughts and beliefs. Exposure homework assignments constitute behavioral experiments for the client to use to ascertain experientially the difference between his or her catastrophic expectations and the events as they actually occur.

One early part of Jenny's treatment involved reversing avoidance using graded exposure. She developed a hierarchy of increasingly anxiety-provoking situations, ranging from driving one block away from home alone (anxiety rating of 5) to driving alone and being caught in rush-hour traffic (100). She began practicing doing at least one of the lower level hierarchy items each day. She was very eager to get better and worked hard at her hierarchy items, so that she was able to drive alone to her therapy sessions by the third session and was very proud of herself. This experience was then used to challenge her belief that "if I drive alone, I'll panic and crash."

This distinction between using behavioral experiments to test cognitions and using desensitization to decondition anxiety is more than a semantic one and has definite implications for treatment. In classic systematic desensitization, because the goal is to break any possible connection between the stimulus and anxiety, it is crucial to proceed through the hierarchy slowly and systematically, making sure that the client does not at any point experience high levels of anxiety. In the cognitive approach to graded exposure, however, it is not considered crucial to protect the client from any anxiety. In fact, with agoraphobics, the belief that they cannot tolerate anxiety must be challenged, so it is important that during the course of treatment the client does experience anxiety and even panic attacks, learning that he or she can indeed tolerate and cope with them.

Teaching clients to tolerate anxiety lends itself nicely to the use of paradoxical techniques. Beck and his colleagues (Beck et al., 1979) initially expressed disapproval with these techniques, primarily because of the belief that use of paradoxical techniques would risk disrupting the collaboration that is such an important part of treatment. As paradoxical techniques were originally used, the therapist would instruct the client to intensify a symptom, whereas the therapist, unbeknown to the client, assumed that this would actually decrease the symptom. Obviously, interventions based on this sort of hidden agenda could easily leave the client feeling manipulated and disrupt collaboration. With anxiety clients, however, this type of secrecy is unnecessary, and full collaboration can be maintained simply by sharing the rationale for the assignment with the client. For example, the type of paradoxical intervention that is most useful with clients who have panic attacks is that of prescribing the symptom, or in this case, asking the client to deliberately have a panic attack. It can be explained to the client that fear of the panic attack helps to maintain and intensify the panic. Therefore, the client is informed that the strongest way to combat this "fear of the fear" is to intentionally induce a panic attack by deliberately making the symptoms worse and then tolerating the anxiety without attempting to avoid it. Also, because it is necessary to have panic attacks in order to practice ways to cope with them, deliberately having a panic attack provides a good opportunity to practice coping skills. Thus the situation is set up as a no-lose situation: If fear of the fear is one of the major components of the panic, intentionally trying to panic may reduce the likelihood or the intensity of the panic. Even if the client does panic, this will then provide a useful opportunity to prove that he or she can survive the panic attacks and that the panic attacks do not lead to disaster. The task is paradoxical in that the client is trying to intensify something that he or she ultimately wants to eliminate, but because the rationale is fully shared with the client, no deception or loss of collaboration is involved. Whenever paradox is used, it is essential that the therapist and client have a good working relationship, that the client trust the therapist, and that the rationale is fully understood by the client. The same paradoxical intervention (such as saying, "Go ahead, let's see if you can have a heart attack") could be seen as cruel, sarcastic, or demeaning in one therapy relationship but seen as humorous, supportive, and caring within the content of a different therapeutic relationship.

Paradox can be particularly effective when used in a group therapy context, whether with agoraphobics or social phobics. Often, when the concept of paradox is first introduced, no matter how carefully the rationale is explained, the client comments, "Well, you clearly haven't had panic attacks, or you'd know that they are so awful that no one would deliberately encourage one." Of course, that idea can be challenged verbally, but in a group context, the client has the opportunity to watch other clients using paradox and hear their success stories, so it is much easier to convince him or her that it is worth a try. Also, the group can go out to a public place and practice paradox together, deriving a great deal of social support and encouragement for their attempts.

To actually address Jenny's fear of fear, it was necessary to have her experience panic attacks and deal with them rather than always working to keep her anxiety down. She was initially resistant to the idea of deliberately inducing panic because she had been able to cope well and had not been having spontaneous panic attacks. Unfortunately, there was no agoraphobia group available for her to join so that she could see how useful paradox had been to other clients. She decided to go ahead and try paradox after she spontaneously did have another panic attack and realized that she could not count on never panicking again no matter how skilled she was at coping. Because her main fear was of getting dizzy and fainting, she chose to go into a situation that was high up on her hierarchy (going to a restaurant where she had had a particularly bad panic attack 2 years before) and deliberately try to get dizzy and faint. She did get quite anxious, but as she tried to make it worse, she found that the symptoms decreased, and she was able to enjoy her lunch. Encouraged by the success of her attempt at not fighting the panic, she tried paradox in a variety of situations, especially when she felt that a panic attack was coming on.

Before attempting any behavioral experiments (whether paradoxical or part of a gradual exposure program), it is useful to go through a process of cognitive review in the office. Using imagery or verbal discussion to plan out the behavioral experiment step by step, the therapist can begin to desensitize the client to the situation, but it can also be a big help in identifying the automatic thoughts that are the most likely to occur in the actual situation. Once these have been identified, the therapist and the client can work together to develop an active coping plan and practice ways that the client can challenge the thoughts as they occur. It is particularly useful to attempt to identify and address all of the client's major fears about the particular situation before attempting a behavioral experiment in order to improve the chances that the client will prove willing to follow through with it. If the client changes his or her mind at the last minute, it is likely that this indicates that an important fear has not been addressed sufficiently.

The most commonly discussed behavioral treatment for Obsessive-Compulsive Disorder is response prevention, which can be seen in cognitive terms as the behavioral experiment of refraining from the obsessive-compulsive behavior as a test of whether or not the feared consequences occur. This intervention is appropriate and useful for both cognitive and behavioral rituals that are anxiety-reducing in nature because the individual is using the ritual to avoid anxiety, and thus preventing this response serves to help the client confront his or her fears. For example, if a compulsive hand washer is prevented from washing his or her hands even though he or she feels contaminated, the anxiety increases substantially, peaks, and begins to subside with no catastrophe following. The client discovers that the hand washing is unnecessary and that his or her anxiety can be reduced more effectively by confronting the fears.

Response prevention, however, would not be appropriate for obsessions that are anxiety evoking. For the treatment of anxiety-evoking obsessions, flooding with feared cognitions is necessary. These thoughts are maintained by the individual's fears and horror at the thoughts, and attempts at preventing these thoughts through procedures such as thought stopping could serve to support the view that the thoughts are terrible and could actually make the disorder worse. If the client is induced to confront the feared thoughts, images, or impulses and sufficient time is allowed for his or her anxiety to come to a peak and then subside, he or she discovers that they are unpleasant but not dangerous, breaking the cycle that perpetuated them.

Studies by Foa and her colleagues (Foa, Steketee, Grayson, Turner, & Latimer, 1984; Foa, Steketee, & Milby, 1980; Steketee, Foa, & Grayson, 1982) have shown that a combination of response prevention and prolonged exposure to obsessional cues was clearly superior to either component used alone for the treatment of Obsessive-Compulsive Disorder. For a detailed discussion of how to implement these procedures, see Steketee and Foa (1985).

Once the client has learned to successfully challenge his or her automatic thoughts and is actively confronting feared situations, the focus of treatment shifts to the underlying assumptions that predispose that person to anxiety. After having collected several weeks of automatic thoughts in a variety of situations, basic themes can generally be identified. In addition, the "downward arrow" technique (discussed in Chapter 3) can be used to pinpoint the specific underlying assumptions that seem most prominent for that client. Even though many anxious clients may share similar underlying assumptions, it is important not to assume that a given client holds a given belief. It is the most useful to identify the central idiosyncratic assumptions of the individual client and to specify them in the client's own words, so that challenging the assumptions will have the maximal impact.

As treatment went on, it became clear that Jenny strongly held the belief that because she was the minister's wife and a pillar of the community, she should be able to be perfect at whatever she did, which included not having any strong negative emotions. The prohibition against strong emotions included not only anxiety but also anger and sadness as well. She had already begun to see how fighting anxiety only made it worse and accepting it worked much better, so that was used as evidence that accepting strong emotions in general might be a more useful strategy than prohibiting them. With anger, she realized that she tended to hold her feelings in and pout when she was mad at her husband, which was not very useful because he was so busy he generally did not notice. Instead, she decided to accept her anger and work on assertive ways of expressing it. While working on assertion, she was able to pinpoint another underlying assumption: She felt she needed approval from everyone and that other people's reactions were extremely important. Assertion training served as a continual, and powerful, challenge to that assumption.

Many of the behavioral experiments being used to test out automatic thoughts will also serve as tests of some of the client's underlying assumptions, but it cannot be assumed that the client will draw those connections on his or her own. It is necessary to repeatedly restate the underlying assumption and discuss explicitly how a given behavioral experiment could be used as a challenge to that assumption. For example, an agoraphobic client may be practicing hierarchy items that involve being alone but may not spontaneously draw the connection that each successfully completed hierarchy item is further evidence to challenge the belief that he or she is incapable of functioning independently in the world.

In addition to consistently pointing out the steps the client is already taking to challenge his or her underlying assumptions, specific new behavioral assignments can be set up to directly test out these beliefs. For example, if a client has the belief that he or she needs to always be competent in all respects, an experiment could be set up where he or she deliberately does a task less than perfectly and observes the consequences. If the individual believes that total control over emotions is necessary at all times, he or she could practice being out of control (either by having a panic attack, or allowing him- or herself to have other strong emotions). The person who believes that it is necessary to get approval from everyone could deliberately do something that will clearly be disapproved of by someone else to test out that assumption.

Other basic beliefs can be successfully challenged by examining the advantages and disadvantages of maintaining those beliefs. Anxious over-concern, catastrophizing, problem avoidance, and helplessness are beliefs for which it is particularly useful to examine the price the client pays for holding the belief. Once the client can see that there is a choice as to whether to continue to pay that price, it can be useful to write out a new, more adaptive underlying assumption. For example, a client who decided that he no longer wants to maintain the belief that it is essential to be loved and approved of by everyone at all times could write a new belief, such as "It feels good to be loved and approved of, but it's even more important that I approve of what I'm doing." Then, without assuming that the client can change his or her belief automatically, the therapist can help the client outline how he or she would behave differently *if* he or she did endorse the new belief. Once the changes are elaborated sufficiently, the client could practice acting for 1 week *as if* he or she believed the new belief and observe the consequences (fixed-role therapy, Chapter 3).

In the treatment of Social Phobia, "decentering" is the process of having the client challenge the basic belief that she or he is the focal point of all events. The client is asked to collect concrete evidence to determine how often he or she actually is the focus of attention and what behaviors are being attended to by others. Thus, for example, a client may be asked to go to a mall or restaurant and count how many people actually are watching him or her sitting there. This exercise in itself requires a shift in focus because the person is required to adopt the perspective of other people.

Because control is often a major issue for individuals with anxiety disorders, it can be useful to help the client understand the distinction between the two different types of control discussed by Weisz, Rothbaum, and Blackburn (1984). Most American writings on the psychology of control focus on the view that perceived control results when individuals shape existing physical, social, or behavioral realities to fit their perceptions, goals, or wishes. This is what Weisz and his colleagues define as "primary control." For example, if a person begins to get anxious and uncomfortable in a crowded room when the lecturer continues to speak past the allotted time, he or she could exert primary control by changing the situation (leaving the room, opening a window, asking the lecturer to conclude his talk, etc.). In addition to this primary control, however, Weisz *et al.* argue that control is often sought via alternative paths that they label as *secondary control*. In secondary control, individuals attempt to align themselves with existing realities, leaving the realities unchanged but exerting control over the situation's psychological impact. In the above mentioned situation, the individual could exert secondary control by trying to better adapt to the situation as it is (deciding the information being imparted is worth running overtime, doing deep breathing to feel more comfortable, accepting that he or she gets anxious at times but does not have to do anything about it, etc.). Weisz *et al.* conclude that both types of control can be useful and that an important goal is to find an optimally adaptive blend of primary and secondary control. Anxiety clients, however, often feel out of control because they focus only on the aspects of the situation over which they feel no control. A discussion of primary versus secondary control and teaching the client to enumerate which factors are under his or her control can be very useful.

A 32-year-old male accountant was afraid to fly. When on an airplane, his thoughts focused on all the ways he was out of control, such as "I can't get out and leave no matter how much I want to" and "I have no say over how the pilot flies this plane." When the issue of primary versus secondary control was discussed with him, he realized that there are always many aspects of life over which he really had little or no control (i.e., the weather) but that he simply did not focus his attention on them so they did not bother him. He made up a list of all the things he did have control of during a flight (i.e., whether to read or nap, have a drink or eat, go to the bathroom or stay seated, write and challenge his dysfunctional thoughts, or practice relaxation training), and he found it very helpful to him to review this list when he took his next plane flight.

The final stage in therapy is work on relapse prevention. In addition to the usual process of identifying high-risk situations and planning how to handle them if they arise, it is important for clients recovering from anxiety disorders to understand the risks inherent in avoidance. The tendency to avoid situations that evoke anxiety is a very natural one; however, if a previously avoidant client gradually begins to again avoid the situations he or she avoided previously, the anxiety may well begin to return. In return, the client can expect that for some time following treatment, if he or she goes for some time without confronting a previously feared situation, mild anxiety will return. This is not a sign of relapse. All the client needs to do is to go ahead and confront the situation and the anxiety will fade quickly.

Later in Jenny's treatment, she wanted to get off of the medication, so it was necessary to address her attributions about her medications and fade her off of them (with the full cooperation of her physician). She was concerned that perhaps all her improvement was due to the medications, so she and her therapist conducted a behavioral experiment, having her redo all her hierarchy items once she was off of the medications. She also did thought sheets whenever she felt concerned about being medication free, and except for some initial anxiety when she first went off the medication, she was able to go through her hierarchy very quickly and successfully.

As Jenny and her therapist reviewed her goals and realized that she had made significant headway toward them, they decided to increase the time between sessions so that she could build up her confidence that she could continue her progress on her own. In the final sessions, treatment focused on getting her some time away from her son, increasing her involvement in activities she found rewarding without her husband, and scheduling enjoyable activities alone with her husband to improve their marriage. The therapy was terminated by mutual agreement after a total of 20 sessions, and contact 2 years later showed that she had maintained her progress and continued to improve further. She had had to deal with a number of serious stressors including the birth of a second child and her husband's having a serious illness, and she had found it difficult to resume her normal activities after long periods stuck at home with a new baby and sick husband; but she had managed to get through it all without a recurrence of the agoraphobia.

CONCLUSIONS

Although Cognitive Therapy is effective for the full range of anxiety disorders, Cognitive Therapy of anxiety appears to be somewhat more time consuming than Cognitive Therapy of depression. Whereas for depression the treatment is often effective within 10 to 12 weeks, Cognitive Therapy for anxiety often can take between 6 months and 1 year to be completed. This may be because individuals with anxiety disorders seem to have less access to their dysfunctional cognitions and also because avoidance behaviors can become so comfortable that they are difficult to change.

Research evidence for the efficacy of cognitive-behavioral therapies for anxiety has been accumulating over recent years, and several meta-analytic reviews have shown promising results (Barrios & Shigatomi, 1980; Dushe, Hurt, & Schroeder, 1983; Miller & Berman, 1983). In studies of the treatment of agoraphobia in particular, however, the findings are less clear. Some studies show an advantage to cognitive-behavioral approaches over behavioral treatments, but other studies show no such advantage, and other studies demonstrate a superiority of straight behavioral treatments over the cognitive-behavioral approaches (summarized in Michelson, 1987). Although further research is clearly needed, Michelson concludes that "a multimodal treatment approach would represent a more state-of-the-art treatment of this complex anxiety disorder by simultaneously addressing the three dimensions of the disorder (behavior, cognition, and physiology). Treatment integration of this nature is likely to result in improved outcome, synchrony, and maintenance and generalization effects" (1987, p. 264). Cognitive Therapy can provide such a multimodal, integrated approach.

III

Personality Disorders

Personality Disorders are long-standing, inflexible patterns of perceiving, interpreting, and responding to one's environment and to oneself that are characteristic of the individual's functioning across a wide range of situations. These disorders are generally recognizable by adolescence or early adulthood and, without effective intervention, tend to be characteristic of much of the affected individual's adult life.

In recent years, the importance of developing effective approaches to the treatment of clients with personality disorders has become increasingly apparent. The finding that over 50% of the subjects who participated in the DSM-III field trials satisfied diagnostic criteria for one or more personality disorders makes it clear that the incidence of clients with these problems is quite high, at least in some settings. When this finding is considered along with the observation that clients with personality disorders typically respond poorly and slowly to "standard" psychotherapeutic interventions even when they seek treatment for apparently commonplace problems, it raises the possibility that the presence of personality disorders may account for a substantial proportion of those clients who do not benefit from therapy. Certainly, it is commonly observed that clients with personality disorders are among the most difficult and frustrating clients encountered in practice. Theorists with orientations ranging from psychoanalytic (e.g. Masterson, 1978) to cognitive behavioral (Pretzer, 1983) argue that in order to be effective with this group of clients, therapists must recognize the presence of personality disorders and modify their interventions appropriately.

Much of the rapidly growing literature on the treatment of personality disorders has been based on psychoanalytic theory and is of limited use to therapists who do not care to practice long-term, psychoanalytically oriented psychotherapy (e.g., Goldstein, 1985; Gunderson, 1984; Kernberg, 1975; Lion, 1981; Millon, 1981; Saul & Warner, 1982). Behavioral and cognitive-behavioral theorists have a long tradition of rejecting explanations of psychopathological behavior that are based on the idea of enduring personality traits in favor of explanations that are based on the stimuli, consequences, and cognitions experienced in the particular situations in which the problems occur. As a result, many were quick to assume that it would not be possible to understand personality disorders by such a perspective because, by definition, these disorders are manifested in a wide range of situations over an extended period of time. Fortunately, this has not proved to the case. Millon's (1981) biopsychosocial view of personality disorders is compatible in many ways with behavioral and other non-psychoanalytic approaches and he has been quite influential in shaping approaches to diagnosis and conceptualization of personality disorders. Following an interval during which personality disorders received little attention from behavioral and cognitive-behavioral authors, a number of clinically based approaches to Personality Disorders have been developed (Fleming, 1983, 1985; Linehan, 1987a,b; Pretzer, 1983, 1985; Simon, 1983, 1985; Young, 1987) and the initial steps toward developing an empirically based approach to the conceptualization and treatment of personality disorders has begun (Turkat & Maisto, 1985). Although the perspectives of these behavioral and cognitive-behavioral authors vary in many ways, they agree that in order to treat clients with these complex disorders effectively, one must plan interventions carefully on the basis of a clear understanding of the client and his or her problems, that one must pay more careful attention to the therapist–client relationship than is usually the case, and that therapy with these clients requires substantially more time than does treatment of simpler disorders.

Cognitive Therapy proves to be well suited to the treatment of clients with personality disorders. The inclusion of clients' basic assumptions as well as their immediate cognitions in problem situations permits clear conceptualization of these complex disorders, the use of a collaborative approach to therapy based on guided discovery aids in addressing the interpersonal complexities of therapy with these clients, and the cognitive-behavioral interventions prove effective despite the clients' complexity. The following chapters present cognitive approaches to conceptualizing and treating each of the currently recognized personality disorders.

These chapters are organized roughly according to DSM-III-R's division of personality disorders into three clusters. Cluster A includes Paranoid, Schizoid, and Schizotypal Personality Disorders, persons who are often seen as odd or eccentric. Cluster B includes persons who are seen as dramatic, emotional, or erratic, that is, Antisocial, Borderline, Histrionic, and Narcissistic Personality disorders. The final cluster, Cluster C, consists of persons who often appear anxious or fearful, including Avoidant, Dependent, Obsessive-Compulsive, and Passive Aggressive Personality Disorders.

7

Paranoid, Schizoid, and Schizotypal Personality Disorders

PARANOID PERSONALITY DISORDER

In many ways, Paranoid Personality Disorder is a primarily cognitive disorder. It is characterized by a set of extreme and unrealistic beliefs regarding the motivation and likely actions of other persons. The paranoid individual is certain that people in general have malicious intentions and will take advantage of any opportunity to deceive, attack, or take advantage of him or her. This "paranoid" world view is firmly held and is not substantially changed by interactions in which the client is treated well by others. However, these unrealistically suspicious views are not accompanied by a thought disorder or by systematized delusions. Although individuals with Paranoid Personality Disorder are prone to a variety of intrapersonal and interpersonal problems, these stem from the paranoid world view. The individual's beliefs about the nature of other persons and his or her interpretations of their actions are responsible for most of the problems he or she encounters.

It might appear that a disorder such as this, where cognition plays such a central role, would be ideally suited to cognitive-behavioral interventions. However, simply establishing a working relationship with these clients can be difficult and, as most therapists can attest, attempts to directly challenge the paranoid individual's view of others typically prove ineffective or counterproductive. Psychodynamically oriented writers have concluded that modest gains achieved slowly over extended periods of time are the best that can be expected with Paranoid Personality Disorder (Weintraub, 1981). Cognitive Therapy's more active, collaborative approach offers some advantages in working with paranoid clients, but for cognitive-behavioral techniques to be effective, they must be used strategically.

Assessment

Persons with Paranoid Personality Disorder are reputed to rarely enter therapy because they do not see their suspiciousness as a problem, are reluctant to accept help, and rarely function so poorly that they require hospitalization (Weintraub, 1981). However, it may be the case that individuals with Paranoid Personality Disorder often enter therapy without the disorder being diagnosed. Although it is true that these individuals rarely seek therapy for their paranoia, they may well seek therapy due to difficulty handling job stress, conflicts with superiors or colleagues, problems with anxiety, depression, marital problems, and substance abuse, perhaps without their underlying suspicions of others being recognized.

These clients have a strong tendency to blame others for interpersonal problems. Thus when the assessment is based on the client's self-report, an impression may be created that their problems are due to mistreatment by others and that their suspicions are justified. In addition, the client may well realize that a paranoid world view is not socially acceptable and actively conceal his or her paranoia. When this is the case, indications of paranoia may emerge only gradually over the course of therapy and may easily be missed.

The DSM-III-R diagnostic criteria for Paranoid Personality Disorder are shown in Table 15. Sometimes Paranoid Personality Disorder is obvious. For example:

"Ann" was a married secretary in her mid-30s who sought help with stress management because of problems with tension, fatigue, insomnia, and being short-tempered, which she attributed to job stress. When asked what the main sources of stress were she said, "People at work are constantly dropping things and making noise just to get me" and "They keep trying to turn my supervisor against me." She

TABLE 15. DSM-III-R Diagnostic Criteria for Paranoid Personality Disorder

---

A. A pervasive and unwarranted tendency, beginning in early adulthood and present in a variety of contexts, to interpret the actions of people as deliberately demeaning or threatening, as indicated by at least *four* of the following:
  1. Expects, without sufficient basis, to be exploited or harmed by others
  2. Questions, without justification, the loyalty or trustworthiness of friends or associates
  3. Reads hidden demeaning or threatening meanings into benign remarks or events, e.g., suspects that a neighbor put trash out early to annoy him
  4. Bears grudges or is unforgiving of insults or slights
  5. Is reluctant to confide in others because of unwarranted fear that the information will be used against him or her
  6. Is easily slighted and quick to react with anger or to counterattack
  7. Questions, without justification, fidelity of spouse or sexual partner
B. Occurrence not exclusively during the course of Schizophrenia or a Delusional Disorder.

was unwilling to consider alternative explanations for their actions and described herself as typically sensitive, jealous, easily offended, and quick to anger.

However, the diagnosis can be much more difficult to make:

"Gary" was a radiologist in his late 20s who was single with a steady girlfriend. He was working while going to graduate school part-time and living with his parents in order to afford tuition. He described himself as chronically nervous and reported problems with worry, anxiety attacks, and insomnia. He was seeking therapy because his symptoms had intensified due to school pressures. He talked openly and seemed forthright. The initial interview was remarkable only for his not wanting his family to know he was in therapy because they did not believe in seeking help for problems and his not wanting to use his health insurance because of concerns about confidentiality.

Cognitive Therapy focusing both on learning skills for coping more effectively with stress and anxiety and on examining his fears proceeded unremarkably and effectively for six sessions. At the beginning of the seventh session he described a number of occasions on which progressive relaxation techniques "didn't work." In discussing these episodes, he said, "It's like I don't want to relax," "Maybe I'm afraid of people just taking from me," "I don't want him stealing my idea," "Every little thing you say is used against you," and finally that people are "out to take you for what they can get." Further discussion made it clear that a suspicious, defensive approach to interpersonal situations was characteristic of his long-term functioning and played a central role both in his problems with stress and anxiety and in his difficulty using relaxation techniques effectively.

The distinctive characteristic of Paranoid Personality Disorder is a long-standing, pervasive, and *unwarranted* suspiciousness and mistrust of people. Although guardedness, mistrust, or suspicion may be both justified and adaptive in a variety of difficult situations, well-functioning individuals are willing to look critically at their suspicions and are willing to abandon them in the face of contradictory evidence. The individual with Paranoid Personality Disorder overlooks or rejects evidence that conflicts with his or her suspicions and may become suspicious of persons who challenge his or her suspicious beliefs. This suspiciousness is not confined to situations in which there are grounds for vigilance or suspicion but is characteristic of the individual's overall functioning.

Individuals with this disorder are typically hypervigilant, quick to interpret ambiguous situations as threatening, and quick to take precautions against perceived threats. They expect others to be devious, deceptive, disloyal, and hostile and act on the assumption that these expectations are accurate. As a result, they frequently are perceived by others as devious, deceptive, disloyal, and hostile and also are often seen as stubborn, defensive, and unwilling to compromise. They often have little recognition of the

TABLE 16. Possible Indications of Paranoid Personality Disorder

Constant vigilance, possibly manifested as a tendency to scan the therapist's office during the interview and/or to frequently glance out the window.

Greater than normal concern about confidentiality, possibly including reluctance to allow the therapist to maintain progress notes and/or requests that the therapist take special steps to assure confidentiality when returning telephone calls from the client.

A tendency to attribute all blame for problems to others and to perceive himself or herself as frequently mistreated and abused.

Recurrent conflict with authority figures.

Unusually strong convictions regarding the motives of others and difficulty considering alternative explanations for their actions.

A tendency to interpret small events as having great significance and thus react strongly, apparently "making mountains out of molehills."

A tendency to counterattack quickly in response to a perceived threat or slight and to be contentious and litigious.

A tendency to receive more than his or her share of bad treatment from others or to provoke hostility from others.

A tendency to search intensely and narrowly for evidence that confirms his or her negative expectations regarding others, ignoring the context and reading (plausible) special meanings and hidden motives into ordinary events.

Inability to relax, particularly when in the presence of others, possibly including unwillingness or inability to close his or her eyes in the presence of the therapist for relaxation training.

Inability to see the humor in situations.

An unusually strong need for self-sufficiency and independence.

Disdain for those he or she sees as weak, soft, sickly, or defective.

Difficulty expressing warm, tender feelings, or expressing doubts and insecurities.

Pathological jealousy.

impact their behavior has on others' perception of them, blaming others for all interpersonal problems and refusing to accept their share of responsibility for the problems. Table 16 presents a number of possible indications of a paranoid personality style that may warn the clinician to be alert for other indications of Paranoid Personality Disorder.

It is important to note that the discussion in this chapter applies to Paranoid Personality Disorder, not to Paranoid Disorder or Paranoid Schizophrenia. Paranoia is also a symptom of these other disorders; however, in these disorders, there are persistent psychotic symptoms such as delusions and hallucinations. According to the DSM-III-R diagnostic criteria, psychotic symptoms are never part of Paranoid Personality Disorder except for brief periods at times of extreme stress. Although many of the principles discussed in this chapter may apply with Paranoid Disorder or Paranoid Schizophrenia, it is not clear what impact the presence of thought disorder or a formalized delusional system will have on treatment. The principles often apply well to individuals who abruptly develop paranoid symptomatology without thought disorder in response to a stressor such as an illness or an unexpected failure.

Conceptualization

The topic of paranoia in general has received extensive attention from psychodynamic writers from Freud to the present. A lucid discussion of the traditional view is presented by Shapiro (1965, pp. 54–107). Following a clear and extensive discussion of the paranoid cognitive style, he argues that the disorder is a result of "projection" of unacceptable feelings and impulses onto others. A similar view of paranoia has been presented in the cognitive-behavioral literature by Colby and his colleagues (Colby, Faught, & Parkinson, 1979). These investigators have developed a computer simulation of a paranoid client's responses in a psychiatric interview based on their model of paranoia. This computer simulation is sufficiently realistic that experienced interviewers are unable to distinguish the responses of the computer model from the responses of an actual client as long as the domain of the interview is sufficiently restricted. Colby's model is based on the assumption that the paranoid individual strongly believes that he or she is inadequate, imperfect, and insufficient. It is proposed that these beliefs are activated when relevant events or thoughts occur and that, at that time, the individual experiences distress due to the resulting "shame-humiliation." Colby and his colleagues suggest that by concluding that other persons are the source of his or her distress, the paranoid individual is able to reduce the shame-humiliation by attributing the distress to the inadequacy of others rather than the inadequacy of the self. Thus the paranoid cognitive style is seen as being motivated and perpetuated by its distress-reducing effects. On the basis of this model, the authors speculate that it might be most effective to use interventions that focus on (1) challenging the client's belief that he or she is inadequate or insufficient, (2) restricting the scope of events that are accepted as evidence of inadequacy, and (3) counteracting the client's external attributions regarding the sources of his or her distress. They argue that directly challenging specific suspicions and allegations will prove ineffective as well as difficult because it has little effect on the factors producing the disorder. The authors make it clear that these suggestions are based purely on their computer simulation and have not been clinically validated. Also, Colby's theoretical model is of paranoia in general, and it is not clear to what extent it provides a comprehensive understanding of Paranoid Personality Disorder.

Paranoid Personality Disorder *per se* has received less attention from cognitive-behavioral authors. In a discussion of personality disorders in general, Marshall and Barbaree (1984) comment briefly that the paranoid client's suspiciousness plays a central role in the disorder through its dual impact on cognition and on social interaction, but they go no further in discussing the disorder or in proposing interventions. The most detailed discussion to date is Turkat and Maisto's (1985) case example of treatment in progress with Mr. E., a client with Paranoid Personality Disorder, in a paper presenting their experimentally based behavioral approach to the treatment of personality disorders.

The core of the conceptualization of Mr. E. proposed by Turkat and Maisto is that, as a result of childhood learning, he had developed a hyper-sensitivity to others' evaluations of him but did not acquire good social skills. This is seen as resulting in a self-perpetuating cycle in which the client was concerned about the opinions of others, attempted to gain their approval and/or to avoid their disapproval but did so in a way that instead elicited criticism. In response, he withdrew and ruminated about his failures and his mistreatment by others. Mr. E.'s cognitions about persecu-tion at the hands of others were seen as a rationalization used to cope with his recurrent failures and his ruminations about failures. On the basis of this conceptualization, Turkat and Maisto (1985) selected interventions focused on decreasing the client's anxiety regarding evaluation by others and on improving his social skills as being most appropriate, paying only limited attention to his paranoid thought style. Although treatment had not been completed at the time of publication, the authors document con-siderable progress that had been made after 7 months of twice-weekly therapy.

Observations made in the course of Cognitive Therapy with clients with Paranoid Personality Disorder suggest conclusions that are somewhat different from those of Colby et al. (1979) or Turkat and Maisto (1985). For example, Figure 12 summarizes the cognitive and interpersonal compo-nents of Gary's paranoid approach to life that were uncovered in the course of his therapy. He held three basic assumptions quite strongly: "People are malevolent and deceptive." "They'll attack you if they get the chance," and "You can be OK only if you stay on your toes." Obviously these assump-tions led to the expectation and deception, trickery, and harm in interper-sonal interactions and to the conclusion that vigilance for signs of decep-tion, trickery, and malicious intentions was necessary. However, this vigilance produced an unintended side effect. If one is vigilant for subtle indications that others are untrustworthy (and not equally vigilant for signs of trustworthiness and benign intentions), one quickly accumulates considerable evidence to support the view that people cannot be trusted. After all, people are not uniformly trustworthy, and many interactions are ambiguous enough to leave room for them to be interpreted as revealing malicious intentions even if such is actually not the case. Thus, Gary's vigilance produced substantial evidence to support his assumptions about human nature and tended to perpetuate his paranoid approach to life.

Also, Gary's negative expectations about interpersonal interactions

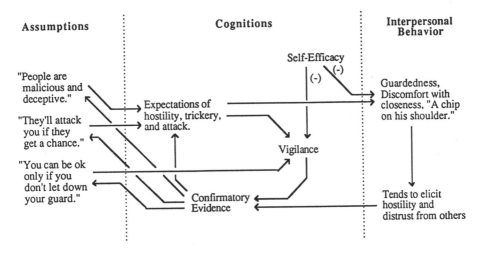

FIGURE 12. Cognitive conceptualization of paranoid personality disorder.

had a major impact on his interactions with colleagues and acquaintances. He avoided closeness in relationships for fear that the emotional involvement and greater openness involved in close relationships would make him more vulnerable to being hurt. In addition, he was generally guarded and defensive, tended to react strongly to small slights, and was quick to respond to perceived provocation with hostility. Naturally, these characteristics did not endear him to others or establish the types of relationships that would encourage others to be kind and generous toward him. Instead, he tended to provoke distrust and hostility from others. His beliefs regarding human nature led Gary to interact with people in a way that provided him with the repeated experience of being badly treated, and these experiences supported his negative view of human nature.

As noted in the previous discussion of anxiety disorders (Chapter 6), self-efficacy, the individual's estimate of his or her ability to handle a particular situation effectively, plays a major role in individuals' responses to situations perceived as presenting risk or danger. If one is faced with a dangerous situation but is confident that he or she can handle it effectively, the emotional and behavioral responses will be quite different from those experienced by a person in the same situation who has serious doubts about his or her ability to handle it. If Gary had been confident that he could see through the deceptions of others and thwart their attacks, he would have felt less need to be constantly on guard. However, he doubted his ability to deal effectively with others and felt that it would be quite dangerous to lower his guard.

Many aspects of paranoia follow naturally from the pattern of cognition and behavior observed in Paranoid Personality Disorder. The assumptions that people are malevolent and deceptive and that one can be safe only through vigilance lead to vigilance for signs of danger and results in selective attention to experience that supports the paranoid's world view. However, these assumptions also contribute to paranoid interpretations of experiences that would otherwise be incompatible with the assumption that others are malicious. If one assumes that people cannot be trusted, then interactions in which other people seem benign or helpful can easily be interpreted as revealing deception on their part, as being an attempt to trick one into trusting them. If this interpretation of benign acts as deceptive occurs, the "fact" that people are trying to deceive the client by acting nice is seen as clear evidence that their intentions are malicious. This pattern leads to the commonly observed tendency to reject "obvious" interpretations of the actions of others and to search for the "real" underlying meaning, a search that continues until an interpretation consistent with the paranoid individual's preconceptions is found.

In many ways, the paranoid reacts as anyone would in a dangerous situation that he or she confronts rather than avoids. Vigilant for signs of danger, he or she acts cautiously and purposefully, avoiding carelessness and unnecessary risks. Because the most important danger is seen as coming from others and others are seen as potentially deceptive, the paranoid is alert for signs of danger or deception during interactions, constantly scanning for subtle cues of the individual's true intentions. In such a "dog-eat-dog" world, to show any weakness is to court attack so the paranoid carefully conceals his or her insecurities, shortcomings, and problems through deception, denial, excuses, or blaming others. What others know about you may be used against you, so the paranoid carefully guards his or her privacy, striving to suppress even trivial information and, in particular, suppressing signs of his own emotions and intentions.

When one is facing a hostile situation such as the paranoid believes he or she faces, any restrictions on one's freedom can leave one trapped and vulnerable. Thus the paranoid has a low tolerance for rules and regulations unless they serve his or her plans. The more powerful an individual is, the more of a threat he or she is seen as posing. As a result, the paranoid is keenly aware of power hierarchies, both admiring and fearing persons in positions of authority, hoping for a powerful ally but fearing betrayal or attack. He is typically unwilling to "give in" because the appearance of weakness might encourage attack, yet is reluctant to challenge powerful individuals and risk provoking attack.

When one is vigilant for signs of threat or attack and presumes malicious intentions, it follows that any slights or mistreatments are intentional and malicious. When others protest that their actions were unintentional, accidental, or justified, their protestations are seen as evidence of deception. Because attention is focused on mistreatment by others whereas any apparently good treatment by others is discounted and any mistreatment of others is justified, situations constantly seem unfair and unjust. The perception that others are making unjustified intrusions on the client's personal domain elicits anger that is expressed aggressively, passive-aggressively, or explosively rather than assertively.

The primary difference between this view of Paranoid Personality Disorder and those presented by Colby *et al.* (1979) and by Turkat and Maisto (1985) is that there is no need to make the traditional psychodynamic assumption that the paranoid individual's suspicions of others are due to "projection" of unacceptable impulses or to attribute them to attempts to avoid shame and humiliation by blaming others (Colby *et al.*, 1979) or a rationalization used to cope with recurrent failures (Turkat & Maisto, 1985). Each of these views argues that the paranoid individuals' suspicions, which seem central to the disorder, are actually complex side effects of other, more important factors. However, the model of Paranoid Personality Disorder presented here permits a more parsimonious explanation of the paranoid's suspicions and assigns them a more central role. Both the "expectation of malevolence-vigilance-perception of malevolence" cycle and the "expectation of malevolence-defensiveness-hostility from others" cycle discussed can easily result in a "self-fulfilling prophecy" and thus be self-perpetuating. In addition, these cycles are rendered largely impervious to experiences that would conflict with the assumption that others have malicious intentions by the concomitant assumption that people are deceptive as well. This results in a strong tendency for the paranoid individual to assume that apparently benign or benevolent actions on the part of others are deceptive rather than genuine and, as a result, the paranoid searches for concealed meanings in apparently benign events. This view suggests that rather than being peripheral, the paranoid client's suspicions are an important component of the cognitive, and interpersonal cycles that perpetuate the disorder and should be considered as potential targets for intervention.

Any conclusions regarding the etiology of Paranoid Personality Disorder are purely speculative because no reliable data have been collected regarding the developmental histories of persons who develop Paranoid Personality Disorder and because paranoid clients' views of others and their recollections of previous events are known to be distorted in a paranoia-congruent way. However, it is interesting to note that a paranoid stance would be adaptive if one were faced by a truly dangerous situation where others were likely to prove to be overtly or covertly hostile. Many paranoid clients describe growing up in families that they experienced as quite dangerous. For example, Gary described a long history of being ridiculed for any sign of sensitivity or weakness, of being lied to and cheated by parents and siblings, and of verbal and physical assaults by family members. In addition, he reported being explicitly taught by his parents that the world was a "dog-eat-dog" place where one must be tough

to survive. Such accounts give the impression that growing up in a generally hostile or paranoid family where vigilance is truly necessary could
contribute substantially to the development of Paranoid Personality Disorder. Such a hypothesis is appealing, but it will remain speculative until it is
possible to obtain more objective data regarding the histories of these
individuals. A comprehensive theoretical treatment of the etiology of Paranoid Personality Disorder would also need to account for studies that find
an unusually high incidence of "schizophrenic spectrum" disorders among
relatives of individuals diagnosed with Paranoid Personality Disorder (Kendler & Gruenberg, 1982). Such findings raise the possibility of a genetic
link, but the mechanisms through which such a link could occur are not yet
understood.

Intervention Strategies and Techniques

The model of Paranoid Personality Disorder that has been presented
here may appear to provide little opportunity for effective intervention.
Obviously, one goal of intervention would be to modify the basic assumptions that are the foundation of the disorder, but how can one hope to
challenge these assumptions effectively when the client's vigilance and
paranoid approach to interactions constantly produce experiences that
seem to confirm the assumptions? On the other hand, how can the therapist hope to induce the client to relax his or her vigilance or to treat others
more appropriately as long as the client is convinced that they have malicious intentions? If these two self-perpetuating cycles were the whole of
the cognitive model, there would be little prospect for effective cognitive-
behavioral intervention with these clients.

Fortunately, the client's self-efficacy has an important role in Paranoid
Personality Disorder. The paranoid individual's intense vigilance and defensiveness is a product of the belief that constant vigilance and defensiveness is necessary to preserve his or her safety. If it is possible to increase the client's sense of self-efficacy so that he or she is confident of
being able to handle problems as they arise, then the intense vigilance and
defensiveness would seem less necessary, and it might be possible for the
client to relax both to some extent. This would reduce the intensity of the
client's symptomatology substantially, making it much easier to address
the client's cognitions through conventional cognitive techniques and making it more possible to persuade the client to test more adaptive ways of
handling interpersonal conflicts. Therefore, the primary strategy in the
cognitive treatment of Paranoid Personality Disorder is to work to increase
the client's sense of self-efficacy before attempting to modify other aspects
of the client's automatic thoughts, interpersonal behavior, and basic
assumptions.

The first issue in Cognitive Therapy with Paranoid Personality Disorder is establishing a working relationship. This obviously is no simple task when working with someone who assumes that others are likely to prove malevolent and deceptive. The paranoid is certain that it can be very dangerous to trust other people and quickly realizes that the therapist–client relationship is a relationship in which he or she will be quite vulnerable at times. It rarely is productive to try to establish trust through persuasion, argument, or pointing to one's credentials. The paranoid is not foolish enough to trust someone simply because they say that they can be trusted or because they have a diploma. Trust is most effectively established through explicitly acknowledging and accepting the client's difficulty in trusting the therapist once this becomes evident and then being careful to behave in a trustworthy manner in order to provide the evidence on which trust can be based. It is important to exercise more than the usual amount of care in communicating clearly, assertively, and honestly, avoiding misunderstandings, maintaining congruence between verbal statements and nonverbal cues, and following through on agreements. It is important not to press the client to take risks in therapy until a sufficient level of trust has been established, and it is important to make it clear that he or she has the option of not talking about sensitive topics until they feel ready to do so.

Collaboration is always important in Cognitive Therapy, but it is especially important in working with paranoid individuals because they are likely to become intensely anxious or angry if they feel coerced, treated unfairly, or placed in a "one-down" position. Because these clients rarely present their paranoia as a problem they wish to work on, it is important to focus on the client's stated goals for therapy. There is no need to worry that by focusing on their stress, marital problems, or whatever, the "real problem" of their paranoia will be missed. A guided discovery approach to pursuing their goals will quickly reveal the ways in which their paranoia contributes to their other problems, creating a situation where it is possible to work collaboratively on their distrust of others, feelings of vulnerability, and so on, rather than it being a matter of the therapist insisting that these issues be addressed.

The initial phase of therapy can be quite stressful to paranoid clients even when it seems to the therapist that the focus is on superficial topics that should not be very threatening. It is important to remember that simply participating in therapy requires the client to engage in a number of activities, such as self-disclosure, acknowledging weakness, and trusting another person, which he or she experiences as being quite dangerous. The stress that results from simply participating in therapy can be reduced somewhat by focusing initially on the least sensitive topics, by starting with more behavioral interventions, and by discussing issues indirectly (i.e., through the use of analogies or through talking about how "some people" react in such situations) rather than pressing for direct self-disclosure. One of the more effective ways to increase a paranoid client's comfort with therapy is to give the client even more than the usual amount of control over the content of sessions, homework assignments, and the scheduling of sessions. These clients may be much more comfortable and progress more quickly if sessions are scheduled less frequently than usual. With a number of paranoid clients, scheduling sessions about once every 3 weeks has seemed optimal.

As the focus of therapy shifts from establishing a working relationship to working toward the client's initial goals, it is generally most productive for the therapist to focus on increasing the client's sense of self-efficacy in problem situations. There are two main ways in which this can be done. If the client is actually capable of handling the situation but overestimates the threat posed by the situation and/or underestimates his or her capacity for handling the situation, interventions that result in a more realistic appraisal of his or her ability to cope will increase self-efficacy. If the client is not capable of handling the situation or if there is room for improvement in his or her coping skills, interventions that improve his or her coping skills will increase self-efficacy. In practice, it often works best to use the two approaches in combination.

With Ann (the secretary mentioned before), it would have been ineffective to challenge her paranoid ideation ("They are making noise just to get me"), but it proved quite helpful for the therapist to help her to reevaluate how much danger such actions would pose if her co-workers were indeed trying to provoke her and to reevaluate her capacity for coping with the situation:

Therapist: You're reacting as though this is a very dangerous situation. What are the risks you see?

Ann: They'll keep dropping things and making noise to annoy me.

Therapist: Are you sure nothing worse is a risk?

Ann: (After a moment of thought) Yeah.

Therapist: So you don't think there's much chance of them attacking you or anything?

Ann: Nah, they wouldn't do that.

Therapist: If they do keep dropping things and making noises, how bad will that be?

Ann: Like I told you, it's real aggravating. It really bugs me.

Therapist: So it would continue pretty much as it has been going for years now.

Ann: Yeah it bugs me, but I can take it.

Therapist: And you know that if it keeps happening, at the very least you can keep handling it the way you have been, holding the aggravation in, then taking it out on your husband when you get home. . . . Suppose we could come up with some ways to handle the aggravation even better or have them get to you less, is that something you'd be interested in?

Ann: Yeah, that sounds good.

Therapist: Another risk you mentioned earlier was that they might talk to your supervisor and turn her against you. As you see it, how long have they been trying to do this?

Ann: Ever since I've been there.

Therapist: How much luck have they had so far in doing that?

Ann: Not much.

Therapist: Do you see any indications that they're going to have any more success now than they have so far?

Ann: No, I don't guess so.

Therapist: So your gut reaction is as though the situation at work is really dangerous. But when you stop and think it through, you conclude that the worst they're going to do is to be really aggravating and that even if we don't come up with anything new, you can handle it well enough to get by. Does that sound right?

Ann: Yeah, I guess so!

Therapist: And if we can come up with some ways to handle the stress better or handle them better, there will be even less they can do to you.

Obviously this interchange alone was not sufficient to transform Ann dramatically, but following this session she reported a noticeable decrease in vigilance and stress at work. Additional interventions focusing on re-evaluating perceived threats, on stress management and assertion, and on improving marital communication resulted in rapid improvement. According to her husband's report as well as her own, she continued to be somewhat guarded and vigilant but no longer overreacted to minor provocations, was able to be assertive rather than hostile, and no longer exploded at her husband as a result of aggravations at work.

Gary's Paranoid Personality Disorder was not recognized until the seventh session of Cognitive Therapy that up to that point, had focused on coping with chronic stress and anxiety. By that point, successful stress-management interventions had already raised his sense of self-efficacy substantially. It was possible to further boost his sense of self-efficacy by helping him to reevaluate his perfectionistic, dichotomous standards for himself. He had previously assumed that if one were truly competent, one would handle situations without any stress or difficulty, and therefore he assumed that if he experienced any distress, this showed that he was incompetent. A reevaluation of these beliefs led him to conclude that his ability to handle difficult situations well despite considerable stress and anxiety was actually a sign of his capabilities rather than being a sign of incompetence. His shift from a dichotomous view of competence to a continuous one enabled him to set more manageable standards for himself and thus experience more frequent successes. Following these increases in his sense of self-efficacy, he was much more willing to disclose thoughts and feelings, to look critically at his beliefs and assumptions, and to test new approaches to problem situations. This made it possible to use standard cognitive techniques with greater effectiveness.

One intervention that had a particularly strong impact was using the continuum technique (Chapter 3) to challenge his dichotomous view of trustworthiness. Once he delineated the behaviors that he saw as being characteristic of truly trustworthy and completely untrustworthy individuals and considered whether his acquaintances completely fit into one category or the other, it became clear that few people actually fell at either extreme. However, because Gary had little idea of how to determine how trustworthy a particular individual might be or of how to deal with persons who were at intermediate levels of trustworthiness, it was necessary to introduce the idea that he could learn which persons were likely to prove trustworthy by noticing how well they followed through when trusted on trivial issues and then could choose whether to risk trusting them on more important issues. When this was followed by raising the question of whether his (consistently malevolent) family was typical of people in general, he was able to gradually risk trusting colleagues and acquaintances in small things and was pleasantly surprised to discover that the world at large was much less malevolent than he had believed.

Concurrently with these cognitive interventions, it is important to work to modify the client's dysfunctional interpersonal interactions so that the client no longer provokes hostile reactions from others that would seem to confirm his or her paranoid views. In Gary's case, this required focusing on specific problem situations that arose and both addressing the cognitions that blocked appropriate assertion and working to help him develop adequate skills in assertion and clear communication. The resulting improvements in his relationships with colleagues and his relationship with his girlfriend helped him recognize the ways in which his previous interaction style had inadvertently provoked hostility from others. The improvements in interpersonal interactions also supported his new belief that the world contained benevolent and indifferent people as well as malevolent ones.

Toward the close of therapy, it was possible to "fine-tune" Gary's new perspective on people and new interpersonal skills by working to help him develop an increased ability to understand the perspectives of others and to empathize with them. This was done through asking questions that focused on anticipating the impact of his actions on others, considering how he would feel if the roles were reversed, or infering the thoughts and feelings of the other person from his or her actions, and then examining the correspondence between his answers and the available data. Initially he found these questions difficult to answer and was often off the mark, but as he received feedback both from the therapist and from subsequent interactions, his ability to accurately understand the other person's perspective increased steadily. He found that aggravating actions by others were not necessarily motivated by malicious intentions and that these actions were less aggravating when he could understand the other person's point of view.

At the close of therapy Gary was noticeably more relaxed and was bothered by mild symptoms of stress and anxiety only at times when many people experience mild symptoms, such as immediately before major examinations. He reported being much more comfortable with friends and colleagues, was socializing more actively, and seemed to feel no particular need to be vigilant. When he and his girlfriend began having difficulties, due in part to her discomfort with the increasing closeness in their relationship, he was able to suspend his initial feelings of rejection and desire to retaliate long enough to consider her point of view. Then he was able to take a major role in resolving their difficulties by clearly communicating his understanding of her concerns, his own fears and doubts, and his commitment to their relationship.

Conclusions

The authors' clinical experience in working with individuals with Paranoid Personality Disorder has been quite promising. The interventions—increasing self-efficacy, seeing trustworthiness as a continuum, learning a more assertive approach to interpersonal conflicts, and developing an increased awareness of the other person's point of view—are all changes that would be expected to have broad intrapersonal and interpersonal impacts. It appears that major "personality change" can occur as a result of Cognitive Therapy with these clients, but at this point we do not have the follow-up data that would be needed to determine how well the improvements generalize and persist.

Schizoid Personality Disorder

The diagnosis of Schizoid Personality Disorder is probably one of the most confusing of the Axis II diagnoses. The construct or label *schizoid* has been a diagnostic category that has been in transition for almost 100 years. The original use of the term *schizoid* can be traced to Manfred Bleuler of the Swiss Burgholzi Clinic (Siever, 1981). It is composed of the prefix *schizo* from the Greek word meaning *cleaving* or *splitting* and the suffix *oid* that means "like or representing." Traditionally, the schizoid was seen as an individual who was quiet, shy, and reserved and was schizophreniclike (Kraeplin, 1913). In reviewing historical conceptions of schizoid individuals, Siever (1981) cites several authors who saw the schizoid behavior as part of the schizophrenic process and a precursor to schizophrenia. Alternatively, Campbell (1981) argues that the schizoid behavior can represent either a chronic vulnerability to a schizophrenic process that may be genetically dictated or can be due to a partial recovery from schizophrenia. He utilizes the traditional definition when he states that the schizoid personality disorder resembles "the division, separation, or split of the personality that is characteristic of schizophrenia" (p. 563).

Kretschmer (1936) described a number of subtypes of schizoid personality. Some were stiff, formal, and correct in social situations, indicating a keen awareness of social requirements. Others were isolated and eccentric, either not caring about social conventions or being unaware of them. Still others appeared fragile, delicate, and hypersensitive. In Kretchmer's view, the schizoid diagnosis was not necessarily synonymous with disability. The schizoid personality could be very creative in occupations that allowed for solitary work. More frequently, the schizoid was employed at simple jobs that were below his or her level of ability. A number of early studies examined the premorbid adjustment of schizophrenics and found that a premorbid schizoid adjustment was prognostically related to the severity of the schizophrenic illness and a poorer chance of a favorable outcome, though it was not necessarily a precursor to schizophrenia (Frazee, 1953; Gittleman-Klein & Klein, 1969; Longabaugh & Eldred, 1973; Mellsop, 1972, 1973; Morris, Soroker, & Burrus, 1954; Roff, Knight, & Wertheim, 1976).

The view of schizoid individuals presented in the past three editions of the *Diagnostic and Statistical Manual of Mental Disorders* differs markedly from the traditional view. Here, Schizoid Personality Disorder is not seen as a precursor to an eventual movement into schizophrenia but rather the schizoid individual is seen as chronically reclusive and isolated. In both DSM-III and DSM-III-R, the schizoid diagnosis has been separated from another diagnostic group, the schizotypal group that is seen as more closely related to the schizophrenic disorders (Baron 1983; Kendler & Gruenberg, 1982) and that will be discussed later in this chapter.

In DSM-II (APA, 1965), schizoid was defined as follows:

> This behavior pattern manifests shyness, oversensitivity, seclusiveness, avoidance of close or competitive relationships, and often eccentricity. Autistic thinking without loss of capacity to recognize reality is common, as are daydreaming and the inability to express hostility and ordinary aggressive feelings. These patients react to disturbing experiences and conflicts with apparent detachment. (p. 42)

In DSM-III (APA, 1980) and most recently, DSM-III-R (APA, 1987), the diagnostic criteria have been expanded (Table 17). The basic themes of emotional constriction, aloofness, and lack of desire to form relationships still remain as basic elements of this disorder.

Assessment

Schizoid individuals often appear odd or eccentric, and their solitary behavior in the midst of a generally sociable milieu stands out in sharp relief. However, although these individuals may be noticed by their neighbors and labeled as *strange*, the clinician who is assessing a client often will not have access to data about the client's social behavior other than that which he or she observes within the session. Schizoid individuals gener-

TABLE 17. DSM-III-R Criteria for Schizoid Personality Disorder

A. A pervisive pattern of indifference to social relationships and a restricted range of emotional experience and expression, beginning by early adulthood and present in a variety of contexts, as indicated by at least four of the following:
  1. Neither desires nor enjoys close relationships, including being part of a family
  2. Almost always chooses solitary activities
  3. Rarely, if ever, claims or appears to experience strong emotions, such as anger or joy
  4. Indicates little if any desire to have sexual experiences with another person (age being taken into account)
  5. Is indifferent to the praise and criticism of others
  6. Has no close friends or confidants (or only one) other than first-degree relatives
  7. Displays constricted affect, e.g., is aloof, cold, rarely reciprocates gestures or facial expressions, such as smiles or nods
B. Occurrence not exclusively during the course of Schizophrenia or a Delusional Disorder.

ally do not seek treatment of their own volition and often do not describe substantial problems when interviewed. Often those individuals come to the attention of mental health professionals when their behavior is noticed by physicians, employers, or family members. These persons are likely to be concerned because the client seems unusual, avoids interactions with staff, co-workers, and others, avoids relating personal information, and generally is nonresponsive in group settings. As is the case with the other personality disorders, even when schizoid individuals do seek treatment, they do not generally seek to change their schizoid way of dealing with the world. These individuals usually present complaints of depression, anxiety, somatic problems, or vague, general dysphoria.

Schizoid individuals may function well in settings where a preference for social isolation is acceptable or is actually an asset. In occupational settings that encourage or require working in isolation such as computer work, typing, or research, these individuals may be very successful. For example:

Evan, aged 37, was a graduate of a prestigious law school and a partner in a large law firm. He sought therapy for a mild depression after his medical doctor recommended doing so. His position in his law firm was centered around his being a research expert and drafter of briefs for the other partners. He would be given a legal problem to deal with, would utilize library and computer search facilities to investigate the relevant cases, and then write a brief for other attorneys to use. He rarely attended office parties, had no friends in the office, and could generally be counted on to work evenings and weekends.

As can be seen from Table 17, one of the key factors in assessing Schizoid Personality Disorder is the individual's isolated life-style. The diagnostician is often faced with a question of whether a client is schizoid or avoidant, because both share the common threads of difficulty in interpersonal relationships and an avoidance of contact with others. In both disorders, the problems begin by the early adult years and are pervasive in a variety of life contexts. A lively debate regarding the similarities and differences between these diagnoses has been conducted (Livesley, West, & Tanney, 1986; Millon, 1986; Reich, 1987a). The DSM-III-R criteria agree with the view advocated by Millon, treating the disorders as quite different. Millon (1981) differentiates the reasons for the asocial behavior of the asocial individual (schizoid) and the withdrawn individual (avoidant). When the schizoid individual observes others in social situations, he or she can acknowledge that other people choose to affiliate with each other but cannot understand why they do so and personally feels no desire to socialize. The avoidant individual, on the other hand, sees others in social situations and would very much like to join them. The following clinical vignette illustrates the schizoid response:

Alan, a 38-year-old draftsman, came for therapy because of his depression. He had worked in the same company for the past 7 years and shared a workspace with 6 other men. When asked whether he had friends at work, he said, "No, I'm not friends with them. We work together." In fact, he did not even speak with them during the day. The other men shared a coffee pot and would contribute periodically for coffee, sugar, etc. Alan had his own pot. His drafting table faced a wall, and he insisted that the other men call him by his family name. When asked why he insisted on the title "Mr.," he responded, "We're not friends, we just work together." In point of fact, Alan had no friends. One of the therapeutic recommendations was for Alan to participate in a group. He asked why, and the therapist explained about the advantages of getting feedback from others, practicing social skills, and simply being social. Alan looked quite bewildered and asked, "Why would I want to do those things?"

Conceptualization

The social isolation and emotional constriction of the schizoid seem to follow directly from a lack of positive thoughts about closeness coupled with positive thoughts about being alone. Typical views expressed by schizoid clients include: "There are few reasons to be close to people." "I am my own best friend." "Stay calm, displays of emotion are unnecessary and embarrassing." "What others say is of little interest or importance to me." "Sex is okay, but just for release." For example:

Dan, a 66-year-old retired chemist, came for therapy because of his reported high level of anxiety. His Beck Anxiety Inventory score at intake was 33. He had never married but was presently dating a woman he had dated for the past 8 years. He would see her once a week on a Saturday night. They would have dinner in a restaurant, see a movie, and then go to her home and have sex. Dan would then go home. When asked why he did not ever have dinner at her home, stay over at her home after sex, or stay at her home and watch television, he said, "Why stay over? I did what I came for. That's pretty funny, what I *came* for".

Dan described himself as "low keyed" and stated, "I never get angry." The therapeutic goals with Dan were first to lower his anxiety and then to explore his avoidance or lack of understanding as to why people spend time together. He came for weekly therapy sessions and seemed to respond positively to the sessions but did not show much emotional involvement. When the therapist informed Dan of the therapist's impending vacation, in a month, Dan replied, "So what! You deserve a vacation. Why tell me at all? We just won't schedule any appointments for those days." The therapist said that he wanted to tell Dan early enough so that any reactions to the therapist's absence could be talked over. Dan replied, "I don't understand. If you're away, you're away. What is that to me?"

The schizoid client's expressed view is that there is no point to social interaction, and this lack of motivation for social interaction, in combination with the subsequent low frequency of social interaction, is sufficient to explain the primary characteristics of the disorder. The schizoid typically denies having any desire for close relationships and denies having any significant fears of close relationships. Despite this, it is tempting to hypothesize that both a desire for closeness and fears regarding closeness are present but are being suppressed. However, it is not at all clear whether this is the case or not.

Although it is difficult to judge the accuracy of clients' reports of their history, it is interesting to note that, when historical information can be obtained, schizoid clients often report experiences that could contribute to a neutral or negative view of interpersonal closeness and a positive view of social isolation. In Dan's case:

Dan reported that when he was 2 years old, his mother became quite ill with tuberculosis and was sent to a sanitarium for 2 years. She returned home for several months and then had to return to the sanitarium where she died a year later. During his mother's illness, he lived with his maternal grandmother. After his mother's death, he continued to live with his grandmother until age 6 or 7. At that time, his father remarried, and Dan had to return to live with his father and stepmother. He did not want to leave his grandmother and barely knew his father. Dan's lack of a family feeling and his difficulty in seeing himself as connected with others probably stemmed from these early unsuccessful affiliation experiences. Through childhood, adolescence, and his young adult years, he avoided relationships. In Dan's case, a major assumption was "Getting attached to people is not a good idea. They'll probably leave me."

Intervention Strategies and Techniques

From the conceptualization presented here, it is obvious that a major goal of intervention with schizoid individuals is to establish or increase positive views of social interaction and personal closeness and to reduce positive views of social isolation. This need not be done primarily through verbal interventions. The therapist can use the therapeutic relationship as a prototype for other interpersonal relationships as well as working to increase the client's range and frequency of interpersonal interactions outside the session.

The schizoid individual may not enter therapy with any strong interest in altering his or her manner of relating to other people. Therefore, the initial goals of treatment need to focus on the client's presenting problems. As the client and therapist work on the explicit presenting problems, the therapist can begin to make the nature of the schizoid adjustment pattern explicit, pointing out some of the advantages and disadvantages of this pattern and showing how this adaptation effects the presenting problems.

Schizoid clients typically show little understanding of interpersonal relationships and may have quite poor social skills. The therapist working with the schizoid client may find him- or herself explaining very basic patterns of human interaction that the client has apparently managed not to observe or experience. At times, it is as though the therapist were explaining human interactions to a Martian, newly arrived on our planet and completely naive about humans. Therapist–client interactions within the session can provide valuable opportunities for the therapist to point out characteristic interaction patterns and to provide the client with feedback regarding his or her impact on others. As the client gradually develops a greater understanding of interpersonal relationships, it is important to also help him or her to master any social skills in which he or she is deficient and to test these new understandings and skills both in interactions with the therapist and in interactions outside of the therapy session.

In using the therapist–client relationship to establish a more positive view of interpersonal relationships and in attempting to broaden the client's social interactions, the therapist must work carefully so as to not have the client's anxiety increase to a point where he or she would choose to leave therapy. Because schizoid clients are usually quite unexpressive, it is particularly important for the therapist to make a point of soliciting feedback from the client on a regular basis as well as being sensitive to nonverbal indications of stress or anxiety.

Although the therapeutic relationship can be very useful in working with schizoid clients, it can also present problems. The therapist may find it difficult to maintain a warm, supportive, empathic stance with an individual who, because of his or her lack of interpersonal involvement, cannot be an equal partner in the therapeutic collaboration. Therapy with these clients can often be frustrating because the therapist is accustomed to having considerable leverage for influencing clients, including the close personal relationship that develops between therapist and client, the client's desire to "get better," the client's desire to please the therapist, and the client's responsiveness to even mild praise or criticism from the therapist. However, with the schizoid client much of this leverage is unavailable. Fortunately, reason is still available as a tool for motivating change. If the therapist clearly presents the rationale for the therapy, the reasons for acting differently, the pros and cons of changing behavior, and the concrete gains that are possible, the schizoid client can be induced to make the necessary changes. However, this can be a slow and tedious process, and it is important for the therapist to be alert for annoyance, resentment, or resignation on his or her part that could impede therapy.

From the beginning, therapy with Dan focused on increasing his interactions with others. He eventually began to spend weekends with his girlfriend, attend her family's functions (weddings, Thanksgiving dinner, Christmas, and funerals) and went away on a 2-week vacation with her. Dan was not opposed to spending time with another person; it was just never something that he ever really understood. Although it was not his first thought or choice, he was able to use self-instructional strategies to help him to be with others. His self-instruction was, "When in doubt, don't be alone." In an attempt to increase Dan's motivation for social interaction, his therapist argued that spending time with his girlfriend would make her happier, and she might then want to make him happier. In discussing the pros and cons of spending more time with his girlfriend, the therapist observed that among other things there was an opportunity for increased sex. Dan did not see the need for the increase. "After all, I can use sex once a week. Why push it?"

At that point, Dan's behavior had been altered, although the underlying assumptions remained the same. With continued interpersonal contacts, the older schemas were gradually modified to include the idea of pleasing others because this would lead to more positive responses from them and the idea of pleasing others simply because it is a nice thing to do.

Conclusions

Our experience with Schizoid Personality Disorder has been less encouraging than our experience with Paranoid Personality Disorder. With persistence, it is possible to improve the client's social skills, increase his or her frequency of social interaction, and decrease their "strangeness." However, they typically continue to be relatively distant and passive in interpersonal relationships, and they seem to develop little capacity for warmth and intimacy.

SCHIZOTYPAL PERSONALITY DISORDER

Individuals with Schizotypal Personality Disorder are definitely "eccentric." As described in DSM-III-R,

> The essential feature of this disorder is a pervasive pattern of peculiarities of ideation, appearance, and behavior and deficits in interpersonal relatedness, beginning by early adulthood and present in a variety of contexts, that are not severe enough to meet the criteria for Schizophrenia. (p. 340)

These are individuals who would be diagnosed as *borderline*, if one were using the term to refer to persons who seem to lie on the border between neurosis and psychosis but do not manifest the characteristics of Borderline Personality Disorder. Other diagnostic labels that have been used to refer to these individuals have included *pseudoneurotic schizophrenia* (Hoch & Polatin, 1949) and *psychotic personality* (Frosch, 1964).

Assessment

The differential diagnosis between Schizotypal Personality Disorder and Schizophrenia is based on an assessment of the severity of the disorder rather than on symptoms that clearly differentiate between the two disorders. As can be seen from Table 18, comparison of the diagnostic criteria for the two disorders reveals broad areas of overlap once the acute psychotic episode has passed, and the distinction between the two seems to depend on subjective judgments regarding the severity of symptoms. It is possible that attempts to clearly differentiate between Schizotypal Personality Disorder and Schizophrenia are unnecessary. Millon writes that this distinction is "one more of nosologic consistency than of substantive discrimination" and goes on to say that

> Since schizotypals ostensibly experience transient psychotic episodes, usually those of a schizophrenic nature, then it would appear that they [Schizotypal Personality Disorder and Schizophrenia: Residual Type] must always coexist multiaxially—except before the schizotypal's first schizophrenic episode. (Millon, 1981, p. 422)

Conceptualization

It has often been assumed that Schizotypal Personality Disorder has much in common with schizophrenia. In particular, the term *schizotypal* is derived from *schizotype*, an abbreviation of *schizophrenic genotype* coined by Sandor Rado (1956), and the theory that this disorder is genetically related to schizophrenia has been popular. Millon (1981) presents a conceptualization of the development of this disorder that integrates genetic, social-learning, and cognitive factors. He suggests that Schizotypal Personality Disorder can be viewed as an extreme form of either Schizoid or Avoidant Personality. This may be due to a learning history that would predispose the individual to the development of one of these two disorders interacting with biological vulnerabilities that further impair development and functioning.

TABLE 18. Comparison of DSM-III-R Criteria for Schizotypal Personality Disorder and Schizophrenia

Schizotypal Personality Disorder

A. A pervasive pattern of deficits in interpersonal relatedness and peculiarities of ideation, appearance, and behavior, beginning by early adulthood and present in a variety of contexts, as indicated by at least five of the following:
   1. Ideas of reference (excluding delusions of reference)
   2. Excessive social anxiety, e.g., extreme discomfort in social situations involving unfamiliar people
   3. Odd beliefs or magical thinking, influencing behavior and inconsistent with subcultural norms, e.g., superstitiousness, belief in clairvoyance, telepathy, or "sixth sense," "others can feel my feelings" (in children and adolescents, bizarre fantasies or preoccupations)
   4. Unusual perceptual experiences, e.g., illusions, sensing the presence of a force or person not actually present (e.g., "I felt as if my dead mother were in the room with me")
   5. Odd or eccentric behavior or appearance, e.g., unkempt, unusual mannerisms, talks to self
   6. No close friends or confidants (or only one) other than first-degree relatives
   7. Odd speech (without loosening of associations or incoherence), e.g., speech that is impoverished, digressive, vague, or inappropriately abstract
   8. Inappropriate or constricted affect, e.g., silly, aloof, rarely reciprocates gestures or facial expressions, such as smiles or nods
   9. Suspiciousness or paranoid ideation

Schizophrenia

A. Presence of characteristic psychotic symptoms in the active phase: either 1, 2, or 3 for at least 1 week (unless the symptoms are successfully treated):
   1. Two of the following:
      (a) Delusions
      (b) Prominent hallucinations (throughout the day for several days or several times a week for several weeks, each hallucinatory experience not being limited to a few brief moments)
      (c) Incoherence or marked loosening of associations
      (d) Catatonic behavior
      (e) Flat or grossly inappropriate affect
   2. Bizarre delusions (i.e., involving a phenomenon that the person's culture would regard as totally implausible, e.g. thought broadcasting, being controlled by a dead person)
   3. Prominent hallucinations [as defined in (1)(b)] of a voice with content having no apparent relation to depression or elation, or a voice keeping up a running commentary on the persons behavior or thoughts, or two or more voices conversing with each other
B. During the course of the disturbance, functioning in such areas as work, social relations, and self-care is markedly below the highest level achieved before the onset of the disturbance (or, when the onset is in childhood or adolescence, failure to achieve expected level of social development).
C. Schizoaffective Disorder and Mood Disorder with Psychotic Features have been ruled out, i.e., if a Major Depressive or Manic Syndrome has ever been present during an active phase of the disturbance, the total duration of all episodes of the mood syndrome has been brief relative to the total duration of the active and residual phases of the disturbance.

(continued)

TABLE 18. (*Continued*)

D. Continuous signs of the disturbance for at least 6 months. The 6-months' period must include an active phase (of at least 1 week, or less if symptoms have been successfully treated) during which there were psychotic symptoms characteristic of Schizophrenia (symptoms in A), with or without a prodromal or residual phase, as defined later.

Prodromal phase: A clear deterioration in functioning before the active phase of the disturbance that is not due to a disturbance of mood or to a Psychoactive Substance Use Disorder and that involves at least two of the symptoms listed later.

Residual phase: Following the active phase of the disturbance, persistence of at least two of the symptoms listed next, these not being due to a disturbance of mood or to a Psychoactive Substance Use Disorder.

Prodromal or residual symptoms
1. Marked social isolation or withdrawal
2. Marked impairment in role functioning as wage earner, student, or homemaker
3. Markedly peculiar behavior (e.g., collecting garbage, talking to self in public, hoarding food)
4. Marked impairment in personal hygiene and grooming
5. Blunted or inappropriate affect
6. Digressive, vague, overelaborate, or circumstantial speech, poverty of speech, or poverty of content of speech
7. Odd beliefs or magical thinking, influencing behavior and inconsistent with cultural norms, e.g., superstitiousness, belief in clairvoyance, telepathy, "sixth sense," "others can feel my feelings," overvalued ideas, ideas of reference
8. Unusual perceptual experiences, e.g., recurring illusions, sensing the presence of a force or person not actually present
9. Marked lack of initiative, interests, or energy

Examples: Six months of prodromal symptoms with 1 week of symptoms from A; no prodromal symptoms with 6 months of symptoms from A; no prodromal symptoms with 1 week of symptoms from A and 6 months of residual symptoms.
E. It cannot be established that an organic factor initiated and maintained the disturbance.
F. If there is a history of Autistic Disorder, the additional diagnosis of Schizophrenia is made only if prominent delusions or hallucinations are also present.

Millon (1981) suggests that, in the subtype of Schizoid Personality Disorder he refers to as "schizoid-schizotypals," a relative insensitivity to social stimuli, deficient learning of social attachment behaviors, and learning of a disjointed, unfocused thought style result in an extremely passive, unresponsive interpersonal style. This disengaged interpersonal style is hypothesized to contribute to increasing social isolation that perpetuates the lack of social skills and social attachments. He suggests that these individuals then become increasingly preoccupied with personal fantasy "unchecked by the logic and control of reciprocal social communication and activity" (Millon, 1981, p. 424) and eventually present the full schizotypal picture.

Millon (1981) refers to another subgroup, as "schizotypal-avoidants," who may be genetically predisposed to "muddled" thinking and thus may initially be fearful and easily overwhelmed by stimulation. If this elicits deprecation and humiliation from parents, siblings, and peers, the resulting low self-esteem and avoidance of social interaction results in deficiencies in social skills and continuing avoidance of social interaction. Withdrawal into personal thought and fantasy is seen as a consequence of this cycle. Then, when the individual's tendency toward "muddled" thinking is combined with the lack of corrective feedback from interpersonal interactions, the individual's functioning can easily deteriorate into a schizotypal rather than avoidant pattern.

These conceptualizations are certainly plausible and compatible with a cognitive point of view. Unfortunately, it is not possible to elaborate further on the cognitive aspects of this disorder with any confidence because the combination of the extreme difficulty relating to others coherently and the bizarre thought processes characterizing this disorder greatly complicate the process of identifying specific automatic thoughts and underlying assumptions in the course of therapy.

Intervention Strategies and Techniques

Millon's (1981) view that Schizotypal Personality Disorder can be viewed as an extreme form of Schizoid Personality Disorder or Avoidant Personality Disorder might suggest that the intervention approaches recommended for use with each of those disorders might be useful with schizotypals. However, the preponderance of illogical, "magical" thinking requires a somewhat different approach, at least initially. The major goals in working with these patients are similar to those in working with Schizophrenics, that is, improving social skills (including grooming, interpersonal skills, and generally appearing less peculiar), anxiety reduction, and improving social problem solving. The interventions used in working toward these goals are typically more behavioral than cognitive, focusing on teaching skills rather than monitoring thoughts and developing responses to them (Bellack & Hersen, 1985). Over time, as the client becomes somewhat less peculiar and as interactions with the therapist provide "the logic and control of reciprocal social communication and activity" to which Millon refers, the intervention strategies suggested for use with schizoid and avoidant clients may be quite appropriate.

Conclusions

The bizarre thinking of individuals with Schizotypal Personality Disorder greatly complicates intervention and particularly interferes with the use of purely cognitive interventions. Our experience is that the outcome is similar to that observed with clients with Schizoid Personality Disorder. If the therapist is persistent and active, schizotypal clients can learn to behave in more socially appropriate ways, and their vocational functioning and ability to cope with day-to-day problems can improve substantially. However, they are likely to remain somewhat withdrawn and eccentric.

8

Borderline Personality Disorder

Borderline Personality Disorder is apparently common (APA, 1987, p. 347); it typically produces substantial impairment, and it has been cited as a major cause of negative outcome in psychotherapy (Mays & Franks, 1975). Furthermore, it is a diagnostic category with which many clinicians have limited familiarity and that has received limited attention from authors presenting cognitive-behavioral approaches to psychotherapy. The bulk of the literature on psychotherapy with Borderline Personality Disorder has been based on object-relations theory or other psychoanalytic approaches, and it has been argued that psychoanalytic psychotherapy is the treatment of choice for borderline clients (Kernberg, 1977). Some have asserted that Cognitive Therapy is not effective with this complex, long-standing problem (Rush & Shaw, 1983). However, our clinical experience suggests that, when properly applied, Cognitive Therapy can be effective with Borderline Personality Disorder and may have some distinct advantages over alternative treatment approaches.

ASSESSMENT

The term *borderline* has been used in a variety of ways during its short career as a diagnostic category. It was originally used to refer to clients who presented both "neurotic" and "psychotic" types of symptoms and who were thus seen as falling on the "borderline" between neurotic and psychotic. In common usage, this term often meant "nearly psychotic" or "somewhat psychotic," and it was not unusual to hear some professionals talk of borderline clients who had "gone south of the border," when referring to clients who might be appropriately diagnosed as experiencing a Brief Reactive Psychosis.

With the rise of object-relations theory, many authors began to use the term *borderline* to refer to a particular type of personality organization rather than as a diagnostic category *per se* (e.g., Kernberg, 1975). With this usage of "borderline," an individual could be considered to be borderline if a borderline personality structure was judged to be present, independent of the pattern of symptoms present at the moment. Conversely, an individual presenting a mixture of neurotic and psychotic symptoms would not be considered borderline if his or her personality organization did not correspond to the expected pattern of "poorly integrated identity," "primitive defensive operations," "relatively firm self–object boundaries," and "reasonably intact reality testing" (Bauer, Hunt, Gould, & Goldstein, 1980).

As with many other poorly understood diagnostic categories, the term *borderline* has often been used simply to refer to individuals who do not seem to belong to other diagnostic categories and has therefore functioned as an "unspecified" or "miscellaneous" category. This often results in *borderline* being used to refer to a heterogeneous group of individuals who differ from each other in significant ways. For example, when Grinker, Werble, and Drye (1968) performed a cluster analysis on data from 51 subjects who had been labeled *borderline*, they found four distinct subgroups rather than one group of individuals sharing a core of common characteristics.

Given this mixture of conflicting and overlapping meanings for "borderline," it is not surprising that some of the authors of DSM-III argued that it would be best to drop the term and choose a new label (Millon, 1981, pp. 331–335). Although this idea was not adopted, DSM-III-R provides a new definition of "borderline" in its diagnostic criteria for Borderline Personality Disorder. The DSM-III-R criteria clearly identify a group of individuals who manifest many of the features previously discussed under the label "borderline" and who share many important characteristics. When the term *borderline* is used in this discussion, it will refer to Borderline Personality Disorder as defined in DSM-III-R unless otherwise noted. In comparing the present chapter with other literature regarding psychotherapy with "borderline" clients, it is important to remember that other authors may be referring to quite different groups of clients unless they are explicitly using DSM-III-R criteria. For example, one study found that in a sample previously diagnosed as "Personality Disorder with a Borderline Personality Organization" using structural criteria, only 44% met DSM-III criteria for Borderline Personality Disorder (Hamilton, Green, Mech, Brand, Wong, & Coyne, 1984).

In DSM-III-R, Borderline Personality Disorder is defined as an enduring pattern of perceiving, relating to, and thinking about the environment and oneself in which there are problems in a variety of areas including interpersonal behavior, mood, and self-image. No single feature is invariably present, and variability is one of the hallmarks of Borderline Personality Disorder. Therefore, assessment and diagnosis is more complex than with some of the other diagnostic categories. Using DSM-III-R criteria,

TABLE 19. DSM-III-R Diagnostic Criteria for Borderline Personality Disorder

A pervasive pattern of instability of mood, interpersonal relationships, and self-image, beginning by early adulthood and present in a variety of contexts, as indicated by at least *five* of the
following:
1. A pattern of unstable and intense interpersonal relationships characterized by alternat-
    ing between extremes of overidealization and devaluation
2. Impulsiveness in at least two areas that are potentially self damaging, e.g., spending,
    sex, substance use, shoplifting, reckless driving, binge eating (Do not include suicidal or
    self-mutilating behavior covered in [5])
3. Affective instability: marked shifts from baseline mood to depression, irritability, or
    anxiety, usually lasting a few hours and only rarely more than a few days
4. Inappropriate, intense anger or lack of control of anger, e.g., frequent displays of tem-
    per, constant anger, recurrent physical fights
5. Recurrent suicidal threats, gestures, or behavior, or self-mutilating behavior
6. Marked and persistent identity disturbance manifested by uncertainty about at least two
    of the following: self-image, sexual orientation, long-term goals or career choice, type of
    friends desired, preferred values
7. Chronic feelings of emptiness or boredom
8. Frantic efforts to avoid real or imagined abandonment (Do not include suicidal or self-
    mutilating behavior covered in [5])

diagnosis is based on the presence of at least five of eight categories of
problems (shown in Table 19) as a part of the individual's long term functioning, not simply their presence during a period of acute disturbance.

A recent empirical study of diagnostic criteria for Borderline Personality Disorder (Clarkin, Widiger, Frances, Hurt, and Gilmore, 1983) examined the diagnostic efficiency of each of the criteria used in DSM-III. The
study showed that when the symptoms of identity disturbance and unsta-
ble/intense relationships were both present or when impulsivity, unsta-
ble/intense relationships, and intense/uncontrolled anger appeared together, the probability of the individual meeting diagnostic criteria for
Borderline Personality Disorder was quite high. These two patterns were
characteristic of approximately 80% of the borderline sample.

Clinically, the most striking features of borderlines are the intensity of
their reactions, their changeability, and the great variety of symptoms they
present. They may abruptly shift from a pervasive depressed mood to
anxious agitation or intense anger or may impulsively engage in actions
that they later recognize as irrational and counterproductive. They may
present a problem with obsessive ruminations in one therapy session,
depression in the next session, and a specific phobia in a third session.
They typically present an erratic, inconsistent, unpredictable pattern of
problems that can include their functioning effectively and competently in
some areas of life while encountering dramatic problems in other areas. For
example:

A young woman seen by a trainee was doing quite well as a social work intern in a residential setting for disturbed adolescents and was making better progress on her master's thesis than was her therapist. However, at the end of the day, she would lapse into an immobilizing depression and struggle with impulses to slash herself with broken glass. She reported a long history of excellent academic and vocational performance coexisting with severe problems in her personal life, and the mental health professionals with whom she worked were apparently unaware of the intensity of her problems.

Individuals with Borderline Personality Disorder are not necessarily in constant turmoil and may even experience extended periods of stability, but they typically seek therapy at times of crisis and present a complex and somewhat chaotic clinical picture. The unstable pattern of symptoms can make diagnosis of Borderline Personality Disorder complex. The task is further complicated by the fact that borderline individuals often present with other disorders as well. Millon (1981) reports that borderline clients often manifest Generalized Anxiety Disorder, Panic Disorder, Obsessive-Compulsive Disorder, Somatoform Disorders, Psychogenic Fugue states, Major Depression, Bipolar Disorder, Schizoaffective Disorder, Brief Reactive Psychosis, or additional personality disorders. Clarkin *et al.* (1983) found that even when consensus of three raters on the presence or absence of each of the DSM-III-R criteria was required for diagnosis, 60% of their borderline sample met the criteria for other personality disorders as well. These diagnoses included Paranoid, Schizotypal, Histrionic, Narcissistic, Avoidant, and Dependent Personality Disorders.

With this complex picture, it would be convenient if psychological testing could provide a simple index of Borderline Personality Disorder. Research to date with traditional psychological tests has provided evidence that borderline clients tend to score high on both "neurotic" and "psychotic" scales on the MMPI, especially on Scales 2, 4, 6, 7, and 8 (Widiger, Sanderson, & Warner, 1986), and has provided some support for the hypothesis that borderline individuals tend to perform well on structured tests such as the WAIS while performing poorly and showing signs of thought disorder on unstructured projective tests. However, no simple "borderline profile" has been identified. Traditional psychological testing can provide information that is useful in identifying clients with Borderline Personality Disorder, but its value depends on the skill with which it is interpreted.

A number of measures designed specifically to assess Borderline Personality Disorder are included by Reich (1987b) in his review of instruments measuring personality disorders. These include self-report questionnaires (Bell, 1981; Edell, 1984; Hurt, Hyler, Frances, Clarkin, & Brent, 1984), personality inventories (Millon, 1982), and structured interviews (Baron, 1981; Frances, Clarkin, Gilmore, Hurt, & Brown, 1984; Kolb &

TABLE 20. Possible Indications of Borderline Personality Disorder

In presenting problems and symptoms
1. A diverse assortment of problems and symptoms that may shift from week to week
2. Unusual symptoms or unusual combinations of symptoms
3. Intense emotional reactions that are out of proportion to the situation
4. Self-punitive or self-destructive behavior
5. Impulsive, poorly planned behavior that is later recognized as foolish, "crazy," or counterproductive
6. Brief periods of psychotic symptoms that meet DSM-III-R criteria for Brief Reactive Psychosis (but that may have been misdiagnosed as schizophrenia)
7. Confusion regarding goals, priorities, feelings, sexual orientation, etc.
8. Feelings of emptiness or void, possibly localized in the solar plexus

In interpersonal relationships
1. Lack of stable intimate relationships (possibly masked by stable nonintimate relationships or relationships that are stable as long as full intimacy is not possible)
2. Tendency to either idealize or denigrate others, perhaps switching abruptly from idealization to denigration
3. A tendency to confuse intimacy and sexuality

In therapy
1. Frequent crises, frequent telephone calls to the therapist, or demands for special treatment in scheduling sessions, making financial arrangements, etc.
2. Extreme or frequent misinterpretations of therapists' statements, intentions, or feelings
3. Unusually strong reactions to changes in appointment time, room changes, vacations, or termination of therapy
4. Low tolerance for direct eye contact, physical contact, or close proximity
5. Unusually strong ambivalence on many issues
6. Fear of change or unusually strong resistance to change

In psychological testing
1. Good performance on structured tests such as the WAIS combined with poor performance or indications of thought disorder on projective tests
2. Elevation of both "neurotic" and "psychotic" MMPI scales or indications of an unusually wide variety of problems

Gunderson, 1980; Perry & Klerman, 1980; Stangl, Pfohl, Zimmerman, Bowers, & Corenthal, 1985). Each shows potential for use in screening but all will need further development and validation before they are ready for clinical use. Thus the clinician cannot rely on any of these new measures to make the diagnosis for him or her.

However, the diagnosis of Borderline Personality Disorder need not be difficult. The DSM-III-R diagnostic criteria are sufficiently clear to permit reliable diagnosis if the clinician considers a diagnosis of Borderline Personality Disorder and obtains the necessary information. For many clinicians, the primary difficulty lies in recognizing when it might be appropriate to consider a diagnosis of Borderline Personality Disorder. Table 20 lists a number of characteristics that often serve as indications of Borderline Personality Disorder. These are not intended as additional diagnostic criteria but may be useful as cues to the clinician to consider the possibility of an undiagnosed personality disorder.

A clinical example may illustrate the complexities involved in correctly diagnosing Borderline Personality Disorder:

Mary, a 30-year-old mother of two, requested treatment for chronic problems with depression, anxiety, isolation, and alienation. She said that she had been depressed her whole life but had first realized that she was depressed about 10 years previously. During the period following her realization that she was depressed, she had sought treatment from five different therapists but had not been helped by psychoanalytic psychotherapy and was frightened of psychotropic medication. As a part of the intake procedure, she was asked to complete the Beck Depression Inventory, the Beck Anxiety Checklist, and the Minnesota Multiphasic Personality Inventory. Her responses indicated that she was severely depressed, that she experienced frequent periods of intense anxiety, and that she was uncomfortable in social situations. The psychological testing results alone indicated that she was likely to have a strongly negative self-image, unrealistically high standards for herself, and difficulty expressing anger or acting assertively, and suggested a diagnosis of Major Depression.

In the initial therapy session, we discussed her goals and priorities, and between the first and second sessions she developed the list of goals and priorities shown in Table 21. This list reveals several types of anxiety disorder (Panic Disorder with Agoraphobia, possible Social Phobia, possible Obsessive-Compulsive Disorder) as well as difficulty trusting others, low stress tolerance, difficulty handling anger adaptively, and confusion over her sexual orientation. In the second session, she reported serious suicidal impulses resulting from a complex marital conflict. In the third session, she was extremely confused over whether to leave her husband, whether to return to her previous therapist, and whether to ask for medication and was pleading for someone to take care of her. Within 2 months, these issues had largely been resolved, and she was preoccupied with panic attacks elicited by a planned trip to Jamaica.

Although Mary's intake interview and her MMPI scores suggested a diagnosis of Major Depression, it was clear within the first few sessions that she also manifested many features of Borderline Personality Disorder. She presented a wide range of problems, had difficulty choosing her goals, and her goals and problems varied from week to week. Her emotional reactions were intense, changeable, and tended to switch from one extreme to another. She described a very difficult childhood, periods of impulsive behavior, and an apparent psychotic period following recreational drug use. She had a long history of uneven performance and continued to do well in graduate school despite periods of personal and marital crisis.

It is common for symptoms of a Borderline Personality Disorder to become apparent only gradually. In a problem-focused therapy approach such as Cognitive Therapy, it is possible for such a personality disorder to go unrecognized for an extended period of time. This is because the indi-

TABLE 21. Problem/Goal List (in order of priority)

A1. The anxiety symptoms are driving me nuts. I want them gone before the problems have been solved!

1. I feel my mental/emotional problems are so severe they will never be resolved. . . . I fear and believe I'm beyond help.
2. There's nobody I trust completely to help me if I'm ever unable to help myself . . . this causes me terrible anxiety and hostility.
3. I'd like to feel less isolated, alienated, alone and unique . . .
4. I'm very ambivalent about having a third child. . . . I'd like to resolve this dilemma once and for all.
5. I'm terrified of the idea of being "out of control." I'd like to be able to . . . risk lessening control.
6. I suffer from agoraphobic symptoms at times. . . . I'd like . . . to put an end to them.
7. I want to be able to display hurt and anger better instead of withdrawing into a shell. The only people in the world to whom I can express affection freely . . . are my children. I'd like to feel more comfortable being demonstrative.
8. I want to find better ways of dealing with my negative feelings about my mother . . .
9. I feel the majority of my life's energies and talents are going to waste because I spend so much time worrying . . .
10. I'd like to examine my "God/shit" complex—sometimes feelings superior to others, other times feeling so inferior . . .
11. The more I respect, admire, or care about a particular couple, the more anxious I get going out socially with them.
12. I'm really obsessive/compulsive. As soon as one obsession disappears, I must immediately have something else to obsess about.
13. I have this nagging fear that something awful will happen to one of my children.
14. I want to define what I can realistically expect of myself as a parent and become comfortable with that.
15. I worry, if I begin to feel close to another female, that my feelings could be sexual.
16. I'm so perfectionistic that I'm perpetually frustrated, disappointed, or afraid to risk failure. But I'm also afraid of success beyond a certain point.
17. I become overwhelmed by tight, demanding schedules—getting almost unbearably hyper.

vidual's relationship history, his or her characteristic ways of handling anger, or whether or not he or she has a clear sense of identity may not be discussed in detail unless they seem related to the treatment goals. Mary was unusual in that her intelligence, verbal fluency, and insights gained through years of psychoanalytic therapy allowed her to present the salient issues much more clearly and concisely than is often the case.

CONCEPTUALIZATION

The most widely known conceptualizations of Borderline Personality Disorder have been based on object-relations theory or other contemporary psychoanalytic approaches (e.g., Guntrip, 1969; Kernberg, 1977; Masterson, 1978). Unfortunately, the vocabulary used in these analyses renders these conceptualizations inaccessible to many clinicians who are not fluent in psychoanalytic terminology.

It appears that, when translated into cognitive-behavioral terminology, the core of the object-relations view is: The borderline individual holds extreme, poorly integrated views of relationships with early caregivers and, as a result, holds extreme, unrealistic expectancies regarding interpersonal relationships. These expectancies are seen as consistently shaping both behavior and emotional responses. It is assumed that the most appropriate way to resolve this situation is to conduct therapy in such a way that these expectancies will be manifested in an intensely emotional relationship with the therapist where they may be resolved through the application of psychoanalytic techniques.

Millon (1981) provides a competing view based on social learning theory in which he attributes a central role to the borderline individual's lack of a clear, consistent sense of his or her own identity. He argues that this lack of a clear sense of identity includes a lack of clear, consistent goals and results in poorly coordinated actions, poorly controlled impulses, and a lack of consistent accomplishment. In addition, he suggests that as a result of unstable or unsure identities, borderlines become dependent on others for protection and reassurance and become vulnerable to separation from these sources of support. He asserts that this situation is complicated by intense conflicts regarding dependency and assertion and by their realization that their anger over being trapped by dependency could result in their losing the security they gain from dependency.

Although these two theoretical approaches focus on aspects of the borderline experience that are widely considered to be important, only limited attention has been paid to the cognitive aspects of Borderline Personality Disorder. A cognitive perspective can make important contributions to the treatment of Borderline Personality Disorder. Not only can examination of the content of clients' thoughts in specific situations make apparently extreme responses much more comprehensible, but, more importantly, an understanding of the cognitive distortions and basic assumptions common among borderlines can form a basis for a conceptualization that permits a strategic approach to intervention.

Borderlines are notorious for their intense emotional reactions and abrupt mood swings. Mary, the depressed mother of two previously discussed, initially did well in therapy, but when her depression had subsided substantially and she had been doing reasonably well for several weeks, she arrived for her weekly appointment having suddenly become quite agitated and suicidal. It turned out that her husband had suggested that they take a vacation in Jamaica; she had begun experiencing panic attacks thinking about it and had decided that no matter what she did, she was doomed to have her marriage break up and consequently lose her husband and children. Fortunately she had completed a "thought sheet" regarding

Daily Record of Automatic Thoughts		
Situation Briefly describe the situation	**Emotion(s)** Rate 0–100%	**Automatic Thought(s)** Try to quote thoughts then rate your belief in each thought 0–100%
Thinking about trip to Jamaica	Scared 100% Anxious 100% Guilty 100% Pessimistic 75% Inadequate 75% Hopeless 75%	It will be just like it always is; I'll spend all the time till we go away being afraid of "freaking out", when we actually go, my fears will become a self-fulfilling prophecy, & I'll ruin the vacation for both of us. 100% I'm scared to death of the incapacitating, all-consuming panic attacks I've always had before on vacations. I want to avert them, but I don't think I'll be able to. 100% I'm tired of being an emotional cripple, but I don't think I'll ever be better. 100% I feel so guilty about going away – first because we can have this vacation & others can't; second, because I'm going some place other than to visit my parents. 100%

FIGURE 13. Example thought sheet from Mary, a borderline client.

her reaction to the proposed vacation, seen in Figure 13. As you can see, knowledge of her thoughts while anticipating the trip provides a simple explanation of her apparently strange reaction. Further exploration of her expectations regarding the trip made it clear that she was certain that recurrent, inescapable panic attacks would ruin the vacation and inevitably lead to the alienation of her husband and the loss of her husband and children. Because she was also certain that refusing to go to Jamaica would alienate her husband and result in divorce and the loss of her children, she saw the trip to Jamaica as presenting an inescapable catastrophe rather than a pleasant vacation.

One particular distortion, which Beck refers to as "dichotomous thinking," is particularly common among borderlines and contributes substantially to the extreme reactions and mood shifts characteristic of these clients. Dichotomous thinking is the tendency to evaluate experiences in terms of mutually exclusive categories (e.g., good or bad, flawless or defective, love or hate) rather than seeing experiences as falling along continua. The end result of this "black-or-white" thinking is to force extreme interpretations on relatively neutral events. Because there is no neutral category, only a choice between two extreme categorizations, persons and events are necessarily evaluated in extreme terms. These extreme evaluations are then accompanied by extreme emotional responses and extreme actions. In addition, dichotomous thinking leads to abrupt shifts in mood and behavior because the absence of intermediate categories means that when the individual's perception of a situation changes, it necessarily changes from one extreme to another. In dichotomous thinking, a person who is believed to be trustworthy is seen as completely trustworthy until the first time he or she falls at all short of expectations; then he or she suddenly is seen as completely untrustworthy. The idea that a person might be trustworthy *most of the time* or might be *fairly* trustworthy would be incompatible with dichotomous thinking.

The borderline individual also holds basic assumptions that play a central role in the disorder. In Mary's case, as with many other borderline clients, three key basic assumptions were uncovered: "The world is dangerous and malevolent," "I am powerless and vulnerable," and "I am inherently unacceptable." These assumptions have an important impact on the borderline's cognition and behavior.

Viewing the world as a dangerous place in which one is relatively powerless has important consequences. It leads directly to the conclusion that it is dangerous to relax vigilance, to take risks, to reveal one's weakness, to be "out of control," to be in a situation where one cannot escape easily, and so on. Not only does this result in chronic tension and anxiety, but vigilance for signs of danger results in the individual's noticing many apparent signs of danger and thus tends to perpetuate the view of the world as a dangerous place.

Some persons who view the world as a dangerous, malevolent place feel able to rely on their own strengths and abilities in dealing with it (and develop a paranoid pattern), but the borderline's belief that he or she is weak and powerless blocks this alternative. Other persons who see themselves as not being capable of dealing effectively with the risks presented by daily life are able to resolve this dilemma by becoming dependent on someone whom they see as capable of taking care of them (and develop a dependent pattern). However, the borderline's belief that he or she is inherently unacceptable leads to the conclusion that dependence entails a serious risk of rejection, abandonment, or attack. The borderline individual therefore faces quite a dilemma, convinced that he or she is relatively helpless in a hostile world with no easy source of security.

The combination of dichotomous thinking coupled with the borderline's basic assumptions is particularly potent. We all recognize that the world presents risks and threats, but dichotomous thinking results in the world's being seen as deadly. We all have our faults and shortcomings, but the borderline's dichotomous categorization of people as either "okay" or "not okay" leads to the conclusion that he or she is irrevocably "not okay" and must hide this fact from others in order to be accepted. A desire for closeness and security conflicts with this world view and self-concept; and dichotomous thinking leads easily to this conclusion: "I'll never get what I want. Everything else is pointless."

The dichotomous thinking also creates and perpetuates some of the borderline's conflicts. For example, frustration (or anticipated frustration) of the borderline's desire for closeness and dependency often leads to intense anger, which is seen by the borderline as being so devastating that it would destroy any chance of a close relationship if expressed. However, satisfaction of the desire for closeness and dependency is seen as being intolerably dangerous because, in a hostile world, to be dependent is to be helpless and vulnerable. This intense conflict over dependency and anger would vanish if it were possible for the borderline to take a more moderate view and say, "It would be good to be diplomatic in expressing my dissatisfactions so that this doesn't cause additional problems. . . . Depending on someone opens me to the possibility of being hurt or disappointed, so I should try to use good judgment about whom to depend on and how dependent to be." However, without help, borderlines seem to have great difficulty shifting from dichotomous thinking to thinking in terms of continua.

The final component that seems to play a central role in Borderline Personality Disorder is a weak or unstable sense of identity. Confusion regarding goals and priorities makes it difficult to work consistently and effectively toward long-term goals, especially in the face of abrupt emotional shifts. A low sense of self-efficacy leads to low motivation and low persistence and thus to limited success in the face of adversity. A lack of a clear sense of self makes it difficult to decide what to do in ambiguous situations and also makes it difficult to maintain a clear sense of oneself as separate from the other person in an intimate relationship.

The basic assumptions, dichotomous thinking, and weak sense of identity do not simply each contribute separately to Borderline Personality Disorder. They form a mutually reinforcing and self-perpetuating system that is quite complex. For example, viewing a situation as dangerous may encourage dichotomous thinking; dichotomous thinking can encourage the idea that one is inadequate; and the belief that one is inadequate supports the idea that the situation is dangerous. Similarly, viewing the situation as dangerous discourages risk taking; avoidance of risk taking deprives the individual of the experiences that could serve as a basis for a positive sense of self-efficacy; and a low sense of self-efficacy supports the idea that risk taking should be avoided. The complexity of the resulting pattern can be seen easily when an attempt is made to present it graphically as in Figure 14.

STRATEGIES FOR INTERVENTION

When the "standard" Cognitive Therapy described in Chapter 4 is used with borderline clients, problems soon arise. Establishing a collaborative working relationship requires some degree of trust and intimacy; however, trust and intimacy are major issues for most borderline individuals. Strategic, problem-focused psychotherapeutic approaches such as

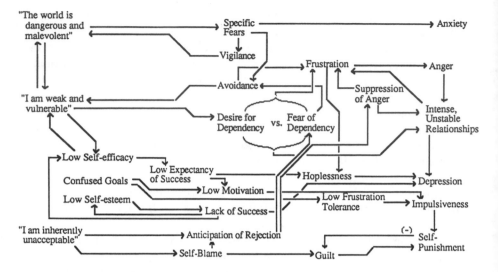

Figure 14. Cognitive conceptualization of borderline personality disorder.

Cognitive Therapy and many other cognitive-behavioral therapies require the therapist and client to agree on specific goals and to maintain a consistent focus on these goals; however, many borderline individuals have great difficulty determining what their goals are, and their priorities may change from week to week. Cognitive-behavioral therapists are generally accustomed to establishing straightforward, businesslike relationships with their clients that minimize transference and other interpersonal complications; however, therapy with borderline individuals necessarily involves working with intense emotional interactions within the therapy session. Cognitive Therapists are oriented toward helping clients change quickly and efficiently, but borderline individuals often fear and resist sudden change. Cognitive Therapy is often seen as a short-term therapy; but borderline individuals often need much more than 10 or 20 weeks of treatment. Therapists who attempt to work with borderline individuals without taking these features into account run the risk of providing an ineffective treatment, having the client terminate therapy prematurely or precipitating a serious crisis (Mays & Franks, 1975; Rush & Shaw, 1983).

In working with borderline clients, it is particularly important to maintain a collaborative, strategic approach based on guided discovery rather than on theoretical preconceptions. Borderline clients often have idiosyncratic cognitions underlying apparently commonplace problems, and interventions based on the therapist's preconceptions can easily miss the mark. When the therapist adopts a guided discovery approach rather than a cookbook approach, the therapist and the client are constantly obtaining new data. This alerts the therapist to any unusual patterns behind apparently ordinary symptoms and provides the information needed for them to select key problems for intervention.

The interpersonal aspects of therapy are much more important with clients who have personality disorders than is usually the case in Cognitive Therapy, and this is particularly true with borderlines. Not only does the borderline client have problems involving interpersonal relationships that are manifested in the client's relationship with his or her therapist, but these problems can arise abruptly and change suddenly and unexpectedly. In addition, the client's strong emotional responses to the therapist, the complexity of the client's problems, and the intensity of the client's responses may elicit strong emotional responses in the therapist that can have an important impact on therapy.

Psychodynamic therapists spend much time discussing the phenomenon of transference, in which the client responds to the therapist on the basis of experiences in previous relationships rather than responding to the therapist's behavior. This is a phenomenon that is not prominent in Cognitive Therapy with many clients but is quite likely with borderline clients. And it can present difficulties for therapists who are not used to dealing with strong emotional responses from their clients. For example:

A 38-year-old medical technician consulted her physician regarding difficulties handling stress, and he began providing biofeedback training. Treatment proceeded uneventfully until the patient suddenly began to experience a strong sexual attraction to her physician and decided she was in love with him. The physician decided he could not continue to work with her, given these feelings, so he had his secretary call the patient to tell her that he could no longer treat her but that his wife would be able to continue the biofeedback training. The patient became increasingly preoccupied with the physician, her behavior became increasingly inappropriate, and she was eventually hospitalized with a Brief Reactive Psychosis.

A more sensitive response on the physician's part might well have averted the psychotic reaction.

"Transference" can be easily understood in cognitive terms as the client's responding to the therapist on the basis of generalized beliefs and expectancies rather than as an individual. In an ambiguous interpersonal situation, such as psychoanalytic psychotherapy, many of the individual's responses are based on his or her beliefs and expectancies because the therapist's behavior is difficult to interpret. An active, directive therapeutic approach such as that used in Cognitive Therapy avoids this situation because the therapist takes a straightforward, unambiguous role. However, this does not completely eliminate these intense emotional responses. This is especially the case with clients, such as borderlines, who are vigilant for any indication that their hopes or fears may be realized. When intense emotional responses do occur, it is essential to deal with them promptly and directly. This is done, first, by developing a clear understanding of what the client is thinking and feeling and then clearing up the misconceptions and misunderstandings directly and explicitly. It is particularly important to make it clear to the client that he or she will be neither exploited nor rejected in therapy.

Borderline clients are particularly likely to experience strong emotional reactions and potential crises at the termination of therapy. This is especially true if it is necessary to terminate therapy before treatment is completed. It is important for the therapist to initiate discussion of the client's expectations, fears, and feelings well in advance of the termination date and to return to this discussion on several occasions even if the client initially insists that termination is not a major concern. Clinical experience suggests that it is often advisable to initiate this process 3 months or more in advance of the anticipated termination date. When terminating therapy because the client's goals have been achieved, it is often quite helpful to taper treatment gradually, moving from weekly appointments to biweekly sessions, then monthly sessions.

Therapists working with borderline clients are likely to discover that, from time to time, interactions with clients elicit in themselves strong emotional reactions ranging from empathic feelings of depression to strong anger, hopelessness, or attraction. It is important for the therapist to be aware of these reactions and to look at them critically so that they do not unduly bias his or her responses. However, far from being an impediment, these feelings can be quite useful if the therapist is able to understand his or her emotional responses to the client. Emotional responses do not occur randomly. If a therapist experiences an unusually strong response to a client, this is likely to be a response to some aspect of the client's behavior, and it may provide valuable information if it can be understood. It is not unusual for a therapist to respond emotionally to a pattern in the client's behavior long before that pattern has been recognized intellectually. Accurate interpretation of emotional responses can speed recognition of these patterns. However, judgment must be exercised in deciding whether to express these emotional reactions. Self-disclosure by the therapist increases the level of intimacy and may be threatening to the client. On the other hand, denial of an emotional response that is apparent to the client from nonverbal cues may decrease trust and encourage the client's fears. Whenever a therapist is having difficulty understanding his or her responses to a client or is uncertain about how to handle them, he or she should consult an unbiased colleague.

Throughout therapy it is advisable for the therapist to strive for a calm, methodical approach and to resist the tendency to respond to each new symptom or crisis as an emergency. Many new symptoms and crises will turn out to be transitory problems that vanish as quickly as they appeared. For those problems that do become the focus of therapy for a period of time, it is important to evaluate the situation in detail before intervening rather than reflexively trying "standard" interventions that may be off the mark. In particular, if the borderline client begins to manifest extreme agitation, signs of thought disorder, or other indications of a Brief Reactive Psychosis, a calm, measured response from the therapist may be sufficient to calm the client and avert the psychotic episode. If it is not possible to prevent the psychosis from developing, this need not be tragic. Although a brief hospitalization may be necessary and psychotrophic medication may be useful, these psychotic reactions rarely produce lasting effects as long as the client and therapist do not decide that this is a sign of "craziness" and give up. Although the symptoms manifested during a Brief Reactive Psychosis may resemble Schizophrenia, a duration of at least 6 months is required for the diagnosis of Schizophrenia, whereas a Brief Reactive Psychosis often lasts only a few days (APA, 1987).

In short, when working with borderline clients, it is particularly important to "stay close to the data" rather than relying on clinical or theoretical preconceptions, to pay close attention to the therapist–client relationship, and to think strategically rather than slipping into a "cookbook" approach. The intensity of the client's emotions (and the therapist's responses) calls for a calm, measured approach and for sufficient therapist self-understanding so that the therapist's responses can be used to facilitate therapy rather than serving as impediments.

Cognitive and Behavioral Techniques

The first problem in Cognitive Therapy with borderline individuals is establishing a collaborative working relationship. The borderline is not foolish enough to trust others simply because they say they can be trusted or because they have a diploma. Trust is most effectively established by using the approach discussed in Chapter 7. This involves acknowledging and accepting the client's difficulty in trusting the therapist, once this becomes evident, and thereafter being careful to behave in a trustworthy manner so as to provide evidence on which trust can be based. It is important for the therapist to exercise more than the usual amount of care in communicating clearly, assertively, and honestly, avoiding misunderstandings, maintaining congruence between verbal statements and nonverbal cues, and following through on agreements. In addition, the therapist will need to be alert for indications that his or her actions are being misinterpreted and to act quickly to clear up misunderstandings. Finally, the therapist should make a point of not pressing clients to take risks in therapy until a sufficient level of trust has been established and making it clear that the client has the option of not talking about sensitive topics until he or she feels ready to do so.

Crises, emergency telephone calls, and requests for special arrangements are common during the early stages of therapy with many borderline clients. Traditionally this behavior has been viewed as a "test" of the therapist's reliability and caring. Although it is not clear that crises early in therapy are intentionally staged as tests of the therapist, they often function as such, and it is important for the therapist to handle emergency phone calls and requests for special treatment effectively if he or she wishes the client to continue in treatment. However, it is not necessarily important for the therapist to agree to the client's requests or encourage midnight telephone calls. It is important for the therapist to consider how far he or she is willing to go in being responsive to the client and for the therapist to be both responsive to the client and to set clear, consistent limits. If the therapist is unresponsive or is inconsistent in setting limits, the client is likely to become angry, terminate therapy abruptly, or become increasingly demanding. If the therapist fails to set suitable limits and begins to resent the client's demands, this resentment is likely to interfere with therapy. It often works well to set a policy of keeping emergency telephone sessions brief and limiting them to crisis intervention and then offering to schedule a therapy session as soon as possible as an alternative to lengthy phone contacts. Also, it is generally advisable for the therapist to make no special arrangements for one client that he or she would not be willing to extend to other clients. Most borderline clients adapt quickly to clear, consistent guidelines, and if a client is not willing or able to accept reasonable limits, he or she is not likely to be able to benefit from the collaborative approach inherent in Cognitive Therapy.

Often a borderline individual's discomfort with intimacy will extend to some aspects of the therapy setting, and subtle aspects of the interpersonal interaction may sometimes elicit intense anxiety in the client. For example:

> After several weeks of therapy, a client hesitantly mentioned that several times in each session she would become intensely anxious for no apparent reason and would have to resist a strong desire to run from the room. As this problem was explored, it gradually became clear that whenever the therapist leaned forward in his chair and made direct eye contact, the level of intimacy became higher than the client could tolerate at that point in therapy.

It may be necessary to limit the amount of direct eye contact, to increase the distance between chairs, and to avoid handshakes, familiarity, or therapist self-disclosure early in therapy in order to avoid excessive discomfort that could impede therapy or lead to premature termination. It can be quite helpful to explicitly involve clients in this process by soliciting their feedback and making it clear that you will seriously consider any suggestions they have for making therapy more comfortable for them. The client's realization that he or she has some control over the seating arrangements, the topics discussed, and so on, in itself renders the intimacy of the therapeutic relationship less threatening by making it clear that the intimacy is not inescapable.

An initial focus on concrete behavioral goals can be very useful in reducing the impact of the borderline's difficulties with intimacy and trust. Most borderline individuals find it less threatening to work on problems for which little introspection is required, where the focus is on behavior rather than on thoughts and feelings. However, this provides an opportunity to build trust and increase their tolerance for intimacy while making demonstrable progress toward their goals and thereby increasing their motivation to persist in therapy.

When working with borderline clients, there is a conflict between being responsive to the client's immediate concerns and maintaining a focused strategic approach. If each session deals with a different issue as the client's concerns and problems shift from week to week, little will be accomplished; but if the therapist unilaterally insists on sticking to a fixed set of goals and priorities, the therapist has abandoned Cognitive Therapy's collaborative approach and risks alienating the client. Cognitive Therapy with borderline individuals calls for greater flexibility than conventional Cognitive Therapy. It may be possible to maintain a consistent focus in therapy either by discussing the pros and cons of maintaining a steady focus or by agreeing to set aside part of the session for the current crises and then use the remainder of the session to work on ongoing goals. However, with some clients, it is necessary to focus on a different immediate crisis each week and to maintain continuity by addressing the issues underlying the immediate crisis. For example, a problem such as failure to anticipate the consequences of one's actions can be manifested in many different problem situations, and consequently it is possible to maintain a consistent focus while responding to a series of different but related problems if the therapist draws attention to the underlying issue.

Both the client's belief that the world is a dangerous place and that he or she is helpless can be gradually challenged through helping the client to test his or her expectancies against previous experience, developing behavioral experiments that can be used to test expectancies, and helping the client to develop new competencies and coping skills. For example, when Mary developed her fear of vacationing in Jamaica, which was presented in Figure 13, it was possible for her therapist to approach this in much the same way as was recommended for working with other clients with Panic Disorder. He worked initially to help her examine her extensive experience with previous panic attacks and realize that her panic attacks were not continuous, that the attacks were not likely to ruin the whole trip, and that although the attacks were intensely unpleasant, they were not dangerous. Over the course of the next several sessions, it was possible to help her to learn to cope more effectively with anxiety and panic attacks through focusing techniques, progressive relaxation training, and related techniques (see Chapter 6). In addition, it was possible to challenge some of the thoughts that contributed to her anxiety, such as her conviction that her husband would leave her if her anxiety ruined the vacation. When the time for the vacation arrived, it was possible to use the vacation itself as a behavioral experiment by planning how to handle the situation, having her state her expectancies clearly before the trip, and then comparing these expectancies with her actual experience on the trip. Mary found that she was able to cope with intense anxiety well enough to prevent panic attacks, was able to have a very good time, and was able to cope effectively with unexpected problems as they arose. As a result, she began to look more skeptically at her tendency to anticipate that new challenges would always turn into disasters because of her incompetence.

Dichotomous thinking is often such a pervasive component of the borderline individual's cognitive functioning that it is difficult for him or her to conceive of thinking in terms of continuous dimensions. However, dichotomous thinking can be challenged effectively by using the continuum technique discussed in Chapter 3. By identifying a clear example of dichotomous thinking, helping the client operationalize his or her definitions of the two extremes, and then testing to see whether the dichotomous view is really consistent with the available evidence, it is possible to demonstrate that dichotomous thinking is neither realistic nor adaptive. With a little practice, borderline clients can become skilled at challenging their own dichotomous thinking, and the frequency of dichotomous thinking gradually declines.

This decrease in dichotomous thinking often results in a decrease in the frequency of sudden mood swings and in the intensity of emotional reactions as the client evaluates problem situations in less extreme terms. In addition, the client can attain even greater control over emotional responses through increasing his or her ability to look critically at thoughts in problem situations, by developing alternative ways to respond to problem situations, and by learning adaptive ways to express emotional responses. Although techniques used in monitoring and challenging thoughts and developing active, assertive responses to problem situations with borderline clients are no different from those used with other clinical groups (Chapter 3), it is particularly important not to rush the borderline client and to be alert for complications. For example, many borderline clients believe that if they express certain feelings, such as anger, they will be immediately rejected or attacked. As a result, they often attempt to suppress any expression of these emotions and are extremely reluctant to consider an active, assertive approach that might include expressing annoyance or mild levels of other problematic emotions. The therapeutic relationship may provide a situation in which the client can experiment with expressing these emotions in safety. The therapist can facilitate this by gently asking

Possible Interventions

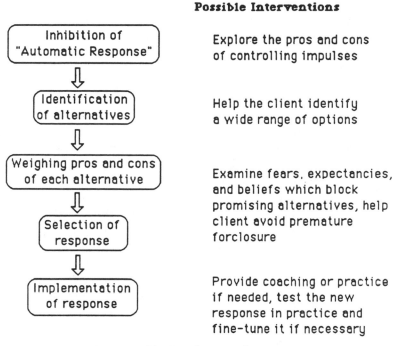

FIGURE 15. The impulse control process.

how the client is feeling when situations occur that might produce annoyance or other unpleasant emotions in the average client and making a
point of explicitly acknowledging and accepting the emotional responses
that the client is willing to express. It is better for the therapist to take
advantage of naturally occurring situations than for him or her to stage
situations in order to elicit feelings because the therapist's genuineness and
honesty is important for maintaining a trusting working relationship.

Impulsive behavior is a very common problem with borderline clients.
Figure 15 shows a series of possible interventions for helping clients develop better impulse control. With borderlines, the first step is to help the
client explore the advantages and disadvantages of impulse control in
order to ensure sufficient motivation. Often the client has had extensive
experience with authority figures who tried to force him or her to be less
impulsive, and he or she may well respond to the idea of improving impulse control with "Why the hell should I?" This can be addressed by
working to help the client to recognize the ways in which it is in his or her
best interest to better control impulses and to realize that the option of
choosing to act on the impulses if he or she wishes to will remain available.
The next step is to examine the cognitions preceding impulsive behavior
and to use self-instructional training (Meichenbaum, 1977), if necessary to

enable the client to inhibit his or her reaction long enough to choose an adaptive option. The therapist may also need to help the client to identify adaptive options and to master the skills needed to use them.

Self-destructive impulsive behavior may be a significant problem for the borderline, and it may be necessary to eliminate this behavior quickly. First, it is important to develop a clear understanding of the motivation for self-destructive behavior by examining the thoughts leading up to the self-destructive impulses or behavior. It is then possible to ask the questions: "What do you want to accomplish through this action? Is there another way to accomplish this which is likely to be more effective or have fewer bad side effects?" If it is possible to identify alternative responses that are more effective and less destructive than the problem behaviors, these can be substituted for the problem behaviors. As a stopgap measure, it is sometimes possible to substitute a minimally self-destructive behavior, such as marking oneself with a marking pen, for a more self-destructive act, such as slashing oneself. This less destructive act can then be replaced with a more adaptive alternative as time allows.

A clearer sense of one's own goals, priorities, competencies, and accomplishments is, to some extent, a side effect of choosing specific goals for therapy and working to adopt an active, assertive approach in dealing with problem situations. However, it is possible to further facilitate the client's development of a clearer sense of identity by helping him or her to identify positive characteristics and accomplishments, by providing positive feedback about good decisions and effective coping, and by helping the client realistically evaluate his or her own actions. It is generally wise to provide feedback in moderation and to avoid effusiveness because borderline clients may be very uncomfortable with positive feedback at first. It is also important for feedback to be honest because unrealistic positive feedback simply lowers the therapist's credibility.

Borderline clients are often quite sensitive to issues of control; and in an active, directive therapy it is quite easy for therapist and client to become locked in a power struggle over agenda setting or homework assignments. It is important to remember that it is very difficult for a client to stage a power struggle if the therapist does not participate actively in it. If the therapist adheres to the collaborative model underlying Cognitive Therapy and allows the client to have a part in developing agendas and homework assignments, is responsive to his or her requests, and is careful to work with the client, power struggles are less likely. It is important to remember that there is no magic to one particular format for monitoring and challenging thoughts, learning to relax, and so on. The therapist may need to use some flexibility in tailoring standard techniques to the individual client's needs and preferences.

When problems with noncompliance do occur, it is rarely productive for the therapist to take a parental role and simply insist that the client do the assignments. Often it is much more productive to explicitly acknowledge that the client has the power to refuse to do whatever he or she wishes but then to explore with the client the pros and cons of choosing to do homework versus choosing not to do it. If the rationale behind the assignment is clear and the clients recognize that they are choosing to do it, not being forced to do it, then there is much less chance of problems with noncompliance. If noncompliance persists, exploration of the client's thoughts at moments when he or she decides not to do the homework should be useful in identifying additional issues that need to be addressed.

One factor that often contributes to problems with noncompliance and that can also produce increased distress during therapy or lead to premature termination is fear of change. Because borderlines typically assume that the world is a dangerous place and often have a low tolerance for ambiguity, it is not surprising that they often find change, even change for the better, to be quite threatening. When persons are in a dangerous situation (or one that they view as dangerous), they have a tendency to rely on their usual coping responses because they realize that trying novel solutions involves risking failure and increases their uncertainty about the outcome. The borderline client's usual coping responses may be quite unsatisfactory, but at least they are familiar, and the outcomes are predictable. Trying a new response involves taking a step into the unknown, and even if the client is intellectually convinced that the proposed change will be a change for the better, he or she is likely to experience a significant amount of anxiety If the fear of change is not recognized and discussed, the client may interpret this anxiety as a sign that the change really is dangerous and become quite opposed to it.

The borderline client's fear of change can be reduced to some extent by addressing it openly when it becomes apparent and by examining the risks involved in trying new responses in this particular situation. However, it is generally necessary to be careful to make changes in a series of small steps and not to press for change too quickly. Therapists often experience a desire to "go for the kill" when they see an opportunity to make a dramatic intervention that could produce a sudden change; however, with borderline clients, it is generally better to err on the side of caution. It is much easier to work with a client who sees gradual change and is eager to continue than it is to work with a client who is terrified by sudden changes and is reluctant to continue therapy. Clients can be valuable guides in pacing therapy if the therapist solicits their feedback and is attentive to signs of increased distress or reluctance. Fear of change can be intensified by the client's assuming that therapy will end as soon as the problems are overcome, and he or she may fear an abrupt abandonment by the therapist. When such fears are present, it is important to make it clear to the client that therapy will not be terminated abruptly in any case, and that termination will be a joint decision based on many considerations, only one of which is the client's improvement.

CONCLUSION

Working with borderline clients is more complex than working with clients with isolated problems of depression or anxiety, and it takes longer. However, it is often possible to not only alleviate clients' anxiety or depression but also help them to gradually resolve long-standing problems such as identity confusion and inability to maintain stable intimate relationships. Because no follow-up studies have been done, we cannot be certain that these improvements persist. However, clients maintain these improvements over a gradual "tapering-off" period at the close of therapy, and it seems likely that clients who receive adequate preparation for dealing with future problems would be able to maintain the improvements achieved in therapy.

To date, no empirical research has been done either in the cognitions of borderline individuals or on the outcome of Cognitive Therapy with borderline clients, although it has been reported that such research is in progress (Linehan, 1987b). It goes without saying that such research is needed and that it will not be possible to adequately test the theoretical analysis and treatment approach here until such data have been collected. However, the experiences of clinicians who have used Cognitive Therapy with borderline clients suggests that it can be quite effective if skillfully applied.

It appears that Cognitive Therapy may have significant advantages over the leading treatment alternative—psychoanalytic psychotherapy. First, because psychoanalytic psychotherapy for Borderline Personality Disorder is a transference-based treatment that does not focus on treating specific symptoms (Kernberg, 1977), Cognitive Therapy typically produces improvement in important symptoms much more quickly. Second, psychoanalytic authorities on the treatment of Borderline Personality Disorder report that therapy typically requires 5 to 7 years (Masterson, 1982), whereas cognitive therapists more commonly report completing treatment in 1½ to 2½ years. Cognitive Therapy with borderline clients is not at all quick and easy, but it shows promise of proving an effective treatment approach that is more efficient than the currently available alternatives.

9

Histrionic Personality Disorder

The use of the term *hysteria* has varied widely over its 4,000-year-history and has often been a source of controversy (Vieth, 1977). Hysteria has at times been used to refer to conversion disorder, Briquet's syndrome, a personality disorder, and a personality trait. Perhaps most commonly, it has been used pejoratively to describe hyperexcitable female clients who are difficult to treat. The concept of hysteria has been strongly rejected by feminists who view it as a sexist label due to the denigrating use of the term *hysterical* to discount the problems presented by the female client. Perhaps as an attempt to reduce the confusion regarding the use of the term *hysteria*, the American Psychiatric Association does not include hysteria in DSM-III-R. Instead, separate categories of Somatization Disorder, Conversion Disorder, Hypochondriasis, Dissociative Disorders, and Histrionic Personality Disorder have been designated.

This chapter will focus on the treatment of people who fit the DSM-III-R criteria for Histrionic Personality Disorder (Table 22), a disorder that is most similar to the previous classification of hysterical personality. According to DSM-III-R (APA, 1987, p. 348),

> The essential feature is a pervasive pattern of excessive emotionality and atten-
> tion seeking, beginning by early childhood and present in a variety of contexts.

These clients are lively, dramatic, and, as the label implies, histrionic in style. They constantly draw attention to themselves and are prone to exaggeration. Their behavior is overly reactive and intense. They are emotionally excitable and crave stimulation, often responding to minor stimuli with irrational, angry outbursts or tantrums. Their interpersonal relationships are impaired, and they are perceived by others as shallow, lacking in genuineness, demanding, and overly dependent. Although this chapter will focus on clients who meet the full criteria of Histrionic Personality Disorder, many of the concepts may also be applied to clients who show a strong histrionic style and features of the histrionic client without the depth of impairment of a full personality disorder.

As noted in DSM-III-R, the client with a Histrionic Personality Disor-

Table 22. DSM-III-R Diagnostic Criteria for Histrionic Personality Disorder

A pervasive pattern of excessive emotionality and attention seeking, beginning by early adulthood and present in a variety of contexts, as indicated by at least *four* of the following:
1. Constantly seeks or demands reassurance, approval, or praise
2. Is inappropriately sexually seductive in appearance or behavior
3. Is overly concerned with physical attractiveness
4. Expresses emotion with inappropriate exaggeration, e.g., embraces casual acquaintances with excessive ardor, uncontrollable sobbing on minor sentimental occasions, has temper tantrums
5. Is uncomfortable in situations in which he or she is not the center of attention
6. Displays rapidly shifting and shallow expression of emotions
7. Is self-centered, actions being directed toward obtaining immediate satisfaction; has no tolerance for the frustration of delayed gratification
8. Has a style of speech that is excessively impressionistic and lacking in detail, e.g., when asked to describe mother, can be no more specific than "She was a beautiful person."

der has been conceptualized as a caricature of what is defined as femininity in our culture—vain, shallow, self-dramatizing, immature, overly dependent, and selfish. This disorder is most frequently diagnosed in women, and when it is diagnosed in men it has been associated with a homosexual arousal pattern. This gender differential, however, may be more a product of our societal expectations than a true difference in occurrence. It has been suggested that Histrionic Personality Disorder is more appropriately seen as a caricature of sex roles in general, including extreme masculinity as well as extreme femininity (Kolb, 1968; MacKinnon & Michaels, 1971; Malmquist, 1971). The caricature of femininity is fairly commonly diagnosed as histrionic, yet a caricature of masculinity (an overly "macho" male who is dramatic, sensation seeking, shallow, vain, and egocentric) is rarely diagnosed as Histrionic Personality Disorder and is even less likely to seek treatment.

As is generally the case with personality disorders, people do not seek treatment with Histrionic Personality Disorder as their presenting problem. Individuals with this disorder often experience periods of intense dissatisfaction and depression, sometimes making dramatic suicide attempts. Due to their dependence on the attention of other people, they are especially vulnerable to separation anxieties and may seek treatment when they become intensely upset over the breakup of a relationship. Anxiety disorders such as Panic Disorder with and without Agoraphobia are also common presenting problems in people with Histrionic Personality Disorders. In fact, Goldstein and Chambless (1978) suggest that one of the defining characteristics of the agoraphobic personality is a "hysterical response style," which they define as the inability to accurately connect feeling states with their eliciting stimuli and the inability to appropriately label current feeling states. Other common complications of Histrionic Personality Disorder that may lead to the seeking of treatment include alcoholism and other substance abuse, Conversion Disorder, and Somatization Disorder.

ASSESSMENT

The strongest indication of Histrionic Personality Disorder is an overly dramatic self-presentation. These clients express intense emotionality but often do it in an exaggerated or unconvincing manner, as if they are playing a role. In fact, when talking with these clients, the clinician may have a sense of watching a performance rather than experiencing empathy for the individual. Histrionic clients can appear quite warm, charming, and even seductive; yet as the session goes on, their charm begins to seem superficial, as if it lacks genuineness. They often present their symptoms, thoughts, and actions as if they were external entities involuntarily imposed upon them. They tend to throw up their hands (literally) and proclaim, "These things just always seem to be happening to me!" Histrionic clients often use strong, dramatic words, include much hyperbole in their speech, and seem to have a proclivity for meaningless generalizations. They use theatrical intonation with dramatic nonverbal gestures and facial expressions. They often dress in ways that are likely to attract attention, wearing striking and provocative styles in bright colors and using cosmetics and hair dyes extensively.

Although these indications of a dramatic portrayal of the self can serve as useful cues to the presence of a Histrionic Personality Disorder, a dramatic style or unusual clothing alone certainly does not prove that the client has a Histrionic Personality Disorder. Professionals in the past have seemed all too eager to label women *hysteric* whenever they presented complaints that were not easily explained or when they made demands that seemed excessive. If the term *histrionic personality disorder* is going to be clinically useful and more than just another term used to denigrate women, clinicians must be careful not to classify clients as histrionic merely on the basis of indications of dramatic flair. These characteristics, however, can serve as useful cues for the clinician to probe carefully for further information that will be useful in arriving at a diagnosis.

In the diagnosis of Histrionic Personality Disorder, it is crucial to explore interpersonal relationships in depth. Details should be obtained as to how previous relationships started, what happened, and how they ended. Indications to watch for would include an overly romantic view of relationships with hopes or expectations of Prince Charming riding along on his white horse. Do their relationships start out as idyllic and end up as disasters? How stormy are their relationships, and how dramatic are the endings? Another area to ask about is the way that they handle anger, fights, and disagreements. The clinician should ask for specific examples and look for any signs of dramatic outbursts, temper tantrums, and the manipulative use of anger.

Many of the characteristics of histrionic personality are generally considered to be negative traits, and most people would not readily acknowledge them. It is certainly not productive to ask people if they are shallow, egocentric, vain, and demanding; however, it may be possible to obtain some relevant material regarding these factors by asking them how other people tend to view them. One way to phrase this would be to ask what complaints the other person made about them, while exploring previous relationships that did not work out. With any client, details should be gathered about suicidal ideation, threats, and attempts to determine whether there is currently a risk of a suicide attempt. With a client who is potentially histrionic, this information is also useful to help determine whether or not there is a dramatic or manipulative quality to the threats or attempts. It can also be useful to ask for details of the types of activities the client most enjoys: Does he or she especially enjoy being the center of attention? Does he or she show a craving for activity and excitement?

Two brief clinical examples may help to illustrate the variations in people who fit the criteria for Histrionic Personality Disorder:

Suzy was a 31-year-old unmarried high-school teacher with a master's degree in education. The reasons she gave for seeking therapy were vague and included phrases like "getting it all together." She was a recovering alcoholic who had not had a drink for the past 6 months but was worried that she would not be able to stay sober. She reported a variety of complaints including depression, anxiety, social isolation, procrastination, financial problems, and dissatisfaction with her job. She was overweight and sloppily dressed with long, frizzy hair and torn jeans with flowers embroidered all over them. She looked somewhat like a burned-out hippie, out of place in the Midwest of the 1980s. She began the first session with an angry outburst because she had been asked to fill out a variety of evaluation forms, and she felt this meant that the therapist was more interested in the forms than in her. When the purpose of the forms was explained to her, however, her mood changed rapidly to one of eager compliance. In fact, her mood fluctuated wildly throughout the session. She had the voice of a little girl, and when she described situations involving other people she would imitate their voices, as if she were acting out their roles. She repeated her adjectives several times for emphasis, saying that she had a "real, real, real, real aversion to medications" and describing someone she barely knew as "just a beautiful, beautiful, beautiful person." She used dramatic, yet confusing statements, such as "It was as if all my synapses were thrown into the air and came down I know not where." In describing her history, she said, "I killed myself in 1975," and only when she was asked to explain did she add, "Well, maybe not literally but that's how I look at it since so much of me died that day." She had recently broken up with her boyfriend and described that relationship saying, "I was madly in love with him. . . . He came along and I flipped out. . . . Then he turned into a real rat."

Suzy was fairly easy to diagnose as Histrionic Personality Disorder, given her unconventional appearance, strongly dramatic style, labile mood, and attitudes toward relationships. Fred initially seemed to be completely different from Suzy, yet he also fit the diagnosis of Histrionic Personality Disorder.

Fred was a 60-year-old married man who was very successful in advertising. He looked businesslike in his three-piece suit and sought treatment due to panic attacks that led him to avoid being alone at all and to avoid driving. His voice was powerful and dramatic, and he began our first session by explaining (in hushed tones) how vital confidentiality was because he had so many prominent accounts and people would be appalled to learn he had these problems. He proceeded to regale the therapist at every opportunity with stories of his big business deals and even brought brochures of his more successful jobs. He was disappointed to hear that his therapist was new in town and therefore could not appreciate the importance of his various clients. When it was possible to pin him down to discuss his reasons for seeking therapy, it became clear that whenever he had any physical symptom at all he immediately concluded that he was having a heart attack or going to die of suffocation. His wife was constantly at his beck and call, and he actually demanded that she wear a beeper and drop everything whenever he became upset (which was quite frequent). He worked hard to maintain his businesslike image with other people but had frequent angry outbursts toward his wife, throwing and breaking things when she had displeased him in some small way.

Conceptualization

Most of the conceptualizations of Histrionic Personality Disorder have been psychodynamic in nature. Early dynamic descriptions emphasized unresolved Oedipal conflicts as the primary determinant of this disorder, whereas later dynamic theorists focused on the presence of a more pervasive and primitive disturbance arising during the oral state of development (Halleck, 1967). Shapiro, although primarily psychodynamic in orientation, discusses many of the cognitive aspects of the "neurotic style" of the hysteric (1965). More recently, Millon (1981) has presented what he refers to as a biosocial learning theory view of personality disorders, including the Histrionic Personality Disorder. In his application of cognitive theory to a wide range of psychopathology, Beck (1976) discusses hysteria but examines conversion hysteria rather than Histrionic Personality Disorder. When the thoughts and beliefs of histrionic clients are examined, however, it seems that a cognitive conceptualization that combines some of the ideas of Millon and Shapiro with Beck's cognitive theory could clarify many of the aspects of the behavior of histrionic clients and suggest areas for useful clinical intervention.

One of the basic beliefs of the person with a Histrionic Personality

Disorder seems to be, "I am inadequate and unable to handle life on my own." Depressives with this underlying assumption might dwell on the negative aspects of themselves, feeling worthless and hopeless. Histrionic persons, however, seem to draw the conclusion, "Well, then, I'll need to rely on others to take care of me," and actively set about finding ways to insure that their needs are sufficiently met by others. As Millon (1981, pg. 131) observes, both the dependent personality and the histrionic personality are dependent upon others for attention and affection, but the dependent personality gets taken care of by emphasizing his or her helplessness and taking a passive role, whereas the histrionic person takes the initiative in actively seeking attention and approval.

Because attention and approval are seen as the only way to survive in the world, histrionic clients tend to hold the underlying assumption that it is necessary to be loved by everyone for everything one does. Any rejection at all is seen as devastating, even when the person doing the rejecting was not previously important to the client. Just the idea that one can be rejected at all reminds the client of his or her tenuous position in the world. Feeling basically inadequate yet desperate for approval as their only salvation, persons with a Histrionic Personality Disorder are not willing to relax and leave the acquisition of approval to chance. Instead, they work diligently to seek this attention in the most effective ways they know—often by fulfilling an extreme of their sex-role stereotype. Female histrionics (as well as some of the males) seem to have learned from an early age that they are rewarded for cuteness, attractiveness, and charm rather than for competence or for any endeavor requiring careful thought and planning. The more "macho" male histrionics have learned to play an extreme masculine role, being rewarded for the appearance of virility, toughness, and power rather than actual competence or problem solving. Understandably, then, both male and female histrionics learn to focus attention on the playing of roles, on "performing" for others, and on the responses of their intended "audience." Although winning approval from others is the primary goal, histrionics have not learned to systematically plan ways to please or impress others. Instead, the histrionic person has been frequently rewarded for the global enactment of certain roles, so it is in the enactment of these roles that he or she learns to excel. This striving to please others is not necessarily dysfunctional in and of itself. Histrionic people, however, get so involved in this strategy that they take it beyond what is actually effective. They can get carried away with dramatics and attracting attention, losing sight of their actual goal and eventually seeking stimulation and drama for its own sake.

People with a Histrionic Personality Disorder view themselves as sociable, friendly, and agreeable, and, in fact, they are often perceived that way at the beginning of a relationship. Given their basic assumption that acceptance from others is essential, they tend to engage in a variety of subtle (and sometimes not so subtle) maneuvers to elicit favorable responses. As a relationship continues, they gradually are seen as overly demanding and in need of constant reassurance. They tend to overreact to anything they interpret as rejection and are prone to dramatic outbursts and tantrums. Because asking directly for what they want involves the risk of rejection, they often use manipulation to achieve their ends but will resort to threats, coercion, temper tantrums, and suicide threats if their more subtle methods fail.

Histrionic people become so preoccupied with external approval that they learn to value external events over their own internal experience. With so little focus on their own emotions, wants, and preferences, they are left without any clear sense of identity apart from other people and see themselves primarily in relation to others. This lifelong focus on what others think and feel has prevented them from learning to deal with their own inner thoughts and feelings. In fact, their own internal experience can feel quite foreign and uncomfortable, and at times they actively avoid self-knowledge, not knowing how to deal with it. Being somewhat aware of the superficial nature of their affections may also encourage them to shy away from true intimacy with another person for fear of being "found out." Because they have paid little attention to their own internal resources, histrionics individuals are at a loss when any depth is required in a relationship. Thus their relationships tend to be stormy and shallow.

The histrionic's focus on the external and the dramatic may lead to the characteristic thought style that has been described by Shapiro (1965). The thinking of the histrionic client is seen as impressionistic, vivid, and interesting but lacking detail and focus. This seems to result not only from the histrionic's lack of introspection but also from the fact that he or she simply does not attend to details and specifics in the first place. What is not clearly perceived cannot be recalled in a specific manner, so histrionics' memories of events must necessarily remain global and diffuse. Their resulting objective deficiency in knowledge of specific details and facts, along with a lack of experience in systematic problem solving, can lead to serious difficulty in coping constructively with conflicts or problems that arise. This serves to further reinforce the histrionic's sense that he or she is inadequate to cope with life alone and needs to rely on the help of others.

With a "vague" cognitive style, the histrionic individual's sense of self remains impressionistic rather than being based on specific characteristics and accomplishments. It is difficult to maintain a realistic impression of oneself if one does not view one's own actions and feelings in a sufficiently detailed fashion. In addition, if thoughts exert a strong influence on emotions (as is argued by cognitive theory), then it follows that global and exaggerated thoughts would lead to global and exaggerated emotions. Global emotions can be very intense and labile, so the client may get carried away by affect even though it does not feel totally connected to him or her. Without the availability of complex, cognitive integration, these undifferentiated emotions can be very difficult to control, leaving the person subject to explosive outbursts.

The histrionic client's characteristic style of thinking can manifest itself in several of the cognitive distortions outlined by Beck (1976). Because these clients tend to be struck by impressions rather than thinking things through, they are especially susceptible to all-or-nothing thinking. They react strongly and suddenly, jumping to extreme conclusions whether good or bad. Thus one person is seen immediately as Mr. Wonderful, whereas someone else is seen as a totally repulsive, evil figure. Due to the intensity of their felt emotions and lack of sharp attention to detail and logic, histrionic clients are also prone to the distortion of overgeneralization. If they are rejected once, they dramatically conclude that they always have been rejected and always will be. Unlike the depressive, however, they can be equally extreme in their positive conclusions about people and relationships and can easily switch between the two extremes. Due to their inability to look at responses critically, they are also subject to emotional reasoning—taking their emotions as evidence for the truth. Thus histrionic individuals tend to assume that if they feel inadequate, they must truly be inadequate; if they feel stupid, they must be stupid; and conversely, if they feel charming, they must be irresistibly charming.

STRATEGIES FOR INTERVENTION

Since the days of Freud's work with Dora, psychoanalytic treatment has generally been seen as the treatment of choice for the various classes of hysteria. Little has been written about the treatment of hysteria from a behavioral point of view (summarized by Bird, 1979) and even less has been presented about behavioral treatment specifically for the client with a Histrionic Personality Disorder. Given the problems that global, diffuse thinking causes for histrionic clients, it seems that a specific, focused approach to treatment might be useful, if they are able to accommodate to it.

Although admittedly an oversimplification, there is some truth to the statement that we need to "teach the hysteric to think and the obsessive to feel" (Allen, 1977, p. 317). Because the characteristic thought style of clients with Histrionic Personality Disorder is dysfunctional to them in many ways, Cognitive Therapy could be seen as a particularly appropriate treatment. Cognitive Therapy is a systematic and structured treatment, focusing on specific target problems and goals. The cognitive therapist tries to be well organized and comes to the session prepared to help the client work systematically toward the achievement of specific goals. The histrionic client, although perhaps cooperative and eager to work, comes to the session with an approach to life that is diametrically opposed to the systematic, structured nature of Cognitive Therapy. With such different basic styles, both the therapist and the client may find Cognitive Therapy quite difficult and frustrating; but, if this conflict in styles can be gradually resolved, the cognitive changes facilitated by therapy can be particularly useful to the client. The therapist needs to maintain a steady, consistent effort and to be flexible, if clients are to accept an approach that is so unnatural to them.

Teaching the histrionic client to use the techniques of Cognitive Therapy involves teaching an entirely new approach to the perception and processing of experience. Before the client can even begin to monitor thoughts and feelings, he or she needs to learn to focus attention on one issue at a time. Only then can details of events, thoughts, and feelings be identified. In treating many other disorders, cognitive techniques are basically tools used to help the client to change feelings and behavior. With Histrionic Personality Disorder, however, learning the process of Cognitive Therapy is more than just a means to an end; in fact, the skills acquired just by learning the process of Cognitive Therapy can constitute the most significant part of the treatment.

Because the histrionic client is generally dependent in relationships, the use of collaboration and guided discovery is particularly important. The client is likely to view the therapist as the all-powerful rescuer who will make everything better, so the more active a role he or she is required to play in the treatment the less this image will be maintained. When he or she brings a series of problems to the therapist and asks for quick solutions, the therapist must be careful not to be seduced into the role of savior but rather to use questioning to help the client arrive at his or her own solutions.

As one aspect of teaching these clients to focus their attention and to identify thoughts and feelings, it is important to reinforce them for competence and attention to specifics rather than for their more commonly reinforced emotionality and manipulation. If they can learn ways that attention to details and assertion can pay off in the sessions, they may also be able to learn that being assertive and doing active problem solving can pay off more than manipulation and emotional upheaval in the real world. Thus it is important for the therapist to be aware of attempts at manipulation within the therapy, so that they are not rewarded. Histrionic clients often maneuver to earn "special status" as clients by getting the therapist to agree to unusual fee arrangements or scheduling considerations. Their demands may seem insatiable, and yet any refusal to comply may be seen by the client as rejection. These clients, therefore, need to learn that there are limits to the demands they can successfully make, and that limits are not necessarily a sign of rejection. Thus, the therapist needs to set clear limits in therapy and be firm about enforcing them, while rewarding assertive requests within these limits and demonstrating caring in other ways.

An example of the importance of maintaining clear limits is Suzy (discussed previously), who complained of financial hardship and was concerned that she would be unable to pay the agreed-upon fee. Rather than making special concessions for her, the standard fee arrangements were explained clearly, and she was told that if she could not afford to be seen at this clinic, the therapist would be sorry but would help her try to find a therapist with a lower fee. It was also explained that letting her build up a large bill that she was unable to pay would not be useful to her or the treatment; thus, if she was ever two sessions behind in payments, she would need to wait until she was caught up before meeting again. She tested this arrangement once, and the therapist expressed regret that it would be necessary to postpone the next session but remained firm in the face of tears and pleas. From that point on, she kept up with her fee payments. Later it was discovered that in another therapy she had been given special fee considerations and abused them, racking up a substantial bill and not being able to pay it. When the consequences are clear, concrete, and immediate, the histrionic client finds it difficult to manipulate the situation and can learn to behave more adaptively.

Cognitive and Behavioral Techniques

The initial step in Cognitive Therapy with any client involves learning to set an agenda. This generally straightforward and brief method of jointly making a plan for the session helps to enhance the collaborative relationship between the client and the therapist and structures the session to allow for focusing on goals. Because the inability to focus attention is one of the major problem areas for the client with a Histrionic Personality Disorder, the process of learning to set an agenda takes on additional significance. Before any real problem solving can take place, the client needs to learn to focus attention on specific topics within the therapy session, and the setting of an agenda is an excellent place to begin working on this. Because setting a clear, specific agenda is likely to be a foreign concept to the histrionic client, it is necessary to use a graded task approach along with a great deal of patience. Getting the client to agree on even very broad, vague agenda items without going into extensive elaboration on each area can be quite an accomplishment. If the therapist remains flexible, however, and gradually works to impose more structure, even the most histrionic client can learn to cooperate with the setting of an adequate agenda.

Because focusing attention on specific goals is difficult for histrionic clients and their natural tendency is to want to come into the session and dramatically fill the therapist in on all the traumatic events of the week, it may be important to schedule a part of each session for that purpose. Thus one agenda item could be to review how things went during the week (with a clear time limit) so the therapist can be empathic and the client can feel understood; then the rest of the session can be used to work toward goals.

After setting the agenda, the next step in any Cognitive Therapy is the setting of specific goals for the treatment. This is a challenging but crucial stage in the treatment of the histrionic client. One of the largest problems in the treatment of these clients is that they often do not stay in therapy long enough to make significant changes because, as with other activities and relationships, they tend to lose interest and move on to something more exciting. One key to keeping histrionic clients in treatment is to set goals that are genuinely meaningful, that are perceived as urgent to them, and that present the possibility of deriving some short-term benefit as well as longer term accomplishments. They may have a tendency to set broad, vague goals that sound "noble" and impressive and fit their image of what is expected from a therapy client. They may talk about "feeling better," "living a happier life," "being a better wife and mother," or "being more of a success."

It is crucial, however, that the goals be specific and concrete and that they also genuinely feel important to the clients (and not just an image of what they think they "should" want). The therapist can help clients to operationalize their goals by asking questions like "How would you be able to tell if you had achieved your goal?" "What exactly would look and feel different, in what ways?" "Why exactly would you want to accomplish that?" It may be useful to have clients fantasize in the session about how it would feel to have changed their lives, in order to help them begin to fit their ideas together into a tentative model of who they would like to become. Because one of the main ways the therapist will be able to keep the client in treatment is by demonstrating actual changes toward the goals, the importance of goal setting cannot be overemphasized.

Once the goals have been set, they can be enlisted as an aid to help teach the client to focus attention. When an agenda has been set but the client continually wanders off the subject (as he or she invariably will), the therapist can gently but persistently ask questions such as "Now, that's very interesting, but how is that related to the goal we agreed to discuss?" If he or she continues to oppose efforts to focus on the agreed-upon topic (despite having had time scheduled for ventilation), the therapist can introduce one of the primary cognitive techniques in the treatment of histrionic clients: the listing of advantages and disadvantages.

Helping the client to make conscious choices within the therapy session by examining the "pros and cons" of various courses of action is a useful antecedent to learning to make such choices in daily life. The histrionic client tends to react emotionally and dramatically to situations, rarely stopping to think or paying attention to the possible consequences.

As a result, he or she tends to feel helpless and out of control over what happens. Exploration of the advantages and disadvantages of changing and working toward goals early in the treatment can help both to minimize resistance and to make any resistance that does occur obvious to both the client and the therapist. Often, when asked about the disadvantages of changing in the desired ways, the client will adamantly exclaim that it would be wonderful to change and there could not possibly be any disadvantages. With careful examination, it will become clear that changing does have its costs, including that of having to acknowledge some responsibility for actions rather than blaming external forces. If the therapist simply insists that the client focus attention on goals, the client can fight this, and a power struggle may ensue with the client arguing that the therapist is "mean" and "doesn't understand." On the other hand, if the therapist consistently points out that it is the client's choice how to spent the therapy time but that achieving the desired goals will require some focus of attention, the client is left to make the decision, and whatever the client chooses is experienced as coming more from the client than from the therapist.

After the initial stages of the treatment, the actual focus of therapy will depend to some extent on the client's particular presenting problem and goals. In general, the same Cognitive Therapy techniques would be used with histrionic clients as would be used to treat similar problems in other clients. The therapist, however, would need to be prepared to spend additional time in the initial stages of each technique, helping the client to adapt to the structure and to the focus of attention required. Given the hypothesis that histrionic clients' problems are exacerbated by their global, impressionistic thought style, and their inability to focus on specifics, it seems that teaching the client to monitor and pinpoint specific thoughts will be the crux of the treatment, regardless of the presenting problem.

For example, in helping histrionic clients reduce depression, the therapist would use the well-established procedures for the Cognitive Therapy of depression (Beck *et al.*, 1979). In teaching them to monitor thoughts using dysfunctional thought sheets, it is likely that a great deal of time will have to be spent on the first three columns, specifying events, thoughts, and feelings. It is unrealistic to expect histrionic clients to be able to go home and monitor thoughts accurately after a simple explanation and demonstration in the session, although this may be possible for many other types of clients. More commonly, histrionic clients will forget the point of monitoring thoughts and will instead bring unstructured pages of prose describing their stream of consciousness throughout the week. They should be reinforced for trying to do the homework, but the procedure will need to be explained again with a focus on the idea that the goal is not just to communicate with the therapist but to learn the skill of identifying and challenging thoughts in order to change emotions.

Daily Record of Automatic Thoughts

Date	Situation Briefly describe the situation	Emotion(s) Rate 0-100%	Automatic Thought(s) Try to quote thoughts then rate your belief in each thought 0-100%
	Drove to Chester to look at car, took son with me, had to get back to get Mary to swim class, drove Volvo, liked it and salesman said make up your mind because this is last one. I said I'll buy it & signed paper. Then I said but I want to drive an Olds to make certain & I liked that too, so I said forget it & he said he would bring the car over that night to drive. I tried to talk my husband into signing papers, but he said we will sleep on it. Will probably buy it today. Was delighted to find car dealer near costume shop.	Couldn't make up mind & felt pressured, felt stupid for signing papers & then asking him to forget it.	

FIGURE 16. An example thought sheet from early in therapy with a histrionic client.

If clients strongly feel the need to communicate all of their thoughts and feelings to the therapist in the hope that the therapist can understand them better and be more able to help them, they can be encouraged to write unstructured prose in addition to the thought sheets, not as a substitute. Figure 16 gives an example of a "thought sheet" written by a histrionic client early in her treatment. She had a driving phobia and had been asked to write her automatic thoughts and feelings when driving. Although she was writing on the appropriate form, she wrote a narrative of her experience rather than using the form to identify and challenge her thoughts. Figure 17 shows a thought sheet from later in her treatment, after she had learned to identify thoughts more specifically.

Once clients have learned to identify their cognitions to some extent, they can begin to make gradual changes in their problematic thought style. The dysfunctional thought records, most widely known for their use in treating depression, can also be used to help clients challenge any thoughts that prove to be dysfunctional for them. Cognitive distortions can be pinpointed and modified, and care can be taken to help them to distinguish reality from their extreme fantasies. Thought sheets can be especially useful in the process of reattribution: For example, Fred (discussed before)

Daily Record of Automatic Thoughts			
Date	Situation Briefly describe the situation	Emotion(s) Rate 0-100%	Automatic Thought(s) Try to quote thoughts then rate your belief in each thought 0-100%
	Driving on Ventura Blvd, guy drives over yellow line	Anxiety 50%	What if there was a car next to me? He would kill me. 50% What if lots of people get killed on this road and it just doesn't make the headlines? 50%
	Drove on highway with husband	Anxious 50%	I will get stuck on the hill and my husband will get impatient and scream at me. 70%

FIGURE 17. An example thought sheet from later in therapy with the same histrionic client.

would attribute any slight change in his physical condition to a terrible disease and immediately conclude that he was going to have a heart attack and die. To him, it made no difference whether he became slightly light-headed due to inhaling gasoline fumes from pumping his own gas, smelling ammonia in a restroom that had just been cleaned, or having a panic attack. Whatever the actual cause of his slight lightheadedness, he immediately concluded he was dying. Teaching him to stop and explore the possible alternative causes for his physical symptoms helped him to make more appropriate causal attributions and interrupt his cycle of panic.

Because histrionic clients have vivid imaginations, their cognitions often take the form of vivid imagery of disaster rather than verbal thoughts. Challenging cognitions is not restricted to verbal thoughts; in fact, imagery modification is an important part of Cognitive Therapy with the histrionic client. The therapist needs to specifically ask them what images go through their minds at upsetting times because otherwise, clients may not realize that imagery is important. Because images can serve as powerful emotional stimuli, neglecting them in the treatment by focusing only on verbal thoughts can greatly decrease the effectiveness of treatment (Beck, 1970).

In addition to helping clients challenge automatic thoughts, the self-monitoring of cognitions can be used to help them begin to control their impulsivity. As long as situations occur to which they automatically react emotionally and in a manipulative manner, it is very difficult to make any change in their behavior. If they can learn to stop before they react (or, using a graded task approach, stop in the early stages of their reactions) long enough to note their thoughts, they have already taken a major step toward self-control. Thus, even before they learn to effectively challenge their cognitions, the simple pinpointing of cognitions may serve to reduce impulsivity.

As histrionic clients begin to learn to pause before reacting, they can also benefit from specific problem-solving training. Because they are rarely aware of the consequences before they act, it is helpful for them to learn to do what has been called "means–ends thinking" (Spivack & Shure, 1974). This problem-solving procedure involves teaching the client to generate a variety of suggested solutions (means) to a problem and then accurately evaluate the probable consequences (ends) of the various options.

The treatment goals of histrionic clients often involve improving their interpersonal relationships. They are so concerned about maintaining attention and affection from others that they often attempt to dominate relationships in indirect ways that do not seem to carry the risk of rejection. The methods that they most generally use to manipulate relationships include inducing emotional crises, provoking jealousy, using their charm and seductiveness, withholding sex, nagging, scolding, and complaining. Although these behaviors seem sufficiently successful in the short term for the clients to maintain them, they have long-term costs that are not apparent to the clients. Once they are able to pause and examine their thoughts when they begin to have a strong emotional reaction, histrionic individuals can learn to challenge them.

Challenging their immediate thoughts may not be sufficient, however, because histrionic individuals so often use emotional outbursts as a way to manipulate situations.

Martha was a 42-year-old woman who was married to a man who worked long hours and did not pay as much attention to her as she wanted. Often when her husband came home late from work, Martha would have a temper tantrum, with automatic thoughts, such as "How can he do this to me? He doesn't love me any more! I'll die if he leaves me!" As a result of her tantrum, however, she got a great deal of attention from her husband, and he would make clear statements of his love for her, which she found to be very reassuring. Thus, in addition to directly challenging her thoughts when she got emotionally upset, Martha also needed to learn to ask herself, "What do I really want now?" Only when she realized that what she really wanted at that point in time was reassurance from her husband could she begin to explore alternative ways of achieving this.

Once clients can begin to stop and determine what they want from the situation, they can be taught to explore the various methods for achieving that goal and look at the advantages and disadvantages of each. Thus, they are presented with a choice between having a temper tantrum and trying other alternatives. Instead of asking them to make permanent changes in their behavior, the therapist can suggest that they set up brief behavioral experiments to test out which methods are the most effective with the least long-term cost. Setting up brief behavioral experiments can be much less threatening to clients than the idea of making long-term behavior changes and may help them to try out some behaviors that they might otherwise be unwilling to try.

Once histrionic clients are able to explore various means of attempting to get what they want, the therapist can help them to consider the advantages of a method that may be quite new to them—assertiveness. The process of assertiveness training with histrionic clients involves more than just helping them learn to more directly communicate their wishes to others. Before they can communicate their wishes, they need to learn to identify those wishes and attend to them. Having spent so much time focusing on how to get attention and affection from others, these clients have lost sight of what it actually is that they want. Thus effective assertiveness training with histrionic clients will involve using cognitive methods to help them pay attention to what they want, in addition to the behavioral methods of teaching them how to communicate assertively.

Of course, the experience of the client in the session needs to reinforce the idea that assertion and competence can be just as rewarding as manipulation and dramatics, if not more so. Thus the therapist must be careful to reward attempts at clear communication and assertion, without falling into the patterns of so many of the client's previous relationships. This can be quite a challenge even to the experienced therapist, because the style of the histrionic client can be very appealing and attractive, and dramatic renditions of experience can be quite absorbing, entertaining, and amusing. The unwary therapist can easily be maneuvered into taking on the role of "rescuer," taking on too much of the blame if the client does not work toward change and giving in to too many demands. This may lead the therapist to feel manipulated, angered, and deceived by the histrionic client. A therapist who strongly wants to be helpful to others may inadvertently reinforce the client's feelings of helplessness and end up embroiled in a reenactment of the client's usual type of relationship. The methods of Cognitive Therapy can be useful for therapists as well as clients. When the therapist finds himself or herself having strong emotional reactions to the histrionic client and being less than consistent in reinforcing assertive and competent responses, it may be time for the therapist to monitor his or her own cognitions and feelings for inconsistencies that might be interfering with the process of the treatment.

At the same time that clients work to improve their relationships, it is important that they also challenge their beliefs that the loss of a relationship would be disastrous. Even though their relationships may improve, as long as they still believe that they could not survive if the relationship ended, they will have difficulty continuing to take the risks of being assertive. Fantasizing about the reality of what would happen if their relationship should end and recalling how they survived before this relationship began are two ways to begin helping the client to "decatastrophize" the idea of rejection. Another useful method is to set up behavioral experiments that deliberately set up small "rejections" so the client can actually practice being rejected without being devastated.

Ultimately, clients need to learn to challenge their most basic assumption: the belief that "I am inadequate and have to rely on others to survive." Many of the procedures discussed (including assertion, problem solving, and behavioral experiments) can increase self-efficacy and help the client to feel some sense of competence. Given the difficulty these clients have in drawing connections, however, it is important to systematically point out to them how each task they accomplish challenges the idea that they cannot be competent. It can also be useful to set up small, specific behavioral experiments designed to test the idea that they cannot do things by themselves.

Even clients who are able to see the advantages of thinking clearly and using assertion may become frightened by the idea that if they learn more "reasonable" ways of approaching life, they will lose all the excitement in their lives and become drab, dull people. Histrionic people can be lively, energetic, and fun to be with, and they stand to lose a lot if they give up their emotionality completely. It is therefore important to clarify throughout the treatment that the goal is not to eliminate emotions but to use them more constructively. For example, clients can be encouraged to be dramatic when writing their rational responses, making the rational responses more powerful. Thus, when Suzy was challenging the automatic thought, "I'm too busy," while she was procrastinating about doing her homework, her most influential rational response was, "That's a pimply white lie and you know it!"

Paula was a 33-year-old cashier who had been married to an alcoholic and whose life had consisted of constant crisis, including being beaten regularly by her husband and making frequent suicide attempts. After she divorced her alcoholic husband and became involved in a more stable relationship, she in some ways felt the loss of the stimulation and excitement. She had found the period of making up after a violent fight to be very reassuring and had not yet found other ways of getting reassurance that she was loved. Through her work in therapy she was able to find assertive ways to ask for reassurance from her husband and began to learn to recognize some of the less obvious signs of his affection. She also went back to school to add more challenge into her life.

Other constructive avenues for sensation seeking can include involvement in theater and drama, participating in exciting activities and competitive sports, and occasional escape into dramatic literature, movies, and television.

For clients who feel reluctant to give up the emotional trauma in their lives and insist that they have no choice but to get terribly depressed and upset, it can be useful to help them gain at least some control by learning to "schedule a trauma." Clients can pick a specific time each day or week during which they will give in to their strong feelings (for example, depression, anger, a temper tantrum, and so on), but rather than being overwhelmed whenever such feelings occur, they learn to postpone the feelings to a convenient time and keep them within an agreed-upon time frame. This often has a paradoxical effect. When clients learn that they can indeed "schedule depression" and stick to the time limits without letting it interfere with their lives, they rarely feel the need to schedule such time on a regular basis. It always remains as an option for them, however. Thus, long after therapy has terminated, they will have a less destructive way to give in to such strong emotional experiences.

Because the histrionic client is so heavily invested in receiving approval and attention from others, a structured cognitive group therapy can be a particularly effective mode of treatment. Kass, Silvers, and Abrams (1972) demonstrated that the help of group members could be enlisted to reinforce assertion and extinguish dysfunctional, overly emotional responses. One histrionic client continually focused on her physical symptoms of anxiety, complaining loudly, dramatically, and in graphic detail, despite the therapist's efforts. When she was placed in a Cognitive Therapy group, the feedback from the other group members, their consistent lack of reinforcement for physical complaints, and their positive reinforcement when she discussed other issues was much more successful at reducing her focus on her symptoms than her individual therapy had been. When Suzy entered a Cognitive Therapy group, her manipulative patterns of interacting with men became much more obvious than they had been while she was in therapy with a female therapist. If the client is involved in a significant relationship, couple therapy can also be especially useful. In couple therapy, both spouses can be helped to recognize the patterns in the relationship and the ways in which they each facilitate the maintenance of those patterns.

CONCLUSION

Most of the behavioral research that has been conducted in the area of hysteria has been confined to the treatment of conversion hysteria and somatization disorders (Bird, 1979). Woolson and Swanson (1972) presented an approach to the treatment of four "hysterical women" that included some behavioral components, and they report that all four clients made substantial gains toward all of their stated goals within 4 months of initiating therapy. Kass *et al.* (1972) describe an inpatient behavioral group treatment of five women who had been admitted for suicidal intent and diagnosed as having a hysterical personality. Clients were required to adhere to a tight daily schedule, including therapeutic exercises to teach appropriate self-assertion. The clients were taught to identify their dysfunctional reactions to stress and systematically modify them. The group members were responsible for specifying each other's hysterical behaviors (which had been operationally defined) and providing the rewards and penalties which had been agreed upon. There was no control group, but multiple and concrete measures of progress were kept. Four of the five clients showed symptomatic improvement and more adaptive behavioral responses at the end of treatment and after an 18-month follow-up. Thus, fairly positive results were obtained in two studies of largely behavioral treatments with a population that is generally acknowledged to be very difficult to treat.

The efficacy of Cognitive Therapy for the treatment of Histrionic Personality Disorders has not yet been tested empirically. It does show clinical promise in that several therapists have used these strategies over the past 6 years with a variety of histrionic clients and report it to be an effective treatment that results in less frustration on the part of both therapist and client than the more traditional approaches to treatment.

10

Antisocial and Narcissistic Personality Disorders

ANTISOCIAL PERSONALITY DISORDER

Perhaps because of the societal impact of its symptoms, its refractoriness to traditional treatment, and the easy availability of imprisoned subjects for research, Antisocial Personality Disorder is distinguished from other personality disorders by the large volume of empirical research that has been conducted on this disorder (for a recent overview, see Marshall & Barbaree, 1984). Unfortunately, the voluminous research has resulted in neither a consensus on how to best conceptualize the disorder nor in an effective approach to outpatient treatment. Frosch (1983) expresses a widely held view when he writes:

> The person with antisocial personality is the least popular of patients. Many would question whether these people should be considered patients at all, rather than criminals. The common view is that they are unable to experience guilt, incapable of empathy, and unresponsive to treatment. . . . Almost everybody does agree that outpatient therapy, when it is the sole treatment, is of little benefit, no matter what the approach. (pp. 98–99)

This pessimism presents a dilemma for the clinician practicing in an outpatient setting. When a client with Antisocial Personality Disorder enters therapy, whether at the behest of others or voluntarily, what is the therapist to do? Frosch's cited view suggests that it is fruitless to offer outpatient therapy, and some would argue that it is unethical to offer a treatment known to be ineffective. However, is it reasonable or ethical for the therapist to refuse treatment in the hopes that the person will eventually be arrested and sentenced to one of the few inpatient treatment programs that have been reported to be effective (for examples, see Carney, 1986; Matthews & Reid, 1986; Reid & Solomon, 1986)? Fortunately, there are recent indications that short-term outpatient cognitive-behavioral therapy can be effective for at least some clients with Antisocial Personality

TABLE 23. DSM-III-R Diagnostic Criteria for Antisocial Personality Disorder

A. Age at least 18.
B. Evidence of Conduct Disorder with onset before age 15, as indicated by a history of 3 or
   more from a list of 12 categories of antisocial activities.
C. A pattern of irresponsible and antisocial behavior since the age of 15, as indicated by at
   least four of the following:
   1. Is unable to sustain consistent work behavior
   2. Fails to conform to social norms with respect to lawful behavior, as indicated by
      repeatedly performing antisocial acts that are grounds for arrest (whether arrested or
      not), e.g., destroying property, harassing others, stealing, pursuing an illegal occupa-
      tion
   3. Is irritable and aggressive, as indicated by repeated physical fights or assaults (not
      required by one's job or to defend someone or oneself), including spouse- or child
      beating
   4. Repeatedly fails to honor financial obligations, as indicated by defaulting on debts or
      failing to provide child support or support for other dependents on a regular basis
   5. Fails to plan ahead, or is impulsive, as indicated by one or both of the following:
      (a) Traveling from place to place without a prearranged job or clear goal for the
          period of travel or a clear idea when the travel will terminate
      (b) Lack of a fixed address for a month or more
   6. Has no regard for the truth, as indicated by repeated lying, use of aliases, or "con-
      ning" others for personal profit or pleasure
   7. Is reckless regarding his or her own or others' personal safety, as indicated by driving
      while intoxicated, or recurrent speeding
   8. If a parent or guardian, lacks ability to function as a responsible parent, as indicated
      by one or more of the following:
      (a) Malnutrition of child
      (b) Child's illness resulting from lack of minimal hygiene
      (c) Failure to obtain medical care for a seriously ill child
      (d) Child's dependence on neighbors or nonresident relatives for food or shelter
      (e) Failure to arrange for a caretaker for young child when parent is away from home
      (f) Repeatedly squandering, on personal items, of money required for household
          necessities
   9. Has never sustained a totally monogamous relationship for more than 1 year
   10. Lacks remorse (feels justified in having hurt, mistreated, or stolen from another)
D. Occurrence of antisocial behavior not exclusively during the course of Schizophrenia or
   Manic Episodes.

Disorder (Woody, McLellan, Luborsky, & O'Brien, 1985). This chapter will
present a treatment approach that may offer a viable option for therapists
faced with attempting outpatient therapy with clients with Antisocial Personality Disorder or with significant antisocial features.

Assessment

The diagnosis of Antisocial Personality Disorder is not simply a matter
of the individual's having engaged in criminal behavior (see Table 23). The

disorder is characterized by a pattern of irresponsible and antisocial behavior beginning in childhood or early adolescence and continuing through adulthood. However, it also includes problems that extend beyond criminal behavior. These individuals are typically irritable and impulsive to an extent that makes it difficult for them to succeed in prosocial activities if they do make an attempt to conform to social norms. Also, despite the common impression that "sociopaths" or "psychopaths" are free of guilt and subjective distress, they typically complain of tension, inability to tolerate boredom, and depression as well as problems in relationships with family, friends, and sexual partners. These emotional and interpersonal problems tend to persist even if flagrant antisocial activity declines later in adulthood.

Consider this example:

"Rex" was a swarthy man of average build who appeared for his first appointment dressed in skin-tight pants, a bold print shirt unbuttoned far down his chest, several gold chains, and alligator shoes. His physician had referred him for evaluation because the pain and impairment that Rex reported as resulting from his rheumatoid arthritis was out of proportion to the physical findings and because Rex repeatedly referred to himself as a "cripple" and as "decrepit." The physician suspected that this "negative thinking" might amplify the pain produced by Rex's medical problems and result in increased impairment. Rex rejected this suggestion but accepted referral for an evaluation anyway.

Rex was cooperative but vague in the initial interview and managed to provide little information without seeming closemouthed. For example, in describing a typical day he said, "Well, ya know, I see some people, run some errands, make a couple'a deals. . . . Ya know how it is." Later in the interview he seemed to relax and begin to enjoy telling tales of his exploits. As a child he had "hung around" with older kids "on the street," and he described himself as quite streetwise, making sharp deals, exploiting loopholes, and taking advantage of the rules. As a boy he had become involved with illegal gambling operations, first as an errand boy and then gradually advancing to the point where he was nearly indicted by the Grand Jury and "had to leave town for a while." He had earned his living as a bookie at one time and later had a lucrative position about which he was quite vague but that involved frequent trips to exotic locations. By this point in the interview, the therapist had decided not to ask for more detailed information than Rex volunteered.

When asked about stressors, Rex acknowledged that a recent problem was constantly on his mind and that his physician was probably right in suspecting that emotional factors were affecting his health. Shortly before his arthritis had started "acting up," Rex had learned through unofficial channels that an associate who he had befriended was informing on him. He felt that he should "snuff the bastard" but didn't want to do so. He found himself unable to stop ruminating about this situation despite fears that the resulting stress would have a lasting impact on his health and concluded that "this bastard is crippling me!" This view of the situation led to additional anger and intensified Rex's conflict over what action to take.

Rex fits the common stereotype regarding Antisocial Personality Disorder in many ways, including his apparent freedom from guilt and remorse. However, this did not mean that he was free from distress. In addition to being greatly distressed by his physical symptoms and the impact they had on his life, he was experiencing considerable stress as a result of his indecision and was experiencing sadness as well as anger in response to his betrayal by a man whom he had considered a close friend.

The diagnosis of Antisocial Personality Disorder is not at all difficult if the necessary information can be obtained. However, it may take some time to determine if the individual meets full criteria for Antisocial Personality Disorder or simply manifests some antisocial features. Individuals involved in criminal activity may be reluctant to provide detailed information about such activity for obvious reasons or may enjoy boasting about their exploits to an extent that raises questions about the veracity of the tales. Similarly, some therapists may be cautious about seeking detailed information for fear of "knowing too much" or angering the client, whereas others may be intrigued by the client's life-style and seek much more information than is needed because the stories are fascinating. Clearly, neither extreme is productive. Ideally, the therapist would pursue the information that is needed for assessment and treatment without undue timidity but would not be distracted by anecdotes that are interesting but unnecessary.

Because individuals with Antisocial Personality Disorder are typically quick to deny personal problems and blame difficulties on mistreatment by others, it is important for the therapist to be alert for data that are inconsistent with such denials and to explore apparent inconsistencies. When information from other sources is available, the therapist has the opportunity to evaluate the accuracy of the client's report of events.

A number of authors have drawn a distinction between "criminal sociopaths" or "unsuccessful sociopaths" (i.e., persons with Antisocial Personality Disorder who get caught) and "creative sociopaths" or "successful sociopaths" who are clever enough to profit from their freedom from socially imposed limitations on behavior without being imprisoned. It is obviously impossible to devise an empirical test of the hypothesis that there are many persons with Antisocial Personality Disorder who elude detection (How can one locate subjects who, by definition, escape detection?). However, the authors of DSM-III assert that individuals who engage in antisocial or "shady" acts with the forethought and planning required for them to consistently profit from such acts rarely meet the full criteria for Antisocial Personality Disorder. The discussion that follows applies both to persons who meet the full diagnostic criteria for Antisocial Personality Disorder and to persons who manifest some of the features of this disorder without meeting the full diagnostic criteria.

Conceptualization

The traditional view of Antisocial Personality Disorder is that these individuals have failed to internalize family and societal standards for behavior and consequently have no conscience and feel no guilt. It is typically assumed that without a conscience to inhibit unacceptable behavior and without guilt to serve as punishment for such behavior, anyone would frequently act on aggressive, self-centered, antisocial impulses. The various authors who adopt this view disagree as to whether this failure to develop conscience and guilt is a result of genetic factors, family factors, or the interaction of the two; but, whatever the cause, this view implies that, in order to be effective, treatment would need to somehow instill a conscience. Unfortunately, no effective way to do so has yet been developed.

Although it is easy to see how persons who view criminal behavior in moral terms would assume that absence of guilt is responsible for antisocial behavior, it is possible to explain much antisocial behavior without reference to the individual's conscience or to the amount of guilt he or she experiences. It is interesting to note that, to a large extent, the constellation of behaviors that constitute Antisocial Personality Disorder can be accounted for by inadequate impulse control, poor means–ends thinking, a lack of adaptive control over anger, and low frustration tolerance. In fact, a lack of guilt alone would not explain the behavior of a person with Antisocial Personality Disorder. Antisocial behavior is counterproductive for the individual as well as for society. Even the minority of persons with Antisocial Personality Disorder who manage to avoid jail and who are financially successful pay a heavy price in terms of the disorder's impact on interpersonal relationships. An individual who simply was not inhibited by conscience and acted purely out of self-interest would be more of a hedonist than a criminal and could lead a far happier, more successful life than that which results from Antisocial Personality Disorder.

A cognitive model of Antisocial Personality Disorder is presented graphically in Figure 18. The reader may note similarities to the cognitive model of Paranoid Personality Disorder (Chapter 7) in that the individual sees others as being "out to get what they can for themselves" and thus sees the world as a hostile place where one must be sure to look out for oneself. As a consequence, persons with Antisocial Personality Disorder anticipate mistreatment by others, avoid revealing any vulnerabilities, and tend to avoid closeness. However, although the paranoid individual attempts to cope with perceived dangers through carefully analyzing situations and planning his or her actions, the antisocial individual assumes that planning ahead will prove ineffective. Thus he or she acts impulsively without giving much consideration to the long-term consequences of his or her actions. This tendency to act on the basis of momentary impulses or on

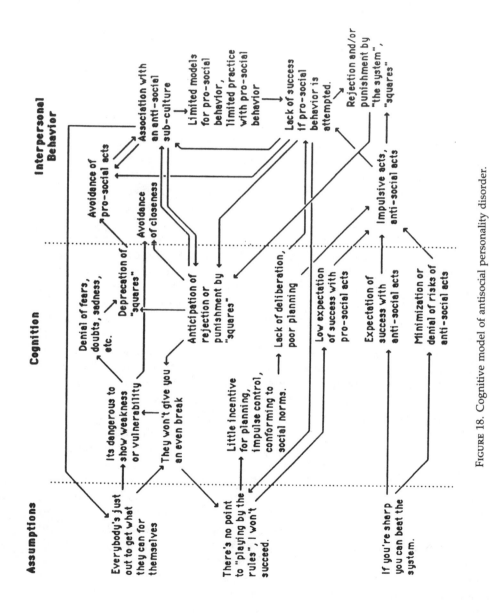

FIGURE 18. Cognitive model of antisocial personality disorder.

the basis of the expected short-term consequences of actions results in erratic behavior, contributes to impulsive acts that are self-defeating, and makes it difficult for the individual to work consistently toward long-term goals. As a result, such individuals are generally unsuccessful when they do try to plan ahead or "play by the rules," and these experiences support their view that there is no point in trying to do so.

The self-defeating nature of the antisocial pattern and the frequency of antisocial acts is greatly increased by the individual's tendency to overestimate the likelihood of being able to "get away with it," and, at the same time, to minimize the likelihood and significance of negative consequences. This strongly biases him or her toward acting on each impulse as it occurs unless there are obvious and undeniable reasons not to do so, resulting in impulsive behavior that is not governed by conventional ideas of what actions are appropriate. The combination of a lack of success at prosocial behavior and impulsive antisocial behavior provides the individual with recurrent experiences of rejection and punishment at the hands of "the system." This provides the individual with grounds for anticipating similar experiences in the future and results in generalized anger at society as well as anger over specific incidents. The anger contributes to the antisocial, destructive nature of the individual's impulses, whereas his or her anticipation of rejection or punishment by those within the mainstream of society encourages the individual to associate with an antisocial or criminal subculture.

This selective association provides the individual with many experiences that support the view that "everybody's just out to get what they can for themselves"; it provides him or her with few models of effective prosocial behavior and strongly reinforces antisocial attitudes and behaviors. The antisocial subculture also presents a disparaging view of "squares," and this can result in reluctance to engage in prosocial behavior even if the client's ability to control impulses and anticipate the consequences of his or her actions have improved to the point that he or she could be successful in doing so. This is particularly true when combined with previous lack of success with attempts at prosocial activities and with a desire to maintain links with criminal friends and associates.

Intervention Strategies and Techniques

The view of Antisocial Personality Disorder presented here provides the therapist with more viable treatment options than that of trying to find some way to instill a conscience. If these clients can develop a more enlightened view of their self-interest and recognize that it is in their own best interest to anticipate the long-term consequences of their actions, they may find that they have an incentive for working to control their impulsivity long enough to consider the consequences of possible actions.

Because the long-term consequences of prosocial behavior are typically better than those of antisocial behavior,* a client who is able to anticipate the consequences of his or her actions realistically is likely to engage in less antisocial activity. In working to more effectively pursue his or her long-term self-interest, the antisocial client will find that in addition to controlling his or her impulsiveness it is necessary to develop more adaptive ways of handling anger, to develop the ability to tolerate frustration, and make a number of other changes. Cognitive-behavioral interventions for helping clients become less impulsive, handle anger more adaptively, find more effective solutions to interpersonal problems, and increase their frustration tolerance can be used to good effect once therapist and client are working collaboratively and the client can see that it is in his or her self-interest to work to make such changes. Such interventions are typically ineffective when the client does not clearly realize "what's in it for me?"

It might appear that there would be a risk that in working with a client to help him or her more effectively pursue his or her long-term self-interest the therapist would be helping him or her become a more successful criminal. However, in practice this does not become a problem. The cliche, "crime doesn't pay," is often untrue when only the immediate consequences of antisocial acts are considered. However, when the long-term effects of antisocial behavior on relationships, on one's life-style, and on one's self-esteem are considered along with the risk of being apprehended, antisocial behavior "pays" less well than prosocial behavior.

The idea of intervening with clients with Antisocial Personality Disorder by helping them to take a more realistic, long-term view of their self-interest seems deceptively simple. The actual implementation of this strategy can be considerably more complex. Simply establishing a working relationship can be a major undertaking. These clients are a difficult population to work with in several ways: first, they tend to distrust therapists and to be uncomfortable accepting help; second, motivation for therapy is usually a problem, particularly if treatment is involuntary; and, finally, the therapist's reactions to the client often are a problem.

A collaborative approach to therapy with these clients is essential but a challenge to achieve. One major advantage of the treatment strategy discussed here is that it provides a general goal toward which therapist and client can work collaboratively: overcoming impediments to the client's successfully pursuing his or her self-interest. A client with Antisocial Personality Disorder is not going to be willing to work to become less im-

---

*Skeptics can test this assertion by trying to find specific situations where the long-term consequences of lying or cheating, or stealing, or violence are superior to the alternatives. When the individual has mastered the social skills needed for effective prosocial behavior and when the risk of getting caught and the impact such acts have on interpersonal relationships and on the actions of others is considered, it is difficult to identify many situations where self-interest would call for antisocial acts.

pulsive simply because the therapist thinks it would be a good idea or because doing so would be socially acceptable. However, he or she may be quite willing to work on impulse control and other issues if it is clear that doing so will lead to greater success in dealing with others. These clients are strongly motivated to pursue their own self-interest, and it is possible to use this self-interest to develop motivation for therapy if a guided discovery approach is used to identify the ways in which impulsive actions, inappropriate expression of anger, failure to anticipate the consequences of actions, and so on, block the client from attaining goals he or she desires. Given the difficulty these clients typically have in recognizing the long-term consequences of their actions, the connection between interventions made in therapy and the client's goals will probably need to be pointed out frequently. However, by doing so, it is possible to maintain a collaborative relationship.

Antisocial clients enter therapy with a long history of punishment and rejection at the hands of authority figures and upstanding members of society, and with extensive practice in devising alibis, resisting coercion, and concealing their true intentions. This, of course, greatly complicates therapy. It is important for the therapist to avoid taking an authoritarian approach to the client and to anticipate the client's repeatedly testing whether the therapist is genuine in presenting a collaborative approach. However, it is also important to avoid appearing nonauthoritarian in a way that makes the therapist appear weak and easily deceived. Although it requires some delicacy to establish oneself as strong but not authoritarian, this can be done through emphasizing collaboration, setting clear, firm limits, and being alert for attempts at deception or manipulation. When confronted by inconsistencies in the client's statements, it is generally most productive for the therapist to work nonpunitively to clarify the apparent inconsistencies and to make it clear that attempts at deceiving the therapist are counterproductive because they make it more difficult for the therapist to help the client work toward their shared goals. Attempts to "cross-examine" the client to determine the truth, to get the client to confess that he or she was lying, or to punish the client are usually counterproductive.

It is particularly important for the therapist to monitor his or her own responses to the client because disgust, impulses to punish the client, fear of the client, and anger at the client's attempts to deceive the therapist are common and can easily disrupt therapy. Because the client expects punishment or rejection from the therapist (as a representative of society), he or she is likely to be vigilant for indications of such reactions and may be quite quick to perceive and react to unacknowledged reactions on the therapist's part. Although it obviously would be ideal not to have problematic emotional reactions in the first place, the therapist's openly acknowledging his or her reactions can reduce the risk of their being misinterpreted or exploited as well as providing the client with a model for being open without being weak or vulnerable.

Antisocial clients typically adopt a "tough guy" role and refuse to acknowledge fears, doubts, and insecurities, as well as tenderness and caring, for fear of revealing vulnerabilities that others could exploit. Although this often makes it difficult for the therapist to obtain needed information, it is important to minimize the need for the client to acknowledge weaknesses early in therapy in order to reduce the risk of premature termination. If the therapist works gradually to establish trust, handles confidences sensitively, and explicitly acknowledges the client's strengths and capabilities, the client's discomfort with self-disclosure and with accepting help will gradually decrease.

In the initial phase of therapy, once the goals have been agreed upon, it is most productive to focus on specific problem situations and use of a problem-solving-training (Coché, 1987) type of approach. This consists of clarifying the nature of the situation, the desired outcomes, and the problems encountered and then identifying possible solutions, anticipating the likely outcome of each alternative, working to overcome impediments to potentially adaptive responses, and testing the most promising alternative(s) in practice. If this process is conducted collaboratively through guided discovery, resistance is minimized, and the client gradually masters the skills needed for effective problem solving. For example:

Rex's primary goal for therapy was to minimize the degree to which his medical symptoms interfered with his life. By focusing on identifying the situations, thoughts, and feelings that coincided with exacerbations of his arthritis, it was possible to demonstrate a clear relationship between subjective stress and amount of pain and to develop a treatment plan that included mastering stress management techniques, working to deal more effectively with situations that were recurrent sources of stress, and working to develop more adaptive responses to pain. By simply comparing the effects of staying in bed because of the pain with the effects of going ahead with his day despite the pain, it was possible to help him find a better way to handle his physical symptoms as well as to demonstrate the value of considering more than just the immediate consequences of his actions. Staying in bed resulted in less pain at the moment but on days when he remained in bed, his pain persisted for much of the day, he become increasingly depressed, and he tended to ruminate about having been betrayed by his friend. However, on days when he got out of bed and went on with his activities despite the pain, he initially experienced substantially more pain, but the pain passed fairly quickly, and he felt much better for the remainder of the day.

Given the evidence suggesting that antisocial clients are less affected by aversive consequences than others are (see Marshall & Barbaree, 1984), it may be most productive to focus more on pursuing desired outcomes than on avoiding negative outcomes while working on problem solving. When poor impulse control or inappropriate expression of anger are problems, the intervention approaches discussed in Chapter 8 may be useful.

As the client begins to control impulses and to anticipate the consequences of his or her actions more successfully outside of the therapy session, it is useful to help him or her to recognize that an accurate understanding of the motivations and feelings of others can help in anticipating the interpersonal consequences of his or her actions. Such questions as "How do you think he felt when you said that?" and "How would you feel if you were in her place?" can be used to focus the client's attention on the other person's perspective and to encourage the development of understanding and possibly even empathy. The client may initially be confident that he or she is accurately understanding the motivation of others, whereas it seems to the therapist that the client is mistaken. When this occurs, it is useful to treat the client's view as a hypothesis to be tested through a review of the available evidence or through behavioral experiments, rather than the therapist's trying to convince the client that he or she is wrong. If the client attributes selfish or malicious intentions to virtually everyone and he or she is heavily involved in a criminal subculture or has managed to alienate those around him or her, this negative view of others may be accurate for those with whom the client interacts regularly. In this case, it may be necessary to devote substantial time to helping the client develop new relationships or repair damaged relationships.

Over the course of therapy, there is likely to be a gradual transition from a largely behavioral focus that does not require the client to disclose his or her own thoughts and feelings in detail, to a more cognitive focus where the client's cognitions and emotions receive considerable attention. As the client is more willing to acknowledge doubts, fears, and longings, it becomes easier to identify the beliefs and assumptions that underlie the client's responses in various situations and to address these beliefs and assumptions as well.

With outpatient treatment, premature termination is likely to be a major problem. Even when the therapist is able to establish a collaborative relationship with the client and intervene effectively, there is a substantial risk of the client's terminating therapy if his or her distress is somehow alleviated. For example:

Rex reluctantly agreed to a treatment plan directed toward alleviating the stress that aggravated his medical symptoms. He was making good progress toward recognizing the consequences of his typical ways of responding to stressful situations and exploring his alternatives when he learned that the former friend who had betrayed him had also offended important crime figures elsewhere in the country, and that they planned to have the former friend killed. This resolved Rex's dilemma regarding whether to take the direct action himself, and the stress and physical symptoms that brought him into therapy quickly subsided. Not surprisingly, he immediately decided to terminate therapy and insisted that similar problems would never reoccur in the future.

When faced with this situation, the therapist can best handle it by pointing out, as clearly as possible, the ways in which continuing in therapy is in the client's best interest and by identifying any remaining distress that the client may be minimizing or denying. In a study of the effectiveness of psychotherapy with clients in a methadone maintenance program for addicts, Woody *et al.* (1985) found that antisocial clients who were depressed benefitted substantially from short-term cognitive-behavioral therapy, whereas antisocial clients who were not depressed did not. If the client is truly free of distress, he or she is likely to terminate despite the therapist's efforts or invest little effort in therapy. However, if some distress remains, this may provide sufficient motivation for continued treatment.

As the close of therapy approaches, if not before, it is important to pay special attention to the social pressures the client faces for continued antisocial behavior. The obvious solution would be for the client to work to establish new friendships with persons not associated with his or her previous life-style. However, in order to do this, the client may need to work on the social skills needed to fit in with prosocial groups, face his or her anticipation of rejection, and modify his or her derogatory attitudes toward "squares." In working on relapse prevention, it is particularly important to prepare for situations where the client is treated unfairly, rejected, or punished despite having tried to "play by the rules." Obviously, "playing by the rules" does not guarantee success, but a client who has recently adopted a prosocial approach can easily misinterpret unfair treatment or rejection as an indication that it does not work at all.

The approach to intervention described here can be conducted in individual therapy or in group or family therapy. Group and family therapy are likely to have substantial advantages and to prove superior to individual intervention when they are feasible. Family intervention presents the possibility of obtaining information from family members as well as the client, of using feedback from family members to help the antisocial individual recognize the consequences of his or her actions, and of working to modify the family system that otherwise may tend to perpetuate antisocial behavior. Therapy with a group of antisocial clients presents an opportunity for group members to provide each other with feedback about the impact of their behavior within the session as well as presenting an opportunity for using role playing to develop problem-solving skills (see Coché, 1987). In addition, group members may be particularly perceptive in confronting other group members' attempts at evasion or manipulation and may be especially credible in pointing out the ways in which antisocial behavior is counterproductive.

Conclusions

If the antisocial client stays in therapy long enough to complete the tment approach outlined here, much can be accomplished, not only in decreasing antisocial behavior but in enabling the client to adopt a life-style that is more rewarding both to the client and to his or her acquaintances. However, clients with Antisocial Personality Disorder often discontinue therapy prematurely unless treatment is involuntary or the client is experiencing continued distress. Therefore, the impact of outpatient Cognitive Therapy on clients with Antisocial Personality Disorder is likely to be limited unless the client suffers from problems in addition to his or her personality disorder that provide an incentive for persistent work in therapy.

Narcissistic Personality Disorder

The diagnosis of Narcissistic Personality Disorder was a new addition to DSM-III (APA, 1980) and has been maintained in DSM-III-R (APA, 1987). The concept of narcissism, however, goes back to the earliest history of the psychoanalytic movement. The term itself is based on the Greek myth of Narcissus, the young boy who was so enamoured of his own image that he ended up rooted to his position, fascinated by his reflection. The earliest reference to the myth of Narcissus as a metaphor for psychological functioning was made by Havelock Ellis (1898). The term *narcissistic* and the use of the concept as a clinical description of a style of responding originated with Nacke (cited in Freud, 1914). The concept of narcissism has been central to psychoanalytic thinking over the years (Campbell, 1981), but, unfortunately, narcissism has received little attention from behavioral and cognitive-behavioral writers to date.

Assessment

According to DSM-III-R, the individual with a Narcissistic Personality Disorder suffers from a "pervasive pattern of grandiosity (in fantasy or behavior), lack of empathy, and hypersensitivity to the evaluation of others" (see Table 24). This pattern of grandiosity occurs whether or not an objective evaluation of talent, accomplishment, physical prowess, intelligence, achievement, or beauty would validate the idiosyncratic view of the individual. The self-focus inherent in this grandiosity is accompanied by a lack of empathy for others. For example, a young woman was "insulted" because when she paid a condolence call on the parent of a co-worker who had died, no one noticed her new dress.

As with most personality disorders, clients with Narcissistic Personality Disorder are usually referred because of problems with depression or anxiety rather than because of narcissism *per se*. The Axis II problems often become apparent quite quickly in therapy as the client complains about not receiving the recognition or approval that he or she deserves or indirectly reveals the lengths to which he or she goes in order to assure receipt of this recognition and approval. Narcissistic Personality Disorder is grouped in

TABLE 24. DSM-III-R Diagnostic Criteria for Narcissistic Personality Disorders

---

A pervasive pattern of grandiosity (in fantasy or behavior), lack of empathy, and hypersensitivity to the evaluation of others, beginning by early adulthood and present in a variety of contexts, as indicated by at least *five* of the following:
1. Reacts to criticism with feelings of rage, shame, or humiliation (even if not expressed)
2. Is interpersonally exploitative: takes advantage of othes to achieve his or her own ends
3. Has a grandiose sense of self-importance, e.g., exaggerates achievements and talents, expects to be noticed as "special" without appropriate achievement
4. Believes that his or her problems are unique and can be understood only by other special people
5. Is preoccupied with fantasies of unlimited success, power, brilliance, beauty, or ideal love
6. Has a sense of entitlement: unreasonable expectation of especially favorable treatment, e.g., assumes that he or she does not have to wait in line when others must do so
7. Requires constant attention and admiration, e.g., keeps fishing for compliments
8. Lack of empathy: inability to recognize and experience how others feel, e.g., annoyance and surprise when a friend who is seriously ill cancels a date
9. Is preoccupied with feelings of envy

Cluster B, because of the "dramatic, emotional, or erratic" manner of relating to the world (APA, 1987, p. 337), and these clients may manifest a hyperreactivity or overresponsiveness to others that may appear to have histrionic or antisocial features. The constant pursuit of reinforcement and acknowledgment of a special status requires considerable effort and often leaves the narcissist feeling empty and depressed. When the desired reactions from others are received, this often gives the narcissist a brief period of happiness, but it is usually followed by a letdown resulting from the cessation of the acknowledgment.

The narcissistic individual may go beyond merely fantasizing about outstanding success and accomplishment and may be powerfully motivated to succeed in order to receive the recognition he or she desires. This may result in what might appear to be a driven compulsive striving for wealth, fame, or recognition. For example:

Sam was a 64-year-old surgeon and professor of surgery at a major university medical school. He had become internationally known after developing several new techniques for cardiac surgery over many years. Although acclaimed and invited to address medical groups around the world, he strove to receive awards that were, in fact, meaningless in search of proof of his skills and abilities. Each award would give him a transient sense of accomplishment but would be followed by a feeling of emptiness.

Narcissistic individuals will often go to considerable lengths to maintain their high opinion of themselves. Maintaining physical health may become exaggerated into fad dieting to maintain strength, health, or beauty. The need for academic success may result in a joyless, educationless school experience that centers on grades and recognition rather than on learning. For example:

Jack, a 20-year-old male college student, was referred by the dean because of suicidal remarks. The student had asked the dean to investigate his grade in a course where he had received an "A." He requested a review because he had received an "A−" on the final exam, and he wanted an opportunity to retake the examination to achieve an "A" on the exam as well as in the course. He stated that he could not live his life knowing that his grade was "so poor" and not commensurate with his assessment of himself as "one of the finest students in the class."

There is, for the narcissist, little joy in succeeding, because any success is perceived as "due and owing" rather than as an accomplishment worth savoring. The achievement of one of the highest grades in a course is mitigated by the fact that it was not the highest and that others did equally well. If someone else has a greater accomplishment, the narcissistic individual often responds with envy and jealousy.

In some cases, the narcissistic behavior may be less problematic in that it is consistent with societal expectations. The handsome or beautiful movie star is expected to be aware of his or her beauty and to demand special treatment because of it. Those who have become famous whether through achievement or through birth are often seen as deserving special treatment. Few are surprised when these individuals act as "prima donnas." However, even the "socially acceptable" narcissist may encounter problems in relationships with peers, when the aging process can no longer be stayed by medicines or surgery, or when the individual's career declines for other reasons.

Conceptualization

Freud's paper, "On Narcissism: An Introduction" (1914), was among his most important in that it first introduced the basic concepts of the ego ideal and the self-observing portion of the psyche that Freud was later to describe as the superego. The early, self-involved behavior of the infant was seen by Freud to be a transitional state, eventually maturing into the ability to transfer this self-love to others. The basic psychoanalytic model of narcissism posits a disruption in the maturation process that fixates the individual's ability to love at the level of self-love.

The object-relations theorists (Kernberg, 1967, 1970; Kohut, 1968, 1971) view narcissism as a paradoxical response to emotional deprivation during the early developmental stages. In effect, the exaggeration and overvaluation serve the defensive purpose of protecting the real self that is threatened and weak. There is, however, little empirical research validating the notion that early deprivation will lead to an inflated sense of self. Studies of emotional deprivation have, in fact, presented evidence that emotional deprivation in infancy leads to apathy, withdrawal, poor social skills, and an avoidance of social interaction (Harlow, 1971).

Theories regarding the development of the "self-concept" provide another perspective on narcissism. During normal development, a major part of the parental role is to help a child develop a positive self-image and a strong sense of self-concept or self-esteem (Hamner & Turner, 1985). This would ideally translate into a sense of personal efficacy, a feeling of satisfaction that is derived from successfully dealing with stressors and limitations imposed by one's environment. This may lead to what van der Waals (1965) calls "healthy narcissism," that is, a positive sense of self that is developed by having an awareness and acceptance of one's abilities and limitations and a striving to develop one's abilities. Hamner and Turner (1985) make three assumptions about the development of self-concept. First, that it is learned; second, that this learning occurs early in the socialization process; and third, that the self-concept is a powerful determinant of behavior. This view implies that inappropriate early socialization could result in the individual's learning an unrealistically high appraisal of his or her capabilities and developing a pathological level of narcissism but does not specify what problems in socialization would produce this problem.

Millon (1969, 1981) has proposed a social-learning hypothesis for the development of narcissistic characteristics or the Narcissistic Personality Disorder that is compatible with this developmental view. Several elements may combine to establish the early exaggeration and overvaluation of self. The parental style of manifesting self-esteem will often be reflected by the child. If a parent is narcissistic, he or she will model certain behaviors and a general style for the child. Furthermore, narcissistic parents will want to have special and wonderful children that enhance parental self-esteem and will thereby tend to exaggerate the accomplishments or abilities of the child. This modeling and reinforcement of exaggerated self-valuation behavior could easily establish a narcissistic pattern for the child. In other cases, the parents may be unable or unwilling to assist the child in setting realistic boundaries within which to view him- or herself. The parent who accepts the young child's grandiose visions of self, experience, or future possibilities, without offering realistic feedback and pointing out the child's limits and boundaries, reinforces this overinflated and eventually dysfunctional self-image. Schools may further contribute to the lack of limits by offering special treatment and excessive positive feedback to children who are seen as special. For example:

When Tom, a 15-year-old male, was referred because of school truancy the therapist learned that he had been allowed to miss more than the usual number of classes before the school was forced to take action. The rationale offered by the teacher was that the boy was doing well, could easily catch up on the work, and was gifted.

The same special attention might be offered to a child who appeared gifted athletically or in other ways. Such special attention would not be expected to establish a narcissistic pattern if it was the only such influence or if the child received sufficient reality-based feedback from some other source. However, if a narcissistic pattern has already been encouraged by family interactions, the child may interact with others in ways that tend to elicit special treatment and excessive attention from teachers and peers who thus unintentionally perpetuate the pattern.

Narcissistic Personality Disorder is characterized by the cognitive distortions of selective abstraction and all-or-nothing thinking. These individuals constantly scan the environment for evidence of their superiority and place great weight on the evidence they find. They may ignore any evidence that points to their being average, or they may respond to any indications that they are "normal" with anger, anxiety, or overcompensatory words or actions. In either case, their view of the data is quite selective and leads to extreme conclusions. These problems may be exacerbated by poor problem-solving and reality-testing skills.

It is no doubt obvious that the central dysfunctional belief underlying Narcissistic Personality Disorder is the assumption that the individual is, or must be, a "special" person. The need to be admired for real or imagined achievement is an overriding factor. The narcissist may exaggerate his or her accomplishments to impress others. The nature of the attempt to impress others may depend on the degree to which the client has histrionic characteristics as well. The greater the hysteria, the more strange or bizarre the behavior. For example:

Ralph, a 41-year-old attorney, was referred because of a number of somatic problems that his internist thought were psychogenic. In the initial session, the client announced that he had been an assistant professor at a university medical school. When questioned further, he had to admit that he was not an assistant professor but had assisted a professor by giving two presentations as part of a lecture on medicine and the law. This same individual would meet women in a bar and speak in a very credible English accent. He would regale these women with stories of his work at Oxford and his practice outside of London. While many women found him intriguing, he could never go out with them because if he did they would then find out the truth about him.

A common corollary to the client's belief in his or her specialness is the client's assumption that, as a result, he or she deserves special treatment and must not be slowed or stopped from seeking pleasure and status. For this individual, the natural course of events involves pleasure seeking and self-aggrandizement, and any deterrent or obstacle is not only to be avoided or destroyed but is also unfair and wrong. This view can generate considerable anger and frequent "temper tantrums" as well as behavior that can seem sociopathic. The client often believes that no one should have more of anything than he or she has and shows an intense envy for any persons who are seen as having more. This may be coupled with an insulting and denigrating manner and attempts to succeed by putting others down or actually destroying the productions of others. For example:

Joe, a 33-year-old insurance salesman would take messages out of the mailboxes of other salesmen so that he could be the most successful salesman in his office and have his name on the "Salesman of the Month" plaque in the office corridor. When he was caught and was barred from winning for a year, he was incensed that such a big deal was being made of it and that he was not going to get the proper recognition for his work.

Obviously, the interpersonal patterns discussed have a detrimental impact on most relationships. Often the narcissistic individual will seek out kindred spirits who will participate in a "mutual admiration society." They may well believe that they should only have to relate to "special" people like themselves and see others as beneath them either socially, financially, or intellectually. They will tend to join only those clubs or organizations that offer them prestige, status, or the opportunity to associate with people who are seen as special, being very conscious of the trappings of status. For example:

James, a 42-year-old male accountant, was referred because of anxiety about his dwindling practice. He would not have anything to do with his clients beyond doing their accounting work because he considered himself above them. He would avoid clients if he met them in a social situation, thinking, "Why should I have to mix with people I consider rabble?" Unfortunately for him, the usual response of his clients was to seek another accountant. The major concern he presented in therapy was that he could not keep up the payments on his Mercedes Benz. His goal was to have the therapist give him ways of responding to his clients so that it would appear that he cared, as long as that did not entail having to have drinks or lunch with them. When the therapist questioned that as a goal of therapy, the client responded by saying, "You are a consultant. I pay you to be whatever I want you to be."

These individuals may also select spouses or partners who admire them greatly or who can be exploited. For example:

Jack, a 32-year-old male client prided himself on being what he called a "shark." He would attend dances or go to bars and pick up the women that he considered the least attractive or least socially skilled. He would almost always have sex and then never have any more contact with them. He said that he kept count of the number of sexual experiences that he had. He described his behavior as, "I'm doing them a favor. I'm giving them what no one else will." He felt no remorse or sense of guilt about his behavior and when questioned as to whether he felt uncomfortable with women that he considered so unattractive, his response was that he only thought about how wonderful these women would see him to be. Because he never took them out, he had no concern of a loss of status.

Intervention Strategies and Techniques

After the initial assessment, the building of a strong collaborative relationship is essential because participation in psychotherapy requires that the narcissistic client be asked to do things that he or she either has had great difficulty doing, has never had to do, or has never learned to do. These tasks include tolerating frustration and bearing anxiety without alcoholism, drug abuse, taking flight, abusive behavior toward others, or other forms of acting out. Unfortunately collaboration can be difficult both because of the characteristics of the client and the reactions the client elicits from the therapist.

One of the first steps in establishing a collaboration is the task of agreeing on goals for therapy. Because the narcissistic client is not likely to present "becoming less narcissistic" or even "getting along with others better" as goals for therapy, it is important for the therapist to focus on clarifying and operationalizing the client's goals rather than on trying to convince the client to work to change his or her narcissism. The client's narcissism most naturally will become a focus of therapy as it impedes progress toward accomplishing more concrete goals. In practice, it may be far more realistic to work on changing specific behaviors and on helping the client be more moderate in his or her narcissism than to plan to change a lifelong narcissistic pattern.

Sam, the surgeon mentioned earlier, came to therapy with great reluctance, as part of marital therapy. He had been married for 42 years to Anita. She had suffered a "nervous breakdown" (Major Depressive Episode), which required hospitalization. The treating resident strongly recommended marital therapy. As part of the assessment, Sam was seen for two sessions. While he made it quite clear that he did not like being in the therapist's office, he was smiling, pleasant, and collegial. He stated that he did not want to be part of the therapy ("I really don't think that I can offer anything useful"), was very busy ("You know how it is. We're all so busy"), and did not think that there was anything wrong with his wife that had anything to do with him ("This is her problem, it always was"). When his pleasant and charming manner did not work to convince the therapist that Sam's involvement in therapy was unnecessary, he became brusque, bordering on rudeness. "Why," he inquired, "am I seeing a therapist who is only an associate professor, when I am a full professor? If I have got to be part of this ridiculous business, I might as well have the best person."

Sam and Anita had been married for 42 years. The primary marital problem revolved around Sam's demanding that his wife wait on him, hand and foot. She had little more than servant status and was expected to provide for his every whim. She had graduated from college and had immediately gotten married, becoming a housewife and mother. Over the last 10 years, Anita had become more and more "down" and finally ceased functioning and was admitted into the hospital. The beginning of her deterioration coincided with the last child's marrying and leaving home. Sam's view of Anita's problem was that she was just "too moody, too weak, too spoiled, and too reluctant to do her job," which was, in his eyes, to do his bidding. Sam considered his position in life as one that was well deserved. He described himself as a tyrant in the operating theater because "I'm damn good." He described, with great relish, how he had his residents and nurses jump whenever he came into a room.

The goal of therapy, within the context of the agreed-upon marital work, was to have Sam respond differently to his wife; the rationale was that this would help Anita return to full functioning. It was pointed out to Sam that if he continued to create stress, his wife would continue to be depressed and would be unavailable to meet his needs. With this as a rationale, he was willing to continue in therapy.

Once clear, manageable goals have been identified, the full range of cognitive and behavioral techniques are available for use. Because revealing one's flaws and shortcomings is incompatible with a narcissistic approach to life, behavioral interventions are often easier to implement because they require less self-disclosure than many of the cognitive interventions. Noncompliance with homework assignments due to the client's belief that "I must have my way in every interaction," his or her desire for special treatment, and power struggles with the therapist are common. The client may, in fact, attempt to bait the therapist into the struggle in an attempt to assert power over the therapist, the ultimate power being leaving therapy. By pointing out what is happening, identifying the automatic thoughts and the underlying beliefs, and reminding the client that the point to the homework is to help the client achieve his or her goals, the therapist can deal with noncompliance without having to try to defeat the client. In time, the client may be able to see that there is no need to struggle and that, in fact, the struggle is counterproductive to reaching his or her goals.

Insofar as possible, the therapist must work with, rather than against, the narcissistic pattern in order to minimize unproductive conflict and to engage the client in therapy. The therapist who is not willing or able to tolerate the narcissistic client's behavior and accommodate to it will have difficulty inducing the client to persist in therapy. However, the therapist who is unwilling to confront the client because he or she is so easily offended is likely to end up being helpless to have any impact.

The narcissistic client's sense of specialness complicates the therapeutic relationship. He or she is likely to expect special privileges and exemption from the standard rules followed by others. Sometimes by direct words, or covert deeds, the client will demand special attention. For example:

Mark, a 42-year-old salesman, would come early for sessions, ask for an empty office so that he could make phone calls, and would give the therapist's secretary xeroxing to do, telling her it was okayed by the therapist. When it was pointed out that the client was impinging on the time of the staff, he responded by asking whether the therapist thought that his work was important. The therapist felt he had been put into the position of "proving" that the client was indeed special to him. This was coupled by the client bringing gifts, coffee, newspapers, and holiday cards to the therapist.

It is essential for the therapist to establish and maintain firm guidelines and limits in therapy. This may be as straightforward as in asking a client to not put muddy shoes on a couch in the office, or it may be more involved. For example, a female client spoke about a possible lump in her breast to her male therapist and asked if he wanted to feel it. When the therapist questioned the appropriateness of that request, the client responded, "You're a doctor aren't you? What's the big deal? Are you embarrassed?"

Often the need to decide to what extent to accommodate to the client's narcissism and to what extent to set limits or confront the client presents itself from the beginning of therapy. For example:

Mr. A. began therapy with a rather involved telephone call to set up an initial consultation. After contacting the therapist, the client said that he could be available on Tuesday at 3 P.M. When informed that that time was not available, the client became irritated and said, "Why must I make myself available only when you think it is best? My time and schedule are just as important as yours." When he was told that that time belonged to another client, he offered to call the other client and "persuade" him or her that they should come another time. When offered an appointment at 4 P.M., he quickly countered with, "How about 4:30?"

One area in which the client is likely to resist limit setting is in the therapist's attempts to agree on a clear agenda and stick to it, and this is an excellent point for beginning to set limits with the client. On this issue it is possible to turn the client's narcissism to the therapist's advantage by pointing out that the purpose of sticking to agreed-upon goals and a clear agenda is not to limit the client's freedom but rather to allow the therapist to most effectively pursue the client's goals and to be sure to address his or her important concerns. (There is no need to mention that all clients receive this form of "special treatment"). This issue of the agenda is also an ideal arena for limit setting because it is generally easy to demonstrate that it is in the client's interest to comply with the limits the therapist proposes. Having demonstrated that, in this one area, it is the client's interest to comply with the limits the therapist sets, it may be easier to get the client to comply with limits in other areas as well.

Like the sociopath, narcissistic clients are not motivated by empathy for others, a desire to do what is right, or a desire to please the therapist. It is important to focus on the client's long-term self-interest in working to help him or her to choose the most adaptive courses of action and in trying to motivate him or her to take that action. As is the case with the sociopath, the client will discover that narcissistic behavior can be quite counterproductive and that it is in his or her self-interest to make substantial changes in his or her interpersonal behavior. The use of significant others in therapy can help to reinforce certain changes and to help the significant others cope more effectively with the client.

In the treatment of Sam and Anita, marital sessions were held weekly, and Sam was seen individually every other week. The therapy work with Sam was quite limited, with much of the treatment consisting of direct instruction on more adaptive ways to behave with Anita. He did, in fact, alter his response to Anita, not because he agreed with the changes but because if he did not make those alterations, he would get even less of what he wanted.

Anita was a dependent individual who wanted to maintain the marriage. She stated that she loved Sam and understood him "like no one in the whole world does." The focus of work with Anita was to have her be more assertive and try to refuse doing things that she did not want to do. If Sam wanted certain things done, they could hire someone and pay that person to do it, or Sam could do it himself. After 6 months of therapy, Sam and Anita terminated the therapy. She was less depressed and described Sam as more responsive. She also pointed out that any response on Sam's part was more response than she had gotten in the past.

Conclusions

Therapy with narcissistic clients can be quite frustrating. These clients are not simply resistant to negative feedback. Any intimation that the therapist holds less than absolute positive regard (bordering on admiration or worship) toward the client may very quickly evoke either a dramatic overreaction with strong anxiety or rage or refusal to acknowledge the therapist's view. The "yes, but . . ." nature of the client's typical response, an almost automatic dismissal of the therapist's statements, and a tendency to see the therapist as taking the side of all of the "others" that do not fully understand or appreciate the value and importance of the client, all serve to make it very difficult for the therapist to intervene effectively. It is essential that the therapist be aware of his or her emotional reactions to the client, not only to prevent the obvious frustration and annoyance from interfering with therapy but also to avoid being inhibited by fear of the client's reactions. In particular, it is counterproductive to spend excessive time being angry at the narcissistic client for being narcissistic or to give in to his or her demands for special treatment, even though this may seem like less trouble than it is to set firm limits.

Despite the difficulties, narcissistic clients can be worked with effectively in Cognitive Therapy. It is far less likely that the narcissistic pattern will be erased than it is that the patterns will be modified or utilized in more productive ways. The best predictors of success may be the degree of narcissism and the therapist's ability to withstand the narcissistic individual's constant pressure for approval and special treatment.

11

Obsessive-Compulsive Personality Disorder

The symptoms of the Obsessive-Compulsive Personality Disorder are characteristics that are common in our culture. They are behaviors that are highly valued in our society when in a less extreme form. For example, perseverance and attention to detail are valued and functional; however, when carried to an extreme, the resulting perseveration and inability to grasp "the big picture" are not. Children are taught to value rumination when adults send them to their room to think about the "error of their ways," but the obsessive-compulsive tends to ruminate constantly. Such homilies as "if it's worth doing, it's worth doing well" and "if at first you don't succeed, try, try again" teach an approach to life that the obsessive-compulsive carries to a pathological extreme.

Because some aspects of compulsive behavior are functional and perhaps even essential to success in our society, treatment presents some complications. The compulsive, like the overeater, cannot totally stop performing the problem behaviors. He or she must learn to use his or her compulsivity in a judicious and functional way rather than simply abandoning attention to detail, thoroughness, and persistence.

CLINICAL ASSESSMENT

Kathy was an 18-year-old girl, who had graduated from high school 3 months before. She had planned to go away to college but decided to postpone these plans because she was depressed. She was attending classes at a local college while living at home with her parents and her younger brother. Kathy complained of being depressed for the past 2½ months: She was anhedonic, self-critical, lethargic, and in her "own little world." She had gained 15 to 20 pounds and was "obsessed" with her weight. She had been a counselor at a summer camp but left early because she felt so bad. Her parents left on a trip to China 3 days later, and Kathy called her mother home because she could not tolerate being alone. Kathy had always done moderately well in school (B/B+ average) but said that she was "lazy and procrasti-nates" and "knows" she will be like that in college. She had always had one to two close friends but felt nervous getting to know new people. She had dated for the past 2 years and felt flattered to be asked out, but the boys had never measured up to her standards.

Ralph was a 21-year-old, white graduate student whose presenting problem was: "I have a problem making decisions. If I decide to choose one possibility—let's say a topic for a paper—I compulsively look to the other options and as a conse-quence the subject I originally chose loses its attractiveness. The symptoms I expe-rience are a sense of helplessness and futility in my intellectual endeavors, a lack of confidence, and an inability to step back and look at my work or even the texts I'm analyzing from any perspective."

The characteristics of Obsessive-Compulsive Personality Disorder specified by DSM-III-R are shown in Table 25. Kathy's initial interview gave ample evidence of Obsessive-Compulsive features and of the possibility that she had the full disorder. Her perfectionism, indecisiveness, rigidity, inability to relax, and tendency to ruminate were quite apparent from the beginning of treatment, as is commonly the case with such clients.

These qualities are characteristic of the individual's long-term func-tioning and are *self-consonant*. That is, they are part of the individual's identity and are rarely considered by the client to be the cause of any problems that may be experienced. Unlike the person with Major De-pressive Disorder, who complains of severe depression, the person with Obsessive-Compulsive Personality Disorder does not tend to complain of compulsivity. This person may enter therapy complaining of any of a large number of problems—including depression, anxiety, or problems with spouses, children, or co-workers—but will rarely recognize the connection between the problem and his or her compulsivity. It is the clinician's job to be alert to the underlying pathology that may be giving rise to the Axis I complaints.

It is important to note the differences between Obsessive-Compulsive Personality Disorder and Obsessive-Compulsive Disorder. As was dis-cussed in Chapter 6, Obsessive-Compulsive Disorder is characterized by obsessions, compulsions, or both. These are recurrent thoughts, images, or actions that the client sees as useless or abhorrent but from which he or she is unable to refrain. It can be seen from Table 25 that despite the name "Obsessive-Compulsive Personality Disorder," obsessions and compul-sions are not symptomatic of this disorder. Although a client may have both disorders, they are separate and distinct. The obsessions and compul-sions experienced by individuals with Obsessive-Compulsive Disorder are *self-dissonant* and are likely to be primary complaints when they enter ther-apy. Persons with Obsessive-Compulsive Personality Disorder are prone to excessive internal debate and rumination and apparently compulsive be-havior such as excessive double-checking of their work. However, these

TABLE 25. DSM-III-R Criteria for Obsessive-Compulsive Personality Disorder

---

A pervasive pattern of perfectionism and inflexibility, beginning by early adulthood and present in a variety of contexts, as indicated by at least five of the following:
1. Perfectionism that interferes with task completion, e.g., inability to complete a project because own overly strict standards are not met
2. Preoccupation with details, rules, lists, order, organization, or schedules to the extent that the major point of the activity is lost
3. Unreasonable insistence that others submit to exactly his or her way of doing things or unreasonable reluctance to allow others to do things because of the conviction that they will not do them correctly
4. Excessive devotion to work and productivity to the exclusion of leisure activities and friendships (not accounted for by obvious economic necessity)
5. Indecisiveness: decision making is either avoided, postponed, or protracted, e.g., the person cannot get assignments done on time because of ruminating about priorities (do not include if indecisiveness is due to excessive need for advice or reassurance from others)
6. Overconscientiousness, scrupulousness, and inflexibility about matters of morality, ethics, or values (not accounted for by cultural or religious identification)
7. Restricted expression of affection when no personal gain is likely to result
9. Inability to discard worn-out or worthless objects even when they have no sentimental value

---

characteristics are typically seen by the client as being signs of appropriate carefulness and thoroughness and are often not presented as problems. The treatment of Obsessive-Compulsive Disorder has been discussed in Chapter 6, and the present chapter will focus on the treatment of Obsessive-Compulsive Personality Disorder.

Assessment of Obsessive-Compulsive Personality Disorder may begin even before the initial session. At the first telephone contact with the client, the therapist may note that it takes an inordinately long time to arrive at a mutually acceptable appointment time. Whereas this task is usually accomplished with other clients within a matter of moments, it may take 5, 10, or more minutes with the compulsive. Even after this, the client may call back moments later to change the time. This is often the result of extreme indecisiveness, anxiety, and the felt need to meet at the "perfect" time. Or, at the first phone contact, the client may start telling the therapist his or her life story in such a way that the therapist finds it difficult to interrupt. Such compulsive talking without regard to consideration of appropriateness is also diagnostic. Or, paradoxically, the client may take an inordinately long time to respond to, seemingly, the most straightforward inquiries. This was the case with Ralph. For example, at his first session, Ralph's therapist asked him how he was feeling and got no response even after waiting almost 1 minute. Although the therapist needs to consider the possibility of a psychotic process, it is more than likely that this is the result of the client's ruminatively considering all possible responses to the question and their relative merit.

The content of the client's speech may also give ample indication of compulsive features, if not Obsessive-Compulsive Personality. The therapist will notice that the client has a tendency to take the worst possible construction of an event or eventuality. Thus, the future is seen as holding all manner of dangers for the client and his or her friends or family. Events that occurred long ago are still worried over. In fact, it may seem as if the person thinks of nothing besides what has gone or may go wrong. This client's speech may give additional evidence of Obsessive-Compulsive Personality by digressing from one worry to the next to the next to the next. Furthermore, the compulsive may frequently say, "Yes, but . . ." to suggestions or comments by the therapist. Because the compulsive thinks he or she must be absolutely correct, this individual has gotten into the habit of considering all points of view regarding any issue. Because there is always a point of view that conflicts with the therapist's statement, the compulsive responds, "Yes, but . . ." Although the passive-aggressive individual also does this a great deal (see Chapter 13), the therapist should entertain the possibility of the presence of Obsessive-Compulsive Personality.

Another aspect of the client that may be suggestive of Obsessive-Compulsive Personality Disorder is his or her job choice and leisure activities. The compulsive frequently gravitates to professions that require focused attention to detail and rigid procedures. As a result, the professions of law or accounting are more conducive to the compulsive style than is art, for example. However, this is by no means absolute, as there certainly are compulsive artists. Choice of leisure activities may be even more indicative of Obsessive-Compulsive Personality Disorder than is job choice. Compulsives rarely if ever take vacations; if their families can get them to take one, these individuals will be unable to relax and enjoy themselves. In fact, it is very difficult for the compulsive to engage in activities for the sake of pleasure alone because he or she feels as if he or she is "wasting time": television viewing must be "educational" or "uplifting," books or magazines must be related to work activities or self-improvement, a day at the pool must include swimming laps or dictating into a tape recorder. The compulsive experiences anxiety in unstructured situations, such as leisure, and therefore tries to avoid them.

The presenting problems that bring the client to treatment are also suggestive of Obsessive-Compulsive Personality. The foremost symptoms are a pattern of long-standing procrastination and chronic anxiety. The compulsive frequently reports a history of procrastination that dates back to college, if not to high school. This procrastination usually presents problems in the workplace whenever a rigid routine cannot be invoked to produce the required result. Compulsive lawyers may report that employers are dissatisfied with the number of billable hours per day on their timesheets or the time it takes them to write a standard letter. Students, such as Ralph, may have incomplete grades because they never complete and turn in papers to professors. Thus procrastination is often the primary presenting problem. Whenever the rigid approach to living stops working for one reason or another, the compulsive experiences anxiety. Because people initiate therapy when their habitual methods of coping stop working, the compulsive who seeks therapy is almost certain to complain of anxiety.

We see in the case of Kathy that she fit this profile very closely: Although she had been a chronic procrastinator all through high school, her crisis did not begin until she graduated. When she found herself entering a new and more personally demanding stage of life away from family and friends, her habitual means of coping stopped working. She became intensely ruminative and anxious (Hamilton Anxiety Rating Scale score of 21) and then became extremely depressed and hopeless (BDI of 31 and Hopelessness Scale score of 13) about her lack of control over her emotional state.

To complete our list of informal indicators of Obsessive-Compulsive Personality Disorder, we look at the client's nonverbal behavior and personal presentation. The woman who looks as if she spent careful hours on her appearance before leaving the house or the man who looks almost too perfectly put together may be individuals with perfectionism underlying a personality disorder. This type of client may also comment on the messiness of the therapist's office or may actually start tidying the therapist's desk.

In summary, from their earliest contact, the therapist will be aware of behavior in the client that may be indicative of Obsessive-Compulsive Personality Disorder. Such behaviors will include speech patterns and content, dress, grooming, life-style, activities, and interpersonal behavior, which are summarized in Table 26. As for all personality disorders, the earlier that correct diagnosis can be made, the greater the likelihood of success in therapy. Early diagnosis is important so that the therapist can avoid prematurely addressing threatening issues before the proper groundwork is set.

CONCEPTUALIZATION

Shapiro (1965) described the compulsive style in terms of three basic features. First, the thinking of compulsives shows extreme *rigidity*. These individuals are frequently considered to be "dogmatic" or "opinionated." Their attention is intensely, sharply focused on one particular detail of a situation at a time. Therefore, they are not able to let their attention wander

TABLE 26. Possible Indications of Obsessive-Compulsive Personality Disorder

In presenting problems
  Severe procrastination
  Indecision regarding fairly commonplace decisions
  Dissatisfaction with own performance despite others viewing his or her performance as
    good
  Stress resulting from own high standards and own pressure to do well
  Inefficiency, inability to maintain an acceptable level of productivity despite having ade-
    quate skills and intelligence
  Depression due to inability to live up to own standards
In personal characteristics
  Insists on neatness and thoroughness even when it is unnecessary or counterproductive
  Prefers activities that involve attention to detail and adherence to clear procedures
  Inability to relax or take vacations, leisure time (if any) is occupied with self-improvement or
    productive activities
  Very controlled, little expression of emotion, little spontaneity or humor
  Discomfort with uncertainty or ambiguity
  Strong reactions when plans are disrupted
In interpersonal relationships
  Insists that others do things his or her way, unable to compromise or delegate responsibility
  Unable to express warmth, tenderness, affection
  Unempathic, shows little understanding of others' feelings
  Moralistic, judgmental, intolerant of others' views
  Critical of others, unable to give positive feedback
  Sensitive to criticism, defensive when criticized
In therapy
  Goes into excessive or irrelevant detail, digresses
  Talks about others in an impersonal, uninvolved way
  Meticulous, precise appearance and mannerisms
  Criticizes therapist's lack of neatness or begins straightening the therapist's desk
  Unusually stiff and formal
  Interprets mild inquiries or suggestions as criticism
In psychological testing
  Requires an excessive amount of time to complete questionnaires
  Excessively detailed, thorough responses
  Discomfort with ambiguous tasks or with questions where there is no "right" answer
  Discomfort with true-false questions when the item is not completely true or completely
    false

or allow it to be captured by some occurrence. For similar reasons, they frequently miss the point in social interactions, rarely get "hunches," and are rarely surprised. As Shapiro says, "It is not that they do not look or listen, but they are looking or listening too hard for something else" (p. 28).

The second significant feature of the compulsive style, according to Shapiro, is the mode of activity. He states that these people have a fairly continuous *absorption in intensive routine or technical activity*. Furthermore, their activity seems to be characterized by a "more or less continuous experience of tense deliberateness, a sense of effort, and of trying" (p. 31).

They never seem to relax. Even on the rare occasions in which their families can induce them to take a vacation, they plan a full schedule for each day so that their time is not spent ineffectively. If they are prevented from following the schedule exactly, they will be upset that their plans went astray, not that they might have missed out on something enjoyable.

The third feature is a *loss of reality*, according to Shapiro. Compulsives often seem to worry about things that do not merely seem unlikely, but often seem absurd, almost delusional. Their attention to detail leads them to focus on some particular trivial bit of data to the exclusion of other relevant data. For example, a male compulsive may notice a sore on his arm; he may remember from a magazine article that Caposi's sarcoma looks like a sore and starts to worry that he has AIDS and is dying. He does not stop to consider that he has none of the other symptoms that normally accompany AIDS or that he does not engage in any high risk behaviors because he is focused so strongly on the one symptom that is present.

Another feature of their "loss of reality" experienced by some, but not all, compulsives is a loss of conviction as to the truth. Such individuals do not experience things as true or false, good or bad, from a sense of conviction, as do most people. They deduce that something "must be" true or good because "it fits" with certain accepted rules or principles. For example, one educated and intelligent client with Obsessive-Compulsive Personality Disorder was unable to answer when asked his opinion about almost anything; however, he was able to say what "should" be true. Another client responded to the question "How do you feel right now?" with "My voice is raised and my fists are clenched. . . . I must be angry."

An understanding of the obsessive-compulsive individual's beliefs and assumptions sheds considerable light on his or her reasons for adhering to extreme forms of normally adaptive strategies, despite the obvious problems. Our conceptualization is based in part on the work of Guidano and Liotti (1983). The central assumption in Obsessive-Compulsive Personality Disorder is "I must avoid mistakes at all costs." He or she believes that "in each situation there is one right answer or right action," that anything else is a mistake, and that mistakes are intolerable. The individual may well fear the consequences of making mistakes, but above and beyond this there is a strong, unreasoning conviction that mistakes are intolerable even when no serious consequences are likely.

Most of the maladaptive aspects of Obsessive-Compulsive Personality Disorder are the result of the strategies the individual uses to avoid mistakes. These individuals assume "the way to avoid making mistakes is to be careful and thorough, to pay attention to details, to try hard, to set high standards for oneself, and to be sure to notice mistakes so that they can be corrected." These certainly are strategies that are often quite useful in minimizing mistakes and doing a good job on a variety of tasks. However, the obsessive-compulsive client is not willing to simply minimize mistakes;

his or her goal is to totally eliminate them. Each time he or she does something that is perceived as a mistake, he or she concludes that the thing to do is to try harder, pay more attention to details, be more careful, and so forth. Thus normally adaptive strategies are carried to such extremes that they become counterproductive, and the obsessive-compulsive's tendency not to see "the big picture" interferes with his or her recognizing this.

One result of the obsessive-compulsive's belief that mistakes must be avoided is his or her strong desire for both self-control and control over his or her environment. The beliefs that in order to successfully avoid mistakes "I must be perfectly in control of my environment as well as of myself" and "loss of control is intolerable" underlie the client's insistence on certainty, predictability, and control over others. Another result of the assumption that mistakes must be avoided that is often particularly destructive is the belief that "to make a mistake is to be deserving of criticism." The obsessive-compulsive hopes that sufficient self-criticism will eliminate mistakes and fears. Furthermore, if this individual is not severely self-critical, he or she is compounding the mistake and will become increasingly imperfect and worthless. Thus, when Kathy followed her diet perfectly for 11 days, but ate one cookie on Day 12, she declared that she had failed, was totally out of control, and was fat and disgusting. When her therapist suggested that her guilt and depression were disproportionate to her "sin," she countered that without guilt she would become increasingly out of control and, ultimately, obese.

In addition, given the individual's strong desire to avoid mistakes and his or her assumption that there is one right answer or action, he or she is highly motivated to find the "right" response in each situation and then to adhere rigidly to it. As a result of dichotomous thinking, any departure from what is "right" is automatically seen as being "wrong." Therefore, the obsessive-compulsive individual has little tolerance for beliefs, values, or ways of doing things that differ from his or her own. Not surprisingly, this leads the individual to be quite uncomfortable with any novel or ambiguous situation where it is not clear what course of action is "right" and with any situation where there are several perfectly acceptable options rather than one right one.

Interpersonal relationships and interactions that involve strong emotions often do not present easily discernible right answers and, in addition, threaten to distract the obsessive-compulsive from his or her work and to cause "mistakes." Thus obsessive-compulsives tend to be uncomfortable both with intimate relationships and with strong emotions and tend to avoid both. Over time, this results in the individual's developing both relatively poor social skills and limited skill at handling emotions adaptively. This tends to lead to further avoidance for fear of making mistakes in interactions and thus tends to be self-perpetuating.

Let us consider the compulsive client who heard on the news that some unfortunate man had a stroke at the wheel of his car and died in the ensuing crash. She responded by becoming terrified of driving alone because she feared having a stroke and dying. It made no difference that the client was a healthy 34-year-old female and the man on the news was a 62-year-old and had a history of high blood pressure and strokes. The compulsive cannot simply acknowledge that something might be dangerous, take steps to reduce its risk, and put it out of his or her mind. He or she feels compelled to worry about it at great length because "if something is or may be dangerous, one must be terribly upset by it." One reason for this is the assumption that "one is powerful enough to initiate or prevent the occurrence of catastrophes by magical rituals or obsessional ruminations." If one worries enough, one can forestall whatever dire consequences one may feel are waiting. Ritualistic acts and obsessional rumination are seen as essential, helpful, and productive; to do anything else would seem foolhardy and dangerous.

Another assumption that gives rise to many clients seeking therapy is: "If the perfect course of action is not clear, it is better to do nothing." Because imperfection carries such terrible consequences, the compulsive will frequently only make choices or act when certain of success. Because there is so much uncertainty in life, it often seems best to do nothing. If one does nothing, one cannot fail, and therefore, one does not risk censure from self or others. The problem with this strategy is obvious when one considers that the environment more often requires productivity than perfection. The procrastination of the student or the lawyer may be an example of this assumption in action.

Given the obvious problems created by the obsessive-compulsive approach to life, it might seem that these individuals would be relieved to discover that they do not have to avoid mistakes at all costs and can safely relax their standards for themselves. However, these individuals typically are convinced that any deviations from doing things the "right" way will lead to disaster. Consequently, if the therapist points out the drawbacks to the client's current approach to life and suggests that some rules or rituals might be modified or abandoned, the compulsive becomes quite anxious. Such interventions are likely to lead to such thoughts such as "I'll stop working altogether," "My work will become low rate," "I'll become promiscuous," and so on.

The effects of dichotomous thinking can be seen in the assumption that any deviation from trying to do things perfectly will lead quickly to total disaster. It can also be seen in the assumption that if one is not in total control, one is out of control and in the assumption that actions are either right or wrong. These dichotomous views make it difficult to induce the client to change his or her obsessive-compulsive approach to life and make the pattern quite resistant to spontaneous change.

Kathy's most problematic distortion was dichotomous thinking: "I'm either perfectly in control, or I am totally out of control." She indicated some of her underlying assumptions on the Dysfunctional Attitude Scale by endorsing such items as: "Criticism must upset the person who receives the criticism." "If I do well, it is probably due to chance; if I do badly, it is probably my own fault." "If I do not treat people kindly, fairly, and considerately, I am a rotten person." "If I fail partly, it is as bad as being a complete failure." Beliefs such as these indicate some of the various pathways Kathy has into anxiety and depression: "Unless I rigidly fulfill my perfectionistic standards, I must be terribly upset."

Although there is little empirical evidence regarding the etiology of Obsessive-Compulsive Personality Disorder, a number of factors seem obvious from clinical observation. First, obsessive-compulsive characteristics are strongly reinforced in our culture. Parents and teachers usually respond quite positively to the boy or girl who is diligent, obedient, and hard working and often devote considerable effort to attempting to inculcate these traits. Second, obsessive-compulsive individuals often describe a history of growing up with a critical, demanding parent who reacted negatively to mistakes, who focused on results rather than effort or intentions, and who did not give an equal emphasis to rewarding achievement. This experience could easily form the basis for a belief that mistakes are intolerable, could lead the individual to emphasize avoiding mistakes rather than striving to achieve, and encourage the individual to adopt self-criticism and self-punishment as a strategy for eliminating mistakes. Although these two factors are probably not sufficient to completely account for the etiology of this disorder, they frequently appear to play a major role in its development.

Strategies for Intervention

Although the obsessive-compulsive individual's intense desire to avoid mistakes appears to be central to the disorder and is an important target for intervention, it is also a major impediment to intervention because it results in a reluctance to experiment with new approaches to problem situations. Even obsessive-compulsive individuals who are in considerable distress frequently fear that the changes their therapists advocate will make the situation worse rather than better. If it were possible to eliminate clients' fear of making mistakes before attempting to induce them to change their behavior, this would greatly simplify treatment. Unfortunately, it is rarely possible to effectively challenge the client's inability to tolerate making mistakes without first inducing the client to change his or her behavior, even though this entails the risk of making mistakes.

The first problem in therapy with an obsessive-compulsive client is simply establishing goals toward which therapist and client can work collaboratively. Once the client's Obsessive-Compulsive Personality Disorder has been diagnosed, it is clear that the client needs to adopt more reasonable standards, become more accepting of ordinary "mistakes" and shortcomings, and so forth. However, these are not goals that the client will endorse initially. The client usually does not recognize the connection between his or her obsessive-compulsive behavior and his or her problems and, in addition, he or she believes that it is imperative that he or she avoid mistakes and would see the changes the therapist would advocate as being certain to lead to his or her making more mistakes. Obviously, it is important to begin treatment by clarifying the client's goals for therapy and then working to identify mutually acceptable goals. Often "increasing my efficiency" is a promising initial goal, one that is endorsed wholeheartedly by most obsessive-compulsives. However, when the therapist and client jointly explore the impediments to efficiency that the client encounters, it is easy for the therapist to demonstrate the ways in which an obsessive-compulsive approach is counterproductive. The therapist and client are then in a position to consider whether specific changes would actually lead to the client's making more mistakes.

The therapist also needs to be aware of the compulsive's rigidity because it is the ritualistic approach to living that is most likely to get this individual into psychological trouble. However, the cognitive therapist deals with rigidity in what is for, many, a nonintuitive way, by introducing additional structure. Individuals with Obsessive-Compulsive Personality Disorder, for all their rigidity, lack structure. Their speech and thinking is disorganized, rambling, and tortuous. When faced by multiple tasks, they are frequently overwhelmed because they lack the skills for prioritizing, managing time, and problem solving. An important part of our approach to the treatment of Obsessive-Compulsive Personality Disorder is to help the client replace his or her rigidity with structure.

Because the obsessive-compulsive individual takes normally adaptive strategies to a pathological extreme, it is not necessary to attempt to induce the client to abandon these strategies but rather to help him or her to learn to use them more adaptively. The foremost problem of the compulsive is his or her rigidity in approaching all situations in the same way whether or not avoiding mistakes is really the most important goal and whether or not a compulsive approach proves effective. If the compulsive client can become able to use his or her ability to carefully focus on details and work diligently in a flexible way that is appropriate to the demands of the situation, these characteristics can work to his or her advantage. If he or she can also learn appropriate ways to handle situations where a careful, detailed approach is not appropriate, the maladaptive aspects of this disorder can be eliminated.

The rigidity that is such a problem for the obsessive-compulsive in daily life is likely to be a problem in therapy as well. The client is likely to approach therapy as though avoiding mistakes in therapy is essential, and approaching therapy compulsively is seen as the way to do this. Thus he or she is likely to have a strong tendency to describe his or her history in excessive detail, to try to give the "right" answer rather than accurately describing thoughts and feelings, to avoid topics and assignments where it is not clear what the "right" answer is, and to tend to rigidly persist in trying to do therapy in the way he or she sees as "right" rather than complying with the therapist's suggestions. Although these tendencies complicate therapy, they also provide abundant opportunities to address the client's rigidity and the underlying fear of making mistakes in the moment rather than simply discussing them in the abstract. In learning that there is considerable value in foregoing irrelevant detail in his or her responses, in sticking to an agenda, and in completing a DTR even if it is not perfect, the client discovers that changes in his or her usual way of doing things can be beneficial rather than leading to disaster. By trying these changes within therapy before attempting them in the real world, the client's fears are reduced somewhat, and, in addition, the therapist is available to address the fears as they arise.

In dealing with the obsessive-compulsive's real-life problems, there are a number of advantages to using a problem-solving approach that consists of analyzing the problem in detail, identifying the options the client has in dealing with the situation, considering the pros and cons of each of the alternatives, and systematically trying the most promising of these. The practical, systematic nature of this approach appeals to the obsessive-compulsive, and it is often possible to begin therapy alleviating some of the client's immediate problems without requiring him or her to take major risks. At the same time, it involves an implicit shift to choosing actions on the basis of their likely consequences rather than on the basis of rigid ideas of the "right" way to respond. Obsessive-compulsive individuals are notorious for transforming therapy into an abstract intellectual exercise where much is discussed but few changes happen outside the therapy session. A problem-solving focus puts the therapist in a good position to work for both behavior change outside the therapy session and attention to emotions within the therapy session rather than allowing therapy to be purely verbal and intellectual.

As with Borderline Personality Disorder, it can be quite useful to attempt to challenge the client's dichotomus thinking early in therapy. The compulsive's rigidity, perfectionism, desire to be in control, and many other problematic characteristics are amplified by his or her dichotomous thinking. If it is possible to help him or her to shift to less dichotomus views in these areas, he or she is likely to become more flexible, and subsequent interventions are likely to be easier.

The client's intolerance of mistakes will need to be addressed throughout therapy. Initially, this can be done by structuring therapy sessions and homework assignments to minimize the need for the client to risk making mistakes. However, it will soon be necessary to work to explicitly verbalize the client's concerns, to examine the likely consequences of specific mistakes, and to consider whether the actions being discussed are really as risky as the client believes them to be. Later in therapy, it is possible to gradually begin to challenge the assumption that mistakes must be avoided at all costs, to help the client accept being a fallible human, and to help him or her to face the interpersonal and emotional situations that he or she has avoided due to this fear of mistakes.

If, at some point in treatment, it appears that medication is indicated for the client, it is important to take the client's personality style into account. For example, obsessive-compulsives are often quite tense and driven even when they are quite depressed. If an antidepressant is indicated, one that tends to have a calming effect may be a better choice than an antidepressant that tends to be energizing. An energizing antidepressant could lead the susceptible client to experience additional hyperactivity and agitation.

Cognitive and Behavioral Techniques

Because the compulsive is rigid but does not structure his or her time and efforts effectively, the structure of cognitive therapy can be used as a model for dealing with problems more effectively. Agenda setting, prioritizing problems, and focusing on one topic at a time are forums for teaching the compulsive to organize his or her life more adaptively. Furthermore, some compulsive clients get caught up in their ruminations during sessions and frequently do not hear or remember portions of what the therapist says. By structuring the session carefully, the tendency to ruminate is reduced. Furthermore, the therapist can provide regular opportunities for the client to respond to the points that have been made or to summarize them. If the client is unable to do so, both therapist and client know that this is an issue they need to address. This can help the compulsive to realize the ways in which rumination is counterproductive both inside and outside of the therapy session and may help to provide the motivation and skills that enable him or her to control the ruminations.

Many obsessive-compulsives are chronically tense, and it is frequently important to help them find a way to reduce tension and anxiety in adaptive ways. Any form of relaxation can be helpful as long as the client uses it regularly (see Chapter 6). The main problem with any relaxation homework is inducing the obsessive-compulsive client to do it regularly. Relaxation is an alien feeling to the compulsive, and he or she may experience it as being "out of control," may see relaxation as "goofing off" and feel guilty about taking time for it, or may fear that he or she will make more mistakes if he or she is not constantly tense and vigilant. The therapist must be alert to this problem and address the client's reactions to the relaxation exercises directly if they become a problem.

The thinking of the Obsessive-Compulsive Personality is often characterized by anxiety-provoking, ruminative thoughts regarding past or future errors, mistakes, and catastrophes. These ruminations are upsetting in their own right, as well as being problematic because they occupy time and attention that could be used more constructively. Thus teaching the client to voluntarily control his or her ruminations can have significant benefits.

It is important to help the client to recognize the differences between constructive, problem-solving thinking and rumination and to appreciate the disadvantages of rumination. This can be done by doing an experiment of having the client intentionally ruminate for a limited period of time and then note the results, which usually include increased anxiety and depression, a feeling of being overwhelmed, and confusion. Then the therapist can assist the client in engaging in problem-solving thinking and compare the results. After the client understands the difference between ruminating and problem solving and has seen that the latter is more beneficial than the former, he or she may be willing to give up rumination entirely. At that point, it is primarily a matter of teaching the client techniques for doing so using the approaches discussed in Chapters 3 and 6 (such as thought stopping and focusing). Certain clients, although seeing the need to reduce rumination, may be unwilling to give it up entirely. Often, providing a time and a structure for rumination, for example, ruminating only during specific times, can be very helpful, in giving the client control over his or her thinking. For example:

> Lisa was a 45-year-old woman who had left a prestigious position in New York, which she loved, to come to Philadelphia at her husband's request. She had immediately gotten a less fulfilling job and spent all her time crying about New York and the job she left behind. Her memories of New York, although upsetting, were also very important to her, and she was unwilling to give them up entirely. Her therapist suggested that she schedule her rumination for 7 to 8 P.M. nightly. She took to this readily, saying that she was "on a diet of New York." In very little time, she got over her depression and was attempting to make herself happy in Philadelphia.

Activity scheduling (see Chapter 3) can be useful in a variety of ways early in therapy. It can be used for raising the mood of depressed clients, overcoming procrastination, and providing structure for dealing with a myriad of tasks and can usually be used without requiring the client to make changes that seem risky. It can be particularly useful when procrastination and inefficiency are caused by the client's feeling overwhelmed by tasks that he or she is not approaching systematically. The obsessive-compulsive who is faced with a number of tasks that need to be completed simultaneously is likely to freeze, not knowing what to do first and experiencing the need to do them all perfectly well. For example:

Sharon needed to find a new job, to cope with an ill parent, and to plan a wedding all in the same month and felt overwhelmed by these tasks. Her therapist first asked her to make a comprehensive list of all the component tasks needed to accomplish her goals in these three areas. When she had done so, her therapist asked her to make a liberal estimate of the time needed to do each step and to schedule each onto her Weekly Activity Schedule as well as allowing appropriate time for socializing and relaxing. When the client saw that it really was possible to do everything that absolutely needed to be done and that each subtask was well within her capabilities when taken one at a time, she stopped avoiding these problems and started working more effectively.

The Daily Record of Dysfunctional Thoughts can be quite useful, not only as a way for clients to identify and challenge their dysfunctional thoughts and cognitive distortions but also as a way to get more accurate information about what clients actually think and feel in problem situations, as opposed to what they believe they should think and feel. Column 2 (specifying emotions) can be especially helpful in getting these clients to pay attention to feelings. Compulsives usually are both reluctant to express their feelings and are unskilled at monitoring and reporting feelings. However, if the client can be persuaded to report some of his or her emotions and the therapist can demonstrate that this provides useful information, it is possible to induce the client to pay attention to his or her emotions regularly, and over time the client will gradually become more comfortable with his or her emotions and more skilled at expressing them.

There is, however, one caveat in using the DTR with obsessive-compulsive clients. The therapist must take more care in teaching and monitoring the use of the DTR with this population than with most others because the compulsive has a tendency to approach this task, as most others, obsessively. Often it takes some effort to persuade the client to complete the DTR because of a fear that he or she will not do it "right." It can be quite helpful to address this fear at the time when the DTR is assigned by first predicting that the concern will arise and then making it clear that the DTR does not have to be done perfectly to be useful.

One common problem encountered once the client is using the DTR is that the compulsive will write one or more automatic thoughts, then write a rational response, and then write a "yes-but" thought to discount the rational response. Some of these clients will jump back and forth between the automatic thoughts and the rational response columns for several pages. This is precisely the mode of thinking to which they are accustomed, constantly jumping from one side of the issue to another with no strategy for resolving the conflicting views, and it may be a way of postponing the risk of making a mistake by reaching the wrong conclusion. Once this problem has been identified, the therapist can help the client learn to address one side of the issue completely before going on to the next. One approach that often works is for the client to list all possible negative thoughts about a situation before going on to the rational responses and then to write rational responses that address all aspects of the automatic thoughts. Alternatively, the client can start with one automatic thought and write rational responses to that one thought until it has been exhaustively dealt with before going on to the next automatic thought.

Another common problem in using the DTR is that the client may start writing negative thoughts, start ruminating about them, and never actually get to the rational responding. Not only does this produce no relief, but the client may well end up feeling worse than before doing the assignment. If the client can effectively use thought-stopping techniques to control his or her tendency to ruminate while listing automatic thoughts, he or she will then be able to complete the DTR and get its benefits. If the client cannot stop the ruminations, then it is better to discard the DTR for the time being and work on the generation of rational responses without it. This can be done by identifying typical automatic thoughts during the therapy session and asking the client to write a one-page essay in support of the *opposite* of the automatic thought. For example, Iris was troubled by the thought that her husband might be having an affair. She was given the homework assignment of writing an essay detailing all the evidence she could muster that was inconsistent with the idea that he was being unfaithful. This helped her to feel much better and, also, gave her ammunition with which to refute subsequent reoccurrences of her negative thoughts.

Although the process of challenging automatic thoughts can be quite effective with obsessive-compulsives, the use of self-instruction techniques (Meichenbaum, 1977) can also be quite useful because the automatic thoughts of the compulsive individual are often extremely redundant. By developing a set of coping statements to use in responding to automatic thoughts that reoccur frequently and writing them on a 3 × 5 card, the client can readily reduce his or her negative affect without having to generate the rational responses anew each time. For example, one client who tended to feel overwhelmed at work made up a card that read: "Slow down and take a deep breath. You can only do one thing at a time. Make a list of what you must do this week. Write each task onto your activity schedule. Then begin working."

The process of identifying the client's underlying assumptions and addressing them as opportunities permit is an important part of Cognitive Therapy with obsessive-compulsive clients, and it becomes an increasingly important focus in the middle and late stages of therapy. As the client increasing recognizes his or her assumptions about the importance of avoiding mistakes and about the most appropriate ways of doing so, the full range of interventions from rational analysis to behavioral experiments can be used to challenge the beliefs. However, the process of doing so can be complicated by the therapist's own "blind spots." The assumptions of the obsessive-compulsive are extreme forms of beliefs that are widely held in our culture and that are particularly prevalent among those who pursue postgraduate education and training in a profession. Thus many therapists find it difficult to look critically at the obsessive-compulsive's assumptions because they themselves hold milder versions of the same assumption or because the assumptions seem reasonable and logical to them.*

For example, a physician who sought treatment because of problems resulting from excessive double checking of his work said, "Sure, tolerating mistakes is OK for some people, but I can't afford to let any mistakes slip by; people could die." His view certainly sounds logical, but is it true that only persons who never make any mistakes should be physicians? If so, how many physicians would there be? Actually, when he and his therapist examined the effects of his frantic attempts to make sure that he would never make the slightest mistake, it became clear that this not only made him anxious and inefficient but also interfered with his effectively using his skills to the point that it greatly increased the risk of his making a serious mistake. As he began to acknowledge that humans are fallible and to accept his own fallibility, he not only became much more relaxed and efficient, but the quality of his medical care improved substantially as well.

It is often quite useful to help obsessive-compulsive clients critically examine their strategies for maximizing their performance and minimizing mistakes because they often hold assumptions that seem reasonable but that are not universally true. Should one always try harder when one encounters difficulty? Redoubling one's efforts can be very effective in some situations, but counterproductive in others. Is it a good idea to set very high standards for oneself? Many persons are surprised that when they switch to setting moderate or even low standards, their motivation and performance improves substantially. Is it a bad idea to take time off to relax in the midst of a busy day? The person may find that a brief relaxation break improves his or her efficiency enough so that he or she is more productive than when he or she toils unceasingly. In examining these assumptions, it is important to look at the evidence rather than simply considering whether the assumption seems logical or reasonable. Obsessive compulsives hold many views which seem reasonable but which turn out not to be true for them.

Given the compulsive's tendency toward selective abstraction, such

---

*It is interesting to note that of all the topics the authors cover in workshops and courses discussing the treatment of personality disorders, it is the discussion of the dysfunctional assumptions held by obsessive-compulsives that elicits the most skepticism and debate from therapists in the audience.

questions as "When is willingness to tolerate mistakes a *good* thing?" that focus the client's attention on evidence that is incompatible with their assumptions can have considerable impact.* Such questions often lead naturally to attempting to formulate a more adaptive alternative assumption. Clients often assume that the therapist is advocating the opposite of the assumption that is being challenged and is trying to convince him or her that mistakes are wonderful. Actually, it is often quite useful to ask the client to think back over the evidence and observations that have been discussed and to formulate an alternative assumption that seems to be both more realistic and more adaptive.

This sets the stage for considering the advantages and disadvantages of the client's continuing to maintain his or her original underlying assumption versus attempting to act on the alternative assumption. It may not be extremely difficult for most of these clients to see how some of their assumptions might be disadvantageous to them, but it is another matter altogether to induce them to put the alternative assumptions into practice. It is important for the therapist and client to design behavioral experiments to empirically test the actual consequences of living by the alternative assumptions. This actual experience in making different attitudinal and behavioral choices is necessary in order for the client to make lasting changes rather than simply giving lip service to the new views.

Obsessive-compulsive clients often have substantial problems in interpersonal relationships. This is due to the client's tendency to pay little attention to his or her emotions and the emotions of others and to act on the basis of assumptions about how relationships "should" be. Often it is quite helpful to focus the client's attention on the actual impact of his or her actions and statements on others. The "empathy-induction" approach discussed in Chapter 7 can be quite useful for this purpose, as can marital, family, or group therapy.

CONCLUSIONS

Obsessive-Compulsive Personality Disorder is a challenging but treatable problem. Through patient, collaborative, and systematic application of the techniques and strategies described in this chapter, the dysfunctional aspects of this disorder can be mitigated. An understanding of the dys-

---

*The reader may find it useful to try this exercise himself or herself. Before going on to read the rest of this footnote, try to think of several situations where tolerating mistakes is a good thing. . . . The most commonly mentioned situations are trying to master a new skill, attempting to "brainstorm" or come up with creative ideas, attempting to be spontaneous and lively, attempting to put others at ease, and attempting to be open and "out front" in a conversation.

functional world view of the compulsive helps the therapist provide sympathetic treatment of a frequently unsympathetic character. As has been shown, the structure of Cognitive Therapy provides a model of functioning as well as an instrument of change for the compulsive person. Beyond this, in the Cognitive Therapy of the Obsessive-Compulsive Personality Disorder, the standard cognitive techniques frequently need to be modified and closely monitored in order to avoid being used by the client as an occasion for ruminative thinking. This approach has been used extensively in the authors' clinical practice and supervision and can be quite effective.

12

Avoidant and Dependent Personality Disorders

AVOIDANT PERSONALITY DISORDER

Withdrawal from other people is characteristic of a variety of disorders, including Avoidant Personality Disorder, Schizoid Personality Disorder, Social Phobia, Panic Disorder with Agoraphobia, Paranoia, Schizophrenia, Major Depression, and ordinary shyness. What distinguishes Avoidant Personality Disorder from these other disorders, according to DSM-III-R, is that the social withdrawal of Avoidant Personality Disorder is due to pervasive social discomfort, fear of negative evaluation, and timidity (Table 27). This withdrawal is a pattern that starts by early adulthood, if not before, and exists in a variety of situations. Individuals with Avoidant Personality Disorder are easily hurt by criticism or disapproval and are unwilling to get involved with people unless certain of being liked. They have at most one close friend other than immediate relatives and generally avoid activities that involve significant interpersonal contact. They are reticent in social situations and worry about being embarrassed in front of other people, exaggerating the potential difficulties and risks involved in ordinary activities that are outside their usual routine. Although this disorder is thought to be common, many such individuals avoid seeking therapy because therapy itself involves interpersonal contact that is outside of their normal routine and has great potential for embarrassment.

Assessment

To determine whether an individual may have an Avoidant Personality Disorder, it is important to explore the client's interpersonal relationships in depth. The therapist needs to pay attention to any tendency on the part of the client to interpret ambiguous actions as rejection or any pattern of leaving or avoiding relationships rather than facing the possibility of rejec-

TABLE 27. DSM-III-R Diagnostic Criteria for Avoidant Personality Disorders

A pervasive pattern of social discomfort, fear of negative evaluation, and timidity, beginning by early adulthood and present in a variety of contexts, as indicated by at least *four* of the following:

1. Is easily hurt by criticism or disapproval
2. Has no close friends or confidants (or only one) other than first-degree relatives
3. Is unwilling to get involved with people unless certain of being liked
4. Avoids social or occupational activities that involve significant interpersonal contact, e.g., refuses a promotion that will increase social demands
5. Is reticent in social situations because of a fear of saying something inappropriate or foolish or of being unable to answer a question
6. Fears of being embarrassed by blushing, crying, or showing signs of anxiety in front of other people
7. Exaggerates the potential difficulties, physical dangers, or risks involved in doing something ordinary but outside his or her usual routine, e.g., may cancel social plans because she or he anticipates being exhausted by the effort of getting there

tion. These people will often state that they wish they could have relationships, if only they could be certain to work out, but that they are not willing to risk any possibility of rejection or humiliation.

In differentiating among the disorders characterized by social withdrawal and isolation, it is important to understand the client's reason for the avoidance of other people. In many cases, the distinction is fairly straightforward. Individuals with Avoidant Personality Disorder avoid others due to the fact that they are extremely uncomfortable with people, timid, and afraid of being viewed negatively. Unlike those with an Avoidant Personality Disorder, individuals in a Major Depressive Episode withdraw from others because of a loss of interest or pleasure in almost all activities, including social activities. In Panic Disorder with Agoraphobia, the individual may avoid social situations due to a fear of having a panic attack and finding it difficult or embarrassing to leave or to get home. Schizophrenics withdraw because of a preoccupation with egocentric and illogical ideas and fantasies. In Paranoid Personality Disorder, individuals may avoid other people based on a belief that other people have malicious intentions. In common shyness, the individual may be reluctant to enter social situations, but the pattern is less pervasive and less severe than in Avoidant Personality Disorder.

A more difficult differential diagnosis is that between Avoidant Personality Disorder and Schizoid Personality Disorder. The distinction between these two disorders was originally proposed by Millon (1969) and has been the source of some controversy in recent years (Akhtar, 1986; Livesley, West, & Tanney, 1985; Millon, 1986). Clinically, however, the distinction seems to be crucial because different interventions would be recommended for these two diagnoses. People with both disorders are socially isolated and avoid close interpersonal contact, having at most one friend other than first-degree relatives. The key distinction is that persons with Schizoid Personality Disorder have little or no desire for social relationships and an indifference to criticism, whereas individuals with Avoidant Personality Disorder yearn for closeness and acceptance and are upset by their lack of ability to develop relationships. Unfortunately, they are too fearful of rejection to attempt to form relationships.

Another complicated differential diagnosis is that between Social Phobia and Avoidant Personality Disorder because in Social Phobia, people tend to avoid specific situations due to a fear of humiliation. If the social phobic's fear is circumscribed, such as an isolated fear of public speaking, or a fear of eating, drinking, or writing in public, the distinction from Avoidant Personality Disorder is straightforward. In other cases, however, the social phobic may fear most social situations, making it possible to merit both a diagnosis of Social Phobia and Avoidant Personality Disorder. In a study comparing Social Phobia with Avoidant Personality Disorder, Turner, Beidel, Dancu, and Keys (1986) found that individuals with a diagnosis of Avoidant Personality Disorder were more sensitive interpersonally and had significantly poorer social skills than did the Social Phobia subjects.

When people with Avoidant Personality Disorders seek treatment, they tend to do so because of depression, anxiety, alcoholism, or anger at themselves for their lack of relationships. Stravynski, Lamontagne, and Lavellee (1986) found that 35.1% of their sample of alcoholics met the criteria for Avoidant Personality Disorder, with 89% of these subjects reporting that the abuse of alcohol developed after the onset of Avoidant Personality Disorder.

One way that avoidant personalities maintain their avoidance is by actively keeping people at a distance. Although these individuals do not seem as cold as the schizoid, they often are experienced as not being very likeable. They are shy, apprehensive, awkward, and uncomfortable in social situations and seem to actively shrink from interaction. Their speech in generally slow and constrained, with frequent hesitations. Behavior tends to be highly controlled and tense or underactive, with a complete lack of spontaneity. Overt expression of emotions are rare.

Laura was a 29-year-old secretary who sought treatment for what she described as a "fear of people." She presented with symptoms of Social Phobia as well as Dysthymic Disorder, but when these symptoms were explored further, it became clear that she had a chronic pattern of avoiding social situations and interpersonal relationships in general since high school. She had had one close friend who had written Laura a note in the past year that Laura interpreted as meaning, "Go away"; so Laura concluded that "if I ever take down my wall of trust, something bad happens, and it goes back up." When Laura came for her first session, she sat in the waiting room in an almost fetal position and did not make eye contact at all with the therapist for several sessions. She reported such thoughts as "I hate being me," "I'm 20 going on 5," "If I go to the party, I'll feel dumb and won't know what to say," and "I'll end up alone, 'cause' no one will talk to me." During her evaluation, she constantly made disparaging remarks about herself, criticizing the way she phrased things.

Conceptualization

Individuals with an Avoidant Personality Disorder are convinced that they are unacceptable to others and that if they try to develop close relationships, they will be hurt, humiliated, and devastated. They see no other alternative but to protect themselves from the pain of this imminent rejection by avoiding relationships as much as possible. Unfortunately, they still very much want affection and acceptance from others and yearn for close relationships. So they are lonely and distressed by their inability to relate comfortably to other people. Millon (1981) describes the Avoidant Personality Disorder as characterized by an "active-detached" coping style. Unlike individuals with a Schizoid Personality Disorder who are passively detached from others because of indifference, people with an Avoidant Personality Disorder are detached from others because they have made an active and self-protective decision to withdraw from social relationships to avoid the intense pain of defeat and humiliation they anticipate.

Because individuals with Avoidant Personality Disorder expect to be hurt and rejected, they are hypervigilant to any possible signs of rejection and tend to overinterpret innocuous behavior as a threat. They show such strong selective attention to negative cues from others that they do not even notice positive responses from other people. This selective attention, along with their avoidance of social interactions, tends to eliminate any evidence which would disconfirm their expectations, so their expectations of rejection are maintained.

Joe was a 21-year-old single male who sought treatment for his extreme social anxiety and depression. He reported automatic such thoughts as "I'll be inferior," "I won't measure up," and "Others will judge me harshly." When taking the elevator and walking through the cafeteria as part of *in-vivo* exposure with his therapist, Joe kept his head down and did not look at the other people at all. When his therapist asked him about this, Joe reported that although he did not actually see the other people, he had a "sense" that they were judging him negatively. When he tried the exposure again, making it a point to look at the other people, he found no evidence to support his assumption that the other people were judging him.

The avoidant individual's focus on the potential for rejection and his or her subsequent social detachment have a number of additional dysfunctional side effects. Between their limited social interaction and their strong focus on possible signs of rejection, avoidant individuals have little opportunity to learn from experience with others, to master social skills, and to develop effective problem-solving strategies. Also, because they do not spend their time relating to other people, they tend to be preoccupied with their own thoughts and impulses, increasing their estrangement from other people.

The self-protective stance of the individual with Avoidant Personality Disorder becomes so prominent that, as summarized by Millon (1981), "their outlook is therefore a negative one; to avoid pain, to need nothing, to depend on no one, and to deny desire" (p. 307). Their efforts to protect themselves from pain extend beyond social situations; in fact, they feel so inadequate to cope with distress that they also try to avoid confronting their own upsetting thoughts and feelings. The dilemma, however, is that they want to ignore painful thoughts and feelings, yet are so often alone and preoccupied with themselves that the pain is difficult to ignore.

There is a hopelessness that characterizes individuals with Avoidant Personality Disorder. They are so convinced that all relationships will necessarily turn out to be rejecting and painful that they choose not even to try anymore. As uncomfortable as social alienation may be, it is less distressing than the anguish of rebuff or ridicule. Avoidant individuals tend also to have a strongly negative view of themselves, minimizing their accomplishments and maximizing their shortcomings. A negative view of self serves to confirm their belief that they will be rejected because they do not feel worthy of acceptance. Joe was certain that either he was fated to be the way he was or that there was something terribly, deeply wrong with him, such as a brain tumor.

Individuals with Avoidant Personality Disorder tend to restrict their range of behavior in order to minimize the chance of rejection. The less they do, the less chance they have of being criticized. For example, Laura went to bed at 6 P.M. on any nights when she did not have a specific appointment. She reported that this was a good way to not have to deal with anything or anyone.

Common automatic thoughts of individuals with Avoidant Personality Disorder include "I'm obviously a loser," "They'll see how anxious I am and judge/criticize me for it," "I'm better off just staying home tonight—I'll just be disappointed if I go and don't fit in," "I'm really a sad, pathetic person without any real friends," "I don't say anything interesting or original," "What's the use in going places? I'm going to always be alone anyway," and "I'd rather live alone than be humiliated again." The basic assumptions of avoidants include "If anyone knew the real me, they would reject me," "Being rejected by someone else would be a disaster," "The only way I can protect myself from the pain of rejection is to keep at a safe distance from others," "Since I've never had friends, I must not have what it takes to make friends," "If I make a mistake, I'll never live it down," "People can't be trusted to care," "It's easier to remain passive than to be active," and, "It's safest to sit still and do nothing." These thoughts and beliefs lead to very persistent avoidance of a wide range of interpersonal interactions.

Intervention Strategies and Techniques

In treatment with the Avoidant Personality, as with so many of the personality disorders, it is crucial not to push for intimacy and self-disclosure too quickly, whether within the therapy session or in homework assignments. It is much more effective to allow the client to maintain a safe distance until he or she feels ready to move closer than to pursue him or her. One way to help build the intimacy gradually is to begin with behavioral strategies and to work toward specific goals, helping the individual learn to cope with difficult situations. It is hoped that these behavioral strategies will enhance the client's sense of self-worth and help him or her to cope with anxiety in a nonthreatening manner, without the client being required to self-disclose too much or to get too close to the therapist. It can be quite useful to maintain more distance than usual from these clients at the beginning of therapy. Even if a therapist generally takes a more casual approach and uses first names with clients, with individuals having an Avoidant Personality Disorder, it may be wiser to introduce oneself by title and address the client formally as well, until the client gives some indication that he or she would prefer less formality.

Not surprisingly, avoidant clients are difficult to keep in therapy. They will often want to terminate therapy during the initial phases of treatment. When they express interest in ending treatment, it is important to use the issue of early termination as an opportunity to identify automatic thoughts and begin to challenge them. Even more common with avoidant clients is a tendency to develop a pattern of canceling appointments or having difficulty in scheduling regular appointments. This is more difficult to confront directly, because clients typically insist that their poor attendance has nothing to do with discomfort with therapy or with their motivation to improve but is due solely to external factors. In addition, when the therapist points out the pattern of poor attendance, this may be seen as criticism and disapproval (hence rejection) by the therapist. The situation is further complicated by the fact that the treatment can be very frustrating to the therapist because progress is so slow. If the therapist is sufficiently frustrated, he or she may become increasingly critical and disapproving and be tempted to agree with the client's desire to terminate and thus allow the therapy to end prematurely. Rather than become increasingly confrontive the therapist might consider scheduling sessions less frequently in the hopes of reducing the client's anxiety. If attendance continues to be a problem, it may be necessary, first, to help the client find ways to make therapy more comfortable, and second, to discuss the advantages and disadvantages of staying in therapy quite explicitly, emphasizing that it is the client's choice but that staying in therapy may be the best way for them to attain their goals.

Building trust in the therapeutic relationship is one of the first major hurdles of therapy because the fears and cognitive distortions common to Avoidant Personality Disorder will occur regularly within the therapy relationship. Trust tests are a common part of early treatment but are less dramatic than those common with Borderline or Antisocial clients. The client carefully observes whether the therapist is going to criticize or disapprove of him or her but is usually not overtly provocative. Given that these clients tend not to be particularly likeable, yet are exquisitely sensitive to indications of rejection, it is important for the therapist to work to find something he or she can like about the client. The therapist may not find it easy to empathize with these clients because they are not at all engaging, but it is crucial to work to see things from their point of view and find some way of genuinely liking them.

Ruth was a 61-year-old housewife who sought treatment for her anxiety. When she first came into therapy, she appeared irritable and distant. Her therapist worked hard to be accepting and was able to empathize with Ruth's fears. It was not until the fifth session that Ruth cautiously confessed that she had had fantasies of having an extramarital affair, something that she was ashamed of and had never discussed with anyone before. At the time of this "confession," she watched the therapist intently to see if there were any signs of disapproval. It was even later in the treatment that she admitted to not having graduated from high school, again watching the therapist's reaction closely. It was not until after the therapist passed these "trust tests" that Ruth began to relax a bit in the therapy sessions and appeared less irritable and distant.

No matter how carefully the therapist works to be accepting, the client is still likely to interpret the therapist's behavior as rejecting at times. Therefore, it is important for the therapist to frequently check for thoughts and images in the therapy session, especially when there is any evidence of mood change in the client. Even if the client is not ready to share something as personal as his or her thoughts about the therapist, if the therapist continues to ask about them, the message is gradually communicated that it is considered acceptable to have thoughts and feelings about the therapy and the therapist and to discuss these in the session. In order to maximize the possibility of the client sharing his or her concerns about therapy, it can be helpful to phrase questions as if you expect and want to hear some negative reactions. For example, in getting feedback at the end of the session, it is better to ask, "What do you wish had been different in this session?" than the more open-ended, "How did you feel about the session?" Asking the client to fill out a written therapy session evaluation form at the end of each session can also be particularly useful with the avoidant individual because the client may be more likely to share thoughts and feelings about the sessions in a less personal way (e.g., in writing) than in a face-to-face situation where potential rejection would be more obvious and immediate.

In the initial stages of treatment, it is important not to move too quickly to challenge automatic thoughts, because such challenges could be seen as criticism. Only gradually, once the client is engaged in therapy and some trust has been established, would the therapist move to more cognitive interventions to test out some of the individual's expectancies in social situations. If the therapist is careful to be collaborative rather than confrontational and is consistent in the use of guided discovery rather than direct disputation of thoughts, it is less likely that the client will view the cognitive work as criticism.

Because Avoidant Personality Disorder is a chronic and pervasive pattern, these clients may never have learned the basics of social interaction and may therefore need structured social skills training. This would include training in the nonverbal aspects of social interaction (such as smiling, eye contact, posture) and conversational skill training (such as learning to make small talk, active listening). They may also need some basic social education so that they can better interpret other people's behavior.

Work on reducing anxiety can be very helpful to these clients, because they are likely to experience high levels of anxiety when they begin to reverse their patterns of avoidance. The techniques discussed in Chapter 6 can be useful for anxiety management. With such chronic and pervasive patterns of avoidance, avoidant individuals need to be taught to do explicit cost–benefit analyses whenever they are tempted to automatically avoid situations, learning to make a conscious, thoughtful decision about whether to avoid or not, rather than automatically taking the easy way out.

Although individuals with Avoidant Personality Disorder are socially isolated and afraid of intimacy, they also often believe that if they could only find the right relationship and be guaranteed acceptance, everything would be all right. Interventions directed toward finding ways to enjoy being alone and developing a positive relationship with themselves can be useful in reducing the pressure of finding the right relationship immediately. One way to do this is to have the client schedule a "date" to enjoy an evening alone at least once a week, treating himself or herself as one would treat a special friend (preparing a nice dinner, planning favorite activities, etc.)

Many avoidant clients arrange their lives in such a way as to avoid unpleasant thoughts and feelings. The use of alcohol is one obvious way to distract oneself, but other less obvious ways include excessive sleep (as in Laura's case), television watching, overeating, or smoking. This pattern of cognitive avoidance can lead to difficulty doing homework assignments, even those as simple as writing down automatic thoughts or listening to an audiotape of a therapy session. Because even the awareness of their own upsetting thoughts and feelings is extremely anxiety provoking to these individuals, it may be necessary to desensitize the client to the experience of their own internal state. Thus the client might be taught to relax and then to expose him or her to gradually increasing amounts of introspection, or the therapist might slowly increase the periods during which distressing thoughts, images, and feelings are the focus of the therapy session. In order to fully expose them to the internal experience they have been avoiding, it may be necessary to help them gradually eliminate the behaviors they use to avoid their thoughts and feelings.

Although it is important to challenge the underlying assumptions that serve to generate the automatic thoughts, it is fruitless to try to challenge these beliefs early in treatment. The client's hopelessness and his or her belief in the dysfunctional underlying assumptions are typically so strong that verbal challenges are ineffective. Later in therapy, when the client has taken some concrete behavioral steps toward his or her goals and has begun to develop some trust in the therapist, attempts to challenge the basic beliefs are more successful.

After just a few weeks in therapy, Joe was able to identify the assumption, "Other people must think very highly of me, and if they don't, I must be a loser." However, he held this belief so strongly that when his therapist tried to challenge this belief in the therapy session, little headway was made. It was only after he had achieved concrete progress in therapy through using activity scheduling to reduce his depression and having success with a variety of exposure homework assignments (e.g., making phone calls to stores, visiting stores, calling the therapist on the phone) that they addressed this basic assumption again. This time, when he was given the assignment of finding ways to challenge this belief at his own pace between therapy sessions, he was able to come up with several good rational responses (listed in Table 28). This helped to accelerate his progress on his social anxiety hierarchy and enabled him to take greater risks.

Although the issue of trust is central throughout the treatment with Avoidant Personality Disorder, it is too sensitive an issue to discuss explicitly for quite some time. It is only in the later stages of the therapy that trust can be explicitly identified and discussed as an issue that helps to maintain dysfunctional patterns in relationships. Once trust is openly acknowledged as an important issue, developing a continuum of trust can be very helpful. For an example of a trust continuum, see the chapter on Paranoid Personality Disorder (Chapter 7). At this point in therapy, the client may be able to acknowledge his or her initial difficulty in trusting the therapist, and the therapeutic relationship can be used as an example of the development of close relationships in general. In fact, once trust is established, the therapeutic relationship can be used as an arena to test out a variety of thoughts and beliefs.

Table 28. Rational Responding as Homework

Homework assignment
   Come up with rational responses to the belief that "others must think very highly of me, and if they don't, I must be a loser."

1. This is an example of the distortions of all-or-nothing thinking, jumping to conclusions and labeling.
2. Having people think highly of me may be desirable, but what people think doesn't necessarily reflect the way things really are.
3. If the theory is correct, it would mean that my worth as a human being would change as peoples' opinions of me changed. My worth would be determined by the thoughts of others.
4. The theory breaks down when you consider that not everybody is going to have the same opinions. Some people will think highly of me and some won't. Who's right?
5. Because I know myself better than anyone else does, my own opinion of myself should be more important than others.

After a few months in therapy, Joe commented that he could not remember anything positive ever happening to him in a relationship and was certain that he had never received a compliment. His selective attention was so strong that he actually had no recollection that, at one point in the treatment, the therapist had disclosed that he really liked Joe. When the therapist reminded him of that session, Joe still could not remember the compliment, but he trusted the therapist enough to believe him. This example was very powerful for Joe, and for the first time in therapy he recognized how he had been selectively focusing on the negative. He was then able to begin to become aware of his selective attention in other relationships besides the therapeutic one.

Once some trust and intimacy have developed in the therapy relationship and the client has achieved greater comfort in superficial social contacts, issues of the risks of developing *close* relationships can be addressed. Ideally, the treatment would continue long enough for some of the practiced social contacts to develop the potential for becoming closer friendships. This will be quite threatening to the client, and it often is helpful to explore the advantages and disadvantages of taking the risks involved in moving closer in a relationship. An entirely new set of automatic thoughts and underlying assumptions regarding intimacy may need to be identified and challenged. Dichotomous thinking is common in regards to intimacy, with the client fearing that if he or she gets at all closer to another person, the relationship will automatically become overwhelmingly intense, leading to sex, marriage, or will have some other frightening prospects. Breaking this process down into steps and outlining a continuum of closeness can be useful. Ultimately, it will be necessary to decatastrophize disapproval and rejection, even in close relationships. It is hoped that at this point in the treatment, the client will have developed enough of a sense of self-efficacy and have had enough success in a variety of different levels of relationships that he or she is able to entertain the idea that disapproval in a close relationship does not necessarily have to be devastating.

After a period of individual treatment, it is desirable to move to a group therapy approach so that the client can learn new attitudes and practice new skills in a more benign and accepting social environment than he or she has come to expect. Group therapy is particularly anxiety provoking for the client with an Avoidant Personality Disorder, but it can be extremely beneficial.

Paula was a 29-year-old businesswoman who inquired about a dating anxiety group that had been publicized. She suffered from acromegaly (giantism) and had long been convinced that she looked grotesque. In addition to her thoughts about her physical appearance, she reported such thoughts as "I have nothing to say," "Whatever I say, I will look like an idiot," and, "I'll regret this [if I go]." Although the idea of being in a group therapy was very anxiety provoking for her, she was so determined to overcome her problems that she was willing to give it a try. In the first two sessions, she was so anxious that she was virtually unable to speak, and she cried in both sessions. Between sessions, she called the group leader expressing her desire to leave the group and asking for reassurance that she should continue. As time went on, however, she was able to use the group to challenge her dysfunctional ideas. The group members were accepting and supportive, she was gradually able to discuss how she had always felt different from other people in her family in many ways, and eventually she was able to discuss her giantism directly.

When including individuals with Avoidant Personality Disorder in therapy groups, it is important to maintain realistic expectations. Turner (1987) has demonstrated that a short-term cognitive behavioral group treatment for Social Phobia was much less effective for clients who had a personality disorder along with Social Phobia than for clients who had Social Phobia alone. Clearly, clients with Avoidant Personality Disorder will need a longer course of therapy than would clients with social anxiety alone, and they may be much more willing to enter a group and more able to make use of group therapy if they have some individual Cognitive Therapy in preparation for the group treatment.

Conclusion

Although some authors have used the term *socially dysfunctional* as interchangeable with Avoidant Personality Disorder, this personality disorder involves a great deal more than just a lack of social skills or just social anxiety. Therefore, social skills training alone is insufficient. Although short-term social skills training has been demonstrated to be effective in improving performance on specific social tasks between sessions

(Stravynski, Marks, & Yule, 1982), improvement did not extend to the development of intimate relationships, even after an 18-month follow-up period. The cognitive components of identifying and challenging automatic thoughts and underlying assumptions and a longer course of treatment may well prove to be crucial to the development of the ability to form relationships that are close and intimate, rather than simply anxiety free.

DEPENDENT PERSONALITY DISORDER

The treatment of unassertive clients has been addressed in considerable detail (summarized in Millman, Huber, & Diggins, 1982), but clients with a Dependent Personality Disorder are much more than simply dependent or unassertive. Some clients with Dependent Personality Disorder are so obviously dependent that it is clear from the start that they are going to be difficult. These are the people who call for an initial appointment and then call back every 5 minutes until their call is returned, leaving the receptionist ready to scream when the therapist gets back from his or her meeting. However, many of these clients seem deceptively simple at first: They are easy to engage in therapy and are so cooperative that they create the expectation that progress will be quite rapid. They are eager to please and act as if the therapist is wonderful, implicitly giving the message, "Doc, you're so powerful, I know you can help me." This promising start to therapy, however, only adds to the therapist's frustration when the treatment bogs down. The client remains passive, cannot understand why the therapy is not helping more, clings to therapy, and resists the therapist's attempts to encourage him or her toward greater autonomy. As demonstrated by Turkat and Carlson (1984) in their case study of a client with Dependent Personality Disorder, recognition of the disorder, a comprehensive case formulation, and strategic planning of interventions based on this formulation are likely to make the treatment more effective and less frustrating than symptomatic treatment alone.

Assessment

According to DSM-III-R, the client with a Dependent Personality Disorder shows a pervasive pattern of dependent and submissive behavior (Table 29). These people are unable or unwilling to make everyday decisions without an excessive amount of advice and reassurance, and they allow others to make most of their important decisions. They have difficulty in doing things on their own. In fact, they are so uncomfortable when alone that they will go to great lengths to avoid being alone. They are devastated when close relationships end and tend to be preoccupied with fears of being abandoned. They are easily hurt by disapproval, tend to

TABLE 29. DSM-III-R Criteria for Dependent Personality Disorder

A pervasive pattern of dependent and submissive behavior, beginning by early adulthood and present in a variety of contexts, as indicated by at least *five* of the following:
1. Is unable to make everyday decisions without an excessive amount of advice or reassurance from others.
2. Allows others to make most of his or her important decisions, e.g., where to live, what job to take.
3. Agrees with people even when he or she believes they are wrong, because of fear of being rejected.
4. Has difficulty initiating projects or doing things on his or her own.
5. Volunteers to do things that are unpleasant or demeaning in order to get other people to like him or her.
6. Feels uncomfortable or helpless when alone or goes to great lengths to avoid being alone.
7. Feels devastated or helpless when close relationships end.
8. Is frequently preoccupied with fear of being abandoned.
9. Is easily hurt by criticism or disapproval.

subordinate themselves to others, and will go to great lengths to get other people to like them. Common presenting problems include depression, anxiety, and alcoholism.

In diagnosing Dependent Personality Disorder, it is important to carefully investigate the client's relationship history, with particular attention to how he or she has responded to the ending of relationships and how other people have said they perceive the client. Careful questioning about how everyday, as well as major, decisions are made can be helpful, as well as information about how the client feels about being alone for extended periods of time. In addition, it can be useful to ask how the client would handle a situation where he or she disagrees with someone else or is asked to do something unpleasant or demeaning. The therapist's own reaction can sometimes be helpful in diagnosing Dependent Personality Disorder. If the therapist feels tempted to rush in and rescue the client or if the therapist finds him- or herself making exceptions for the client without resenting it as one would with a client who had Borderline Personality Disorder, one should suspect Dependent Personality Disorder and collect the data necessary to substantiate this.

Because clients with a variety of disorders may show dependent features, it is important to be careful to differentiate Dependent Personality Disorder from other, superficially similar disorders. For example, although clients with either Histrionic Personality Disorder or Dependent Personality Disorder may appear childlike and clinging, clients with Dependent Personality Disorder are less flamboyant, egocentric, and shallow than those with Histrionic Personality Disorder. Agoraphobics may be dependent on other people, but they are dependent in a very specific way: They need someone to go places with them so that they do not have to worry about being alone if they should have a panic attack. Agoraphobics are often much more active in asserting their dependence than individuals with Dependent Personality Disorder, actively demanding that they be accompanied wherever they go. It is possible, however, for a client to meet the criteria for both Panic Disorder with Agoraphobia and Dependent Personality Disorder.

Sarah fit the criteria for Dependent Personality Disorder very well. She was a 37-year-old housewife who had stayed with her husband 18 years, despite the fact that he was alcoholic and she felt she was unable to get what she wanted or needed from him. She allowed him to make decisions for her, tolerating moves even when they were not good for her. This was clearly a long-standing pattern for her in relationships in general, and she acknowledged that she had a tendency to get into dependent relationships. She stated that "I can't exist without them, even if they are not good for me." Sarah felt disgusted with herself and felt like she was a failure, incapable, and inadequate. She came into treatment presenting with problems of panic attacks, depression, and avoidance of going virtually any place alone.

Conceptualization

The cognitive-behavioral conceptualization of Dependent Personality Disorder is relatively straightforward. These clients see themselves as inherently inadequate and helpless and thus unable to cope with the world on their own. They see the world as a cold, lonely, or even dangerous place that they could not possibly handle alone. Their solution is to try to find someone they view as competent to handle life who is willing to make a trade-off: They will give up responsibility and subordinate their own needs and desires in exchange for having that person take care of them. With Sarah, this pattern was obvious by age 13. She always made a point of having a steady boyfriend whom she saw as being able to take care of her, even if this meant tolerating substantial abuse.

This "solution" creates two dilemmas for these individuals. First, relying on others to handle problems and make decisions results in their having little opportunity to master and exercise the skills needed for independence. Either they never learn the skills of independent living (e.g., problem solving, decision making), or they do not recognize the skills they do have and therefore do not use them. Second, the idea of being more competent is terrifying, because they believe that if they are any less needy, they will no longer be taken care of but will remain unable to cope on their own.

Beyond these dilemmas, this "solution" has several additional disadvantages. First, the individual always has to be very careful to please the other person and avoid conflict for fear of being abandoned and having to fend for himself or herself. Second, the dependent individual may seem so desperate, needy, and clinging, that their partner may feel overwhelmed, or it may become hard to find a willing partner that can meet his or her needs for any length of time. Finally, if the relationship ends, the individual is almost certain to be devastated and to see no alternative to finding someone new to depend upon. For example, Sarah's panic attacks started with the end of a close friendship, and she had a serious relapse with the end of a previous therapy, remaining obsessed with her therapist even after a period of 2 years had passed.

Among the most frequent and characteristic automatic thoughts of the individual with Dependent Personality Disorder are "I can't," "I never would be able to do that," and "I'm much too stupid, weak, etc." Their underlying assumptions include "I can't survive without someone to take care of me," "I'm too inadequate to handle life on my own," "If my spouse (parent, etc.) left me, I'd fall apart," "If I were more independent, I'd be isolated and alone," and "Independence means being completely on your own." The primary cognitive distortion in Dependent Personality Disorder is a strong all-or-none thinking in regards to autonomy. In their eyes, either you are helpless and dependent or you are totally independent and alone, and they can see no options in between.

Intervention Strategies and Techniques

The primary goal in therapy with the person with Dependent Personality Disorder is to help him or her learn to gradually become more independent from significant others (including the therapist) and to increase his or her self-confidence and sense of self-efficacy. However, because these clients typically fear that competence will lead to abandonment, this must be done with considerable delicacy. It is particularly important to pay careful attention to one factor that is too often ignored by cognitive-behavior therapists: The client–therapist relationship. The client's dependent behavior is typically manifested within the therapeutic relationship. This has led some to suggest that humanistic or nondirective approaches may be preferable to more directive, cognitive-behavioral approaches that might encourage the client to remain submissive in relation to a dominant therapist (e.g., Millon, 1981). However, if the cognitive-behavior therapist modifies the treatment appropriately, the interactions between the client and the therapist can provide rich behavioral and cognitive data, leading to cognitive-behavioral interventions within the session that can have a particularly strong impact on the client due to their immediacy.

Because the individual with a Dependent Personality Disorder comes into treatment looking desperately for someone to solve his or her problems, it may be necessary to allow some dependence in the treatment initially in order to engage the client; but the therapist needs to continually monitor the status of the relationship, consistently working to gradually wean the client away from that dependence. As has been stressed before, collaboration does not need to always be 50-50, and at the beginning of treatment, the therapist may need to do more than half of the work. However, that pattern must change during the course of therapy so that the treatment eventually becomes more clearly the client's own.

As with any of the personality disorders, the early stages of treatment involve working toward achieving the client's stated goals, including helping the client to pinpoint and challenge his or her automatic thoughts. Although it may be obvious to the therapist from the beginning that dependence is the major issue for the client, dependence is rarely stated as part of the presenting problem by the client. In fact, even the use of the words *dependence, independence,* or *autonomy* can be quite frightening to the client early in therapy. The issues of dependence will become obvious as the treatment progresses, no matter what goals the therapy is working toward. However, it may be most natural and least frightening to the client to let the actual use of the terms come first from the client when he or she is ready to bring them up.

The structured collaborative approach used in Cognitive Therapy encourages the client to play an active role in the therapy. Even setting an agenda can be an exercise in taking more initiative than the dependent individual customarily does. It is common for these clients to try to give all the power in the therapy over to the therapist, responding to questioning about what they want to focus on in the session, with, "Oh, whatever you want." In the first session or two, if the client has no items to add to the agenda, the therapist can provide a suggested plan and ask if that is acceptable to the client. After that, however, it is important to take it one step further and explain that because this is their therapy, they will be expected to make suggestion each session about how they want to spend the time. This can even be included as part of their written homework assignment for the week. By making it clear that the therapist expects them to contribute items to the agenda, continuing to ask at the beginning of each session even if they repeatedly offer no suggestions and waiting until they do offer some suggestions before moving on, the therapist may be able to foster some initial active involvement in the treatment.

It is particularly important to use guided discovery and Socratic questioning when working with clients who have a Dependent Personality Disorder. These clients are likely to look on the therapist as "the expert" and hang on the therapist's every word. This can be very gratifying for the therapist, who may have spent the rest of the day seeing clients who do not seem to listen. Thus it can be tempting to just tell these clients exactly what the problem is and what they need to do, thereby taking an authoritarian role in the therapy. These clients do need to get some active guidance and practical suggestions from the therapist in order to get engaged in the treatment; a totally nondirective approach could be too anxiety-provoking for these clients to tolerate for long. However, when the client asks the therapist to tell him or her what to do, the therapist will be more successful in using guided discovery and helping the client arrive at his or her own solutions rather than making direct suggestions. Teaching the process of problem solving is much more useful that just giving the client solutions to his or her problems.

As therapy proceeds, progress toward goals can be used as powerful evidence to challenge the dependent person's assumption that he or she is helpless. For example, the process of doing graded exposure to anxiety-provoking situations was an excellent challenge to Sarah's belief in her own helplessness. After having worked on going to guitar lessons for several weeks, Sarah was able to generate the rational response, "Remember last week? No shakes! I played a solo, and the teacher said I did very well!" The client does not need to be working on an anxiety hierarchy, however, to collect systematic evidence of competence. The therapist and client can collaboratively develop a hierarchy of increasingly difficult independent actions. For example, a decision-making hierarchy could range from decision like what type of fruit to have for lunch to decisions regarding jobs and places to live.

When planning interventions, it is important to assess to what extent the client actually has skill deficits versus a lack of recognition of the coping skills that he or she already does possess. It is easy to assume that these clients really are as helpless as they present themselves to be; yet often they have many of the skills needed to function independently and successfully, but they simply do not recognize this. When there is a skill deficit, the client can be trained in skills such as assertion, problem solving (D'Zurilla & Goldfried, 1971), decision making, and social interaction in order to increase their competence. In Sarah's case, however, she was already able to be assertive in some situations that she did not perceive as personal (such as when shopping and in her volunteer work). It was in her close interpersonal relationships that she rarely used assertion. Therefore, she did not need to be taught the basic skills of assertion but needed help in learning to apply these skills to her close interpersonal relationships. This involved looking carefully at the thoughts that were inhibiting her from asserting herself when the relationship was important to her.

The dichotomous view of independence is a crucial area to explore. Holding the belief that one is either totally dependent and helpless or one is totally independent, isolated, and alone makes any movement toward autonomy seem like a commitment to complete alienation. Working with the client to draw a continuum from dependence to independence can be very useful, as it was with Sarah (Figure 19). Seeing that there were many steps in between the extremes of total dependence and total independence made it less frightening for her to take small steps toward independence. One illustration that can be useful with clients is that even independent,

Totally Dependent ├──────────────────────────┤ Totally Independent

0 1 2 3 4 5 6 7 8 9 10

Doesn't do anything alone
Has someone else make all
  decisions
Does whatever she's told
Has someone else always there to
  handle problems
Completely helpless
Subservient, docile
Like a puppy, always acting happy
  and pleased

Does everything alone
Makes her own decisions without
  considering anyone else
Does whatever she wants
Expresses opinions no matter
  what anyone else thinks
Handles all problems on her own
Totally competent
Doesn't need anyone
Outspoken, aggressive, brash
Isolated and alone

FIGURE 19. Independence continuum drawn by Sarah, a dependent client.

well-functioning adults still join automobile clubs in order to have help when they need it; thus, no one needs to be totally independent at all times and it is no disgrace to admit that one might need help from time to time.

Because maladaptive patterns in interpersonal relationships are a major part of the problem with Dependent Personality Disorders, much time in the therapy usually needs to be spent on dealing with interpersonal relationships. In order to most effectively use the therapeutic relationship as an example of an ongoing pattern of dependent relationships, it is necessary to explicitly encourage the client to explore his or her thoughts and feelings about the therapist. These clients may be so focused on other relationships in their lives that it may not occur to them that thoughts and feelings about the therapist are important, or even appropriate, to discuss. Sarah had developed such a dependent relationship with her previous, humanistic therapist (see herself as being madly in love with him) that she initially had great difficulty dealing with her new cognitive therapist, who happened to be a woman. Through the use of thought sheets (see Figure 20), she was not only able to resolve the difficulties she had been having with her new therapist, but she was also able to come to a better understanding of how her previous therapy relationship had been similar to other relationships in her past, fostering her dependency.

Another important part of paying careful attention to the client–therapist relationship is for the therapist to monitor his or her own thoughts and feelings toward the client. The temptation to rescue this type of client is particularly strong, and it can be very easy to either accept the client's belief in his or her own helplessness or try to rescue the client out of frustration with slow progress. Unfortunately, attempts at rescuing the client are incompatible with the goal of increasing the client's independence and self-sufficiency.

Daily Record of Automatic Thoughts				
Situation Briefly describe the situation	**Emotion(s)** Rate 0–100%	**Automatic Thought(s)** Try to quote thoughts then rate belief in each thought 0–100%	**Rational Response** Rate degree of belief 0–100%	**Outcome** Re-rate emotions
Thinking of previous therapist (HN) and current therapist (Mrs. P)	Sad 90% Anxious 90%	1) I don't feel like a person to Mrs. P. She always wants to talk about the homework & the program.	1) We are not here to get close & dependent. I'm here to learn how to deal with my anxiety & function more effectively in the world.	
		2. Mrs. P ignores me outside of sessions, doesn't call me by name.	2. These are valid points – rather than leave, why not discuss these issues and get more of what I want in this relationship?	
		3. HN made me feel like the most important person in the world for that hour. He relaxed me w/his voice & manner & patience.	3. Mrs. P is not HN – I got into a lot of trouble with his approach. I'm not here to make friends. I want to learn to do things for me, not for my therapist.	Sad 30% Anxious 50%

FIGURE 20. Sarah's thought sheet regarding her reactions to her therapist.

A resident came to supervision after an initial session with a new client, reporting how terribly distressed and anxious the client was. Only after the session had been discussed at length did the resident acknowledge that he had prescribed antianxiety medication, even though there is a clear policy of not prescribing medications to new clients until after discussing it in supervision. It became clear that he had automatically accepted her view of herself as totally helpless and had felt good at the time that he could be of so much help to this pathetic woman.

Whenever a therapist feels tempted to be more active and less collaborative with a client or to make exceptions, it may be useful for the therapist to write a thought sheet to clarify whether the exception is going to be in the best long-term interests of the client or whether it will serve to foster dependency.

Because these clients are especially prone to developing overly dependent relationships, it is crucial to set clear limits on the extent of the therapist's professional relationship with the client. Sarah is certainly not the first client with Dependent Personality Disorder to fall in love with her therapist; in fact, our clinical experience indicates that clients with this disorder are more likely than other clients to develop idealized love relationships with their therapists. These are not the clients with whom to use techniques that involve physical contact or intimate settings, nor is it a good idea to bend your usual rules of maintaining a professional distance. If the use of *in-vivo* exercises necessitates your being outside of the office with a client, it is important to be very clear about the goals of the exercise, keep it very professional (for example, takes notes of cognitions and write down anxiety levels at regular intervals), and minimize "chitchat".

At some point in the treatment, these clients will need to explore the belief that if they become more competent they will be abandoned. One useful way to challenge this is by setting up specific behavioral experiments where they behave a bit more competently and observe the reaction from their significant others. Because this type of behavioral experiment involves other people, this truly is an "experiment": neither the client nor the therapist can be certain how it will turn out. Although it may be irrational to believe that one will end up totally abandoned and alone forever if one is assertive, we really do not know if more competence will lead to abandonment by the client's primary significant other or not. Without having even met Sarah's husband Dave, her therapist would have no way of knowing how he would react to changes in Sarah. Many people get involved with dependent individuals because they are attracted to that dependency, so it is possible that a spouse, parent, or some other person will react negatively if the client begins to change and become more assertive and independent. The dependent behavior may be actively reinforced by significant others, and attempts to change may be punished. However, it is also possible that the spouse will react well to these changes, even if the client is positive that the spouse will react negatively. By starting with small steps, one can usually observe the spouse's reaction without risking enormous upheaval or total abandonment. Sarah was certain that her husband would get angry at her if she started to express her feelings and to ask for more support. She did some dysfunctional thought records about this (Figure 21) and eventually built up the nerve to try the behavioral experiment of asking for more support. She was amazed and delighted at his positive reaction and regretted having been too frightened to try this sooner.

In cases where the spouse's reaction to increased assertion is, in fact, negative, it may be necessary to explore other options. Marital or family

Daily Record of Automatic Thoughts				
Situation Briefly describe the situation	**Emotion(s)** Rate 0-100%	**Automatic Thought(s)** Try to quote thoughts then rate belief in each thought 0-100%	**Rational Response** Rate degree of belief 0-100%	**Outcome** Re-rate emotions
Thinking about HN (previous therapist) and Don (husband)	Sad 90% Angry 75%	1) HN really knew how to comfort me - He'd rub my back and speak quietly and reassuringly. 100% 2) HN really cared for me unlike Don, who doesn't comfort me like I want. 100%	1) He did have a very endearing way about him - it felt good what he did & made me aware of what I want and need. But he may not be the only one who could do that for me. 85% 2) HN didn't love me like Don does - Don is my real relation- ship. 100% Don hugged me and rubbed my back when I asked him to and also spoke quietly & reassuringly! He did what I asked and I felt better - He gave me what I wanted! And I could ask! 100%	 Sad 50% Angry 25%

FIGURE 21. Sarah's thought sheet regarding her reactions to her husband.

therapy can often be useful in helping both spouses begin to adjust to the changes and even change together. For example, Louise, a 42-year-old mother of two, finally decided to learn to drive after much therapy focusing on other issues. Her husband had been quite supportive up to that point but suddenly became more irritable, procrastinated about taking her to get a learner's permit and eventually refused to do so. Several marital sessions were required to calm his fears and resolve the crisis. If either the client or the spouse is not willing to pursue conjoint treatment, however, the client may need to explore the advantages and disadvantages of maintaining his or her current approach to relationships.

Whether the person decides to stay in the relationship and work toward change, stay in it and accept it as it is, or get out of the relationship, he or she will eventually need to decatastrophize the idea that relationships can and do end. Even if he or she insists that things are wonderful in the dependent relationship, unexpected difficulties are always possible, so no one can absolutely count on another person always being there. Of course, the therapist would not deny that losing an important relationship can be extremely upsetting. The idea is not to convince dependent clients that other people are not important, but to help them to see that they could and would survive the loss of the relationship.

Although the client with Dependent Personality Disorder is generally very cooperative and compliant in the beginning of treatment, there is often a problem with the client's not following through on homework assignments later in the therapy. This can be the result of frightening the client by moving too quickly and, if so, it may be important to list the advantages and disadvantages of changing, seriously exploring the disadvantages of achieving the client's goals. It is more effective to induce the client to convince the therapist to proceed more quickly than to have the therapist push the client toward autonomy. The therapist should not be working harder than the client; if this occurs, there is a problem in the treatment.

Sometimes, an exploration of the advantages and disadvantages of changing will reveal that the disadvantages of change outweigh the advantages for a particular client.

Dorothy was a 24-year-old woman who sought treatment for depression. She had always been extremely dependent on her mother and never learned to do things on her own. She very rigidly believed that she could not do anything successfully on her own and was therefore terrified to try anything new because she was certain she would fail miserably. She had gotten married the previous May to her high-school sweetheart and moved out of the state. She immediately became very depressed because she felt overwhelmed by the responsibilities of being a wife and felt helpless to handle them without her mother. She ruminated about her inadequacies and believed she would be fine if she could only be back in her hometown. If she became less depressed and learned to accept life away from her hometown, her husband would have no incentive to move back. When she acknowledged that her main goal was to convince her husband to move back to her hometown, it became clear why she had been noncompliant in treatment. In fact, her mood improved not in relation to any interventions but when her husband agreed that they could move back to her hometown within the year.

There may be some good reasons for the dependent person to be ambivalent about changing. Although the person struggling with feelings of helplessness may feel that he or she has no power, taking the helpless role can actually be very powerful and reinforcing (as with Dorothy), and this role can be difficult to give up. If the client can be helped to identify what would be lost if he or she no longer were as helpless, it may be possible to figure out a way to find a more constructive way of achieving the same ends.

One way to foster the progression from dependence in therapy to independence is to change the structure of therapy itself. Moving the client from individual therapy to group therapy (preferably with the individual therapist as one of the co-therapists of the group) can help to reduce the client's dependence on the therapist and serve to dilute the relationship. In a group setting, the client can still get a great deal of support but can begin to derive more support from peers than from the therapist. This serves as a good first step toward finding even more natural means of support in the client's circle of family and friends. Modeling has been found to help increase independent behavior (Goldstein, Martens, Hubben, Van Belle, Schaaf, Wirsma, & Goedhart, 1973), and in group therapy the other clients can serve as models for the development of many skills. In addition, the group therapy setting provides a safe place to practice new skills, such as assertion. After 20 sessions of individual therapy, Sarah moved to group therapy and was able to use the group to practice assertion, to practice difficult hierarchy items (like taking two airplane trips), and eventually as a place to challenge her perfectionism by playing guitar in front of the group.

Another structural change that helps to facilitate the transition from dependence to independence is the "fading" of sessions by meeting less frequently toward the end of therapy, as discussed in Chapter 1. The concept of terminating therapy is an extremely threatening one for the person with a Dependent Personality Disorder, because he or she is likely to believe that it would be impossible to maintain his or her progress without the therapist's support. Rather than trying to challenge this belief in the abstract, the process of fading sessions can serve as a behavioral experiment to test out the belief. If sessions are moved to every other week, the client will be able to see how well gains can be maintained over 2 weeks. If the client sees that he or she is able to function well over the 2-week period, he or she may then be able to move to monthly sessions. If the client is not able to maintain progress over a 2-week period, then perhaps he or she is not ready to fade the therapy, and it may be appropriate to return to weekly sessions for the time being. If clients can be given a great deal of control over the spacing of the sessions, this is likely to leave them feeling less threatened and more willing to try some fading, because the choice is not irrevocable. The therapist can fade sessions further and further, offering to meet every month, every 3 months, or even every 6 months if they choose. When given this type of free choice, however, clients usually come to realize that if they can go a full month without therapy, they really no longer need to be in treatment. After 14 sessions of group therapy, Sarah felt that she had achieved most of her goals and felt ready to begin the process of termination. She moved to meeting every other week for the next six sessions and then met for one last session after a period of one month. This type of fading can be very useful for the individual client but can be disruptive for a group, especially with various clients on different fading schedules. One workable compromise is for the client to end group therapy when he or she feels ready to move toward termination and then do a limited number of fading sessions individually with one of the group co-therapists. If one is going to try this compromise, it is important to be sure that the client is really ready to move toward termination and is not just using the change in therapy modality as a way to get more individual attention (and, hence, more dependency) on the therapist.

Another factor that can make termination easier for the person with a Dependent Personality Disorder is the offer of booster sessions when necessary. Whenever terminating therapy with a client, the therapist explains that if the client experiences any difficulties in the future, either with these or other issues, it is a good idea to recontact the therapist for one or two booster sessions. Such booster sessions often simply serve to get clients back on the track of doing what they had been doing that had helped in the past. Just knowing that they have the option of recontacting the therapist helps to make the transition to termination easier.

Conclusion

Although treatment of the Dependent Personality Disorder can be a slow, arduous process that can be frustrating at times, it can be very rewarding as well. With the proper conceptualization and careful strategic planning throughout treatment, the therapist may have the opportunity to watch the client blossom into an autonomous adult, providing satisfaction not unlike that of watching a child grow up.

13

Passive-Aggressive Personality Disorder

The nature of Passive-Aggressive Personality Disorder is obvious from its name. This disorder has been referred to in many ways including "negativistic personality" (Millon, 1969), "oral-sadistic melancholiac" (Menninger, 1940), "emotionally unstable character" (Klein & Davis, 1969), "oppositional personality," and "active-ambivalent personality" (Millon, 1981). Whatever it is called, it is one of the most frustrating and aggravating personality disorders to treat. As Millon (1981, p. 258) describes:

> The passive-aggressive's strategy of negativism, of being discontent and unpredictable, of being both seductive and rejecting, and of being demanding and then dissatisfied, is an effective weapon . . . with people in general. Switching among the roles of the martyr, the affronted, the aggrieved, the misunderstood, the contrite, the guilt-ridden, the sickly, and the overworked, is a tactic of interpersonal behavior that gains passive-aggressives the attention, reassurance, and dependency they crave while, at the same time, allowing them to subtly vent their angers and resentments.

Because passive-aggressive behavior creates recurrent roadblocks in therapy, as it does in other important areas of life, these clients progress slowly, if at all, and are likely to arouse antagonism in the therapist. Although no statistics are available concerning the frequency with which individuals with Passive-Aggressive Personality Disorder enter psychotherapy, reports by clinicians indicate that clients with the full disorder or with passive-aggressive features appear quite often. When they do, the therapist is likely to find them challenging to treat.

ASSESSMENT

Hal was a 27-year-old white male living alone and employed as an assistant manager in a shoestore. His Beck Depression Inventory score was 33, indicating severe depression, and his Hamilton Anxiety Scale score was 24, indicating moder-

Table 30. DSM-III-R Criteria for Passive-Aggressive Personality Disorder

A pervasive pattern of passive resistance to demands for adequate social and occupational performance, beginning by early adulthood and present in a variety of contexts, as indicated by at least *five* of the following:
1. Procrastinates
2. Becomes sulky, irritable, or argumentative when asked to do something he or she does not want to do
3. Seems to work deliberately slowly or to do a bad job on tasks that he or she really does not want to do
4. Protests, without justification, that others make unreasonable demands on him or her
5. Avoids obligations by claiming to have "forgotten"
6. Believes that he or she is doing a much better job than others think he or she is doing
7. Resents useful suggestions from others concerning how he or she could be more productive
8. Obstructs the efforts of others by failing to do his or her share of the work
9. Unreasonably criticizes or scorns people in positions of authority

ate to severe anxiety. Hal reported feeling depressed due to career frustrations and a lack of satisfaction in his relationships. He believed he was not progressing in his job the way he wished and felt exploited and oppressed by his boss. This sense of being controlled and used by bosses and other authority figures (including professors) had appeared frequently in Hal's past. In addition, he was dissatisfied with his relationships and reported being unable to modulate levels of disclosure, either being too closed or too open. In therapy, Hal kept agreeing to do homework assignments but usually came back the next week with an excuse for not doing them. such as, "I lost my recorder," "I wasn't sure it would work," "I forgot," "I'm not sure I'll like it," or "I'm not sure why I didn't do it."

In the DSM-III-R criteria for Passive-Aggressive Personality Disorder (see Table 30), we see that the problem behaviors of the passive aggressive tend more often to be those of omission rather than commission. Such individuals are able to tell themselves that they did not *do* anything offensive and that therefore the negative reactions of others are unjustified and unfair. As a result, these clients are able to avoid taking responsibility for the consequences of their actions. The passive-aggressive client typically enters therapy complaining about the actions of others. For example, they may complain that they are poorly treated at work, that they are treated unfairly by superiors, that co-workers do less work than they, or that others ridicule or avoid them. These individuals may complain that their spouse never does what he or she should or that their spouse is angry at them all the time. They often complain of depression, tension, and social isolation resulting from this mistreatment by others. In fact, the passive-aggressive individual may be a reluctant participant in therapy—seeing no need to make changes but considering himself or herself to be an innocent victim of others.

Even among individuals with Passive-Aggressive Personality Disorder, there is variability in how the passive-aggressiveness is expressed. First, this variability can be seen in terms of what situations or persons tend to elicit the most unremitting passive-aggressiveness. For purposes of therapeutic intervention, the most relevant distinction here is how consistently the client behaves passive-aggressively in the therapy sessions. For example, some clients express their passive-aggressiveness only intermittently toward their therapists, whereas others express it almost continuously. Although the former group will be easier to treat and more pleasant to work with, the latter will be easier to diagnose.

In addition, this variability in passive-aggressiveness is also seen in the *style* of expression. Thus some of these individuals will fall more on the aggressive side of the passive-aggressive continuum and are likely to be experienced as "obnoxious." Others will fall more on the passive side of the continuum and will be experienced as "innocent, victim types." Although the same principles apply to the treatment of all passive-aggressive clients, the distinction between the subtypes—intermittent or continuous expression and "obnoxious" or "innocent" style—can be helpful during both assessment and the implementation of treatment.

The "obnoxious" passive-aggressive client, who also manifests his or her passive-aggressive behavior constantly within therapy, is usually easy to diagnose. However, even if the behavior is only intermittent and the passive-aggressive behavior is not immediately obvious, the therapist will soon become aware of his or her own resentment and a sense of being "had" by the client. As a result, the therapist may find the client unpleasant to be around and may experience an urge to retaliate against him or her. When the therapist examines the precipitants of these negative thoughts and reactions, he or she typically discovers a pattern of poor collaboration and noncompliance. The client says that he or she sees the merit of the courses of action suggested by the therapist but either agrees to them and does not follow through or constantly comes up with reasons why the suggestion will not work in his or her case.

Depressed or anxious clients, who are not passive-aggressive, may also fail to follow through on homework or may engage in "yes, but" responses. However, the content of the client's automatic thoughts regarding the assignment and the client's associated affect should fairly easily discriminate between noncompliance stemming from these disorders and passive-aggressive noncompliance. The severely depressed client may say, "What's the use? It's hopeless. Nothing can help me." The anxious client may say, "What if I do it wrong? What if it doesn't work? What if I can't do it?" In addition, the affect expressed by the client will be consistent with each of these sets of automatic thoughts: The depressed client will feel discouraged and hopeless, and the anxious client will feel worried or nervous. The passive-aggressive client may report thoughts that appear to explain the noncompliance but will seem argumentative or even triumphant, rather than hopeless or anxious.

As stated previously, the client who does not consistently manifest his or her passive-aggressive behavior in interactions with the therapist can be more difficult to identify. This is especially true if the client is also an "innocent" type of passive-aggressive. This client is certainly not likely to acknowledge his or her passive-aggressive acts and is likely to describe problem situations as though they were due to accidents, misunderstandings, or unreasonable behavior on the part of others. Thus it can take quite some time for the therapist to realize that the client plays an active, if covert, role in the problems that arise. Assessment of this individual reveals a frequent tendency to "forget" obligations or commitments to other people in such a way that he or she seems blameless; thus, he or she may frequently fail to show up for appointments and fail to do homework simply because "It just slipped my mind." This client may have a tendency to giggle while doing or saying things that seem to express affect other than amusement. They are quite indirect in expressing any dissatisfaction; for example they will pay for sessions with checks that bounce, rather than either discussing their dissatisfactions with the fee or directly refusing to pay.

CONCEPTUALIZATION

The underlying assumptions of the passive-aggressive tend to revolve around anger and justice. For example, a very basic belief would be: "I must avoid conflict at all costs," with such conclusions as "It's dangerous to express anger directly"; "It's dangerous to experience anger"; and "It's dangerous to be open and assertive about one's desires." Such assumptions lead to passivity, denial of anger, and avoidance of open hostility. With only these beliefs, however, the individual might be unassertive and episodically passive-aggressive. It is assumptions regarding justice and fairness that lead to his or her chronic anger and, consequently, to chronic passive-aggressiveness. The passive-aggressive individual holds strong beliefs about how he or she *should* be treated, such as "Everyone should know the right way to treat a person," and, therefore, "I should not have to ask for what I want." When these individuals fail to get from others what they want and think they deserve, they interpret it as meaning that others are cruel, withholding, and unfair. And because people are presumed to know what the passive-aggressive individual wants without having to be told, he or she assumes that "if people don't [spontaneously] do what I want, asking for it won't help." Thus beliefs leading to anger and avoidance of assertion occur side by side and lead to the ambivalent solution of the passive-aggressive. Burns and Epstein (1983) condense these beliefs down to three central assumptions of the passive-aggressive: (1) entitlement—the idea that "other people should meet one's expectations," (2) reciprocity—the belief that the person "has earned good responses from others through good behavior," and (3) conflict phobic—the belief that "people who care about each other shouldn't fight."

Some of the characteristic cognitive distortions of the passive-aggressive individual include the following:

1. *Personalization.* Other people's actions and speech are interpreted as being directed toward the individual, and other factors that may be involved are overlooked. For example, "I would have gotten a better raise if my boss didn't have it in for me."
2. *Should/must/ought.* They judge others and themselves according to *shoulds.* They feel inherently entitled to certain types of treatment by others. For example, "She shouldn't treat me like this."
3. *Emotional reasoning.* This is usually manifested in the attitude, "If I feel slighted, then that proves I actually have been slighted."
4. *Mind reading.* The individual is certain he or she *knows* why others do what they do without having to ask, for example, "She is doing that just because she knows I hate it."
5. *Labeling.* The passive-aggressive assigns global negative labels to people who displease him or her, such as *son of a bitch* or *jerk;* this tends to enhance and justify their anger.
6. *Disqualifying the positive.* The passive-aggressive tends to attribute "bad" motives to "good" behavior and therefore gives no credit to others for objectively positive or neutral actions. An example of this would be, "He only did that so I wouldn't get upset, not because he *wants* to."
7. *Selective abstraction.* If some word or action by another can be interpreted as a slight, the passive-aggressive will tend to do so, regardless of the context.
8. *Magnification.* Minor slights and criticisms become scathing attacks and rejections in the mind of the passive-aggressive.
9. *All-or-nothing thinking.* These individuals believe that they are being treated either fairly or unfairly, that the other person is either right or wrong.

To the observer, passive-aggressiveness seems to be a clearly unsatisfactory approach to living. The individual's strong beliefs about what he or she deserves generate much dissatisfaction, but passive-aggressive behavior is an ineffective means for gaining what is desired. Furthermore, passive-aggressiveness tends to lead to more and more difficulty because of the reaction that it tends to elicit from others. The obstructiveness, the glimpses of suppressed rage, and the "innocent" retaliations of the passive-aggressive lead to anger in others as well as the desire to thwart the passive-aggressive in turn. The passive-aggressive individual may notice this reaction but rather than abandoning this strategy, he or she intensifies the passive-aggressive behavior in the hopes of punishing others for their mistreatment of him or her without risking confrontation.

How then can one explain the development and persistence of passive-aggressiveness in the personality-disordered individual? Although passive-aggressiveness produces unsatisfactory results, it may have led to better results than any other approach available to the developing child (Millon, 1981). For example, in a family of origin without assertive models, where direct expression of anger by children is not tolerated, passive-aggressiveness might allow the person to avoid being punished for active hostility while still allowing some expression of hostile feelings. Thus passive-aggressiveness may be seen as a self-protective compromise in such situations. Once established, this pattern may be maintained by the individual's belief that more direct expression of anger will still lead to intolerable conflict.

Strategies for Intervention

It seems obvious that an important goal in working with passive-aggressive clients is to help them find more adaptive ways to handle anger and resentment. However, assertion training alone is not sufficient. In order to effectively modify the client's passive-aggressive behavior, it is first necessary to get the client to recognize both his or her passive-aggressive behavior and the consequences of this behavior. Only then is it possible to collaboratively explore the client's other options for handling anger and resentment and to address the fears and expectations that block adaptive responses. Finally, an important part of treatment is addressing the client's beliefs, expectations, and demands about how he or she "should" be treated, because these are likely to be the source of much of his or her chronic anger and resentment.

Cognitive and Behavioral Techniques

In treating passive-aggressive clients, the first goal, and often the most difficult one, is to make the client aware of his or her own problem behavior. The therapist must gently but persistently draw the client's attention to any indications of the client's discomfort with anger and his or her tendency to express it indirectly until the client can recognize and acknowledge the pattern. For example:

Andrew brought his female therapist a bouquet of flowers "for no special reason." A few minutes later he smilingly handed her a list of automatic thoughts he had written as homework after the previous session. This list included such statements as, "I'd like to punch [my therapist] in the face." The therapist pointed out the inconsistencies between smiling and bringing a gift of flowers on the one hand, yet notifying the therapist of violent wishes on the other, and she asked for an explanation. The patient admitted that he had been "annoyed" at the therapist but did not want her to be angry at him. This provided an opportunity to explore Andrew's fears about expressing anger in therapy and to question whether similar interactions occurred in other settings.

Another client, Sharon, spent hour after therapeutic hour talking about how much she hated the way she was living her life. However, whenever brainstorming about ideas for changes led to discussion of what she could actually do differently, Sharon would find numerous reasons why they were not worth trying. The therapist questioned the apparent contradiction between believing one's life-style is making one miserable, on the one hand, and never trying anything that might help, on the other. After many months of this, Sharon admitted that she was deciding not to follow through on any ideas that derived from therapy sessions because it was the only place she felt free to refuse anyone anything. Once both Sharon and her therapist knew that this was what she was doing, her therapist stopped asking her for commitments to follow through on discussions and waited for Sharon to decide for herself. As a result, Sharon was eventually able to make this decision and to begin actively working to change.

Once the passive-aggressive client is able to acknowledge his or her motivations (for example, anger, annoyance, or irritation) to the therapist and to himself or herself, treatment may progress in a more straightforward manner. Having acknowledged indirect or mixed responses to situations in which he or she is angry, the client can fairly easily be encouraged to examine the disadvantages of his or her usual behavior and to consider alternative responses. In most situations, one of the more adaptive alternatives is assertion. Explicit training in assertion can be quite useful since the passive-aggressive individual typically has little skill in expressing himself or herself effectively and adaptively.

In working to help the client be more assertive, it is particularly important to identify any automatic thoughts, expectations, and beliefs that block assertion. Clients often overestimate the hazards of assertion, thinking, "They won't like me. They'll be angry with me. I'll be demanding and unfair." Or they may confuse assertion with aggression and anticipate massive retaliation. It is important and useful to address these cognitions verbally by examining the available evidence and considering what it would be like to be in the other person's shoes. However, it is rare for the therapist to be able to eliminate the client's discomfort with assertion through verbal interventions alone. Assertion training and behavioral experiments with assertion are almost always needed.

Much has been written on assertion-training methods, and approaches ranging from self-help books to structured assertion-training groups can be used. In working with passive-aggressive individuals, it is important to make frequent use of modeling and role playing rather than simply discussing assertion. The therapy session is an ideal place to teach assertiveness because the behavior can be identified and corrected through encouragement and feedback from the therapist. Most passive-aggressives do not distinguish between assertiveness and demandingness, criticalness, or nastiness. Thus, even if they can be induced to respond in a more direct manner, they will often do so in an objectionable way unless they are explicitly taught by the therapist. For a more detailed discussion of assertion training methods, see Jakubowski and Lange (1978).

As passive aggressive clients attempt to put their new assertive behavior into practice, it is important for them to both monitor their own behavior and to monitor and challenge dysfunctional thoughts that interfere with assertion. For example, Andrew's notions that "my wife will leave me if I ever disagree with her" or that "being assertive will lead to more trouble and conflict than passive-aggressiveness" were major impediments to assertion until they were challenged. When the DTR is used for this purpose, an additional column can be included to leave a place for the client to indicate the "Action Taken" (see Figure 22).

Behavioral experiments need to be designed to gradually test the consequences of non-passive-aggressive behavior in more and more threatening situations. Initially, the client's fears are likely to be strong enough that even very mild assertion is very difficult for him or her; as the individual's confidence in the safety of assertiveness increases, assertiveness can be tried in progressively more difficult situations. Often the least threatening situation for initial attempts at assertion may be in interactions with the therapist within therapy sessions. This can be practiced in role plays, with the therapist and client changing roles until the client has a sense of how to be tactfully assertive in a specific situation. This can also be tried spontaneously when setting agendas, scheduling appointments, and so on. As the client becomes more comfortable with assertion during therapy sessions, it is easier to induce him or her to try assertion outside the therapist's office. The client can then be asked to make a prediction as to the actual effects of specific assertive acts outside the therapy session. The results can be compared to his or her predictions in the next session, in order to develop more realistic expectancies about the consequences of assertion.

It is essential that the therapist provide a safe environment for the client to express feelings of irritation, annoyance, being "bothered," and so on. The client's belief structure is set up on the premise that such feelings and the perception of such feelings by others in oneself are intensely dangerous and must be avoided. Therefore, any direct expressions of anger, however slight, must be accepted and welcomed by the therapist—this

Daily Record of Automatic Thoughts

Date	Situation Briefly describe the situation	Emotion(s) Rate 0–100%	Automatic Thought(s) Try to quote thoughts then rate your belief in each thought 0–100%	Rational Response Rate degree of belief 0–100%	Action Taken	Outcome Re-rate emotions

FIGURE 22. Modified thought sheet.

includes direct expression of irritation regarding the therapist. Once these clients are able to admit that indirect expressions of annoyance or anger are a problem for them, they may actually need to be encouraged to express direct annoyance about the therapist. For example, the therapist may ask the client for criticism and express pleasure and praise the client for taking the risk of doing so.

In addition to working to increase assertion, it also may be necessary to discuss any real advantages of passive-aggressiveness for the individual. For example, when Andrew agreed to do whatever his wife (who had Borderline Personality Disorder) wanted and failed to follow through, she would get angry at him. However, if he actually refused a demand to her face, she would fly into a rage, would insult him, and threaten to divorce him. For Andrew, being assertive with his wife carried a tremendous cost. In this case, it was necessary to encourage him to make his first tentative attempts at assertion with people with whom success would be more likely. After he became proficient at being direct with others and receiving the social benefits and increased self-esteem this produced, he had to make a choice: Was he willing to continue being passive-aggressive with his wife in order to avoid her rage attacks? Was it important enough to him to be assertive that he would be willing to risk her rage? Did he want to stay in a marriage in which being direct carried such negative consequences? And was there any possibility of finding direct ways of communication that were less likely to set his wife off? Couples therapy can be used as an adjunct to individual psychotherapy in this sort of situation. In Andrew's case, after unsuccessful couples therapy, he decided to separate from his wife.

Although Passive-Aggressive Personality Disorder is, by definition, a long-standing problem, under certain conditions, it is not as difficult or time consuming to treat as some of the other Axis II disorders. If the individual expresses his or her passive-aggressiveness intermittently toward the therapist, rather than either being continually passive-aggressive or rarely revealing his or her passive-aggressiveness within the session, the prognosis is better. When passive-aggressiveness is expressed intermittently in treatment, therapy proceeds as described, with no more detours and difficulties than is the case in any course of therapy.

For those clients whose passive-aggressiveness is directed toward their therapist in an unrelenting manner, the course of therapy tends to proceed much more slowly. This type of passive-aggressive reveals a tendency to be actively obstructionistic in therapy (as in other life situations). They tend to cancel sessions at the last minute or may call, for example, at 2:00 to reschedule a 3:00 appointment to 3:15. The anger in these clients is readily obvious to others and is frequently shown in verbal sarcasm. Their tendency to object and find fault leads them to "yes, but" with regard to constructive action. Thus, they tell the therapist why any given homework suggestion is pointless.

The continually passive-aggressive client provides a wealth of opportunities for the therapist to reflect back to the client instances of passive-aggressive behavior. The purpose of this is to induce the client to notice occurrences of this behavior and to begin to introduce some cognitive dissonance about it. The therapist would not usually begin by labeling the behavior as passive-aggressive, but as "confusing," conveying "mixed messages," or something similarly nonthreatening. The therapist would then use gentle Socratic questioning to elicit the client's thoughts and feelings that precede such "confusing" behavior. The therapist will start to experience some progress once the client will admit to some even vaguely negative antecedent emotion. This eventually results in bringing the covert expression of anger into the open.

With this type of client, it becomes especially important to reflect his or her tendency to find fault. This should be done in a sympathetic and nonthreatening manner, for example, "It seems that life is full of disappointments for you; nothing ever seems to go just right." If we can help this individual to become aware of, and admit to, his or her tendency to find fault, we are in a position to explore the cognitions that produce this tendency. Distortions such as shoulds, entitlement, and discounting the positive are likely to be revealed and can be dealt with in the standard Cognitive Therapy manner.

It is essential to discover and explore the cognitions that interfere with therapeutic collaboration. These may be very predictable, given the client's diagnosis, or they may be idiosyncratic, for example, Sharon's statement that "I always end up doing what everyone else wants; therapy is one place where I don't have to, so I am not going to." The therapist, through guided discovery, will want to help the client explore the advantages and disadvantages of noncollaboration and to help him or her develop rational responses to the interfering cognitions.

It is also helpful, albeit tricky, to help the client to become aware of affect such as triumph when finding fault with others. This bolsters the understanding that he or she has some motivation to criticize or thwart others. This motivation will usually be found to be resentment and the desire to resist being "manipulated" or controlled. Once this has been revealed, the therapist may be able to empathize with the desire to resist being controlled by others and may show understanding that the person might feel resentful. However, the therapist will want to go on to question whether there might be other, more effective means of maintaining his or her autonomy—ways that would not produce retaliation from others. This must be done very carefully, using gentle Socratic questioning, or the therapist will encounter great resistance. This is getting to the core of the problem and is very threatening to passive-aggressives because it leads them to realize that part of the blame for interpersonal difficulties lies with them.

The most important strategy in the therapist's armamentarium with the continually passive-aggressive client is persistence and patience. The therapist will have to gently point out passive-aggressive speech and behavior and disinhibit direct expressions of anger many times before this individual will be able to see and admit to the motives for his or her behavior. For one to expect this to progress rapidly is to set oneself up for feelings of anger and discouragement. One of the authors spent 2 years of sessions with Sharon (discussed before) before this stage of therapy was reached; progress was rapid thereafter.

The greatest pitfall for the therapist treating the "obnoxious" type of passive aggressive is the tendency to become engaged in a power struggle with him or her. Power struggles cannot be won, and they damage the collaboration, which is essential and fragile in dealing with the passive-aggressive; thus they sidetrack and may even derail therapy. The passive-aggressive client can very easily bring out the worst in a therapist unless the therapist is very careful to monitor his or her own cognitions and behavior. Once a power struggle begins with this or any other client, there is no chance for a therapeutic result—*unless* it is used as a stimulus for inquiry and discussion in the therapy session. This, of course, requires that the therapist disengage from the struggle and regain his or her equanimity enough to conduct a fruitful investigation.

It is very difficult for any but the most saintly of therapists to interact with a consistently passive-aggressive client without having moderately to strongly negative feelings toward that individual. Thus the therapist must be aware of his or her own emotional reactions—dislike, anger, resentment, feelings of being "had," dread of sessions, desire to "get even," and so on. But it is not enough to be aware of these negative reactions. The Cognitive Therapist must "practice what he or she preaches" and would be well advised to use the Daily Record of Dysfunctional Thoughts to identify and respond to the automatic thoughts provoking such negative reactions. There is little hope of helping a client with whom one has the desire to "get even." On the positive side, however, the therapist, through his or her own emotional reactions, may get some insight into the effect this client has on others. This may serve as a guide for the therapist in the formulation of goals for the client as well as in the direction taken by the therapist in questioning the client. It may also serve as an opportunity for the therapist to model adaptive ways of handling anger and resentment.

Although therapy with the "innocent" passive-aggressive who rarely acts passive-aggressively within therapy sessions is much less aversive than working with the "obnoxious" passive-aggressive, it can be quite difficult in another way. As was noted earlier, it can be challenging to recognize a passive-aggressive behavior pattern in a client who does not manifest it in the therapy session. This is especially true if he or she tends to use more subtle forms of passive-aggressive behavior such as "forgetting."

Because the initial stage in Cognitive Therapy with passive-aggressive clients consists of focusing on instances of passive-aggressive behavior in order to make the chronic pattern apparent to the client, the more subtle the behavior is, the longer it will take to recognize the pattern and make it explicit. Often the "innocent" passive-aggressive reveals his or her passive-aggressive tendencies within therapy through subtle resistance and noncompliance such as "forgetting" appointments and homework assignments. It is important to neither take such "innocent" excuses for noncompliance at face value nor confront them harshly. For example, as soon as a trend toward forgetting begins to be apparent, the therapist could make a point of placing "forgetting" on the agenda. The therapist could use guided discovery in an attempt to understand the forgetting by identifying the context in which it occurs and the thoughts and feelings associated with it. If the forgetting is not passive-aggressive, this approach can lead to practical solutions. If it is passive-aggressive, recognition of the motivation behind "forgetting" can enable the therapist and client to explore more adaptive alternatives.

It is essential that the therapist explore possible reasons for the client's obstructionistic behavior in a nonjudgmental and nonaccusatory way. The "innocent" type of passive-aggressive is usually quite unwilling to acknowledge that he or she has any role in his or her problems with others and is likely to reject any direct assertions by the therapist. An indirect approach can help in circumnavigating this roadblock. It is often useful to avoid strong words such as anger, or even irritation, and instead to inquire about feelings of being "a bit bothered." Instead of asking the client to directly admit to negative feelings at all, the therapist may speak hypothetically, "If you were a bit upset with me, what might be a reason? . . . What might you do?" This indirect approach allows the client to gradually risk acknowledging the angry feelings that he or she fears will prove intolerable.

The most difficult part of working with the "innocent" passive-aggressive client is being perceptive and patient enough to reach the point where the client can acknowledge his or her anger and resentment. From that point on, progress is much quicker and often proceeds unremarkably.

Conclusions

Although the passive-aggressive individual may be one of the more unpleasant clients to work with in the initial phases of therapy, progress can be very satisfactory with the use of Cognitive Therapy. Once the client's passive-aggressive behavior has been explicitly recognized, the process of developing more adaptive alternatives, challenging the client's fears and expectations that block him or her from exercising these alternatives, and addressing cognitions that contribute to chronic anger and resentment is often fairly straightforward. Often the most difficult aspect of therapy is dealing effectively with the client's behavior within the therapy sessions and the therapist's reactions to it.

IV
Conclusion

14

The Practice of Cognitive Therapy

Although the principles on which Cognitive Therapy is based are fairly simple and straightforward, the use of these principles in understanding specific disorders becomes more complex, and the actual practice of Cognitive Therapy can become quite complicated. The purpose of this concluding chapter is to provide suggestions for overcoming problems that are frequently encountered in clinical practice and recommend ways to assess and improve one's skills in the practice of Cognitive Therapy.

OVERCOMING STUMBLING BLOCKS

In an old joke, the question is asked, "How many therapists does it take to change a light bulb?" The answer is, "One. But only if the bulb really wants to change," or alternatively, "None. If the bulb really wanted to change, it would change itself." It is tempting to blame a lack of progress in therapy on the client's noncompliance or "resistance," and many therapists are quick to assume that when progress lags it is because the client does not want to change or "get well," for either conscious or unconscious reasons. However, there are many different problems that can slow or block progress in therapy, and few of them are due to the client's wanting to retain his or her problems. To illustrate this point, think of a "self-improvement" task such as losing weight, exercising regularly, or completing unfinished paperwork that you have been slow to get to work on and then complete Burns's "Possible Reasons for Not Doing Self-help Assignments" (Table 31). To what extent is your lack of followthrough due to a secret desire to remain heavy, out of shape, or behind in your paperwork, and to what extent is it due to a number of more mundane factors?

The first step in overcoming stumbling blocks encountered during therapy is for the therapist and client to identify specific points at which homework assignments are not done, interventions fail to work or backfire, or problematic reactions occur. The therapist can then use guided

TABLE 31. Possible Reasons for Not Doing Self-Help Assignments

The following is a list of reasons that various clients have given for not doing their self-help assignments during the course of therapy. Because the speed of improvement depends primarily on the amount of self-help assignments that you are willing to do, it is of crucial importance to pinpoint any reasons that you may have for not doing this work. As you read the following statements about the self-help assignments, rate each of them with a number between 0 and 5 to indicate how accurately the statement reflects feelings or attitudes you may have. A 5 would indicate that you agree very much with the statement, whereas a 0 would indicate that it does not apply to you at all. Return this memo to the therapist so that he can review the results with you. This might help the two of you understand more clearly why you have difficulty completing the self-help assignments. If you feel you might have difficulty filling out this form and returning it to the therapist, it might be best to do it together during a theapy session.

Rate each statement with a number between 0 and 5. The higher the number the more you agree with the statement.

1. I feel totally hopeless. I am convinced that nothing could help me so there is no point in trying. _____
2. The purpose of these assignments has not been sufficiently explained to me, and I really can't see the point of what the therapist has asked me to do. _____
3. I feel that the particular method the therapist has suggested will not be helpful. It really doesn't make good sense to me. _____
4. I tend to label myself. I say, "I'm a procrastinator, therefore I can't do this." Then I end up not doing it. _____
5. I am willing to do some self-help assignments but I keep forgetting. _____
6. I do not have enough time. I am too busy. _____
7. I feel resentful toward the therapist. He doesn't seem to have a sense of mutual teamwork. _____
8. I have a strong desire to be independent and do things on my own. I feel that if I do something the therapist suggests it's not as good as if I come up with my own ideas. _____
9. If I do the assignments it will mean I'm just a typical patient. This will mean that I am a weak person or that something is wrong with me. _____
10. The therapist has not made it clear to me that the speed of improvement depends on the amount of self-help that I do between therapy sessions. _____
11. I feel helpless, and I don't really believe that I *can* do anything that I choose to do. _____
12. I have the feeling that the therapist is trying to boss me around or control me. _____
13. I don't feel like cooperating with the therapist. He (or she) seems pushy, arrogant, insensitive, mechanical, _____ (fill in). _____
14. I fear the therapist's disapproval or criticism of my work. I believe that what I do just won't be good enough for him. _____
15. I feel that to a certain extent the therapist is missing the point in therapy, and he is not focusing on what is most important to me. _____
16. I have no desire or motivation to do self-help assignments or anything else. Because I don't feel like doing these assignments, it follows that I can't do them, and I don't have time to do them. _____
17. Change seems dangerous to me. The status quo is uncomfortable, but at least it is familiar. _____
18. If I try something new like what the therapist is suggesting, I might make a mistake. _____
19. Because I'm feeling better now, there is no point in doing systematic self-help exercises. I've got my problems licked. _____

Table 31. (*Continued*)

20. Because I'm feeling worse now, there is no point in doing the systematic self-help exercises. Cognitive therapy just won't work for me. _____
21. Because I'm feeling about the same now, it shows that the selp-help exercises cannot help me. _____
22. I have done some things to try to help myself, but they just didn't seem to work. Therefore there's no point in trying anything else. _____
23. I don't trust my therapist. I'm not convinced he is the type of individual I want to make a commitment to work with. _____
24. It's up to the therapist to make me feel better. _____
25. If I start doing something, then I will have to continue to produce, and I couldn't do that. It's safer to be a spectator. _____
26. I notice that when I don't do homework the therapist gets frustrated. This makes me feel even less like participating. _____
27. I thought all you had to do in therapy is go to sessions and talk about your past and express your feelings. So why should I have to *work* in between sessions? _____
28. I want a good personal relationship with a therapist who cares about me and who understands me. That's what I need to get better. All this focus on techniques to control my mood is a lot of hokum. _____
29. These homework assignments are too complicated. The work is just too much for me.
    _____
30. I don't have the patience to do these self-help assignments. _____
31. It's not in the cards for me to feel good. Because of fate or predestination I am bound to feel miserable all my life, no matter how hard I try. _____
32. I don't want to feel happy. I want to be miserable. _____
33. I can't think of anything to do between sessions that would be enjoyable or satisfying or which would have some growth potential. _____
34. This therapy seems too simplistic. It's too much like the power of positive thinking.
    _____
35. It's embarrassing to write down my negative thoughts because someone might see what I'm doing. _____
36. The therapist hasn't given me adequate training in the method he wants me to use. I don't really know how to get started. _____

From Burns (unpublished)

discovery to explore these events with the goal of developing an understanding of how things went awry. An understanding of what went wrong may lead to a simple solution to the problem or reveal an important issue that has not yet been addressed. In many ways, instances where the client is noncompliant or where interventions do not have the desired outcome can be even more useful than instances where the client does the homework as agreed and everything goes smoothly. When everything goes smoothly, and an intervention has the desired result, this confirms the therapist's conceptualization of the client's problems and is a step toward overcoming them. However, when noncompliance or unexpected results occur, the therapist and client have an opportunity to discover a barrier to overcoming the client's problems that they had not yet recognized and can begin to work to overcome this obstacle as well. By using "failures" as an opportunity for discovery, the therapist can revise and fine-tune his or her conceptualization and treatment plan and develop more effective interventions.

Commonly encountered problems that may create stumbling blocks in Cognitive Therapy include the following:

Lack of Collaboration

If the client and therapist have a good working alliance, if the "homework assignment" is clearly related to mutually agreed upon goals, and if both therapist and client have had a voice in developing the assignment, then the client is likely to follow through on the task willingly. If there is no apparent connection between the issues the therapist is working on and the client's goals, or if the therapist is pursuing his or her own goals rather than the client's, active or passive resistance can be expected. For example:

A therapist in training asked for advice in handling a client's noncompliance with behavioral experiments designed to reduce the client's perfectionism. The client's goals for therapy were to resolve some relatively minor marital problems, but the therapist saw the client's perfectionism and the stress and job dissatisfaction that resulted from it as more significant problems. Rather than discussing this issue with the client and reaching an agreement on the goals of therapy, the therapist had unilaterally begun working on perfectionism, and this led to the noncompliance.

Collaboration involves both the therapist and the client and either of them can disrupt it. If the client feels that he or she has no voice in how therapy proceeds, either because this is indeed the case or because of his or her beliefs and expectations, this is likely to interfere with collaboration and produce problems with compliance. It is important for the therapist to actively solicit and value the client's input in setting agendas, determining the focus of therapy, and developing homework assignments, particularly with clients who tend to be unassertive. It is also important to be alert for any cognitions on the part of the client that could block collaboration:

Mary was a 31-year-old married woman who was severely depressed (BDI = 49). Any attempt to establish collaboration was met with, "This won't work, so why bother?" And each homework assignment was received with the same comment. Discussions of options or alternatives were met with a smile and a "Yes, but. . . ." She would often inquire as to whether the therapist thought that she was hard to work with and said that her previous therapists had told her that directly or had implied as much prior to their transferring her to other therapists. Repeated attempts at working collaboratively were stymied until exploration of the client's cognitions during incidents of noncompliance produced the statement, "I have no power anywhere in my life. At least here I can assert my power and win." Once this issue was recognized, the therapist was able to help her find ways of exerting power and "winning" within therapy (and in day-to-day life) that did not block collaboration.

Obviously, the client who does not understand and agree to what is expected of him or her will have difficulty complying with the therapeutic regimen. However, it is easy for therapists to overlook the possibility that their instructions and explanations may not be understood and accepted by the client. It is important for the therapist to repeatedly solicit feedback from the client and to encourage the client to raise any concerns and objections, so that therapist and client can develop a shared understanding of the client's problems that forms a basis for collaboration and so that it is clear that the client understands and accepts the homework assignments. Generally this proves to be sufficient, but when the client holds strong preconceptions about therapy, the therapist may need to compromise to some extent in order to facilitate collaboration. For example:

Ed was a 42-year-old physician referred for Cognitive Therapy after his analyst died. He had been in psychoanalysis three times a week for 15 years and valued his experience in analysis. Ed would come into each session and begin to speak immediately, bringing in dreams and fantasies and generally discussing everything that came to mind despite the therapist's attempts to set an agenda and keep the session focused. Explicit discussions of the value of a more focused, structured approach, and constant redirection by the therapist did not resolve this problem, but the therapist found that scheduling 10 to 15 minutes of free association at the beginning of the session helped to keep the rest of the session directed and focused, with rather good therapeutic results.

Anticipation of Failure

Clients' expectations regarding the likelihood of failure and the consequences of failure can have a strong influence on compliance. For example:

Mitch was a 29-year-old college junior with very limited dating experience. When he was encouraged to try asking a particular girl out, his thoughts included, "How can I ask her out? There's no way in the world she would go out with me. And if I was able to ask her out, what would happen? She'd go out with me once, and never again. So what would I gain? A single date and then if I like her and ask her out again, I'd get turned down. She would tell others what a jerk I am, and the entire school would know that I was a loser. I'm better off not opening myself up to failure and ridicule. In fact, I'm better off dead. No one would even miss me."

Given his conviction that the consequence of his making any attempt to begin dating would result in failure and humiliation, it is not surprising that Mitch was noncompliant until he was able to respond effectively to his negative cognitions. The effects of fear of failure can be reduced by choosing a task that is not too difficult or complex, being sure that the client understands the instructions, and helping the client look objectively at both the likelihood of failure and the potential consequences of failure. If it turns out that failure would indeed entail serious consequences, it may be necessary to reevaluate the assignment.

One aspect of "failure" that inhibits many clients is their anticipations regarding the therapist's reaction if homework assignments are not done "right." If the client anticipates receiving harsh criticism, anger, expressions of disappointment, or other aversive responses from the therapist when the homework is discussed, this can easily result in his or her avoiding the homework and coming up with excuses for not having done it. Obviously, it is important for the therapist to respond to noncompliance without being punitive or authoritarian and instead to work with the client to understand what blocked compliance. However, it is also important for the therapist to be alert for negative anticipations based on the client's previous experience with parents and teachers and to address these explicitly if they impede therapy. In particular, perfectionistic clients often anticipate extreme reactions if the homework is not done perfectly, and it can be quite useful to address these anticipations early in therapy.

Usually it is possible to honestly present the client's task as a "no-lose" situation by pointing out to the client that incidents of noncompliance or unexpected results provide opportunities for making valuable discoveries. For example, the therapist might follow the first homework assignment with, "One of the nice things about this sort of approach is that whatever happens, we come out ahead. If you go ahead and do [the assignment] and it goes the way we expect, great! We're making progress towards your goals. If you expectedly cannot get yourself to do it or if it does not work out the way we expect, then we have an opportunity to look at what happened and at your thoughts and feelings to discover more about what blocks you from your goals. If it goes smoothly, we're making progress and if it doesn't, we're making a discovery." For many clients this greatly reduces the fear of failure.

The Client's Lack of Skill

One major source of fear of failure is the client's belief that he or she is not capable of performing the task that has been assigned. If the client is accurate in believing that he or she cannot handle the situation, the therapist is likely to need to devote time to helping the client to master the necessary skills. If the client is underestimating his or her capabilities, the therapist needs to devote time to boosting the client's confidence. Social skills training can be useful for either of these purposes. For example:

Leo was a 39-year-old lawyer who had recently been divorced after his ex-wife had an affair and bore her lover's child. He entered therapy because of depression due to his conviction that he would never find another woman, and therefore life was not worth living. A homework assignment given during the fourth session involved his calling a woman whose number had been given to him by a colleague. By the seventh session, the call had still not been made. Leo had many excuses for this: He was busy, he left the number at home when he was at work, he left the number at work when he was home. In trying to understand the noncompliance, the therapist asked Leo to roleplay the phone call, and it immediately became clear that he had no idea of how to make such a call or what to say. The therapist then remembered that Leo had not dated throughout college or law school and that his ex-wife had initiated their courtship. Despite having adequate social skills in professional interactions, Leo was quite inexperienced at dating and had not developed the necessary skills. After role-playing several different approaches to the phone call, Leo was willing to attempt the call and was able to do so without additional delay.

The Client's Lack of Motivation

When a client enters therapy because of family pressure, the demands of a spouse, or a court order, he or she may well lack any personal motivation for change and thus fail to participate actively during therapy sessions or to comply with homework assignments. If this is the case, it is essential to devote effort early in therapy to identifying goals or incentives that can provide the individual with motivation for actively engaging in therapy. If no personally relevant reasons for participating in therapy can be identified, therapy is likely to accomplish little.

Lisa was a 14-year-old who was brought in for therapy by her parents after recurrent discipline problems at home and at school and an unsuccessful attempt at family therapy. Her initial stance was quite defiant, and she apparently expected the therapist to take an authoritarian approach and to try to force her to "behave." She relaxed considerably when the therapist explained his understanding of the situation and asked, "Given that you're stuck being here, is there anything you'd like to get out of this?" However, she did not identify any personal goals for therapy until the therapist suggested that they could possibly work on how to get her parents "off her back." When she expressed tentative interest in this goal, the therapist responded, "Obviously you could get them off your back by giving in and doing what they want, but you've made it clear that that's not something you're willing to do. It sounds like the question is whether there's any way to get them off your back without giving in to them." This agreement formed a basis for a very productive course of therapy that resulted in Lisa's learning how to be appropriately independent without having to be rebellious.

Problems in therapy resulting from a lack of motivation are also common with severely depressed clients because a lack of motivation is a common symptom of depression. This can present a substantial problem because the interventions used in Cognitive Therapy for depression require substantial client participation. Fortunately, activity scheduling accompanied by self-motivation training and graded task assignment (all discussed in Chapter 3) is usually quite effective in overcoming this problem. For example:

Sam was a 59-year-old jeweler who had been severely depressed and suicidal for several years as a result of business problems. Though he went to work consistently, he saw no way to regain the income, customers, and status that he had once had and therefore had little motivation to attempt to overcome his business problems. He allowed the store to become piled up with boxes of what he described as "junk" and sought no new business. He came to therapy because his wife, son, and daughter made frequent demands that he seek help; and he approached therapy in the same way as he approached his business, going through the motions but doing little to address the problems. As the therapist helped Sam to identify small but manageable subgoals and to motivate himself to attempt them, Sam discovered that he was not as helpless as he had believed. He was gradually able to take steps that soon helped him to feel better, think of suicide less, and work more energetically to overcome his depression and his business problems.

Antidepressant medication can also be useful in overcoming a serious lack of motivation in a depressed client, but activity scheduling and related interventions are often effective more quickly than pharmacological interventions since medications often take several weeks to have full effect.

Trying to Move Too Fast

The timing and pacing of interventions can be quite important. If the therapist tries to push or rush the client, the result may be the loss of collaboration, poor compliance, poor attendance, or premature termination of therapy.

Bonnie was a predoctoral intern who typically set high standards for herself and worked hard to achieve them. As a result of her desire to succeed as a therapist and to help her clients quickly, she tended to suggest homework assignments that clients found difficult and often attempted to challenge clients' beliefs and assumptions without gathering enough data to support her interventions. As a result, her clients saw her as being quite demanding and as not understanding them. Her immediate reaction to client noncompliance was to assume that she had to work even harder to get her clients to change. However, after meeting with her supervisor, she was persuaded to try a slower pace in therapy, to come up with relatively easy homework assignments, and to try collecting extensive data before attempting to change beliefs and assumptions. To her surprise, she found that not only did her clients perceive her more positively, but she had fewer problems with noncompliance, and therapy actually proceeded more quickly.

An overeager client can rush the pace of therapy just as much as an overeager therapist. Often it is possible to obtain useful feedback about the pacing of therapy by assessing the client's level of anxiety either while discussing the proposed assignment or while attempting it. If the client is completely comfortable, the assignment is probably not breaking any new ground. If the client is quite anxious, the assignment may be too big a step. For example:

John, a chronically overcontrolled accountant, was intrigued by the possibility of his intentionally doing something "out of the ordinary" as a behavioral experiment to test his belief that it was essential for him to always do what others expected of him. He suggested that he could do cartwheels down the hallway at the rather straight-laced firm where he worked, then he immediately became intensely anxious. Upon discussion, it became clear that this was a much more dramatic step than he would actually be able to make. He and his therapist decided that instead, he would try wearing a clashing tie to work. He was somewhat uncomfortable with this more modest assignment but was able to carry it out discovering, to his amazement, that no catastrophe resulted from this unconventional act. After this assignment he quickly became comfortable with sometimes choosing not to conform to the expectations of others.

Concerns about the Consequences of Change

Compliance with homework assignments and active participation during therapy sessions can also be inhibited by the client's concerns about the consequences of successfully making the changes that are the goal of therapy. The concern may be about the effects the changes will have on others. For example:

Marta, a 42-year-old single woman, was employed as a secretary and lived with her mother. By Marta's description, her mother was hypochondriacal and was constantly going to doctors at Marta's expense. When Marta refused to pay for the doctor's appointments any longer, her mother launched into a diatribe about what a bad daughter Marta was. Marta's expressed goals for therapy included being able to assert herself with her mother and being able to move out and live a life of her own. However, she was reluctant to take any steps toward doing so, in part because she believed that if she stayed at home and catered to her mother, this would extend her mother's life. She feared that if she were to succeed in becoming more assertive and independent, her mother would quickly sicken and die, because of the added stress this would subject her mother to and the effects of Marta's spending less time and energy taking care of her. She was able to take steps toward greater autonomy only after these concerns had been addressed.

The concern may also be about the effects the client expects the change to have in his or her own life:

Tom was a hard-driving businessman who came into therapy saying that he had read a number of books by Burns and Ellis and had decided to reduce his perfectionism but was unable to do so. He had an accurate understanding of the cognitions supporting his perfectionism, could produce good "rational responses," and could list many good reasons for reducing his perfectionism but still was unable to put his understanding into practice. When asked what risks there would be in relaxing his perfectionism, he initially said, "None at all!" With additional probing, he went on to describe fears of becoming lazy and unmotivated, of becoming "mediocre," of becoming a "short-term hedonist," of hurting those he cared about, and of eventually losing family and friends. Once these concerns were addressed, he was able to begin changing.

As long as the client believes that he or she risks disaster, either for self or others, by attempting to attain a goal, he or she is likely to hesitate, even if the goal is an important one. It can be quite useful to explore the client's anticipations and expectations about the negative consequences of desired changes before attempting to make the change because it is often possible to address the client's concerns effectively and forestall problems with noncompliance.

As mentioned in our discussion of Borderline Personality Disorder, some clients manifest a fear of change *per se* rather than fearing particular consequences of change. This can often be overcome by acknowledging the client's concerns, giving the client increased control over the pace of change, and pointing out that trying a change does not commit one to persisting with it regardless of the consequences. For a more detailed discussion of this issue, see Chapter 8.

Environmental Impediments to Change

Interactions with family members, the policies of the client's employer, and other environmental factors may work actively against the client making the changes that are a goal of therapy. In many cases, this happens without malice or intent on the part of family, friends, or employer. This can take many forms from family members overtly criticizing the client for talking of "private family matters with a stranger" to trying to be helpful in ways that encourage passivity and dependency. Sometimes these problems can be resolved by working individually with the client, but often marital or family intervention is indicated. Concerns of family members may inadvertently reinforce the client's fears of change:

Al was a 30-year-old single male who lived at home with his parents. He was a college graduate employed as a customer service representative for a large corporation. Even though he made ample money to support himself, his parents continued to press for him to continue living at home. Their concern was that if he lived on his own, he would not take care of himself, and would begin to eat and gain weight, going up to his previous weight of 290 lb. Although he presently weighed 225 lb., was in therapy, and was committed to losing weight, their concern and fears frightened him and kept him from taking steps to live on his own until these fears had been addressed in therapy.

Significant others may resist the changes the client wishes to make because of the impact the changes would have on their own lives:

Ann had never learned to drive, and at the close of Cognitive Therapy for depression she wanted to work on overcoming her anxiety so that she could take driving lessons. Her husband somehow kept "forgetting" to take her to get her learner's permit, started questioning whether her learning to drive was really "necessary," and began having angry outbursts at times when he felt she was being "disobedient." As a result, she was unable to carry out the behavioral experiments needed to effectively challenge her belief that driving safely was beyond her abilities. Marital therapy calmed her husband's insecurities and increased his tolerance for her growing assertion as well as having other benefits. As a result, Ann's husband started actively encouraging her to learn to drive, and her progress in therapy resumed.

Finally, others may resist the changes the client seeks due to their own psychopathology:

After he successfully completed an inpatient treatment program for his alcohol abuse, Roger experienced recurrent difficulty resisting relapse. Several family members had drinking problems of their own, and they not only insisted on drinking in his presence but actively pressured him to drink at a family Christmas party and became offended when he refused. Because his family refused family therapy, it was necessary to devote considerable time to helping him figure out how to best handle pressure from them.

When the client's dysfunctional behavior results in significant interpersonal benefits for him or her, this "secondary gain" can greatly impede progress in therapy. This problem can be overcome by helping the client to consider whether the benefits outweigh the disadvantages of maintaining the dysfunctional behavior, identifying more adaptive ways to attain the same benefits, and/or intervening with the family to eliminate the payoffs to maintaining dysfunctional behavior. For example:

George was a 38-year-old unemployed carpenter who had not worked regularly in 5 years due to a fear that if he exerted himself in any way he would have a heart attack or stroke. His time was spent at home, watching television and doing minimal housework. Even though he had never had any major medical problems, his wife and two children were so concerned about his health that they never asked him to do anything at home. Although George's anxiety was genuine, family members responded in a way that enabled him to avoid doing any work or tolerating any anxiety and that established a powerful disincentive to change. It was only when he realized that the things he had to give up to maintain his life of leisure outweighed its benefits that he was willing to work in therapy.

Unrecognized Problems

No matter how thorough the initial evaluation is, the therapist will sometimes be unable to detect important problems until they are manifested in therapy. When therapy seems "stuck," a reevaluation may be indicated because problems such as substance abuse, Paranoid Personality Disorder, and Passive-Aggressive Personality Disorder are often missed in the initial evaluation and may be discovered only when they begin to disrupt therapy. For example, in the case of Gary, the client with Paranoid Personality Disorder discussed in Chapter 7, his personality disorder was recognized only after he began complaining of times when his progressive relaxation exercises "didn't work." If his personality disorder had not been recognized, therapy would have soon reached an impasse, and his problems with anxiety would have persisted.

Therapist Blind Spots

When the therapist shares the client's dysfunctional beliefs to some extent, it naturally is very difficult for him or her to help the client to challenge them. In fact, unless a supervisor or colleague is available to help the therapist to recognize this problem, he or she is likely to have difficulty even identifying the problem. For example:

Dr. Mason's work was very careful and precise; and she believed that when under stress, extra care, effort, and worry would help to reduce the stress. This approach had resulted in excellent academic achievement, but as a result it often took her much longer than she would have liked to complete her work, and she tended to worry about its completeness and quality. In presenting a client for the first time in supervision, she described the client as a "perfectionistic, obsessive, and internally demanding" person who despaired of ever living up to his standards. When she was questioned by her supervisor as to her goals for this client, Dr. Mason responded, "I would like to help him get rid of all the perfectionism that makes him feel so hopeless." When her supervisor observed that by trying to get rid of all the client's perfectionism, rather than simply modifying it, she was revealing her own perfectionism, the therapist began to argue that it was necessary for her to be perfectionistic in order to succeed at anything.

Obviously, it would have been difficult for this therapist to help the client give up his perfectionism as long as she was convinced herself that becoming less perfectionistic would lead to failure.

Therapist Emotional Reactions

Therapists, being human, can themselves experience the full range of emotions in the course of doing therapy. As was discussed in Chapter 8, emotional reactions can be quite useful if they are recognized and are handled well, but they can also impede therapy at times. In addition to emotions that are largely elicited by the client's behavior, therapists experience emotions that are, to a large extent, a product of their own beliefs and assumptions (see Table 32). When this is the case, it can take some time and effort to eliminate the problem. It may be useful for the therapist to actually write out Dysfunctional Thought Records regarding his or her own thoughts and feelings or to seek the help of a colleague or supervisor.

TABLE 32. Dysfunctional Thoughts and Beliefs
Commonly Encountered by Therapists

---

1. I must be successful with virtually all of my clients all of the time.
   a. I must continually make brilliant statements/interpretations.
   b. I must always show excellent judgement.
   c. I must continually help to move my clients along.
   d. If I fail, it's all my fault.
   e. If I fail, I am a lousy therapist and person.
   f. If I fail, my successes don't count.
2. I must be an outstanding therapist, better than all others.
   a. I must succeed with impossible clients where others have failed.
   b. I must have all good sessions.
   c. I must use a therapy model that is universally accepted.
   d. I must be well known and recognized as a therapist.
   e. I must not have any problems of my own.
3. I must be greatly respected and loved by all of my clients.
   a. I cannot dislike my clients or ever show annoyance.
   b. I must not push clients too hard, or they will dislike me.
   c. I must be very careful to not deal with ticklish issues.
   d. My clients should stay in therapy forever.
   e. I am thoroughly responsible for any client discomfort in the session.
   f. Clients should not disapprove of me.
4. Since I'm doing my best, clients should work as hard.
   a. My clients should not be too difficult.
   b. They should do what I advise them to do.
   c. Clients should do their homework.
   d. I should be blessed with young, bright, attractive, motivated, good-smelling clients.
5. I should enjoy therapy sessions
   a. I should use the therapeutic techniques that I enjoy the most.
   b. I should only have to use techniques that are easy and don't wear me out.
   c. I should be able to make money easily.
   d. I shouldn't have to do any work, reading, thinking, or preparation outside of the therapy session.
   e. I can be late for sessions, cancel sessions, or even miss sessions because I'm the therapist.

And for students and trainees:

6. I must be the best student/trainee ever seen in this setting.
   a. I must be conversant with the most obscure literature.
   b. I cannot do anything in therapy that may be criticized.
   c. I must be better than all of my peers.
   d. My supervisors should all see me as special and brilliant.
   e. My errors or problems should never be pointed out to me.
   f. My supervisors should love me as a person.

After A. Ellis.

Therapist reactions to a lack of progress in therapy can be particularly problematic. Many therapists learning Cognitive Therapy and looking at the promising results reported in outcome research begin to believe that they should be omnipotent, vanquishing all psychopathology quickly and easily. The result can be frustration and anger at the "resistant" client when therapy proceeds slowly, and guilt and self-condemnation when it goes badly. However, effective techniques and polished skills do not make one omnipotent and, as can be seen from the foregoing discussion, a lack of progress in therapy is not necessarily the fault of either therapist or client. When a therapist can acknowledge his or her limitations and take them into account without lapsing into blaming the client or excessive self-criticism, this results in better service to clients and less wear and tear on the therapist. When sessions with a "problem" client produce strong feelings of frustration, discouragement, guilt, or anxiety, even the most seasoned therapist can benefit from consultation with a trusted colleague.

POLISHING SKILLS IN COGNITIVE THERAPY

Obviously, one does not become a skilled cognitive therapist simply by reading this or any other book, any more than one becomes a skilled psychoanalyst by reading a volume or two of Freud. Reading is certainly a good idea because the field of Cognitive Therapy is a rapidly growing one and the only practical way to keep abreast of new developments is to read widely. In addition to the new books that appear on a regular basis and the articles published in "mainstream" journals in psychology and psychiatry, two specialized journals are particularly valuable. *Cognitive Therapy and Research* is a research-oriented journal that publishes many of the new empirical studies as well as a limited number of theoretical or clinically oriented articles. *The Journal of Cognitive Psychotherapy: An International Quarterly* is oriented toward clinical practice and publishes clinical and theoretical papers as well as empirical papers that are clinically applicable. Although reading can provide knowledge about Cognitive Therapy, there is a limit to the extent to which reading alone can convey skill in the practice of Cognitive Therapy. The ideal approach to mastering Cognitive Therapy is to read widely, attend courses and workshops presented by a variety of authorities, and to be personally supervised by a mentor who is expert in Cognitive Therapy. If this is not feasible, however, practitioners have many other options for polishing their skills.

Assessing Skill in Cognitive Therapy

The first requirement for effective learning of any sort is obtaining valid feedback. It is often hard for a therapist to obtain the kind of clear, specific feedback that is needed in order to both identify strengths and to pinpoint the areas in which improvement is needed. A number of Cognitive Therapy rating scales have been developed that can provide a method for assessing the quality of a therapy session and providing this type of feedback (Beck *et al.*, 1979, pp. 404–407). Scales such as these both allow a therapist to assess his or her own performance and allow a supervisor or colleague to provide clear, unambiguous feedback on a therapy session whether observed live or recorded.

One scale that the authors have found particularly useful is the Cognitive Therapy Scale—Revised (CTS–R) shown in the Appendix. The Cognitive Therapy Scale was originally used as a training tool at the Beck's Center for Cognitive Therapy at the University of Pennsylvania, and it was later used to assess the therapists providing Cognitive Therapy in the NIMH Multicenter Collaborative Study of Depression. Shaw, Vallis, and Dobson (1985) studied the psychometric properties of the CTS, and the present revision is designed to remedy the weaknesses and bolster the strengths they observed through greater clarity of description, greater specificity of items, and a more detailed scoring manual.

Cognitive Therapy rating scales can be used most productively if several cautions are kept in mind. Remember that the aim of these scales is to identify the therapist's specific strengths and weaknesses rather than to provide a global rating of the quality of the therapy session; the information it provides is most useful when raters focus on the specific content of each item and base their numerical ratings on the descriptions provided. When Cognitive Therapy rating scales are used for self-assessment, it is important to make audio- or videorecordings of the sessions and then to complete the scale while reviewing the recording because it is virtually impossible to accurately observe a session while fully participating in it. One potential problem to be aware of in utilizing the CTS-R and other Cognitive Therapy rating scales is the "halo effect." When the evaluator perceives a therapist as generally good or bad, this will bias the ratings on individual items unless the evaluator makes a point of adhering to the criteria specified for each item. A second potential problem is that some evaluators use their own idiosyncratic notions of what a particular rating means rather than utilizing the operational definitions given with the scale. In order for the ratings to provide useful feedback, the person using the scale must make an effort to remain objective and to adhere to the scale's definitions of ratings. A brief discussion of each of the CTS-R items follows:

Item 1. Agenda setting. At the beginning of each Cognitive Therapy session, the therapist and client are expected to jointly establish an agenda that specifies both topics to be addressed during the session and how the time will be allocated. This helps insure that the most pertinent issues are addressed and that the available time is used efficiently (this volume, pp. 16–17; Beck et al., 1979, pp. 77–78, 93–98, 167–208; Beck, 1976, pp. 224–300). Some of the most common mistakes observed in agenda setting are (1) failure to agree on specific problems to focus on, (2) a lack of collaboration in agenda setting, (3) a tendency to skip from problem to problem during the session rather than persistently seeking a satisfactory solution to one or two problems at a time, (4) failure to adhere to the agreed-upon agenda, and (5) rigid adherence to the agenda when it would be more appropriate to modify it. If, later in the session, it becomes clear that the agenda should be modified, changes should be made collaboratively and should follow a discussion of the rationale for changing topics.

Item 2: Feedback. It is valuable for the therapist to elicit feedback about the previous therapy session at the beginning of each session and to elicit feedback about the current session at the close of each session. He or she should also check periodically during the session to be sure that the client understands the therapist's interventions, formulations, and line of reasoning, and that the therapist has accurately understood the client's main points (this volume, p. 17; Beck *et al.*, 1979, pp. 81–84). Many therapists fail to do this or do so only intermittently and superficially, thus allowing misunderstandings or other problems to develop to the point that they disrupt therapy.

Item 3. Collaboration. A collaborative approach is central to Cognitive Therapy. It helps insure that the client and therapist have compatible goals at each point in the course of treatment, it minimizes resistance, and it helps prevent misunderstandings between the client and therapist (this volume, pp. 8–16, 310–311; Beck, 1976, pp. 220–221; Beck *et al.*, 1979, pp. 50–54). It is important for the therapist to make *active* efforts to work *with* the client without arbitrarily taking control of the session or passively following the client's direction. This requires establishing a comfortable working relationship, striking a balance between being directive on the one hand and allowing the client to make choices and take responsibility on the other, soliciting and respecting the client's input, and explaining the rationale behind the therapist's recommendations and interventions.

Item 4. Pacing and efficient use of time. The therapist should maintain sufficient control over the session to insure that the agenda is followed; he or she should limit discussion of peripheral issues or unproductive discussion of major topics, and any unfinished business should be rescheduled (this volume, pp. 314–315; Beck *et al.*, 1979, pp. 65–66). The pacing of a session is quite important. If the therapist belabors a point after the client has already grasped the message or gathers much more data than is necessary before intervening, the session will be slow and inefficient. However, if the therapist moves too rapidly before the client has had an opportunity to integrate a new perspective or intervenes before he or she has gathered enough data, interventions are likely to be ineffective.

Item 5. Empathy skills. An important goal is for the therapist to step into the client's world, understand the way he or she sees and experiences life, and convey this understanding to the client (Beck *et al.*, 1979, pp. 47–49). The therapist should be sensitive both to what the client explicitly says and to what the client conveys through tone of voice and nonverbal responses. In addition, he or she should communicate this understanding by rephrasing or summarizing what the client has said and by reflecting what the client seems to be feeling. The therapist's tone of voice and nonverbal responses should convey a sympathetic understanding of the client's point of view (although the therapist must maintain objectivity toward the client's problems).

Item 6. Interpersonal effectiveness. The cognitive therapist should display warmth, concern, confidence, and genuineness in addition to empathy (this volume, p. 10; Beck et al., 1979, pp. 45–47, 49–50). He or she should not act in a manner that seems patronizing, condescending, or indifferent, nor evade client's questions. In the course of questioning the client's point of view, it is important to avoid appearing critical, disapproving, or ridiculing of the client's perspective.

Item 7. Professionalism. It is important for the therapist to convey a relaxed confidence and a professional manner without seeming distant or cold. This can serve as a partial antidote for any pessimism or hopelessness the client feels and make it easier for the therapist to take a directive role in therapy and to be convincing in expressing alternative points of view. This involves acting and dressing the part of the professional while remaining warm and supportive.

Item 8. Guided discovery. One of the most basic strategies of Cognitive Therapy is the use of exploration and questioning to help patients see new perspectives rather than debating, persuading, cross-examining, or lecturing (this volume, pp. 9–10; Beck et al., 1979, pp. 66–71). This is not to say that the effective cognitive therapist relies solely, or even primarily, on guided discovery in all sessions. There are times when it is important for the therapist to provide information, confront, explain, teach, self-disclose, and the like rather than use questions to guide the client in finding his or her own solutions. The balance between questioning and other modes of intervention depends on the particular problem being dealt with, the particular client, and the point of therapy. However, guided discovery generally has many advantages. Clients often adopt new perspectives more readily when they come to their own conclusions than when they are persuaded to adopt the therapist's conclusions. In addition, at the same time that the client is gaining a new perspective through guided discovery, he or she is also learning an approach to dealing with problems that, hopefully, will eventually enable the client to handle problem situations effectively without the therapist's help.

Item 9. Case conceptualization. As has been stressed previously, Cognitive Therapy is intended as a strategic approach in which the therapist's conceptualization of the client's problems forms a basis for a systematic approach to intervention (this volume, pp. 8–9; Beck, 1976, pp. 6–131, 233–300 (esp. 257–262); Beck et al., 1979, pp. 104–271). Obviously, unless the therapist happens to discuss his or her conceptualization with the client in the course of a given session, an observer will not be certain what the therapist's conceptualization is. However, the effects of the therapist's conceptualization (or lack thereof) will be apparent. If the various interventions used during the session seem to "hang together," make sense to the observer, and appear to be "on target," this suggests that the therapist is basing interventions on a coherent and adequately correct view of the client's problems. Without a coherent conceptualization to provide a framework to guide intervention, the session is likely to appear disorganized, interventions are likely to appear disconnected, and the session is less likely to be productive.

Item 10. Focus on key cognitions. A focus on specific cognitions is clearly central to Cognitive Therapy. Throughout each session, the therapist needs to constantly choose which automatic thoughts, beliefs, attributions, and the like to focus on, and which to postpone until a later date or to overlook completely. Obviously, session time will be used most productively if he or she focuses on cognitions that are both important and appropriate for intervention at that point in therapy (this volume, pp. 12–13, 37–40; Beck, 1976, pp. 6–131, 246–257; Beck et al., 1979, pp. 142–152, 163–166, 244–252).

Items 11 and 12. Application of cognitive techniques, application of behavioral techniques. A wide range of intervention techniques are available for use in Cognitive Therapy (this volume, Chapter 3; Beck, 1976, pp. 233–300 (esp. 257–262); Beck et al., 1979, pp. 142–166, 168–206, 345). However, in order to be effective, these techniques must be used skillfully. Commonly observed problems include the therapist's overlooking promising intervention techniques, overusing a few techniques rather than choosing from a large repertoire of techniques, persevering with a technique that has proven ineffective rather than trying alternative approaches, attempting to use a technique clinically before having mastered it, and failure to integrate individual techniques into a coherent treatment approach.

Item 13. Homework. Cognitive Therapy does not occur exclusively within the hour or two per week spent with the therapist. Homework assignments "custom tailored" to help the client test hypotheses, incorporate new perspectives, or experiment with new behavior outside the therapy session are crucial for progress (this volume, p. 14; Beck et al., 1979, pp. 272–294). Near the beginning of a typical session, the therapist should review the results of the homework from the previous session and address any problems with noncompliance. Toward the close of the session, the therapist needs to collaboratively develop a new assignment, make sure the rationale for it is clear, and elicit the client's reactions to it. Commonly observed problems include failing to develop a homework assignment, reviewing the previous assignment superficially (or not at all), assigning homework rather than developing assignments collaboratively, using assignments that are not sufficiently clear and specific, and using assignments that are not tailored to the individual client and the goals of therapy at the moment.

Some therapists learning Cognitive Therapy assume that some of the emphasis placed on the "details" of Cognitive Therapy such as agenda setting and soliciting feedback is unnecessary and that all they need to do is master the general concepts and the major techniques. However, the emphasis on these details is based on extensive experience both in the practice of Cognitive Therapy and in the training of therapists. We strongly recommend that therapists master the ability to do Cognitive Therapy "by the book" and exercise caution in modifying the approach to suit their personal preferences. Although it is a foregone conclusion that there is room for improvement in Cognitive Therapy and that some modifications of the approach will do no harm or may even enhance the effectiveness of therapy, several studies have found that cognitive therapists who adhere to the model (as assessed by the various Cognitive Therapy rating scales) are more effective than those who deviate from it (Luborsky, McLellan, Woody, O'Brian, & Auerbach, 1985).

Obtaining Feedback in the Course of Ongoing Therapy

A therapist can obtain valuable feedback about his or her practice of Cognitive Therapy in a variety of ways. By maintaining session notes and reviewing them periodically, the therapist can obtain a clearer view of the process and progress of therapy than is possible on a session-by-session basis. If scores on the Beck Depression Inventory or other relevant measures are used weekly to monitor progress (as was recommended in Chapter 2), a graph of the client's progress from week to week can be combined with a review of the therapist's notes to identify both problems that arise and interventions that are particularly effective. The most valuable feedback can come from one's clients. As discussed in Chapter 1, Beck suggests (Beck et al., 1979, pp. 81–83) that the therapist encourage client feedback throughout the session and explicitly invite client feedback at the beginning and end of each session. This feedback lets the therapist know whether he or she is understanding the client and can be particularly valuable in identifying problems in the therapist–client relationship before they disrupt therapy. In addition to soliciting feedback verbally during sessions, the Client's Report of Session Form (Figure 23) can be used as well. Although it may seem redundant to use this form if verbal feedback has been requested during the session, the written form has several important advantages. First, some clients who are hesitant to express negative feedback are more willing to communicate it in writing than they are in a face-to-face conversation. Second, this written feedback can be quite useful when reviewing a case longitudinally as discussed before. Finally, the therapist can obtain useful information about the accuracy of his or her self-perception by completing the Therapist's Report of Session Form (Figure 24) and comparing his or her ratings of the session with the client's.

Patient's name _____

Date of session _____ Time session began _____ AM/PM

Therapist's name _____

Part I. Please circle your response to each of the following:

1. Before you came in today, how much progress did you expect to make in dealing with your problems in today's session?

    Much   Some   No
    progress   progress   progress

2. In today's session, how much progress do you feel you actually made?

    Much   Some   No   Things got
    progress   progress   progress   worse

3. In future sessions, how much progress do you think you will be able to make in dealing with your problems?

    Much   Some   No
    progress   progress   progress

4. How satisfied are you with today's session?

    Very
    satisfied   Satisfied   Indifferent   Dissatisfied

5. In today's session, how well do you think your therapist understood your problems?

    Very well   Fairly well   Poorly

6. How well were you able to convey your concerns or problems in this session?

    Very well   Fairly well   Poorly

7. In today's session, how much did you trust (have confidence in) your therapist?

    Very
    much   Some   Not at all

Part II. Please answer the following questions about homework.

1. Was homework assigned last session?   Yes   No
2. Did you discuss last week's homework
   in today's session?   Yes   No
3. How helpful was the homework and the discussion of it?

    Very   Some   Not at all   Not applicable

4. How pleased are you with the homework that was assigned for this coming week?

    Very   Some   Not at all   None was assigned

Part III. Rate the extent to which you believe you gained the following skills in this therapy session. Please refer only to this session, realizing that not all of these skills can be gained in any one session.

	Very much	Some	None
1. Better insight into and understanding of my psychological problems	2	1	0

FIGURE 23. Client's report of therapy session.

	Very much	Some	None
2. Methods or techniques for better ways of dealing with people (i.e., asserting myself)	2	1.	0
3. Techniques in defining and solving my everyday problems (i.e., at home, work, school)	2	1	0
4. Confidence in undertaking an activity to help myself	2	1	0
5. Greater ability to cope with my moods	2	1	0
6. Better control over my actions	2	1	0
7. Greater ability to *recognize* my unreasonable thoughts	2	1	0
8. Greater ability to *correct* my unreasonable thoughts	2	1	0
9. Greater ability to *recognize* my self-defeating or erroneous assumptions	2	1	0
10. Greater ability to *evaluate* my self-defeating or erroneous assumptions	2	1	0
11. Better ways of scheduling my time	2	1	0

Part IV. Rate the extent to which your therapist was the following in this session:

	Very much	Some	Not at all
1. Sympathetic and caring	2	1	0
2. Competent (knows what he/she is doing)	2	1	0
3. Warm and friendly	2	1	0
4. Supportive and encouraging	2	1	0
5. Involved and interested	2	1	0

Part V. Please circle the response which applies to your reaction to today's session:

1. My therapist acted condescending (talked down to me).	Yes	No
2. My therapist was too quiet and passive.	Yes	No
3. My therapist talked too much.	Yes	No
4. My therapist was too bossy.	Yes	No
5. My therapist seemed to miss the point.	Yes	No
6. This therapy (Cognitive Therapy) does not seem to be suited to me and my problems.	Yes	No

Part IV. In the remaining space, please describe the most outstanding aspect of today's session:

FIGURE 23. (Cont.)

Therapist's name _____

Date of session _____ Time session began _____ AM/PM

Patient's name _____

Part I. Please circle your response to each of the following:

1. Before this session, how much progress did you expect to make in dealing with this patient's problems?

Much progress		Some progress		No progress		Things got worse
4	3	2	1	0	−1	−2

2. In this session, how much progress do you feel you actually made?

Much progress		Some progress		No progress		Things got worse
4	3	2	1	0	−1	−2

3. How much progress do you think will be made in dealing with this patient's problems in future sessions?

Much progress		Some progress		No progress
4	3	2	1	0

4. How hopeful or optimistic do you think the patient is about making progress in future sessions?

Very hopeful		Somewhat hopeful		Not at all hopeful
4	3	2	1	0

5. How satisfied were you with this session?

Very satisfied		Satisfied		Indifferent		Dissatisfied
4	3	2	1	0	−1	−2

6. How satisfied do you think your patient was with this session?

Very satisfied		Satisfied		Indifferent		Dissatisfied
4	3	2	1	0	−1	−2

7. In this session, how well do you think you understood your patient's problems?

Very well		Fairly well		Poorly
4	3	2	1	0

8. How well do you think your patient was able to convey his/her concerns or problems in this session?

Very well		Fairly well		Poorly
4	3	2	1	0

9. In today's session, how much do you think your patient trusted you (had confidence in you)?

Very much		Some		Not at all
4	3	2	1	0

10. How likeable is this patient to you?

Very much		Some		Not at all
4	3	2	1	0

FIGURE 24. Therapist's report of therapy session.

11. How much do you think your patient likes you?

Very much		Some		Not at all
4	3	2	1	0

12. How frustrated were you with this patient today?

Very much		Some		Not at all
4	3	2	1	0

13. In this session, how difficult was it to apply the methods of Cognitive Therapy?

Very difficult		Somewhat difficult		Not at all difficult
4	3	2	1	0

14. How typical was today's session (compared to other sessions with this patient)?

Very much		Some		Not at all
4	3	2	1	0

Part II. Please answer the following questions about homework.

1. Was homework assigned last session?   Yes   No
2. Did you discuss last week's homework in today's sesssion?   Yes   No
3. How helpful was the homework and the discussion of it?

Very helpful		Somewhat helpful		Not at all helpful	Not applicable
4	3	2	1	0	N/A

4. How satisfied are you with the homework that was assigned for this coming week?

Very satisfied		Somewhat satisfied		Not at all satisfied	None was assigned
4	3	2	1	0	N/A

Part III. Rate the extent to which you believe your patient gained the following skills in this therapy session:

	Very much		Some		None
1. Better insight into and understanding of his/her psychological problems	4	3	2	1	0
2. Methods or techniques for better ways of dealing with people (i.e., asserting him/herself)	4	3	2	1	0
3. Techniques in defining and solving his/her everyday problems (i.e., at home, work, school)	4	3	2	1	0
4. Confidence in undertaking an activity to help him/herself	4	3	2	1	0
5. Greater ability to cope with his/her moods	4	3	2	1	0
6. Better control over his/her actions	4	3	2	1	0

FIGURE 24. (Cont.)

	Very much		Some		None
7. Greater ability to *recognize* his/her unreasonable thoughts	4	3	2	1	0
8. Greater ability to *correct* his/her unreasonable thoughts	4	3	2	1	0
9. Greater ability to *recognize* his/her self-defeating or erroneous assumptions	4	3	2	1	0
10. Greater ability to *evaluate* his/her self-defeating or erroneous assumptions	4	3	2	1	0
11. Better ways of scheduling his/her time	4	3	2	1	0

Part IV. Rate the extent to which you showed yourself to be the following towards your patient in this session:

	Very much		Some		Not at all
1. Sympathetic and caring	4	3	2	1	0
2. Competent	4	3	2	1	0
3. Warm and friendly	4	3	2	1	0
4. Supportive and encouraging	4	3	2	1	0
5. Involved and interested	4	3	2	1	0

Part V. Please circle the response which applies to your reaction to today's session:

1. I appeared to act condescending.	Yes	No
2. I appeared too quiet and passive.	Yes	No
3. I appeared to talk too much.	Yes	No
4. I appeared too bossy.	Yes	No
5. I appeared to miss the point.	Yes	No
6. Cognitive Therapy does not seem to be suited to this patient and his/her problems.	Yes	No

Part IV. In the remaining space, please describe the most outstanding aspect of today's session:

FIGURE 24. (Cont.)

The forms in Figures 23 and 24 were developed at the
Center for Cognitive Therapy, University of Pennsylvania.

Formal Training in Cognitive Therapy

Formal workshops and courses in Cognitive Therapy can clearly offer much that is difficult to obtain through reading, self-assessment, and client feedback alone. Because Cognitive Therapy is a relatively new approach, there are many clinicians who are interested in it but who did not have access to courses in Cognitive Therapy as part of their clinical training. Training programs in Cognitive Therapy are now much more accessible to practicing therapists than has been the case in the past. At one time, persons interested in training in Cognitive Therapy had no recourse but to travel to Philadelphia to study with Beck and his colleagues. This training generally consisted of a 1- to 2-year, fulltime fellowship that involved seeing clients under supervision, didactic seminars, case discussions, and participation in research. The total number of therapists that can be trained in this intensive and comprehensive manner is, of course, limited; and therapists already in practice would have great difficulty suspending their practices for a year or two to pursue this type of training. Fortunately, there now are Cognitive Therapy programs in many locations across the United States and in Europe,* and training is offered in many different formats.

Workshops and seminars offer some of the most accessible training in Cognitive Therapy that is available. These are often sponsored by state and regional associations, hospitals, mental health centers, or colleges and universities and are available at a number of national conventions. In particular, the annual convention of the Association for the Advancement of Behavior Therapy (AABT) usually offers a number of workshops and preconvention institutes on Cognitive Therapy as well as many papers and symposia that are relevant to Cognitive Therapy. Many workshops last for a single day or less and thus allow little time for anything but didactic presentations. When longer workshops are offered, this often allows the workshop participants to have an opportunity to practice the techniques presented in role plays or other experiential exercises and to discuss clients with whom they are working. The ideal format is for a 1- or 2-day workshop to be followed by a final session a few weeks later so that workshop participants have the opportunity to try the interventions they have learned in practice and then discuss their experiences.

Obviously, a more extended training format would have substantial advantages. Several centers in the United States presently offer year-long training programs in Cognitive Therapy that are designed for practicing mental health professionals. These programs generally meet regularly over

---

*At this time, the authors are aware of Cognitive Therapy training programs in Atlanta, GA; Baltimore, MD; Buenos Aires; Cleveland, OH; Gainesville, FL; Gothenburg, Sweden; Los Angeles, CA; Nashville, TN; Newport Beach, CA; New York, NY; Philadelphia, PA; Rome; San Diego, CA; San Francisco, CA; Seattle, WA; Stockholm; Trondheim, Norway; Umeå, Sweden; and Washington, DC.

a period of 10 months and cover the principles of Cognitive Therapy, the application of these principles with a range of disorders, and ongoing consultation on clients seen by course participants.

Supervision in Cognitive Therapy

When expert supervision is available, this is the most effective way to develop skill in the practice of Cognitive Therapy. Several models of supervision have been used in training cognitive therapists, including the traditional preceptor model in which supervisor and supervisee meet regularly to discuss the supervisee's experiences and problems with clients, an apprenticeship model of training in which the trainee works along with a more experienced therapist and gradually takes increasing responsibility for conducting the therapy session as his or her skill grows (Mooney & Burns, 1983), and group supervision (Burns & Childress, 1983). Whatever the format of supervision being used, it is important that the approach to supervision in Cognitive Therapy parallel the approach used in therapy. After the supervisor assesses the trainee's skills and background in Cognitive Therapy, the supervisor and supervisee(s) should agree on mutual goals for supervision and endeavor to work collaboratively and efficiently toward those goals. Practices such as agreeing on an agenda for each session, emphasizing guided discovery, focusing on specific problem situations, use of "homework assignments," and encouraging explicit feedback are as valuable in supervision as they are in therapy.

It is especially valuable to use more than just verbal discussion in supervision. By reviewing videotapes or audiotapes of therapy sessions or observing live therapy sessions, the supervisor can get a clearer picture of exactly what goes on in the therapy session and can use the Cognitive Therapy rating scales discussed earlier to provide valuable feedback. Role playing of therapist–client interactions with the supervisor or another trainee can give valuable practice in executing interventions and can provide an opportunity to experiment with alternative approaches to a particular problem. By reversing roles so that the supervisee plays the client and the supervisor plays the therapist, supervisees can learn from the therapist's example as well as gain insight into the client's perspective. Finally, by framing conceptualizations of clients as hypotheses to be tested in subsequent therapy sessions, the supervisor and supervisee frequently can replace theoretical debates with data collection and avoid being misled by misconceptions.

It is important for supervision not to focus solely on conceptualizations and intervention techniques. The supervisor must be alert for therapeutic "blind spots" that the supervisee may have. The use of audio- and videorecordings or direct observation of therapy sessions is invaluable for this purpose, because the clinician's blind spots may not be apparent from his or her description of the session. Although the supervisor–supervisee relationship does not have to become psychotherapeutic, it may well be necessary to help the supervisee address some of his or her dysfunctional thoughts and/or beliefs in order to overcome his or her difficulty with certain problems or types of clients. Although supervision may well be personally beneficial for the trainee, there is a major difference between supervision and therapy. The goal in supervision is to develop the trainee's skills in therapy, and his or her personal problems need to addressed only insofar as they interfere with his or her being an effective therapist.

Workshops and courses in Cognitive Therapy are available in many areas, but supervised experience may be more difficult to obtain if one does not live near an established Cognitive Therapy program. One valuable, but underutilized, option for developing skill in Cognitive Therapy is a regularly scheduled consultation group consisting of peers who are also interested in improving their skills in Cognitive Therapy. Although it might seem at first glance that consultation with peers who are no more expert than oneself would have little to offer, one does not have to be a superior player to be an excellent coach. Nonexpert peers can offer each other valuable feedback and support, particularly if audiotapes or videotapes of therapy sessions are reviewed using one of the Cognitive Therapy rating scales. It is important for consultation groups to collaboratively set an agenda, to regularly elicit feedback from all group members, and to establish an atmosphere of mutual respect and openness to criticism. Time spent in presenting detailed case histories or in abstract theoretical discussions is often minimally productive. Groups generally find it much more useful to make sure that the goal of each discussion is clear, to present background information concisely, to focus on specific therapist–client interactions or problem situations, and to use videotapes and role plays when possible.

Extramural Training

One response to the limited availability of training and supervision in Cognitive Therapy has been the development of extramural training programs. This involves the participants coming to a center that offers such training for an initial workshop and for three or four weekend workshops throughout the year. Between workshops, each participant submits a weekly video or audiotape of a therapy session by mail for supervision. The supervisor evaluates the tapes, and supervision sessions are conducted by phone. This provides training and supervision in areas where neither is readily available.

Conclusions

For both the experienced clinician and the neophyte, the task of developing skill in the practice of Cognitive Therapy is much simpler when formal training and expert supervision are easily available. However, if one is receptive to feedback from clients, assesses one's own performance on a regular basis, and takes advantage of opportunities for peer consultation, those without access to training programs can master the skills as well. It is important to remember that skill in Cognitive Therapy is not a static entity that is permanently ingrained once it has been obtained. It is incumbent upon even the most skilled therapist to periodically assess his or her performance, to consult with colleagues regularly, and to keep abreast of new developments in this rapidly developing field.

Appendix

Appendix

Cognitive Therapy Scale

Therapist _____ Patient _____ Date _____
Evaluator _____ Date of Evaluation _____
Session _____ ( )Videotape ( )Audiotape ( )Live observation

DIRECTIONS: For each item, rate the therapist on a scale from 0 to 6 and record the rating next to the item number. The descriptions are provided for even-numbered points on the scale. If you assess the therapist as falling between two scale points interpolate the odd number. Please evaluate every area; do not leave any item blank. If there are circumstances that preclude your evaluating an area, indicate that by writing N/A and explaining the nonapplicability at the end of the scale.

I. General Interview Procedures

_____ 1.   Agenda Setting

    0 The therapist did not set an agenda
    2 The therapist set an agenda that was vague, incomplete, or uni-laterally set (i.e., feeling less depressed)
    4 The therapist worked with the patient to set a mutually accept-able agenda that included specific target problems (i.e., anxiety at work)
    6 Therapist worked with the patient to set an appropriate agenda with discrete target problems, suitable for the available time. Priorities were established and generally followed.

_____ 2.   Eliciting Patient Feedback

    0 The therapist did not, at any point, ask for feedback to determine the patient's understanding of or response to the session.
    2 The therapist occasionally elicited some feedback from the pa-tient but did not ask enough questions to be sure the patient understood the therapist's line of reasoning during the session *or* to ascertain the patient's reaction to the session.
    4 The therapist frequently elicited feedback from the patient to determine the patient's reactions to the session *both* during and after the session.
    6 The therapist continually checked with the patient to determine the patient's understanding of the strategies and techniques being utilized in the session. Worked with the patient to summa-rize main points of the session at the end of the session.

_____ 3.   Collaboration

       0 The therapist did not attempt to establish a collaborative set with the patient.

       2 The therapist attempted to establish a collaborative set with the patient, but had difficulty. Neither defining mutually acceptable problems nor establishing rapport was accomplished at any point.

       4 The therapist was able to establish a collaborative set with the patient, focus on a problem that both patient and therapist considered important, and establish rapport.

       6 Collaboration seemed excellent. The therapist encouraged the patient throughout the session to be active in the therapy session. Clear team work.

_____ 4.   Pacing and Efficient Use of Time

       0 The therapist made no attempt to structure the therapy time. The session seemed aimless.

       2 The session had some direction, but the therapist had difficulty in pacing the session work (too slow, too fast) *or* therapist was inflexible or nonadaptive to the session work.

       4 Therapist was able to use time efficiently. Therapist maintained appropriate control over the flow of discussion.

       6 Therapist paced the session well so the session time allowed for a clear beginning, middle, and closing of the session. Peripheral and unproductive digressions were appropriately handled by the therapist.

II. Interpersonal Effectiveness

_____ 5.   Empathic Skills

       0 The therapist demonstrated poor empathic skills by continually failing to understand what the patient *explicitly* said.

       2 The therapist was usually able to reflect or rephrase what the patient *explicitly* said, but appeared to have difficulty with implicit or subtle communication. Good ability to listen and empathize.

       4 The therapist generally seemed to grasp the patient's "internal reality" as reflected by both what the patient explicitly said and what the patient communicated more subtly. Good ability to listen and empathize.

       6 The therapist demonstrated an understanding of the patient's internal reality and was able to restate or reflect the subtle communication in a way that was acceptable to the patient. Excellent listening and empathic skills.

_____ 6.   Interpersonal Effectiveness

       0 The therapist had poor interpersonal skills. Seemed aloof, hostile, demeaning, sarcastic, by word or action.

       2 While not destructive to the patient, the therapist had significant interpersonal problems. At times the therapist appeared impa-

tient, aloof, insincere *or* had difficulty in conveying a sense of confidence.

   4 The therapist displayed warmth, concern, confidence, and genuineness without significant interpersonal difficulty. Patient and therapist seemed compatible though therapist occasionally appeared ill at ease.

   6 The therapist displayed high levels of warmth, concern, confidence, and genuineness. Therapist seemed at ease throughout the session.

_____ 7. Professionalism

   0 The therapist appeared unprofessional or unethical in action, verbal content, or dress.

   2 The therapist's actions, dress, or session behavior was minimally acceptable. There did not appear to be any unethical behavior or verbalizations. The therapist appeared unconfident.

   4 The therapist conveyed a professionalism in action, dress, and verbal behavior. The patient seemed to respond to the therapist's confidence.

   6 The therapist appeared confident of his or her ability and was able to communicate that confidence to the patient. Dress, action and verbalizations were at the highest professional level.

III. Specific Cognitive-Behavioral Techniques

_____ 8. Use of Guided Discovery

   0 The therapist relied primarily on debate, persuasion, or lecturing. Therapist seemed to be cross-examining the patient. Patient appeared on the defensive as therapist appeared to force his/her view on the patient.

   2 Therapist relied heavily on persuasion and debate rather than on guided discovery. Therapist's style was supportive so that patient did not seem to feel attacked or defensive.

   4 Therapist, for the most part, worked to help the patient see new perspectives through guided discovery rather than debate. Used a primarily questioning format.

   6 Therapist was adept at using guided discovery. Used a questioning format in the therapy and worked to assist the patient in reaching conclusions.

_____ 9. Case Conceptualization

   0 Therapist did not appear to have developed a conceptualization of the case. The session therefore seemed to be poorly focused and to have a "shotgun" approach.

   2 The therapist seemed to have begun to develop a rudimentary conceptualization of the case, and the interventions appeared to have a focus and direction.

   4 The session had a coherent focus that demonstrated a conceptualization of the case.

6 There was a clear treatment conceptualization that eventuated in a series of organized treatment interventions.

_____10.   Focus on Key Cognitions

0 Therapist did not attempt to elicit specific thoughts, assumptions, images, meanings, or beliefs. No use of the DTR or double/triple column technique.

2 The therapist elicited thoughts, assumptions, images, meanings, and beliefs; however, the focus of the cognitive work was vague or irrelevant. Used the DTR and double/triple column technique to collect thoughts.

4. The therapist focused on key cognitions relevant to the target problems in the agenda. The collection of the cognitive material showed promise for progress. Used the DTR or double/triple column technique with skill and was able to teach the patient the use of the tool.

6 The therapist focused on key thoughts and was able to help the patient to clearly delineate the content and nature of the dysfunctional thinking. Used the DTR or double/triple column technique both concretely and verbally.

_____11.   Application of Cognitive Techniques

0 Therapist's application of cognitive techniques was poorly executed.

2 The therapist seemed to have a limited repertoire of technique, *or* attempts to successfully execute different cognitive techniques were incomplete.

4 The therapist seemed to have a variety of cognitive techniques in his or her repertoire and seemed to apply them with skill. There was, however, difficulty or inflexibility in moving easily from one technique to another.

6 The therapist had a broad repertoire of cognitive techniques and was able to move easily and quickly between various techniques, as appropriate.

_____12.   Application of Behavioral Techniques

0 Therapist's use and application of behavioral technique was poorly executed.

2 The therapist seemed to have a limited repertoire of technique, *or* attempts to successfully execute different behavioral techniques were incomplete.

4 The therapist seemed to have a variety of behavioral techniques in his or her repertoire and seemed to apply them with skill. There was, however, difficulty or inflexibility in moving easily from one technique to another.

6 The therapist had a broad repertoire of behavioral techniques and was able to move easily and quickly between various techniques, as appropriate.

_____13. Use of Homework

    0 The therapist did not utilize homework in the session.

    2 The therapist utilized homework but *either* did not review previous agreed-upon homework, suggested inappropriate homework, did not explain the rationale for the homework in sufficient detail for the patient to have success, or assigned homework at the end of the session without collaboration.

    4 The therapist reviewed previous homework. Future homework assigned rather than arrived at collaboratively. Homework explained in detail but not clearly relevant to the therapy work.

    6 Homework carefully and collaboratively agreed upon. Homework drawn directly from session material to allow the patient to test ideas, try new experiences, experiment with new ways of responding.

IV. Additional Factors in Therapy

14. Were there any circumstances that would have you believe that this session is not representative of the therapist's general work?
    ( )Yes   ( )No
    If yes, please describe.

15. Did this patient seem to be resistant to the therapist or to the therapy generally? ( )Yes ( )No
    If yes, please describe.

16. Were there any unusual factors in this session that you feel justified the therapist's departure from any of the standard approaches assessed by this scale? ( )Yes ( )No
    If yes, please describe.

This evaluation has been shared and discussed with the therapist. (The therapist's signature does not in any way indicate agreement with the evaluation.)

Evaluator's signature _____ Date _____
Therapist's signature _____ Date _____

Therapist's comments

References

Abend, S. M., Porder, M. S., & Willick, M. S. (1983). *Borderline patients: Psychoanalytic perspectives.* New York: International Universities Press.

Akhtar, S. (1986). Differentiating schizoid and avoidant personality disorders [letter to the editor]. *American Journal of Psychiatry, 143,* 1060–1061.

Allen, D. W. (1977). Basic treatment issues. In M. J. Horowitz (Ed.), *Hysterical personality.* New York: Jason Aronson.

American Psychiatric Association. (1965). *Diagnostic and statistical manual of mental disorders* (2nd ed.). Washington, DC: Author.

American Psychiatric Association. (1980). *Diagnostic and statistical manual of mental disorders* (3rd ed.). Washington, DC: Author.

American Psychiatric Association. (1987). *Diagnostic and statistical manual of mental disorders* (3rd ed. rev.). Washington, DC: Author.

Ansbacher, H. L. (1985). The significance of Alfred Adler for the concept of narcissism. *American Journal of Psychiatry, 142*(2), 203–207.

Ansbacher, H., & Ansbacher, R. (1963). *The individual psychology of Alfred Adler.* New York: Basic Books.

Arnkoff, D. B., & Glass, C. R. (1982). Clinical cognitive constructs: Examination, evaluation, and elaboration. In P. Kendall (Ed.), *Advances in cognitive-behavioral research and therapy* (Vol. 1). New York: Academic Press.

Bandura, A. (1977). *Social learning theory.* Englewood Cliffs, NJ: Prentice-Hall.

Barlow, D. H., & Waddell, M. T. (1985). Agoraphobia. In D. H. Barlow (Ed.), *Clinical handbook of psychological disorders: A step-by-step treatment manual.* New York: Guilford.

Baron, M. (1981). *Schedule for interviewing borderlines.* New York: New York Psychiatric Institute.

Baron, M. (1983). Schizotypal personality disorder: Family studies. *Abstracts of the 136th Annual Meeting of the American Psychiatric Association,* New York, New York.

Barrios, B. A., & Shigatomi, C. (1980). Coping skills training for the management of anxiety: A critical review. *Behavior Therapy, 10,* 491–522.

Bauer, S. F., Hunt, H. F., Gould, M., & Goldstein, E. G. (1980). Borderline personality organization, structural diagnosis and the structural interview: A pilot study of interview analysis. *Psychiatry, 43,* 224–233.

Baumeister, R. F. (1987). How the self became a problem: A psychological review of the historical research. *Journal of Personality and Social Psychology, 52*(1), 163–176.

Beardslee, W. R., Bemporad, J., Keller, M. B., & Klerman, G. L. (1983). Children of parents with major affective disorder: A review. *American Journal of Psychiatry, 140*(7), 825–832.

Beck, A. T. (1963a). *Depression: Causes and treatment.* Philadelphia: University of Pennsylvania Press.

Beck, A. T. (1963b). Thinking and depression. *Archives of General Psychiatry, 9,* 324–333.

Beck, A. T. (1967). *Depression: Clinical, experimental, and theoretical aspects.* New York: Hoeber.

Beck, A. T. (1970). The role of fantasies in psychotherapy and psychopathology. *Journal of Nervous and Mental Disease, 150,* 3–17.

Beck, A. T. (1976). *Cognitive therapy and the emotional disorders.* New York: International Universities Press.

Beck, A. T. (1978). *Depression Inventory.* Philadelphia: Center for Cognitive Therapy.

Beck, A. T., & Emery, G. (1985). *Anxiety disorders and phobias: A cognitive perspective.* New York: Basic Books.

Beck, A. T., and Greenburg, R. L. (1974). *Coping with depression.* New York: Institute for Rational Living.

Beck, A. T., and Young, J. (1980). *The cognitive therapy scale.* Philadelphia: Center for Cognitive Therapy.

Beck, A. T., Laude, R., & Bohnert, M. (1974). Ideational components of anxiety neurosis. *Archives of General Psychiatry, 31,* 319–325.

Beck, A. T., Kovacs, J., & Weissman, A. (1979). Assessment of suicidal intention: The Scale of Suicidal Ideation. *Journal of Consulting and Clinical Psychology, 47,* 343–352.

Beck, A. T., Kovacs, M., & Weissman, A. (1975). Hopelessness and suicidal behavior: An overview. *Journal of the American Medical Association, 234,* 1146–1149.

Beck, A. T., Rush, A. J., Shaw, B. F., & Emery, G. (1979). *Cognitive therapy of depression.* New York: Guilford.

Beck, A. T., Steer, R. A., Kovacs, M., & Garrison, B. (1985). Hopelessness and eventual suicide: A 10-year prospective study of patients hospitalized with suicide ideation *American Journal of Psychiatry, 142,* 559–563.

Bell, M. (1981). *Bell object-relations self-report scale.* West Haven, CT: Psychology Service, VA Medical Center, 1981.

Bellack, A., & Hersen, M. (Eds.). (1985). *Dictionary of behavior therapy techniques.* New York: Pergamon.

Bellack, A., Hersen, M., & Kazdin, A. (Eds.) (1982). *International handbook of behavior modification and therapy.* New York: Plenum Press.

Bellak, L. (1978). *The T.A.T., C.A.T. and S.A.T. in clinical use.* New York: Grune Stratton.

Benson, H. (1978). *The relaxation response.* New York: Avon.

Bernstein, D. A., & Borkovec, T. D. (1976). *Progressive relaxation training: A manual for the helping professionals.* Champaign, Il.: Research Press.

Bird, J. (1979). The behavioural treatment of hysteria. *British Journal of Psychiatry, 134,* 129–137.

Bower, G. H. (1981). Mood and memory. *American Psychologist, 36,* 293–300.

Bower, S. A., & Bower, G. H. (1976). *Asserting yourself: A practical guide for practical change.* Reading, MA: Addison-Wesley.

Bowers, W. A. (1988). Cognitive therapy with inpatients. In A. Freeman, K. M. Simon, L. Beutler, & H. Arkowitz (Eds.). *Comprehensive handbook of cognitive therapy* (pp. 583–596). New York: Plenum Press.

Boyd, J. H. (1986). Use of mental health services for the treatment of panic disorder. *American Journal of Psychiatry, 143,* 1569–1574.

Burns, D. D. (1980). *Feeling good: The new mood therapy.* New York: William Morrow.

Burns, D. D. *Possible reasons for not doing self-help assignments.* Unpublished manuscript.

Burns, D. D., & Childress, A. R. (1983). *The group supervision model in cognitive therapy training.* In A. Freeman (Ed.), *Cognitive therapy with couples and groups* (pp. 323–336). New York: Plenum.

Burns, D. D., & Epstein, N. (1983). Passive-aggressiveness: A cognitive behavioral approach. In R. D. Parsons & R. J. Wicks (Eds.), *Passive-aggressiveness: Theory and practice* (pp. 72–97). New York: Brunner/Mazel.

Byrne, D., & Kelley, K. (1981). *An introduction to personality* (3rd ed.). Englewood Cliffs, NJ: Prentice-Hall.

Caldwell, A. B., & O'Hare, C. (1975). *A handbook of MMPI personality types*. Santa Monica, CA: Clinical Psychological Services.

Campbell, R. J. (1981). *Psychiatric dictionary* (5th ed.). New York: Oxford University Press.

Carney, F. L. (1986). Residential treatment programs for antisocial personality disorders. In W. H. Reid, D. Dorr, J. I. Walker, & J. W. Bonner III (Eds.), *Unmasking the psychopath: Antisocial personality disorder and related syndromes*. New York: Norton.

Casey, P. R., Tryer, P. J., & Platt, S. (1985). The relationship between social functioning and psychiatric functioning in primary care. *Social Psychiatry, 20*(1), 5–9.

Chamberlain, P., Patterson, G., Reid, J., Kavanaugh, K., & Forgatch, M. (1984). Observation of client resistance. *Behavior Therapy, 15*, 144–155.

Chatham, P. M. (1985). *Treatment of the borderline personality*. New York: Jason Aronson.

Clarkin, J. F., Widiger, T. A., Frances, A., Hurt, S. W., & Gilmore, M. (1983). Prototypic typology and the borderline personality disorder. *Journal of Abnormal Psychology, 93*, 263–275.

Coché, E. (1987). Problem-solving training: A cognitive group therapy modality. In A. Freeman & V. Greenwood (Eds.), *Cognitive therapy: Applications in psychiatric and medical settings*. New York: Human Sciences Press.

Colby, K. M., Faught, W. S., & Parkinson, R. C. (1979). Cognitive therapy of paranoid conditions: Heuristic suggestions based on a computer simulation model. *Cognitive Therapy and Research, 3*, 5–60.

Cone, J. D., & Hawkins, R. P. (1977). *Behavioral assessment: New directions in clinical psychology*. New York: Bruner/Mazel.

Conoley, J. C., & Beard, M. (1984). The effects of a paradoxical intervention on therapeutic relationship measures. *Psychotherapy, 21*(2), 273–277.

Corsini, R. (Ed.). (1979). *Current personality theories*. Ithasca, Il: F. E. Peacock.

Costall, A., & Still, A. (Eds.). (1987). *Cognitive psychology in question*. New York: St. Martin's Press.

Craighead, W. E., Kimball, W. H., & Rehak, P. J. (1979). Mood changes, physiological responses, and self-statements during social rejection imagery. *Journal of Consulting and Clinical Psychology, 47*, 385–396.

Curran, J. P., & Monti, P. (Eds.). (1982). *Social skills training: A practical handbook for assessment and treatment*. New York: Guilford.

Davis, M., Eshelman, E. R., & McKay, M. (1982). *The relaxation and stress reduction workbook*. Oakland, CA: New Harbinger Publications.

Deffenbacher, J. L., Storey, D. A., Stark, R. S., Hogg, J. A., & Brandon, A. D. (1987). Cognitive-relaxation and social skills interventions in the treatment of general anger. *Journal of Counseling Psychology, 34*(2), 171–176.

Deffenbacher, J. L., Zwemer, W. A., Whisman, M. A., Hill, R. A., & Sloan, R. D. (1986). Irrational beliefs and anxiety. *Cognitive Therapy and Research, 10*, 281–292.

DiGiuseppe, R. (1983). Rational emotive therapy and conduct disorders. In A. Ellis & M. E. Bernard (Eds.). *Rational-emotive approaches to the problems of childhood* (pp. 111–138). New York: Plenum Press.

DiGiuseppe, R. (1986). The implication of the philosophy of science for rational-emotive theory and therapy. *Psychotherapy, 23*(4), 634–639.

DiGiuseppe, R., Ellis, A., Leaf, R. C., Mass, R., Alington, D. E., & Wolfe, J. (1987). Unpublished data. New York: Institute for Rational Living.

Douglas, C. J., & Druss, R. G. (1987). Denial of illness: A reappraisal. *General Hospital Psychiatry, 9*(1), 53–57.

Dryden, W. (1984). Rational-emotive therapy and cognitive therapy: A critical comparison. In M. A. Reda & M. J. Mahoney, (Eds.), *Cognitive psychotherapies: Recent developments in theory, research, and practice*. Cambridge, MA: Ballinger.

DSM-I—Diagnostic and statistical manual (1st ed.). (1952). Washington, DC: American Psychiatric Press.

DSM-II—Diagnostic and statistical manual (2nd ed.). (1968). Washington, DC: American Psychiatric Press.

DSM-III—Diagnostic and statistical manual (3rd ed.). (1980). Washington, DC: American Psychiatric Press.

DSM-III–R—Diagnostic and statistical manual (rev. 3rd ed.). (1987). Washington, DC: American Psychiatric Press.

Dushe, D. M., Hurt, M. L., & Schroeder, H. (1983). Self-statement modification with adults: A meta-analysis. *Psychological Bulletin, 94,* 408–442.

D'Zurilla, T. J., & Goldfried, M. R. (1971). Problem solving and behavior modification. *Journal of Abnormal Psychology, 78,* 107–126.

Earls, F. (1981). Temperament characteristics and behavior patterns in three-year-old children. *The Journal of Nervous and Mental Disease, 169*(6), 367–371.

Edell, W. S. (1984). The borderline syndrome index: Clinical validity and utility. *The Journal of Nervous and Mental Disease, 172,* 254–263.

Edwards, D. (1989). Cognitive restructuring through guided imagery: Lessons from gestalt therapy. In A. Freeman, K. M. Simon, H. Arkowitz, & L. Beutler (Eds.), *Comprehensive handbook of cognitive therapy* (pp. 283–297). New York: Plenum Press.

Eich, J. E. (1977). State-dependent retrieval of information in human episodic memory. In I. M. Birnbaum & E. S. Parker (Eds.), *Alcohol and human memory.* New York: Erlbaum.

Ellis, A. (1957a). Rational psychotherapy and individual psychology. *Journal of Individual Psychology, 13*(1), 38–44.

Ellis, A. (1957b). Outcome of employing three techniques of psychotherapy. *Journal of Clinical Psychology, 13*(4), 344–350.

Ellis, A. (1958). Rational psychotherapy. *Journal of General Psychology, 59,* 35–49.

Ellis, A. (1969). *Sex without guilt.* New York: Lancer Books.

Ellis, A. (1985). *Overcoming resistance: Rational-emotive therapy with difficult clients.* New York: Springer Publishing Company.

Ellis, A., & Bernard, M. E. (1985). What is rational-emotive therapy (RET)? In A. Ellis, M. E. Bernard (Eds.). *Clinical applications of rational-emotive therapy* (pp. 1–30). New York: Plenum Press.

Ellis, A., & Greiger, R. (1977). *Handbook of rational-emotive therapy.* New York: Springer Publishing Company.

Ellis, A., & Harper, R. (1975). *A new guide to rational living.* North Hollywood, CA: Wilshire.

Ellis, A., Young, J., & Lockwood, G. (1987). Cognitive Therapy and rational-emotive therapy: A dialogue. *Journal of Cognitive Psychotherapy: An International Quarterly, 1,* 205–256.

Ellis H. (1898). Auto-eroticism: A psychological study. *Alienist and neurologist, 19,* 260–299.

Emery, G. (1988). *Getting undepressed: How a woman can change her life through cognitive therapy.* New York: Simon & Schuster.

Ericsson, K. A., & Simon, H. A. (1980). Verbal reports as data. *Psychological Review, 87,* 215–251.

Festinger, L. A. (1957). *A theory of cognitive dissonance.* Stanford: Stanford University Press.

Fleming, B. (1983, August). *Cognitive therapy with histrionic patients: Resolving a conflict in styles.* Paper presented at the meeting of the American Psychological Association, Anaheim, CA.

Fleming, B. (1985). *Dependent personality disorder: Managing the transition from dependence to autonomy.* Paper presented at the meeting of the Association for the Advancement of Behavior Therapy, Houston, TX.

Fleming, B. (1988). CT with histrionic personality disorder: Resolving a conflict of styles. *International Cognitive Therapy Newsletter, 4*(4), 8–9, 12.

Foa, E. B., Steketee, G., & Milby, J. B. (1980). Differential effects of exposure and response prevention in obsessive-compulsive washers. *Journal of Consulting and Clinical Psychology, 48,* 71–79.

Foa, E. B., Steketee, G., Grayson, J. B., Turner, R. M., & Latimer, P. (1984). Deliberate exposure and blocking of obsessive-compulsive rituals: Immediate and long term effects. *Behavior Therapy, 15,* 450–472.

Foon, A. E. (1985). The effect of social class and cognitive orientation on clinical expectations. *British Journal of Medical Psychology, 58*(4), 357–364.

Frances, A. F., Clarkin, J. F., Gilmore, M., Hurt, I., & Brown, I. (1984). Reliability of criteria for borderline personality disorder: A comparison of DSM-III and the diagnostic interview for borderlines. *American Journal of Psychiatry, 141,* 1080–1084.

Frank, J. D. (1973). *Persuasion and healing* (2nd ed.). Baltimore: Johns Hopkins University Press.

Frazee, H. E. (1953). Children who later become schizophrenic. *Smith College Studies in Social Work, XXIII,* 125–149.

Freeman, A. (1981). Dreams and images in cognitive therapy. In G. Emery, S. D. Hollon, & R. C. Bedrosian. *New directions in cognitive therapy* (pp. 224–238). New York: Guilford.

Freeman, A. (1987). *Understanding personal, cultural and religious schema in psychotherapy.* In A. Freeman, N. Epstein, & K. M. Simon, *Depression in the family.* New York: Haworth Press.

Freeman, A., & DeWolf (1989). *Woulda, coulda, shoulda.* New York: Morrow.

Freeman, A., Epstein, N., & Simon, K. M. (1986). *Depression in the family.* New York: Haworth Press.

Freeman, A., & Greenwood, V. (1987). *Cognitive therapy: Applications in psychiatric and medical settings.* New York: Human Sciences Press.

Freeman, A., & Simon, K. M. (1989). *Cognitive therapy of anxiety.* In A. Freeman, K. M. Simon, H. Arkowitz, & L. Beutler, (Eds.), *Handbook of cognitive therapy.* New York: Plenum Press.

Freeman, A., and White, D. (1989). Cognitive therapy of suicide. In A. Freeman, K. M. Simon, II. Arkowitz, & L. Beutler, (Eds.), *Handbook of cognitive therapy.* New York: Plenum Press.

Freud, S. (1914). On narcissism: An introduction. In J. Strachey (Ed.), *The standard edition of the complete works of Sigmund Freud* (Vol. 14, pp. 69–102). London: Hogarth Press.

Frosch, J. P. (1964). The psychotic character: Clinical psychiatric considerations. *Psychiatric Quarterly, 38,* 81–96.

Frosch, J P. (1983). *Personality disorders.* Washington, DC. American Psychiatric Association Press.

Gilberstadt, H., & Duker, J. (1965). *A handbook for clinical and actuarial MMPI interpretation.* Philadelphia: W B. Saunders.

Gibertini, M., Brandenburg, N. A., & Retzlaff, P. D. (1986). The operating characteristics of the Millon Clinical Multiaxial Inventory. *Journal of Personality Assessment, 50*(4), 554–567.

Gittelman-Klein, R., & Klein, D. (1969). Premorbid asocial adjustment and prognosis in schizophrenia. *Journal of Psychiatric Research, 7,* 35–53.

Glass, C. R., & Arnkoff, D. B. (1982). Think cognitively: Selected issues in cognitive assessment and therapy. In P. Kendall (Ed.), *Advances in cognitive-behavioral research and therapy* (Vol. 1). New York: Academic Press.

Glass, C. R., & Merluzzi, T. V. (1981). Cognitive assessment of social-evaluative anxiety. In T. V. Merluzzi, C. R. Glass, & M. Genest (Eds.), *Cognitive assessment.* New York: Guilford Press.

Goldfried, M. (1971). Systematic desensitization as training in self control. *Journal of Consulting and Clinical Psychology, 37,* 228–234.

Goldstein, A. J. & Chambless, D. A. (1978). A reanalysis of agoraphobia. *Behavior Therapy, 9,* 47–59.

Goldstein, A. P., Martens, J., Hubben, J., Van Belle, H. A., Schaaf, W., Wirsma, H., & Goedhart, A. (1973). The use of modeling to increase independent behavior. *Behavior Research and Therapy, 11,* 31–42.

Goldstein, W. (1985). *An introduction to the borderline conditions.* Northvale, NJ: Jason Aronson.

Gorman, J. M., Shear, M. K., Devereux, R. B., King, D. L., & Klein, D. F. (1986). Prevalence of mitral valve prolapse in panic disorder: Effect of echocardiographic criteria. *Psychosomatic Medicine, 48,* 167–171.

Green, C. J. (1982). The diagnostic accuracy and utility of MMPI and MCMI computer interpretive reports. *Journal of Personality Assessment, 46*(4), 359–365.

Greenwood, V. (1983). Cognitive therapy with the chronic young adult patient. In A. Freeman (Ed.), *Cognitive therapy with couples and groups.* New York: Plenum Press.

Grieger, R. M., and Boyd, J. D. (1980). *Rational emotive therapy: A skills based approach.* New York: Van Nostrand Reinhold.

Grinker, R. R., Werble, B., & Drye, R. C. (1968). *The borderline syndrome.* New York: Basic Books.

Guidano, V. F., and Liotti, G. (1983). *Cognitive processes and emotional disorders.* New York: Guilford.

Gunderson, J. G. (1984). *Borderline personality disorders.* Washington, DC: American Psychiatric Press.

Guntrip, H. (1969). *Schizoid phenomena, object relations and the self.* New York: International Universities Press.

Hales, R. E., Polly, S., Bridenbaugh, H., & Orman, D. (1986). Psychiatric consultations in a military general hospital. A report on 1,065 cases. *General Hospital Psychiatry, 8*(3), 173–182.

Halleck, S. L. (1967). Hysterical personality traits. *Archives of General Psychiatry, 6,* 750–757.

Hamilton, N. G., Green, H. J., Mech, A. W., Brand, A. A., Wong, N., & Coyne, L. (1984). Borderline personality: DSM-III-R versus a previous usage. *Bulletin of the Menninger Clinic, 48,* 540–543.

Hamilton, S., Rothbart, M., & Dawes, R. M. (1987). Sex bias, diagnosis, and DSM-III. *Sex Roles, 15*(5/6), 269–274.

Hamner, T., & Turner, P. (1985). *Parenting in contemporary society.* Englewood Cliffs, NJ: Prentice Hall.

Harlow, H. F. (1971). *Learning to love.* San Francisco: Albion.

Harlow, H. F., & Woolsey, C. N. (1958). *Symposium on interdisciplinary research. Biological and chemical bases of behavior.* Madison, WI: University of Wisconsin Press.

Harris, J. C. (1984). *Tar baby and other rhymes of Uncle Remus.* Marietta, GA: Cherokee.

Hartman, L. M., & Blankenstein, K. R. (1986). *Perception of self in emotional disorder and psychotherapy.* New York: Plenum Press.

Henn, F. A., Herjanic, M., & VanderPearl, R. H. (1976). Forensic psychiatry: Diagnosis and criminal responsibility. *The Journal of Nervous and Mental Disease, 162*(6), 423–429.

Hill, E. F. (1972). *The Holtzman Inkblot Technique.* San Francisco: Jossey-Bass.

Hjelle, L. A., & Ziegler, D. J. (1981). *Personality theories.* New York: McGraw-Hill.

Hoch, P., & Polatin (1949). Pseudoneurotic forms of schizophrenia. *Psychiatric Quarterly, 23,* 248–276.

Hollon, S. D., Kendall, P. C., & Lumry, A. (1986). Specificity of depressogenic cognitions in clinical depression. *Journal of Abnormal Psychology, 95*(1), 52–59.

Holmes, T. H., & Rahe, R. H. (1976). The social readjustment scale. *Journal of Psychosomatic Medicine, 11,* 213.

Horowitz, M. (Ed.). (1977). *Hysterical personality.* New York: Jason Aronson.

Hurlburt, R. T., Leach, B. C., & Saltman, S. (1984). Random sampling of thought and mood. *Cognitive Therapy and Research, 8,* 263–276.

Hurt, S. W., Hyler, S. E., Frances, A., Clarkin, J. F., & Brent, R. (1984). Assessing borderline personality disorder with self-report, clinical interview, or semi-structured interview. *American Journal of Psychiatry, 141,* 1228–1231.

Isen, A. M. (1984). Toward understanding the role of affect in cognition. In R. S. Wyer & T. K. Skrull (Eds.), *Handbook of social cognition.* Hillsdale, NJ: Lawrence Erlbaum.

Jakubowski, P., & Lange, A. J. (1978). *The assertive option: Your rights and responsibilities.* Champaign, IL: Research Press.

Jones, R. A. (1977). *Self-fulfilling prophesies, social psychological, and physiological effects of expectancies.* Hillsdale NJ: Lawrence Erlbaum Associates, Inc.

Karno, M., Hough, R. L., Burnam, M. A., Escobar, J. I., Timbers, D. M., Santana, F., & Boyd, J. H. (1986). Lifetime prevalence of specific psychiatric disorders among Mexican Americans and non-Hispanic whites in Los Angeles. *Archives of General Psychiatry, 44*(8), 695–701.

Kass, D. J., Silvers, F. M., & Abrams, G. M. (1972). Behavioral group treatment of hysteria. *Archives of General Psychiatry, 26,* 42–50.

Kelly, G. A. (1955). *The psychology of personal constructs.* New York: Norton.

Kelly, J. A. (1982). *Social skills training: A practical guide for intervention.* New York: Springer.

Kendall, P. C. (1981). Assessment and cognitive-behavioral interventions: Purposes, proposals, and problems. In P. C. Kendall & S. D. Hollon (Eds.) *Assessment strategies for cognitive behavioral interventions.* New York: Academic Press.

Kendall, P. C., & Hollon, S. D. (1981). Assessing self-referent speech: Methods in the measurement of self-statements. In P. C. Kendall & S. D. Hollon (Eds.), *Assessment strategies for cognitive behavioral interventions.* New York: Academic Press.

Kendall, P. C., & Hollon, S. D. (Eds.). (1981). *Assessment strategies for cognitive behavioral interventions.* New York: Academic Press.

Kendall, P. C., & Korgeski, G. P. (1979). Assessment and cognitive-behavioral interventions. *Cognitive Research and Therapy, 3,* 1–21.

Kendler, K. S., & Gruenberg, A. M. (1982). Genetic relationship between paranoid personality disorder and the "schizophrenic spectrum" disorders. *American Journal of Psychiatry, 139,* 1185–1186.

Kernberg, O. F. (1967). Borderline personality organization. *Journal of the American Psychoanalytic Association, 15,* 641–685.

Kernberg, O. F. (1970). Factors in the treatment of narcissistic personalities. *Journal of the American Psychoanalytic Association, 18,* 51–85.

Kernberg, O. F. (1975). *Borderline conditions and pathological narcissism.* New York: Jason Aronson.

Kernberg, O. F. (1977). Structural change and its impediments. In P. Hartocollis (Ed.), *Borderline personality disorders: The concept, the syndrome, the patient.* New York: International Universities Press.

Kernberg, O. F. (1984). *Severe personality disorders: Psychotherapeutic strategies.* New Haven: Yale University Press.

Kety, S., Rosenthal, D., & Wender, P. H. (1968). The types and prevalence of mental illness in the biological and adoptive families of adopted schizophrenics. In D. Rosenthal & S. Kety (Eds.), *The transmission of Schizophrenia.* Oxford: Pergamon Press.

Klinger, E. (1978). Modes of normal conscious flow. In K. S. Pope & J. L. Singer (Eds.), *The stream of consciousness: Scientific investigation into the flow of human experience.* New York: Plenum Press.

Koenigsberg, H. W., Kaplan, R. D., Gilmore, M. M., & Cooper, A. M. (1985). The relationship between syndrome and personality disorder in DSM-III: Experience with 2,462 patients. *American Journal of Psychiatry, 142*(2), 207–217.

Kohut, H. (1968). The psychoanalytic treatment of narcissistic personality disorders. *Psychoanalytic Study of the Child, 23,* 86–113.

Kohut, H. (1971). *The analysis of the self.* New York: International Universities Press.

Kolb, L. C. (1968). *Noyes' clinical psychiatry* (7th ed.). Philadelphia: W. B. Saunders.

Kolb, J. E., & Gunderson, J. G. (1980). Diagnosing borderline patients with a semi-structured interview. *Archives of General Psychiatry, 37,* 37–41.

Kretschmer, E. (1936). *Physique and character.* London: Routlefge & Kegan Paul.

Lange, A. J., & Jakubowski, P. (1976). *Responsible assertive behavior: Cognitive behavioral procedures for trainers*. Champaign, IL: Research Press.

Latimer, P. R., & Sweet, A. A. (1984). Cognitive versus cognitive-behavioral procedures in cognitive-behavior therapy: A critical review of the evidence. *Journal of Of Behavior Therapy and Experimental Psychiatry, 15*(1), 9–22.

Leitenberg, H., Yost, L. W., & Carroll-Wilson, M. (1986). Negative cognitive errors in children: Questionnaire development, normative data, and comparison between children with and without self-reported symptoms of depression, low self-esteem, and evaluation anxiety. *Journal of Consulting and Clinical Psychology, 54*(4), 528–536.

Lester, D. (1983). *Why people kill themselves*. Springfield, IL: Charles C Thomas.

Levi, L. (1975). *Emotions: Their parameters and measurement*. New York: Raven.

Like, R., & Zyzanski, S. J. (1987). Patient satisfaction with the clinical encounter: Social psychological determinants. *Social Science in Medicine, 24*(4) 351–357.

Linehan, M. M. (1977). Issues in behavioral interviewing. In J. D. Cone & R. P. Hawkins, (Eds.), *Behavioral assessment: New directions in clinical psychology*. New York: Bruner/Mazel.

Linehan, M. M. (1987a). Dialectical behavior therapy in groups: Treating borderline personality disorders and suicidal behavior. In C. M. Brody (Ed.), *Women in groups*. New York: Springer.

Linehan, M. M. (1987b). Dialectical behavioral therapy: A cognitive behavioral approach to parasuicide. *Journal of Personality Disorders, 1*, 328–333.

Lion, J. R. (Ed.). (1981). *Personality disorders: Diagnosis and management*. Baltimore: Williams & Wilkens.

Little, V. L., & Kendall, P. C. (1979). Cognitive-behavioral interventions with delinquents: Problem solving, role-taking, and self-control. In P. C. Kendall & S. D. Hollon, (Eds.), *Cognitive-behavioral interventions: Theory, research, and procedures*. New York: Academic.

Livesley, W. J. (1985). Historical comment on DSM-III Schizoid and Avoidant Personality Disorders. *American Journal of Psychiatry, 142*, 1344–1347.

Livesley, W. J., West, M., & Tanney, A. (1985). Historical comment on DSM-III Schizoid and Avoidant Personality Disorders. *American Journal of Psychiatry, 42*, 1344–1347.

Longsbaugh, R., & Eldred, S. H. (1973). Premorbid adjustments, schizoid personality and onset of illness as predictors of post-hospitalization functioning. *Journal of Psychiatric Research, 10*, 19–29.

Luborsky, L., McLellan, A. T., Woody, G. E., O'Brien, C. P., & Auerbach, A. (1985). Therapist success and its determinants. *Archives of General Psychiatry, 42*, 602–611.

MacKinnon, R. A., & Michaels, R. (1971). *The psychiatric interview in clinical practice*. Philadelphia: W. B. Sanders.

MacLeod, C., Mathews, A., & Tata, P. (1986). Attention bias in emotional disorders, *Journal of Abnormal Psychology, 95*(1), 15–20.

Mahoney, M. J. (1977). Some applied issues in self-monitoring. In J. D. Cone & R. P. Hawkins (Eds.), *Behavioral assessment: New directions in clinical psychology*. New York: Bruner/Mazel.

Mahoney, M. J., & Freeman, A. (Eds.). (1985). *Cognition and psychotherapy*. New York: Plenum Press.

Malmquist, C. P. (1971). Hysteria in childhood. *Postgraduate Medicine, 50*, 112–117.

Marlatt, G. A., & Gordon, J. R. (1985). *Relapse prevention*. New York: Guilford.

Marshall, W. L., & Barbaree, H. E. (1984). Disorders of personality, impulse, and adjustment. In S. M. Turner & M. Hersen (Eds.), *Adult psychopathology and diagnosis*. New York: Wiley.

Marsland, D. W., Wood, M., & Mayo, F. (1976). Content of family practice: A data bank for client care, curriculum, and research in family practice—526, 196 client problems. *Journal of Family Practice, 3*, 25–68.

Martin, J., Martin, W., & Slemon, A. G. (1987). Cognitive mediation in person-centered and rational-emotive therapy. *Journal of Counseling Psychology, 34*(3), 251–260.

Masterson, J. F. (1978). *New perspectives on psychotherapy of the borderline adult*. New York: Brunner/Mazel.

Masterson, J. F. (1980). *From borderline adolescent to functioning adult: The test of time.* New York: Brunner/Mazel.

Masterson, J. F. (April, 1982). *Borderline and narcissistic disorders: An integrated developmental approach.* Workshop presented at Adelphi University, Garden City, New York.

Masterson, J. F. (1985). *Treatment of the borderline adolescent: A developmental approach.* New York: Brunner/Mazel.

Mathews, A. M., Gelder, M. G., & Johnston, D. W. (1981). *Agoraphobia: Nature and treatment.* New York: Guilford.

Mathews, A., & MacLeod, C. (1986). Discrimination of treat cues without awareness in anxiety states. *Journal of Abnormal Psychology, 95*(2), 131–138.

Matthews, W. M., & Reid, W. H. (1986). A wilderness experience treatment program for offenders. In W. H. Reid, D. Dorr, J. I. Walker, & J. W. Bonner III (Eds.), *Unmasking the psychopath: Antisocial personality disorder and related syndromes.* New York: Norton.

Mays, D. T., & Franks, C. M. (1975). Negative outcome: What to do about it. In D. T. Mays, & C. M. Franks (Eds.), *Negative outcome in psychotherapy and what to do about it.* New York: Springer.

Maziade, M., Caperaa, P., Laplante, B., Boudreault, M., Thivierge, J., Cote, R., & Boutin, P. (1985). Value of difficult temperament among 7 year-olds in the general population for predicting psychiatric diagnosis at age 12. *American Journal of Psychiatry, 142*(80), 943–946.

McMahon, R. C., & Davidson, R. S. (1985). An examination of the relationship between personality patterns and symptom/mood patterns. *Journal of Personality Assessment, 49*(5), 552–556.

McMullin, R., & Casey, B. (1975). *Talk sense to yourself: A guide to cognitive restructuring therapy.* Lakewood, CO: Counseling Research Institute.

Means, J. R., Wilson, G. L., & Dlugokinski, L. J. (1987). *Self-initiated Imaginal and cognitive components: Evaluation of differential effectiveness in altering unpleasant moods. Imagination, Cognition and Personality, 6*(3), 219–226.

Meichenbaum, D. (1977). *Cognitive-behavior modification: An integrative approach.* New York: Plenum Press.

Mellsop, G. W. (1972). Psychiatric patients seen as children and adults: Childhood predictors of adult illness. *Journal of Child Psychological Psychiatry, 13*, 91–101.

Mellsop, G. W. (1973). Adult psychiatric patients on whom information during childhood is missing. *British Journal of Psychiatry, 123*, 703–710.

Menninger, K. (1940). Character disorders. In J. F. Brown (Ed.), *The psychodynamics of abnormal behavior* (pp. 384–403). New York: McGraw-Hill.

Merbaum, M., & Butcher, J. N. (1982). Therapists' liking of their psychotherapy patients; Some issues related to severity of disorder and treatability. *Psychotherapy: Theory, Research and Practice, 19*(1), 6–76.

Merluzzi, T. V., Glass, C. R., & Genest, M. (1981). *Cognitive assessment.* New York: Guilford Press.

Michelson, L. (1987). Cognitive-behavioral assessment and treatment of agoraphobia. In L. Michelson & L. M. Ascher (Eds.), *Anxiety and stress disorders: Cognitive-behavioral assessment and treatment.* New York: Guilford Press.

Miller, R. C., & Berman, J. S. (1983). The efficacy of cognitive behavior therapies: A quantitative review of the research evidence. *Psychological Bulletin, 94*, 39–53.

Millman, H. L., Huber, J. T., & Diggins, D. R. (1982). *Therapies for adults.* San Francisco: Jossey-Bass.

Millon, T. (1969). *Modern psychopathology: A biosocial approach to maladaptive learning and functioning.* Philadelphia: W. B. Saunders.

Millon, T. (1981). *Disorders of personality DSM-III: Axis II.* New York: Wiley.

Millon, T. (1982). *Millon Clinical Multi-Axial Inventory.* Minneapolis, MN: Interperative Scoring Systems.

Millon, T. (1985). The MCMI provides a good assessment of DSM-III disorders: The MCMI-II will prove even better. *Journal of Personality Assessment, 49*(4), 379–391.

Millon, T. (1986). DSM-III distinction between Schizoid and Avoidant Personality Disorders [letter to the editor]. *Canadian Journal of Psychiatry, 31,* 600–700.

Mizes, J. S., Landolf-Fritsche, B., & Grossman-McKee, D. (1987). Patterns of distorted cognitions in phobic disorders: An investigation of clinically severe simple phobics, social phobics, and agoraphobics. *Cognitive Therapy and Research, 11,* 583–592.

Mooney, S., & Burns, D. D. (1983). The apprenticeship model: Training in cognitive therapy by participation. In A. Freeman (Ed.), *Cognitive therapy with couples and groups* (pp. 303–322). New York: Plenum Press.

Moore, H. A., Zusman, J., & Root, G. C. (1984). Noninstitutional treatment for sex offenders in Florida, *American Journal of Psychiatry, 142*(8), 964–967.

Moreland, K. L., & Onstad, J. M. (1987). *Validity of Millon's computerized interpretation system for the MCMI: A controlled study. Journal of Consulting and Clinical Psychology, 55*(1), 113–114.

Morris, D. P., Soroker, E., & Burrus, G. (1954). Follow-up studies of shy, withdrawn children. I. Evaluation of later adjustment. *American Journal of Orthopsychiatry, 24,* 743–754.

Morrison, L. A., & Shapiro, D. A. (1987). Expectancy: An outcome in prescriptive vs. exploratory psychotherapy. *British Journal of Clinical Psychology, 26*(1), 59–60.

Murphy, G. E., Simons, A. D., Wetzel, R. D., & Lustman, P. J. (1984). Cognitive therapy versus tricyclic antidepressants in major depression. *Archives of General Psychiatry, 41,* 33–41.

Murray, H. A. (1943). *Thematic Apperception Test manual.* Cambridge, MA: Harvard University Press.

Myers, J. K., Weissman, M. M., Tischler, G. L., Holzer, C. E. III, Leaf, P. J., Orvaschel, H., Anthony, J. C., Boyd, J. H., Burke, J. K., Jr., Kramer, M., & Stoltzman, R. (1984). Six-month prevalence of psychiatric disorders in three communities. *Archives of General Psychiatry, 41,* 959–967.

Nay, R. W. (1976). *Behavioral intervention. Contemporary strategies.* New York: Gardner.

Neisser, U. (1976). *Cognition and reality.* San Francisco: W. H. Freeman.

Nisbett, R. E., & Wilson, T. D. (1977). Telling more than we can know: Verbal reports on mental processes. *Psychological Review, 84,* 231–259.

Norton, G. R., Harrison, B., Hauch, J., & Rhodes, L. (1985). Characteristics of people with infrequent panic attacks. *Journal of Abnormal Psychology, 94,* 216–221.

Novaco, R. (1975). *Anger control: The development and evaluation of an experimental treatment.* Lexington, MA: Heath & Co.

Patterson, W. M., Dohn, H. H., Bird, J., & Patterson, G. A. (1983). Evaluation of suicidal patients: The SAD PERSONS scale. *Psychosomatics, 24,* 343–349.

Perris, C. (1986). *Kognitiv terapi i teori och praktik.* Sweden: Natur och cultur.

Perris, C. (1988). Cognitive psychotherapy and millieutherapeutic processes in psychiatric inpatient units. *Journal of Cognitive Psychotherapy: An International Quarterly, 1,* 35–50.

Perris, C., Rodhe, K., Palm, A., Abelson, M., Hellgren, S., Lilja, C., & Soderman, H. (1987). Fully integrated in- and outpatient services in a psychiatric sector: Implementation of a new model of care of psychiatric patients favoring continuity of care. In A. Freeman & V. Greenwood (Eds.), *Cognitive therapy: Applications in psychiatric and medical settings.* New York: Human Sciences Press.

Perry, J., & Klerman, G. (1980). Clinical features of borderline personality disorder. *American Journal of Psychiatry, 137,* 165–173.

Persons, J. B., & Burns, D. D. (1986). The process of Cognitive Therapy: The first dysfunctional thought changes less than the last one, *Behavior Research and Therapy, 24*(6), 619–624.

Piaget, J. (1970). *The child's conception of time.* New York: Basic Books.

Piaget, J. (1974). *Experiments in contradiction.* Chicago: University of Chicago Press.

Piaget, J. (1976). *The grasp of consciousness.* Cambridge: Harvard University Press.

Piaget, J. (1978). *Success and understanding*. Cambridge: Harvard University Press.

Pfohl, B., Coryell, W., Zimmerman, M., & Stangl, D. (1986). DSM-III personality disorders: Diagnostic overlap and internal consistency of individual DSM-III criteria. *Comprehensive Psychiatry, 27*(1), 21–34.

Pretzer, J. L. (1983, August). *Borderline Personality Disorder: Too complex for cognitive-behavioral approaches?* Paper presented at the meeting of the American Psychological Association, Anaheim, CA. (ERIC Document Reproduction Service No. ED 243 007.)

Pretzer, J. L. (1985, November). *Paranoid Personality Disorder: A cognitive view.* Paper presented at the meeting of the Association for the Advancement of Behavior Therapy, Houston, TX.

Pretzer, J. L. (1988). Paranoid personality disorder: A cognitive view. *International Cognitive Therapy Newsletter, 4*(4), 10–12.

Prince, R. (1985). Denial: Is its use in heart disease a bad thing? *Integrative Psychiatry, 3*, 66–67.

Quay, H. C., Routh, D. K., & Shapiro, S. K. (1987). Psychopathology of childhood: From description to Validation. *Annual Review of Psychology, 38*, 491–532.

Rachman, S. J., & Wilson, G. T. (1980). The effects of psychological therapy (2nd ed.) New York: Pergamon Press.

Rado, S. (1956). Dynamics and classification of disordered behavior. In *Psychoanalysis and behavior* (pp. 268–285). New York: Grune and Stratton.

Reich, J. (1987a). Sex distribution of DSM-III personality disorders in psychiatric outpatients. *American Journal of Psychiatry, 144*(4), 485–488.

Reich, J. H. (1987b). Instruments measuring DSM-III and DSM-III-R personality disorders. *Journal of Personality Disorders, 1*, 220–240.

Reid, W. H. (Ed.). (1981). *The treatment of the antisocial syndromes.* New York: Van Nostrand.

Reid, W. H., & Solomon, G. F. (1986). Community-based offender programs. In W. H. Reid, D. Dorr, J. I. Walker, & J. W. Bonner III. *Unmasking the psychopath: Antisocial personality disorder and related syndromes.* New York: Norton.

Rimm, D. C., and Masters, J. C. (1979). *Behavior therapy: Techniques and empirical findings* (2nd ed.). New York: Academic Press.

Robins, E., Gassner, S., Kayes, J., Wilkonson, R. H., Jr., & Murphy, G. E. (1959). The communication of suicidal intent: A study of 134 consecutive cases of successful (completed) suicide. *American Journal of Psychiatry, 115*, 724–733.

Roff, J. D., Knight, R., and Wertheim, E. (1976). A factor analytic study of childhood symptoms antecedent to schizophrenia. *Journal of Abnormal Psychology, 85*, 543–549.

Rosenbaum, R. L., Horowitz, M. J., & Wilner, N. (1986). Clinician assessments of patient difficulty. *Psychotherapy, 23*(3), 417–422.

Rush, A. J., & Shaw, B. F. (1983). Failures in treating depression by cognitive therapy. In E. B. Foa & P. G. M. Emmelkamp (Eds.), *Failures in behavior therapy.* New York: Wiley.

Salkovskis, P. M. (1986). The cognitive revolution: New way forward, backward somersault or full circle? *Behavioral Psychotherapy, 14*, 278–282.

Saul, L. J., & Warner, S. L. (1982). *The psychotic personality.* New York: Van Nostrand.

Schank, R. C., & Abelson, R. P. (1977). *Scripts, plans, goals and understanding.* Hillsdale, NJ: Lawrence Erlbaum Associates.

Scharnberg, M. (1984). *The myth of paradigm shift, or how to lie with methodology.* Stockholm: Almquist & Wiksell International.

Schwartz, R. M., & Gottman, J. M. (1976). Toward a task analysis of assertive behavior. *Journal of Consulting and Clinical Psychology, 44*, 910–920.

Searles, H. F. (1978). *Psychoanalytic therapy with the borderline adult.* In J. F. Masterson (Ed.), *New perspectives on psychotherapy of the borderline adult* New York: Brunner/Mazel.

Seligman, M. E. P. (1975). *Helplessness: On depression, development, and death.* San Francisco: W. H. Freeman.

Shapiro, D. (1965). *Neurotic styles.* New York: Basic Books.

Shaw, B. F., Vallis, T. M., & McCabe, S. B. (1985). The assessment of the severity and symptom patterns in depression. In E. E. Beckham & W. R. Leher (Eds.), *Handbook of depression* (pp. 372–407). Homewood, IL: The Dorsey Press.

Sherman, M. (1979). *Personality: Inquiry and applications.* New York: Pergamon Press.

Shultz, D. (1981). *Theories of personality.* Monterey: Brooks/Cole.

Siever, L. J. (1981). Schizoid and schizotypal personality disorders. In J. R. Lion (Ed.), *Personality disorders: Diagnosis and management.* Baltimore: Williams and Wilkens.

Silverman, S. (1987). Silence as resistance to medical intervention. *General Hospital Psychiatry, 9,* 259–266.

Simon, K. M. (1983, August). *Cognitive therapy with compulsive patients: Replacing rigidity with structure.* Paper presented at the meeting of the American Psychological Association, Anaheim, CA.

Simon, K. M. (1985, November). *Cognitive therapy of the passive-aggressive personality.* Paper presented at the meeting of the Association for the Advancement of Behavior Therapy, Houston, TX.

Simon, K. M., & Fleming, B. M. (1985). Beck's cognitive therapy of depression: Treatment and outcome. In R. M. Turner & L. M. Ascher (Eds.), *Evaluating behavior therapy outcome.* New York: Springer.

Sobel, H. J. (1981). Projective methods of cognitive analysis. In T. V. Merluzzi, C. R. Glass, & M. Genest (Eds.), *Cognitive assessment* (pp. 127–148). New York: Guilford Press.

Speilberger, C. D., Gorsuch, R. R., & Sucherne, R. E. (1970). *State trait anxiety inventory manual for form X.* Palo Alto, CA: Consulting Psychologists Press.

Spivack, G., & Shure, M. B. (1974). *Social adjustment of young children: A cognitive approach to solving real-life problems.* San Francisco: Jossey-Bass.

Stampfl, T. G., & Levis, D. J. (1967). Essentials of implosive therapy: A learning based psychodynamic behavior therapy. *Journal of Abnormal Psychology, 72,* 496–503.

Stampfl, T. G., & Lewis, D. J. (1969). Learning theory: An aid to dynamic therapeutic practice. In D. Eron and R. Callahan (Eds.), *The relation of theory to practice in Psychotherapy.* Chicago: Aldine.

Stangl, D., Pfohl, B., Zimmerman, M., Bowers, W., & Corenthal, C. (1985). A structured interview for the DSM-III personality disorders: A preliminary report. *Archives of General Psychiatry, 42,* 591–596.

Steketee, G., & Foa, E. B. (1985). Obsessive-compulsive disorder. In D. H. Barlow (Ed.). *Clinical handbook of psychological disorders: A step-by-step treatment manual.* New York: Guilford.

Steketee, G., Foa, E. G., & Grayson, J. B. (1982). Recent advances in the treatment of obsessive-compulsives. *Archives of General Psychiatry, 39,* 1365–1371.

Stravynski, A., Lamontagne, Y., & Lavellee, Y. (1986). Clinical phobias and avoidant personality disorder among alcoholics admitted to an alcoholism rehabilitation setting. *Canadian Journal of Psychiatry, 31,* 714–718.

Stravynski, A., Marks, I., & Yule, W. (1982). Social skills problems in neurotic outpatients: Social skills training with and without cognitive modification. *Archives of General Psychiatry, 39,* 1378–1385.

Sundberg, N. D. (1981). Historical and traditional approaches to cognitive assessment. In T. V. Merluzzi, C. R. Glass, & M. Genest (Eds.), *Cognitive assessment.* New York: Guilford Press.

Turkat, I. D., & Carlson, C. R. (1984). Data-based versus symptomatic formulation of treatment: The case of a dependent personality. *Journal of Behavioral Therapy and Experimental Psychiatry, 15,* 153–160.

Turkat, I. D., & Maisto, S. A. (1985). Personality disorders: Application of the experimental method to the formulation and modification of personality disorders. In D. H. Barlow (Ed.), *Clinical handbook of psychological disorders.* New York: Guilford.

Turner, R. M. (1986, March). *The bio-social-learning approach to the assessment and treatment of borderline personality disorder.* Paper presented at the Carrier Foundation Behavioral Medicine Update Symposium, Belle Meade, New Jersey.

Turner, R. M. (1987). The effects of personality disorder diagnosis on the outcome of social anxiety symptom reduction. *Journal of Personality Disorders, 1,* 136–143.

Turner, S. M., Beidel, D. C., Dancu, C. V., & Keys, D. J. (1986). Psychopathology of social phobia and comparison to avoidant personality disorders. *Journal of Abnormal Psychology, 95,* 389–394.

van der Waals, H. (1965). Problems of narcissism. *Bulletin of the Menninger Clinic, 29,* 293–311.

Vieth, I. (1977). Four thousand years of hysteria. In M. J. Horowitz (Ed.), *Hysterical personality.* New York: Jason Aronson.

Ward, L. G., Friedlander, M. L., & Solverman, W. K. (1987). Children's depressive symptoms, negative self-statements, and causal attributions for success and failure. *Cognitive Therapy and Research, 11*(2), 215–227.

Weintraub, W. (1981). Compulsive and paranoid personalities. In J. R. Lion (Ed.), *Personality disorders: Diagnosis and management.* Baltimore: Williams & Wilkins.

Weisz, J. R., Rothbaum, F. M., & Blackburn, T. C. (1984). Standing out and standing in: The psychology of control in America and Japan. *American Psychologist, 39,* 955–969.

Wessler, R. A., & Wessler, R. L. (1980). *The principles and practice of rational-emotive therapy.* San Francisco: Jossey-Bass.

White, P. (1980). Limitations on verbal reports of internal events: A refutation of Nisbett and Wilson and of Bem. *Psychological Review, 87,* 105–112.

Widiger, T. A., & Sanderson, C. (1987). The convergent and discriminant validity of the MCMI as a measure of DSM-III personality disorders. *Journal of Personality Assessment, 51*(2), 228–242.

Widiger, T. A., Williams, J. B. W., Spitzer, R. L., & Frances, A. (1985). The MCMI as a measure of DSM-III. *Journal of Personality Assessment, 49*(4), 366–378.

Widiger, T. A., Sanderson, C., & Warner, L. (1986). The MMPI, prototypal typology, and borderline personality disorder. *Journal of Personality Assessment, 50,* 540–553.

Widiger, T. A., Williams, J. B. W., Spitzer, R. L., & Frances, A. (1986). The MCMI and DSM-III: A brief rejoinder to Millon (1985). *Journal of Personality Assessment, 50*(2), 198–204.

Williams, M. H. The bait-and-switch tactic in psychotherapy. *Psychotherapy, 22*(1), 110–115.

Wolpe, J. (1958). *Psychotherapy by reciprocal inhibition.* Stanford, CA: Stanford University Press.

Woody, G. E., McLellan, A. T., Luborsky, L., & O'Brien, C. P. (1985). Sociopathy and psychotherapy outcome. *Archives of General Psychiatry, 42,* 1081–1086.

Woolson, A. M., & Swanson, M. G. (1972). The second time around: Psychotherapy with the "hysterical woman." *Psychotherapy: Theory, Research & Practice, 9,* 168–175.

Wright, J. H. (1987). Cognitive Therapy and medication as combined treatment. In A. Freeman & V. Greenwood (Eds.), *Cognitive Therapy: Applications in psychiatric and medical settings.* New York: Human Sciences Press.

Young, J. (1987). *Schema-focused cognitive therapy for personality disorders.* Unpublished manuscript.

Young, J., & Swift, W. (1988). Schema-focused cognitive therapy for personality disorders: Part I. *International Cognitive Therapy Newsletter, 4,* 5, 13–14.

Zimmerman, M., Pfohl, B., Stangl, D., & Coryell, W. (1985). The validity of DSM-III Axis IV. *American Journal of Psychiatry, 142*(12), 1437–1441.

Zwemer, W. A., & Deffenbacher, J. L. (1984). Irrational beliefs, anger and anxiety. *Journal of Counseling Psychology, 31,* 391–393.

Index